INTIMACY AND DISTANCE
CONFLICTING CULTURES IN NINETEENTH-CENTURY FRANCE

LEGENDA

LEGENDA is the Modern Humanities Research Association's book imprint for new research in the Humanities. Founded in 1995 by Malcolm Bowie and others within the University of Oxford, Legenda has always been a collaborative publishing enterprise, directly governed by scholars. The Modern Humanities Research Association (MHRA) joined this collaboration in 1998, became half-owner in 2004, in partnership with Maney Publishing and then Routledge, and has since 2016 been sole owner. Titles range from medieval texts to contemporary cinema and form a widely comparative view of the modern humanities, including works on Arabic, Catalan, English, French, German, Greek, Italian, Portuguese, Russian, Spanish, and Yiddish literature. Editorial boards and committees of more than 60 leading academic specialists work in collaboration with bodies such as the Society for French Studies, the British Comparative Literature Association and the Association of Hispanists of Great Britain & Ireland.

The MHRA encourages and promotes advanced study and research in the field of the modern humanities, especially modern European languages and literature, including English, and also cinema. It aims to break down the barriers between scholars working in different disciplines and to maintain the unity of humanistic scholarship. The Association fulfils this purpose through the publication of journals, bibliographies, monographs, critical editions, and the MHRA Style Guide, and by making grants in support of research. Membership is open to all who work in the Humanities, whether independent or in a University post, and the participation of younger colleagues entering the field is especially welcomed.

ALSO PUBLISHED BY THE ASSOCIATION

Critical Texts
Tudor and Stuart Translations • *New Translations* • *European Translations*
MHRA Library of Medieval Welsh Literature

MHRA Bibliographies
Publications of the Modern Humanities Research Association

The Annual Bibliography of English Language & Literature
Austrian Studies
Modern Language Review
Portuguese Studies
The Slavonic and East European Review
Working Papers in the Humanities
The Yearbook of English Studies

www.mhra.org.uk
www.legendabooks.com

EDITORIAL BOARD

Chair: Professor Jonathan Long (University of Durham)
For *Germanic Literatures*: Ritchie Robertson (University of Oxford)
For *Italian Perspectives*: Simon Gilson (University of Warwick)
For *Moving Image*: Emma Wilson (University of Cambridge)
For *Research Monographs in French Studies*:
Diana Knight (University of Nottingham)
For *Selected Essays*: Susan Harrow (University of Bristol)
For *Studies in Comparative Literature*: Duncan Large
(British Centre for Literary Translation, University of East Anglia)
For *Studies in Hispanic and Lusophone Cultures*:
Trevor Dadson (Queen Mary, University of London)
For *Studies in Yiddish*: Gennady Estraikh (New York University)
For *Transcript*: Matthew Reynolds (University of Oxford)

Managing Editor
Dr Graham Nelson
41 Wellington Square, Oxford OX1 2JF, UK

www.legendabooks.com

Intimacy and Distance

Conflicting Cultures in Nineteenth-Century France

Philippa Lewis

Modern Humanities Research Association
2017

*Published by Legenda
an imprint of the Modern Humanities Research Association
Salisbury House, Station Road, Cambridge CB1 2LA*

*ISBN 978-1-78188-513-0 (HB)
ISBN 978-1-78188-514-7 (PB)*

First published 2017

All rights reserved. No part of this publication may be reproduced or disseminated or transmitted in any form or by any means, electronic, mechanical, photocopying, recording or otherwise, or stored in any retrieval system, or otherwise used in any manner whatsoever without written permission of the copyright owner, except in accordance with the provisions of the Copyright, Designs and Patents Act 1988, or under the terms of a licence permitting restricted copying issued in the UK by the Copyright Licensing Agency Ltd, Saffron House, 6–10 Kirby Street, London EC1N 8TS, England, or in the USA by the Copyright Clearance Center, 222 Rosewood Drive, Danvers MA 01923. Application for the written permission of the copyright owner to reproduce any part of this publication must be made by email to legenda@mhra.org.uk.

Disclaimer: Statements of fact and opinion contained in this book are those of the author and not of the editors or the Modern Humanities Research Association. The publisher makes no representation, express or implied, in respect of the accuracy of the material in this book and cannot accept any legal responsibility or liability for any errors or omissions that may be made.

Trademark notice: Product or corporate names may be trademarks or registered trademarks, and are used only for identification and explanation without intent to infringe.

© *Modern Humanities Research Association 2017*

Copy-Editor: Charlotte Brown

CONTENTS

Acknowledgements		ix
Abbreviations for Selected Texts		xi
	Introducing Intimacy	1
1	Cultures of Intimacy	15
2	The Embarrassments of Intimacy	44
3	Intimacy and Irony in the *journal intime*	66
4	Intercultural Encounters, or Intimacy at a Distance	93
5	Experiencing Art: Baudelaire's Intimate Criticism	117
6	Literary Criticism and the Rhetoric of Friendship	140
	Concluding Remarks: Baudelaire *intime*	156
	Bibliography	165
	Index	182

For my parents

ACKNOWLEDGEMENTS

I began the research for this book as a doctoral student at the University of Cambridge, and I would like to thank all those who helped my work take shape, first as a thesis and now as a monograph. My biggest debt of gratitude is undoubtedly to my PhD supervisor, Miranda Gill, who engaged so thoroughly with my work throughout my time at Cambridge, and without whom this book would not exist. Many other colleagues also provided invaluable insights; special thanks go to Alison Finch, Fanny Robles, Claire White, and Emma Wilson. I would like to thank Nick White in particular for being so generous with his time, and advice, over the years.

Beyond Cambridge, the transformation of my thesis into book form owes much to the suggestions of Ann Jefferson, my PhD external examiner, and to Maria Scott, who read my manuscript for Legenda and encouraged me to rethink aspects of it in productive ways. At the University of Bristol, Susan Harrow has offered a fresh perspective on my work. I am grateful to everyone who has commented on the project, whether at seminars, conferences, or elsewhere: each question or suggestion has made its way, in one form or another, into the book. I am very grateful also for the doctoral funding I received from the Arts and Humanities Research Council, and for the institutional support offered by Trinity Hall, St. John's College, and, most recently, the University of Bristol.

At Legenda, Graham Nelson, my editor, and Charlotte Wathey, my copyeditor, have done an excellent job preparing the manuscript for publication; any errors that remain are, of course, my own.

In Chapters Four and Five of this book, I draw on material I have already published in articles, and I am grateful to the editors of the journals *Modern Language Review* and *HARTS and Minds* for giving me permission to do so.

The long time spent working on this project has been enriched by the presence of my friends and family. Although I can't mention everyone here, I would like to thank in particular Barbara Grodecka Lewis, Stephen Lewis, and Anna Lewis; Mary Grodecka; and Jesse Williams.

P.L., Bristol, June 2017

ABBREVIATIONS FOR SELECTED TEXTS

The following abbreviations are used for the primary texts, collected volumes, and dictionaries which are referred to frequently in the book. For all other references, the author-date system is used.

Barbey d'Aurevilly

OCB	*Œuvres romanesques complètes*, ed. by Jacques Petit, 2 vols (Paris: Gallimard, 1966)
LT	*Lettres à Trebutien 1832–1858*, ed. by Philippe Berthier (Paris: Éditions Bartillat, 2013)

Baudelaire

OC	*Œuvres complètes*, ed. by Claude Pichois, 2 vols (Paris: Gallimard, 1975–76)
BC	*Correspondance de Baudelaire*, ed. by Claude Pichois, 2 vols (Paris: Gallimard, 1973)
BD	*Fusées, Mon cœur mis à nu, La Belgique déshabillée*, ed. by André Guyaux (Paris: Gallimard, 1986)

Flaubert

OF	*Œuvres de Flaubert*, ed. by A. Thibaudet and R. Dumesnil, 2 vols (Paris: Gallimard, 1951)
OJF	*Œuvres complètes*, I: *Œuvres de jeunesse*, ed. by Claudine Gothot-Mersch and Guy Sagnes (Paris: Gallimard, 2001)
CF	*Correspondance de Flaubert*, ed. by Jean Bruneau and Yvan LeClerc, 6 vols (Paris: Gallimard, 1973–2007)
VE	*Voyage en Égypte*, ed. by Pierre-Marc de Biasi (Paris: Bernard Grasset, 1991)

Fromentin

OCF	*Œuvres complètes*, ed. by Guy Sagnes (Paris: Gallimard, 1984)
CEF	*Correspondance d'Eugène Fromentin*, ed. by Barbara Wright, 2 vols (Paris: CNRS-Éditions, 1995)

Guérin

GJ	*Eugénie de Guérin, Journal et lettres, publiés avec l'assentiment de la famille par G. S. Trebutien* (Paris: Didier, 1862)

Sainte-Beuve

NL	*Nouveaux lundis*, 13 vols (Paris: Calmann Lévy, 1883–86)
PC	*Portraits contemporains*, ed. by Michel Brix (Paris: Presses de l'université de Paris-Sorbonne, 2008)

PF *Portraits de femmes*, ed. by Gérald Antoine (Paris: Flammarion, 1998)
PL *Portraits littéraires*, ed. by Gérald Antoine (Paris: R. Laffont, 1993)

Dictionaries

Littré Littré, Émile. *Dictionnaire de la langue française* (Paris: Hachette, 1873–74), electronic version created by François Gannaz, <http://www.littre.org> [accessed 25 May 2017]

Petit Robert *Le Petit Robert de la langue française: dictionnaire alphabétique et analogique de la langue française*, Nouvelle édition millésime 2017, ed. by Josette Rey-Debove and Alain Rey (Paris: Le Robert, 2016)

INTRODUCING INTIMACY

In January 1880, Henry James's fourth, and final, essay on Charles Augustin Sainte-Beuve appeared in the *North American Review*. Written in response to the posthumous publication of a selection of Sainte-Beuve's letters, the essay is highly appreciative of the literary giant who, we know with hindsight, would fall from grace in the century to follow. Offering a comparison between Sainte-Beuve's private correspondence and his public criticism, James evokes the remarkably 'intimate' nature of the latter:

> His work offers a singularly complete image of his character, his tastes, his temper, his idiosyncrasies. It was from himself always that he spoke — from his own personal and, as they say in France, intimate point of view. He wrote himself down in his published pages, and what was left for his letters was simply to fill in the details, to supply a few missing touches, a few inflections and nuances. (James 1880: 52)

When James's essay was reissued, with some revisions, in William M. Payne's *American Literary Criticism* of 1904, the adjectival reference to the intimacy of Sainte-Beuve's work was no longer qualified as characteristically French (James 1986: 25).[1] Nonetheless, the presence of this qualification in the original version of James's study is highly significant for the way in which it draws attention, albeit fleetingly, to the phenomenon which this book seeks to elucidate: the self-conscious culture of intimacy present in nineteenth-century France (and in which Sainte-Beuve was indeed a key protagonist). James does not suggest that intimacy itself is peculiarly French, and nor does this book make any such claim. But, in 1880, James does allude to a *language* for speaking about intimacy which, when compared with Anglophone contexts, he considers more prevalent in France. It is this idiom of intimacy and its role in nineteenth-century French literary culture which this book examines, from a study of the culturally coded 'intimate' forms which flourished in the first half of the century — *poésie intime*, the *roman intime*, and the *journal intime* — to a broader examination of the concept of intimacy itself, understood in the French context as that part of the self which is innermost and private (*l'intime*, *l'intimité*), but also as a state in which this inner life is shared with another (*l'intimité*).

In present-day France, the concept of intimacy has become closely enmeshed with notions of sexuality and romantic love. Yet a different set of connotations gathered around it in the post-Revolutionary, and pre-Freudian, era, particularly with regard to literary culture. Indeed, I argue here that literature became an increasingly important cultural space for intimacy in the nineteenth century. This claim may seem surprising: it has become customary in certain strands of scholarship to present the nineteenth century as a period ever-more concerned with practices of detachment, whether in the realm of knowledge-production, ethics, etiquette, or aesthetics.[2] William Reddy, for example, argues that honour codes took on renewed significance in post-Revolutionary France as part of a full-scale 'erasure' (2001: 208) of the legacy of eighteenth-century sensibility. The realist novel was born in the post-1830 period, taking over the novelistic codes previously associated with the shared sentiment of first-person fiction.[3] And the cultivated impersonality of Parnassian poetry, emerging in the second half of the nineteenth century, has been read as a repudiation of the 'stereotypical sentimentalism of Romantic poetry'.[4] These interpretations, however, tell only one side of the story. As will become apparent — and as the title of *Intimacy and Distance* seeks to convey — a persistent, if necessarily conflicted, preoccupation with intimacy existed alongside and in tension with this desire for distance throughout the century, surfacing in diffuse but palpable ways. The pages which follow trace articulations of intimacy across nineteenth-century France, paying particular attention to the periods of the July Monarchy and Second Empire. Focusing on a cluster of both well-known and neglected writers ranging from Sainte-Beuve, Charles Baudelaire, and Jules Amédée Barbey d'Aurevilly to Eugénie de Guérin, Eugène Fromentin, and Gustave Flaubert, the study demonstrates that intimacy was a concept which actively shaped both 'ordinary' and professional writing and reading practices in the domains of the novel, poetry, diary, travel writing, and art and literary criticism.[5] While the principal focus of *Intimacy and Distance* will be on the aspiration for intimacy, it acknowledges that intimacy as both a relational and more specific literary mode was repeatedly questioned and criticised, even by those who engaged with it. Such conflicts, I argue, led writers to reimagine intimacy in ways which allowed them to articulate and even exploit their ambivalent response to it.

Intimacy is an area of growing interest in the international research community, particularly amongst scholars of the arts, humanities, and social sciences.[6] But what do these researchers mean by the term: are the objects of their investigations the same? In French Studies, *intime* has a particular disciplinary currency, used to designate the types of text which in English Studies fall under the rubric of 'personal writing' or 'life-writing'. Elsewhere, however, it is common for scholars to treat intimacy as a synonym or indeed a euphemism for their primary area of research interest, be this sexuality, romantic love, or the family.[7] In English, the adjective 'intimate' can also be employed to suggest a particular method or approach: the term 'intimate history' is popular with publishers, although it is rarely defined and remains vague.[8] The shifting and somewhat frustrating use of the vocabulary of intimacy today might appear inevitable given the polysemy of the term: in the French context, Brigitte Diaz and José-Luis Diaz claim that despite even the most systematic etymological analysis, 'on achoppe toujours sur la mollesse sémantique de la notion' (2009: 118) and the same semantic suppleness is discernible in English. Yet the prevalence of the term, testament to its ability to 'enchant' twenty-first-century writers and readers,[9] appears less frustrating and immediately more productive when seen as an echo, or continuation, of nineteenth-century literary culture.[10]

As Daniel Madelénat remarks, nineteenth-century critics in France frequently reproached writers and publishers for their tendency to 'prodiguer l'adjectif [*intime*] pour couvrir des marchandises diverses' (1989: 173), and we see a similar tendency at work today.

Certain contemporary theorists *have* sought to engage more rigorously with the concept of intimacy itself, however. Diachronic word histories of intimacy — *intime* and *intimité* — will be presented in Chapter One, with special attention paid to nineteenth-century definitions, but this introduction will first summarise the treatment of intimacy in twentieth- and twenty-first-century sociological and psychoanalytic thought. Doing so will shed light on the relevance of intimacy as a concept today; it will also draw out some of the key questions which underpin this book and resurface in subsequent chapters: What models exist for intimacy? How have connotations and evaluations of it changed over time? And how do intimacy, literature, and culture relate to one another?

Theorising Intimacy: Perspectives from Sociology and Psychoanalysis

As Lynn Jamieson points out, in recent decades 'intimacy has become a fashionable word [...] in the social sciences' (1998: 1). In particular, the concept of intimacy has played an important role for social and cultural theorists analysing the relationship between public and private life in the modern era. Within these theories, 'intimacy' operates as something of a shifter: at times used as a synonym for private life and the intersubjective experiences made possible within it; at others, to signify a state which can exist within both private and public spheres and thus alter boundaries between the two.

Jürgen Habermas's highly influential *Structural Transformation of the Public Sphere* [1962] associates an ideal of intimacy (*Intimität*) with the emotional and intellectual experiences fostered by the patriarchal family unit in eighteenth- and nineteenth-century Europe. According to Habermas, ancient Greek and Roman societies typically privileged the male-orientated public sphere over the private sphere, the latter considered obscure and potentially shameful. The expansion of the middle-classes in early-modern Europe, however, coupled with the increasing right to property, saw home life take on enhanced significance in the eyes of bourgeois citizens.[11] Private and public life were not disconnected entities at this particular stage of social transformation; rather, 'the sphere of the public arose in the broader strata of the bourgeoisie as an expansion and at the same time completion of the intimate sphere of the conjugal family' (Habermas 1989: 50). These worlds come together in Habermas's conception of the home as an 'audience-orientated intimate sphere' (1989: 159) which, as a place for discussion and debate, prepared members for participation in public life. Habermas's conception of the bourgeois public sphere is fundamentally shaped by literature: it was through the form of the novel that ideas from the public sphere and notions of subjectivity and selfhood permeated the private sphere. Having outlined the 'golden age' of the bourgeois public sphere in the eighteenth century and first half of the nineteenth century, Habermas's study proceeds to trace its decline: with increased state intervention in the latter years of the nineteenth century, private life retreated and became radically separate from public life. Moreover, the decline in reading and the rise of screen media in the twentieth century meant that, for Habermas, the intimacy of home life was to become increasingly bound up with the passive culture of consumption rather than critical debate.

Habermas's narrative of a transformation from a critical and 'audience-orientated' intimacy to one which is effectively 'closed-off' (1989: 162) bears comparison with models by two other social theorists, Richard Sennett and Lauren Berlant.[12] While Habermas locates intimacy in the family, and endows it with a positive role in the history of societal flourishing, Sennett defines intimacy as a 'field of vision and an expectation of human relations' which leads to painful, antisocial, and 'fratricidal' interpersonal bonds (1993: 338). In *The Fall of Public Man* [1977], tellingly translated into French as *Les Tyrannies de l'intimité*, Sennett charts a different narrative of decline from that of Habermas: for Sennett, it is the gradual invasion of public life by private life, rather than the gradual retreat of the private, which has led to a distorted society. In Sennett's thesis, the eighteenth century is construed as an era in which an ideal of impersonality held sway in public. Eighteenth-century European citizens, bred on the Enlightenment principles of universality, shared natural character, and natural rights, could interact with one another not as idiosyncratic individuals, but rather as actors on a public stage for which Habermas's 'intimate sphere' had little or no relevance. Yet the nineteenth-century processes of individualisation, combined with and exacerbated by the perceived loss of collective, transcendent belief systems, led to an increased cultural fascination with immediate surroundings, immanent beings, and the self. For Sennett, this has resulted in the growth of an interest in 'personality' over natural character, and a society in which relationships evaluated as close or intimate are seen as more significant than bonds which are predominantly functional. In short, an 'ideology of intimacy' has transmuted 'political categories into psychological categories' (1993: 259). For Sennett, this misplaced expectation has had major consequences:

> The belief in direct human relations on an intimate scale has seduced us from converting our understanding of the realities of power into guides for our own political behavior. The result is that the forces of domination or inequality remain unchallenged. (Sennet 1993: 339)

Sennett is joined by sociologists such as Zygmunt Bauman for whom the narcissism and, at the same time, 'craved-for togetherness' (2003: 32) evidenced in contemporary society by celebrity interviews and chat-shows (and, we might now add, social media) is a reaction to the loss of conventional bonds of belief, community, and family (Bauman 2000: 86). This ideal of togetherness achieved through mutual self-disclosure, variously labelled by Bauman as 'closeness, intimacy, "sincerity", "turning oneself inside out", holding no secrets, [and] compulsive and compulsory confessing' (2003: 32), is, he suggests, inadequate for negotiations in the political sphere amongst peoples 'on a war footing: in a shooting, rather than talking mood' (2003: 33).

While they evaluate the history of intimacy differently, Habermas, Sennett, and Bauman each associate twentieth- and twenty-first-century intimacy with a consumer-driven society devoid of any effective critical or political function. The twentieth-century mode of intimacy, tied to capitalism and individualism, comes at the cost of an intellectual 'dumbing-down' and the loss of social engagement. However, not all theorists view intimacy negatively. Lauren Berlant is one of several feminist critics to rethink, but not entirely rewrite, Habermas's view of the changing nature of intimacy and the public-private dichotomy. Her work on 'intimate publics' draws on Habermas's emphasis on literary culture as a producer of an 'audience-orientated' intimacy, but extends it: for Berlant, with a background in 'feminist/queer pedagogy' (1998: 286), intimacy is neither the sole property of the patriarchal family unit nor the 'world of letters' (Habermas 1989: 51), and is neither tyrannical nor escapist. Rather, intimacy is a bond which transcends the distinction between public and private, and can take place in a range of non-institutionally sanctioned forms, via a variety of media. It can thus be implicitly, if not explicitly, political. Berlant distinguishes herself from sociologists such as Niklas Luhmann (1986) who argue that romantic love is the primary model for intimacy in the West. Berlant's concept of 'intimate publics' may originate in the reading and writing communities of nineteenth-century America yet she also sees technologies like cinema and the internet as productive of new forms of intimacy.[13] Her list of 'minor intimacies' (1998: 285) includes:

> Writers and readers, memorizers of songs, people who walk their dog or swim at the same time each day, fetishists and their objects, teachers and students, serial lovers, sports lovers, listeners to voices who explain things manageably (on the radio, at conferences, on television screens, online, in therapy), fans and celebrities. (Berlant 1998: 284–85)

Berlant's work in particular is concerned with intimacies and sexualities which do not fit into conventional, socially acceptable narratives: 'Desires for intimacy which bypass the couple or the life narrative have no alternative plots, let alone few laws or stable spaces of culture in which to clarify and to cultivate them' (1998: 285). The work of Habermas and Sennett is not explicitly concerned with this problem. Moreover, it is clear that each theorist, working in a different intellectual climate and with particular preoccupations, presents a different vision of intimacy, and its meanings, uses, and limitations as a concept. Intimacy is used primarily by Habermas to refer to the 'close relationships of the conjugal family' (1989: 49), and the thoughts and feelings facilitated by eighteenth-century literary culture. Sennett treats intimacy as a damaging expectation of human relationships. Berlant considers intimacy in a more optimistic, 'spreading way', beyond the remit of the nuclear family (1998: 285).

The differences in semantic emphasis within social theory are exacerbated when considering intimacy in the context of psychoanalysis. Here, a key distinction emerges between theories concerned with intimacy as a quality of individual interiority and those which emphasise its relational aspects; between those which approach intimacy as an index of subjectivity or, instead, intersubjectivity.[14] For Julia Kristeva, writing in *La Révolte intime*, psychoanalysis is central to what she calls a major revolution in the conceptualisation of the *intime*, defined as what is 'le plus profond et le plus singulier de l'expérience humaine' (1997: 81). According to her thesis, twentieth-century developments in psychoanalysis have led to a radical reimagining of inner life in which subjectivity is no longer artificially divided between mind, body, and soul, but is considered as a heterogeneous continuity of psychosomatic experience — including but surpassing the unconscious — which 'nous apparaît désormais comme l'essence de l'intime' (1997: 94). While Kristeva's work more broadly places emphasis on the interrelatedness of subjects and indeed also texts, the conception of intimacy which she articulates here recalls the tendency of classical psychoanalysis to focus on the instinctual drives shaping the interiority of the individual at the expense of interpersonal bonds.[15] In response to this initial neglect, Object Relations theorists of the mid-twentieth century, such as Melanie Klein, sought to establish alternative theoretical models in which an individual's intimate relationships with *others*, initially the mother, were granted much greater significance.[16] However, intimacy, when understood in terms of a shared emotional bond, has been accorded most importance for psychic development and well-being by John Bowlby's theories of childhood attachment, as articulated in *Attachment and Loss* (1969–80). Within Bowlby's theoretical framework, 'attachment' is understood as a condition in which an individual is 'linked emotionally', as Jeremy Holmes describes it (1993: 218), to another, desiring and deriving comfort from his or her presence. Bowlby's research concludes that a secure attachment between a child and his or her primary care-giver is an evolutionary necessity in its own right; that bonding is a basic human need distinct from sexual or sensual drives. Attachment Theory is 'in essence a *spatial* theory' (Holmes 1993: 67) in which distance from the preferred figure is associated with anxiety, sadness, or loneliness, and proximity with security, warmth, and comfort: 'The consummation of attachment is not primarily orgasmic — rather, it is, via an achievement of proximity, a relaxed state in which one can begin to "get on with things", pursue one's projects, to *explore*' (1993: 67). Sennett negatively evaluates the soporific effect produced by close and 'warm' relationships (1993: 338), and Melanie Klein has also probed the anxieties that 'excessive [...] closeness to loved people' and dependence on them in childhood can cause in adulthood (1997: 311). Attachment Theory, however, posits secure, comforting bonds as the basis of productive activity.

This brief survey of some significant strands in twentieth- and twenty-first-century sociological and psychoanalytic research into intimacy suggests that it is more apt to talk of the concept in the plural rather than the singular, a tendency already manifest in Berlant's 1998 discussion.[17] The pluralisation of intimacy corresponds, on the one hand, to a desire to legitimise a diversity of 'non-normative' ways of being and relating. On the other hand, particularly evident in the work of Habermas and Sennett, it can also testify to a concern with how one monolithic or 'tyrannical' understanding of intimacy can perpetuate an excessively localised society in which matters beyond the closed world or 'island' (Bauman 2003: 33) of intimates seem to hold little interest. Does being close to certain individuals mean being closed off to others? The tension between the transformative or productive potential of intimacy on the one hand, and its proximity to individualism and solipsism on the other, in fact has a long history and is prefigured in the literature and culture of nineteenth-century France.

Intimacy in the Nineteenth Century: Literary, Cultural, and Emotional Histories

In the literary context, critics have long privileged the aspiration towards 'impersonality' in mid to late nineteenth-century France, invoking the experimental third-person fiction of Flaubert or Émile Zola, for example, or the work of Parnassian poets such as Théodore de Banville, José-Maria de Heredia or Charles Leconte de Lisle.[18] We can, from one perspective, link these historically situated literary trends to what the historian of emotions William Reddy has theorised — in seeming contrast to Sennett's thesis — as the establishment of a normative 'emotional regime' in post-Revolutionary France in which the cultivation of reserve in public was encouraged.[19] Reddy relates the withdrawal of public emotion in France to the traumas of the French Revolution, and the atmosphere of insecurity and suspicion which followed in its wake. Romanticism, Reddy admits, valorised emotional expansiveness, but in an autonomous aesthetic realm firmly cut off from social life (2001: 242): a form of private 'emotional refuge'.[20] Reserve was particularly prevalent as a behavioural style amongst men as the political unrest of the previous century came to be associated with a dangerous degeneration and 'feminisation' of manners. In this light, the literary impulses of Flaubert and the Parnassians, amongst others, emerge as both a reaction to Romanticism and an aestheticisation of 'masculine' behavioural ideals propagated in the public sphere. Similar tendencies are visible in the British context. However, while Reddy offers a narrative of abrupt change from eighteenth-century sentimental susceptibility to nineteenth-century emotional containment, Anderson (2001) stresses the continuity between Enlightenment ideals of rationality or objectivity and their nineteenth-century counterparts, ranging from novelistic realism and scientific method to practices of the self, such as stoicism and dandyism.

If we adopt the views of Reddy and Anderson, intimacy as a state conducive to and dependent on shared emotions appears as a sorry remnant of an outdated paradigm, unsuited to post-Revolutionary French public life (Reddy 2001) and out of touch with the defining ethical and aesthetic preoccupations of the age (Anderson 2001). Yet it is the contention of this book that an awareness of intimacy as both a social and literary mode was in fact strengthened in nineteenth-century France and, rather than becoming a purely 'private issue' removed from the public sphere, remained a compelling part of the collective cultural consciousness, widely written, read, and talked about. Anderson's discussion of Victorian literature offers useful parallels with French literary culture, but the authors selected for her defence of detachment all fall comfortably within the literary canon. If a more diverse range of works of the period is examined, it becomes clear that the public engagement with the sharing of sentiment did not decline in the nineteenth century. Not only did eighteenth-century texts continue to be published and read, but intimacy was imagined afresh in the form of new generic categories (in France, the *roman intime* or *poésie intime*) and new writing, publishing, and reading practices concerning the diary and biographical criticism. Impersonality can certainly be interpreted as a reaction against this phenomenon, and vice versa: indeed, the conflict between intimacy and impassivity is highly significant for nineteenth-century cultural productions, as this book demonstrates. Yet to read the century as one in which detachment was the more visible and *valuable* cultural preoccupation is surely a misrepresentation.

Efforts to develop our understanding of intimacy as a historical and cultural object in France and beyond are evident in, and thus supported by, a number of new directions in the arts and humanities. The current interest in the history of private life has its origins in both the French Annales School and American cultural history, with their shared emphasis on the practices of everyday life.[21] These disciplinary movements have themselves contributed to the emergence of the interrelated and interdisciplinary fields of the history of emotions and the history of friendship, both highly relevant to the topic of intimacy.[22] In French Studies specifically, an emphasis on practice is increasingly evident in literary histories of the *intime*. Building on important early examples of research into literary intimacy, such as Madelénat's 1989 *L'Intimisme*, there has been a shift in focus away from the work of established authors towards the writing and reading activities of nineteenth-century groups of varying levels of education and literacy.[23] There has been a move to consider the history of letter-writing and diary-writing in particular, areas long ignored by academic literary criticism. In French Studies, letters and diaries typically fall under the rubric *intime*. Yet the ability of *écriture intime* to encompass published autobiographies and biographies as well — in short, all forms of life-writing — highlights the complexities inherent in investigating intimacy as a concept or category, given its relevance to literature circulating both inside and outside the public domain. In grappling with these complexities, the collected 2009 volume *Pour une histoire de l'intime et de ses variations*, edited by Anne Coudreuse and Françoise Simonet-Tenant, is one of the most useful contributions of recent years, in particular Brigitte Diaz and José-Luis Diaz's jointly written essay 'Le Siècle de l'intime'. This highly stimulating essay charts the ways in which the language of intimacy began to be used in relation to literature in the nineteenth century, and as such became a new interpretive and evaluative tool for critics and readers, applicable both to texts intended for publication and those letters or diaries written in relative privacy but published posthumously. Even these private writings contain markedly performative or 'spectacular' elements, and Diaz and Diaz's conceptualisations of the *scénographie de l'intime* and the *effet d'intime* provide useful analytic tools with which to approach this paradox.[24] The interest in intimacy amongst a cluster of French literary scholars is further demonstrated by a more recent collection, *Intime et politique* (2013), edited by Véronique Montémont and Françoise Simonet-Tenant, which testifies to a desire to re-politicise a body of writing or, in Sennett's term, 'field of vision' (1993: 338), frequently attacked for its political and social disengagement.[25]

English Studies also offers research paradigms which, if contextual differences are kept in mind, shed light on French material. Two texts epitomise approaches to intimacy in English Studies: Tom Mole's 2007 *Byron's Romantic Celebrity: Industrial Culture and the Hermeneutic of Intimacy* and Nancy Yousef's 2013 *Romantic Intimacy*. Mole's work on the modern origins of literary celebrity investigates the emotional and commercial effects of what he calls the early nineteenth-century 'hermeneutic of intimacy' (2007: 22). For Mole, celebrity culture grew up as a response and, in certain ways, antidote, to the alienating effects of industrial book production: 'Celebrity apparatus relied on the concealed use of new cultural technologies to construct an impression of unmediated contact' (2007: 22). This contact between reader and writer — the latter firmly understood to have a pre-textual existence — might or might not carry erotic undertones. Byron was to exploit these tendencies consciously; Mole cites the nineteenth-century critic John Wilson for whom *Childe Harold* was felt to have 'something of the nature of private and confidential communications', and 'secrets whispered to chosen ears' (2007: 23); such an impression chimes, of course, with Roland Barthes's view of the 'author' as a ruse of capitalist ideology, which exploits the persona to promote the product.[26] Mole draws on twentieth-century theorisations of 'para-social interaction' or virtual and non-reciprocal intimacy fostered through radio and television to elucidate the operations of the intimate hermeneutic between reader and writer within nineteenth-century print culture.[27] Meanwhile, Yousef's *Romantic Intimacy* is a significant contribution to a thriving body of research into Enlightenment sentimentalism and moral philosophy which examines questions of sympathy, empathy, and 'fellow-feeling' in relation to literature.[28] Referring to Jean-Jacques Rousseau, William Wordsworth, and Jane Austen, Yousef preserves a focus on what she calls the 'ethical aspirations and epistemological anxieties' (2013: 1) surrounding theories of moral sentiment but proposes 'intimacy' as a replacement term for 'sympathy'. Yousef argues that 'romantic-era literature' (2013: 4) betrays a complex attitude to shared experience and asserts that, unlike sympathy, intimacy as a concept is able to encapsulate its 'asymmetrical and nonreciprocal forms of relation, attention, and appreciation' (2013: 3), forms which include gratitude, frustration, awkwardness, and humiliation. Yousef's text is one of the most sustained explorations of intimacy in English Studies, but there is an ahistorical leaning in her broadly philosophical approach. While her arguments are convincing on their own terms, the study owes more to contemporary, somewhat idiosyncratic, definitions of intimacy than those of the period she examines. She pays scant attention to historical definitions of the term (2013: 1), and effectively maps a concept onto the period she examines, rather than drawing one from it.

In an effort to counteract this anachronistic approach to the concept of intimacy itself, evident in much work besides that of Yousef (Mole, for example, does not provide nineteenth-century definitions of intimacy either), this book draws on and intersects with the research areas outlined above, but differentiates itself in several ways. Most notably, it pays closer attention to specifically nineteenth-century articulations of intimacy. Moreover, in contrast to Diaz and Diaz's view that the affective charge of intimacy was 'consensuellement positive' (2009: 118) in the period, it argues that the appeal of intimacy was, from the moment of its self-conscious articulation, always in tension with competing cultural and societal values which led the cultural practices and products of intimacy to be stereotyped negatively in terms of class, gender, maturity, taste, and moral worth. As a consequence, the writers I consider acknowledge the potential vanity and futility of intimate writing practices, and the aspiration towards intimacy in the literary field more widely. Yet at the same time, they seek to harness the power and purchase of the concept by employing a variety of imaginative textual strategies which widen its scope and expand its associations. Ultimately, I argue, these writers come to harbour a two-fold conception of intimacy in which trivial, shameful, or dangerous forms act as foils for an ideal version viewed as profound, transformative, and at times even divine.

Focus and Approach

Although it engages with earlier and later periods, the decades following the July Revolution are the principal focus of this study. The year 1830 is conventionally associated with the rise of novelistic realism in France: writers including Balzac and Stendhal were able to profit from the relative relaxation of censorship laws in the early years of the July Monarchy to produce fiction explicitly concerned with contemporary French society and politics.[29] The success of these realist codes, however, has obscured the diversity of other aesthetics generated, altered, or crystallised by the upheavals of 1830. Recent research has restored the place of the idealist novel, sentimental social novel, and 'spectacular' historical novel in the history of the French literary field.[30] However, intimate literature was also born of or, more precisely, *identified* during the proliferation of aesthetic positions which, in José-Luis Diaz's terms, characterised 'cette foisonnante période d'après 1830' (2007: 94). As I outline in Chapter One, the history of intimate literature and many of the texts which came retrospectively to constitute it began long before 1830. However, it was in the 1830s that intimacy came into public and critical consciousness fully as a category and quality of writing, at first in relation to poetry and the novel.

The core group of writers selected for the book are, broadly speaking, part of two distinct but overlapping generations: the first (Sainte-Beuve, Guérin, and Barbey d'Aurevilly) born between 1804 and 1808; the second (Fromentin, Baudelaire, and Flaubert) between 1820 and 1821. In the case of the first generation, these writers have been selected for their engagement with and, to a large extent, popularisation of intimate writing practices; the second, for the mixed feelings with which they inherited this literary legacy, and the cultural products which they forged from this ambivalence. The book focuses predominantly on male-authored texts: the ambivalence regarding intimate writing is often more marked in these works given the gendered connotations of intimacy discussed in Chapters One and Two; the work of Baudelaire in particular is a prominent guiding thread. Yet it is also important to show the way in which women did work with the genres of intimacy in both private and public and I thus investigate female diary-writing in Chapter Three and female-authored literary criticism in Chapter Six. It will be apparent that I also privilege writers who worked across a diverse range of genres. Doing so allows me to trace how the tropes associated with the self-conscious and defining 'intimate genres' — the *roman intime*, *poésie intime* — resurfaced in other forms; *Intimacy and Distance* thus explores the reach of nineteenth-century intimacy and its rhetoric as it spilled from the genres of the *roman intime* and *poésie intime* (Chapter Two) into the diary (Chapter Three), travel writing (Chapter Four), and art and literary criticism (Chapters Five and Six). For the most part, these genres were in flux throughout the century, growing in popularity and prestige and redefining themselves to suit the new spaces being created for the written word. What happened to intimacy when it entered these worlds potentially foreign to it? How were intimate conventions reconfigured alongside competing generic codes or cultural concerns, and what light can this shed on the concept of intimacy itself? Through close textual analysis, fully informed by historical context, each chapter demonstrates how intimacy was both represented and generated by the works in question, and asks what imaginative opportunities, but also ideological conflicts, this engagement with intimacy created for writers and readers.

The choice to make Baudelaire the guiding thread through the pages to follow means, inevitably, that certain writers do not receive the full attention they deserve: neither Stendhal, for example, whose concept of the 'happy few' envisions the reading experience as an essentially intimate encounter, nor Balzac, whose novels teem with carefully etched scenes of private life. (Balzac, moreover, was the object of much readerly attention in the July Monarchy in the form of literary fan mail, illustrative of the growing tendency to conceptualise the author-figure as an intimate.) Indeed, Miyuka Terashima's 2011 study of Zola, 'Le Discours de "l'intime" dans *Les Rougon-Macquart*', points to the ways we might usefully bring realist or naturalist fiction into the discussion of nineteenth-century literary intimacy. Certainly, intimacy and realism are not opposing literary tendencies; there is a compelling case to be made that the success of the latter is linked to the same cultural appetite for intimacy which first sparked the genres of the *roman intime* and *poésie intime*.[31] In this book, however, the consistent focus on Baudelaire is explained by the pervasive ambivalence towards intimacy evident throughout his *œuvre*, from his verse and prose poetry to his travel writing and art and literary criticism. Baudelaire's work, to borrow a phrase from Leo Bersani, stages an 'exemplary drama in our culture' (1977: 2). I do not follow Bersani in his Freudian interpretation of Baudelaire, but I share his notion of Baudelaire's work as 'exemplary', in this case of a tension between competing social, cultural, and literary values in flux. Baudelaire's situation at the crossroads of Romanticism and post-Romanticism has been a major topic of criticism for over a century.[32] It is, moreover, a position of which he himself was acutely aware; indeed, it is the very lucidity with which Baudelaire regards the state of the literary field, and his place within it, which makes close attention to his writings particularly rewarding. Baudelaire's reluctance to 'prostituer les choses intimes de famille' (*BC* 1: 445), articulated in a letter to his mother of 11 January 1858, is well documented, and indicative, in Jacques Dupont's view, of a desire to 'vis[er] de plus en plus nettement une "impersonnalité" qui récuse, dépasse le "je" lyrique traditionnel' (Dupont 1991: 33). Yet 'les choses intimes' do surface in Baudelaire's writing, whether through his employment of culturally coded intimate forms and writing practices, his use of the language of intimacy, or his representation of intimate relationships, often evoked in highly figurative ways. *Intimacy and Distance* seeks to make sense of such contradictions.[33] More broadly, as this Introduction has outlined, it takes intimacy seriously as a historically constructed concept worthy of consideration in its own right and on its own terms: as neither synonym, nor euphemism. Doing so reveals the rich range of resonances attached to intimacy in the nineteenth-century imagination and allows us to assess better the complex — and continued — impact of the concept on French literature and culture.

Notes to the Introduction

1. Why the qualification ('as they say in France') was omitted from the second version of James's essay is uncertain. It has been suggested that while in the 1880 version of the essay James felt the need to explain or even excuse elements of the 'Gallic imagination' to his Anglophone readers, he could assume a greater familiarity with this by 1904; see discussion in James (1986: 39–41).
2. This is the view proposed by Amanda Anderson in her polemical *The Powers of Distance* (2001). Anderson considers nineteenth-century tendencies towards scientific 'objectivity' and literary realism alongside practices of the self such as stoicism, dandyism, and cosmopolitanism.
3. Cf. Margaret Cohen (1999).
4. Seth Whidden (2007: 22).
5. By 'ordinary' writing and reading practices, I refer to a range of non-remunerated literate activities taking place in relative privacy. The term is inevitably contentious; see discussion by Hervé Moëlo (2004). In her *Uses of Literature*, Rita Felski refers to 'folk reading' and 'lay reading', which she contrasts with so-called 'scholarly reading' (2008: 12 & 14); she does, however, stress that there is not a neat dichotomy between the two modes (2008: 12).
6. Consider, for example: the symposium 'Probing the Intimate: Cross-Cultural Queries of Proximity and Beyond' held by the Division of Social Anthropology at the University of Cambridge, 12–13 May 2014; the exhibition 'Closer: Intimacies in Art' at the National Gallery of Denmark, 11 February–8 May 2016; or the workshop 'Ugly Intimacies', held at the University of California, Berkeley, on 17 May 2016, co-organised with the University of Copenhagen.
7. Consider, for example: *La Naissance de l'intime: 3000 foyers parisiens, XVII–XVIIIe siècles* by Annik Pardailhé-Galabrun (1988); *Narrations déviantes: l'intimité entre femmes dans l'imaginaire français du dix-septième siècle* by Marianne Legault (2008); and *Intimités amoureuses: France 1920–1975* by Anne-Claire Rebreyand (2008). In English, see: *Spectacles of Intimacy: A Public Life for the Victorian Family*, ed. by Karen Chase and Michael Levenson (2000); and *The Burdens of Intimacy: Psychoanalysis and Victorian Masculinity* by Christopher Lane (1999). Few of these books define 'intimacy' at any length, or engage with it as a concept distinct from sexuality, romantic love, or domesticity.
8. For example, Theodore Zeldin, *An Intimate History of Humanity* (1994), Joanna Bourke, *An Intimate History of Killing: Face-to-Face Killing in Twentieth-Century Warfare* (1999), and John L. Locke, *Eavesdropping: An Intimate History* (2010).
9. Cf. Jean Baudrillard, 'La Sphère enchantée de l'intime' (1986). For Baudrillard, *intime* is a 'mot chargé d'affect, de vécu' (1986: 15).
10. I focus on French literary culture in this book, but cross-cultural comparison with Britain and other European countries would be highly fruitful.
11. 'Bourgeois' is a complex term. In this book it is used to refer to individuals, families, and groups

associated with what Richard Sennett labels 'nonfeudal, mercantile or administrative work' (1993: 48). For further discussion of the term's often negative connotations, and the extent to which individuals self-identified as bourgeois in nineteenth-century France, see Raymond Williams (1976), Sarah Maza (2003), and Franco Moretti (2013).
12. Other social theorists concerned with intimacy in various forms and contexts include Niklas Luhmann (1986), Anthony Giddens (1992), and Harry Blatterer (2015).
13. For further discussion of 'intimate publics', see Berlant (2008) and Gabriele Linke (2011).
14. Psychology has also begun to develop theories of love and intimacy, see Robert J. Sternberg and Karin Weis (2006).
15. Kristeva is central to the concept of intertextuality; amongst other works, see her *Séméiotiké: recherches pour une sémanalyse* (1969); see also Mary Orr (2003).
16. See Jay R. Greenberg and Stephen A. Mitchell (1983).
17. See also Leo Bersani and Adam Phillips' psychoanalytically informed *Intimacies* (2004).
18. On Flaubertian 'impersonality' as both a narrative technique and public posture, see D. A. Williams (1987), Mary Orr (2000), and Geoffrey Wall (2006). For discussion of the Parnassians, see Gretchen Schultz (1999), Yann Mortelette (2005), and Whidden (2007).
19. For Reddy, an 'emotional regime' is the 'set of normative emotions and the official rituals, practices, and emotives that express and inculcate them' (2001: 129); 'emotive' being a term used by Reddy to illustrate the way in which an expression of emotion is both descriptive and transformative. For discussion of the history of the emotions as an emerging discipline, see Barbara H. Rosenwein (2002), Jan Plamper (2010: 255–58), Susan J. Matt (2011), Monique Scheer (2012), and Jan Plamper (2015).
20. An 'emotional refuge' is defined by Reddy as a 'relationship, ritual, or organization (whether informal or formal) that provides safe release from prevailing emotional norms and allows relaxation of emotional effort, with or without ideological justification, which may shore up or threaten the existing emotional regime' (2001: 129).
21. For a history of the Annales School, see Peter Burke (1990). For discussions of cultural history, see Roger Chartier (1988) and Lynn Hunt (1989).
22. The recently published collected volume *Histoire des émotions* is one of the first sustained interventions by French researchers into the field of emotion history, dominated until now by American, British, and German scholars; its debt to the Annales project is clearly stated. See Alain Corbin, Jean-Jacques Courtine, and Georges Vigarello (2016). For summaries of research into the history of friendship, see Sarah Horowitz (2008: 16–19) and Vanessa Smith (2010: 8–9).
23. For example, Martyn Lyons (2008), particularly Chapter Nine, 'Intimate Writings in Nineteenth-Century France'.
24. Diaz and Diaz (2009: 121–26) propose that nineteenth-century authors of intimate writings frequently created an *effet d'intime* by representing themselves within a spatio-temporal scenographic system which stressed the particular time and place of writing: this 'scene' was the backdrop to, and signifier and facilitator of, the intimate encounter. Privileged times of day included 'les moments crépusculaires' (123) while the spaces alluded to were typically constricted and enclosed. Other key leitmotifs contributing to the 'intimacy effect' include depth, religiosity, ritual, and the utopic.
25. Sarah Horowitz's excellent doctoral thesis, 'States of Intimacy: Friendship and the Remaking of French Political Elites, 1815–1848', reveals similar points of contact between intimacy and politics. Horowitz explores the ways in which the language of intimacy, understood primarily as friendship, came to perform key social and political functions in post-Restoration France. More recently, in his analysis of Victor Hugo, Roger Pearson uses the concept of intimacy to articulate the tension between the personal and the political functions of poetry: 'From the beginning [for Hugo], poetry is synonymous with intimacy [...]. But what kind of intimacy? The sharing of personal experience and private reflection in the manner, say, of Lamartine's *Méditations*? Or a close political complicity with his reader?' (Pearson 2016: 389).
26. Cf. Roland Barthes, 'La Mort de l'auteur' [1968] (1984).
27. For a theorisation of 'para-social interaction' see Donald Horton and Richard Wohl (1956). Horton and Wohl argue that technologies used by the media work to create the 'illusion of

intimacy' (1956: 218); the bonds it gestures to are 'one-sided, non-dialectical, controlled by the performer and not susceptible to mutual development' (1956: 215).
28. See Janet Todd (1986), Julie Ellison (1999), Suzanne Keen (2007), and Miranda Burgess (2011). There is also a French tradition, see Anne Vincent-Buffault (1986) and Anne Coudreuse (1999).
29. 'Realism' was not, however, a coherent literary category at first; see Jann Matlock (1995) and Maurice Samuels (2004: 9–11).
30. See Naomi Schor (1993), Cohen (1999), and Samuels (2004) respectively.
31. For example, Émile Montégut's 1858 review of Ernest Feydeau's popular novel *Fanny*, 'Le Roman intime de la littérature réaliste', published in the *Revue des deux mondes*, shows that realism and intimacy could be yoked together in the nineteenth century.
32. As a sample, see Georges Blin (1939), Paul Valéry (1957: 598–613), and Jacques Dupont (1991).
33. It will become apparent that *Intimacy and Distance* is less concerned with Baudelaire as a poet and precursor of modernity, still a fertile strand in Baudelairean criticism, and more with how he is implicated in the literary paradigms of his time. For a survey of approaches in Baudelairean scholarship from the nineteenth century onwards, see Antoine Compagnon (2003), and André Guyaux (2007).

CHAPTER 1

Cultures of Intimacy

The idiom of intimacy witnessed a remarkable flourishing in nineteenth-century France, employed with unprecedented frequency, and used to evoke a range of social, cultural, and literary practices as well as affective bonds. This chapter situates this trend within its historical context. What was behind the heightened applicability and appeal of the intimate? Which political, social, and cultural factors, both long and short term, might explain it? At the same time, the chapter is also an initial attempt to answer the more elusive question of what the concept of intimacy meant, or was coming to mean, to nineteenth-century French citizens. Which contexts could the concept operate within, and how was it in turn inflected by these contexts? Were understandings of intimacy throughout the nineteenth century marked more by continuity, or by change? And how do twenty-first-century definitions of intimacy relate to those of the past?

This process of excavation begins with a series of etymological analyses. The first part of the chapter charts the word histories of *intime* and *intimité*, from their original inclusion in dictionaries of the seventeenth century through to their usage in the present day; special attention, however, is paid to uses and evaluations of these words in the nineteenth century. In the second part, these findings are complemented by a discussion of the interrelated cultural phenomena which contributed to the growing importance of intimacy as an idea in nineteenth-century France. These phenomena range from the long legacy of eighteenth-century sensibility and sentimentalism and the growing dominance of the middle-classes to the immediate need for consoling, often highly nostalgic, cultural practices and forms in a time of social and political instability. The third and final part of the chapter narrows its focus to consider the function of intimacy in the literary culture of July Monarchy France and, in particular, the emergence of two generic categories newly labelled as 'intimate': the *roman intime* and *poésie intime*. By outlining the range of affective, ethical, and aesthetic associations attached to intimacy in the nineteenth-century French imagination, the chapter provides a context for the close readings of subsequent chapters.

I. Definitions, Applications, and Evaluations of Intimacy

Word Histories

Today, French dictionaries define intimacy in four main ways. First, *intimité* refers to a quality of subjective experience, feeling, or thought. Conceptualised figuratively in terms of space, it refers to that which has a 'caractère intime, intérieur et profond; ce qui est intérieur et secret' (*Petit Robert*). *Intime* in its substantive form shares in this sense of interiority; as an adjective, meanwhile, it is used to qualify '[ce] qui est contenu au plus profond d'un être'; 'qui est tout à fait privé et généralement tenu caché aux autres. *Vie intime*' (*Petit Robert*). Synonyms of *intime* include *intérieur, profond,* and *secret* while antonyms are *public, visible,* and *superficiel* (Table 1.1). Second, however, and as implied in the shift from 'tout à fait' to 'généralement', intimacy can also be used to designate a mode of intersubjectivity in which the privacy of this inner life is shared with another or select few. In this sense, *intime* describes '[ce] qui lie étroitement, par ce qu'il y a de plus profond' (*Petit Robert*) while *intimité* can define 'relations étroites et familières' (*Petit Robert*); synonyms of *intimité* thus include *liaison, amitié,* and *familiarité* (Table 1.2). Third, and by association, *intime* and *intimité* refer to environments which 'crée, favorise ou évoque l'intimité' (*Petit Robert*), connoting 'agrément, confort (d'un endroit intime)' (*Petit Robert*). Fourth, contemporary definitions testify to the frequent conflation of intimacy with sexuality and the erotic in everyday language. In her lexicographic and linguistic study of the *intime*, Véronique Montémont shows that intimacy is employed in contemporary French as a synonym for a variety of sexually related practices and conditions, including genital hygiene (*toilette intime*), sexually transmitted infections (*maladies intimes*), and pornography (*intimes vidéos*) (2009: 21); in the 2017 *Petit Robert*, *relations intimes* are described as a common euphemism for *rapports sexuels*. By explicitly including these everyday applications in their definitions of intimacy, twentieth- and twenty-first century dictionaries break with a long lexicographic tradition erring more on the side of suggestion. From its earliest definitions, intimacy has been associated with the fields of the affective and the relational. Yet, while the associations between intimacy and sexuality might be implied, coyly, in dictionaries of earlier periods, definitions of the seventeenth, eighteenth, and nineteenth centuries are far from explicit about the potentially sexual aspect of intimate relationships. This implicitness is doubtless for reasons of editorial *politesse*, in part, yet it also indicates, and results from, the diversity of meanings attached to intimacy. The term has undergone a series of dramatic semantic shifts since its initial inclusion in dictionaries of the seventeenth century, and these shifts suggest that sexuality was not always the primary concern of the lexicographer.

Intime first appears in seventeenth-century French dictionaries as an adjective used to qualify a bond of friendship: 'L'amitié intime que j'ay à vous' (Jean Nicot, *Le Thresor de la langue françoyse*, 1606).[2] The Richelet dictionary of 1679 defines *intime* as a 'mot qui vient du latin et qui signifie *fort profond*. Il se dit en françois des amis et des amies, & veut dire qui est un particulier et vrai ami, qui est ami du

TABLE 1.1. Synonyms and antonyms for *intime*.
Source: *Dictionnaire électronique des synonymes* du Centre de recherche inter-langues sur la signification en contexte (CRISCO), Université de Caen.[1]

Synonyms
âme, ami, amical, caché, complet, confident, confidentiel, dedans, domestique, essentiel, étroit, familier, foncier, fond, for intérieur, fusionnel, indéfectible, inséparable, intérieur, lié, particulier, personnel, privé, prochain, proche, profond, secret, sexuel, tréfonds, viscéral

Antonyms
dehors, étranger, extérieur, froid, impersonnel, ouvert, public, solennel, superficiel, visible

TABLE 1.2. Synonyms and antonyms for *intimité*.
Source: *Dictionnaire électronique des synonymes* du CRISCO.

Synonyms
abandon, accointance, amitié, attachement, camaraderie, commerce, compagnonnage, confiance, confidence, contact, correspondance, familiarité, fréquentation, intérieur, liaison, liberté, naturel, profondeur, proximité, sanctuaire, secret, simplicité, subconscient, union

Antonyms
distance, éloignement

fonds du cœur'.[3] The 1694 *Dictionnaire de l'Académie française* concurs: 'Il n'a guere d'usage qu'en cette phrase. *Ami intime*, qui signifie, Un ami cordial, un homme avec lequel on a une liaison d'amitié tres-estroite'. *Intime*, it adds, can also be used in substantive form to refer metonymically to the friend as object of intimacy: '*c'est son intime*'. While intimacy appears restricted to male friendship in the latter case, entries in the 1762 and 1798 *Dictionnaire de l'Académie française* privilege the more capacious term *affection* over *amitié*, suggestive of the increasing range of love relationships and practices which might qualify as intimate. Whether platonic, romantic, or sexual, however, it is apparent that intimacy combines a relational, 'other-orientated' axis with an inward-facing or 'introspective' one deriving from its etymological roots in the Latin *intimus,* superlative of *interior*. Montémont uses the spatial terms 'lateral' and 'vertical' to characterise these two modes of intimacy: 'lateral' refers to a 'side-by-side' intimacy *between* subjects, and 'vertical' to intimacy as the experience of interiority within a single subject, or 'self-orientated' intimacy (2009: 18). These two modes of intimacy are, of course, heavily interdependent. Operating within a cultural framework privileging depth over surface, 'vertical' intimacy in seventeenth-century dictionaries is primarily used to affirm the lateral; that is, to describe the profundity of bonds between friends who feel a love for the other 'du fonds du cœur' (as described by Richelet in 1679). Eighteenth-century dictionary definitions impart new significance to the vertical axis of intimacy. In addition to the intersubjective, *intime* can now be used to describe the self-conscious individual and his or her moral sense, evidence of what Charles Taylor (1989) has identified as the modern European tendency to conceive of the divine and the self in terms of 'inwardness'. In the 1798 edition of the *Dictionnaire de l'Académie française*, for example, the term *persuasion intime* is defined as 'une persuasion interiéure et profonde'; the phrase 'sentiment intime de la conscience' is also recorded.

With the connection between intimacy, interiority, and subjectivity firmly established, and the affective dimension retained, nineteenth-century dictionaries testify to an even greater proliferation of uses for *intime*, which comes to operate in a wide range of fields and disciplines, including the material sciences. Scientific methods are now able to examine the *structure intime* or *constitution intime* of biological or physical mechanisms (Montémont 2009: 19), and intimacy can refer to the 'essential' nature of an object, animate or inanimate. The substantive use of *intime* also evolves in the nineteenth century. No longer simply a substitute for 'friend' (*son intime*), the noun is employed to evoke the sense of an inner life which can be shared with, or withheld from, others (Montémont 2009: 30). Moving into the twentieth century, the increasing influence of psychoanalysis means that intimacy comes to refer more readily to sexuality and sexual rapports with others; it can also, as discussed in the Introduction in relation to Kristeva (1997), represent psychic life and psychosomatic experience. Changing contexts have thus contributed to the wealth of uses to which the *intime* can be put.

Historical definitions of *intimité* reveal less complexity and greater consistency than those pertaining to *intime*, yet the same shift from the domain of the interpersonal to that of interiority is apparent. In 1762, the fourth edition of the *Dictionnaire de l'Académie française* defines *intimité*, somewhat tautologically, as a 'liaison intime', illustrated by the example sentence: '*Ces deux personnes vivent ensemble dans la plus grande intimité*'. Jean-François Feraud's *Dictionnaire critique de la langue française* dating from 1787–88 suggests, in a phrase laden with implication, the way intimacy can elide implicitly with sexuality at this time; the sexual aspect of intimacy is affirmed knowingly, and paradoxically, by way of denial: 'Je doute que *leur intimité* soit telle que vous dites'. In the nineteenth century, *intimité* continues to refer to bonds between humans, whether familial, platonic, or sexual. Yet it also becomes a quality of interiority or inwardness, applicable at first to the sciences: intimacy is the 'qualité de ce qui est intime. *L'intimité des rapports qui unissent toutes les parties de ce système*' (*Dictionnaire de l'Académie française*, sixth edition of 1835). By 1872, Littré's dictionary has introduced the concept of *intimité* as personal interiority, specifically relating it to morality: it is now 'le fond caché de l'intérieur de l'homme. Dans l'intimité de la conscience'. As we have seen, twenty-first-century dictionaries retain 'liaison, relations étroites et familières' (*Petit Robert*) as a definition of *intimité*, but they also make new additions: 'la vie intime, privée' and 'agrément, confort (d'un endroit intime)' (*Petit Robert*).

Nineteenth-Century Uses and Evaluations

As the increasing complexity and length of dictionary definitions of *intime* and *intimité* suggest, new meanings of the term have not replaced previous ones, but rather acted as additional and complementary layers, creating a form of palimpsest. Intimacy has not fully abandoned its etymological origins or early significations but rather expanded semantically to incorporate new uses. This has resulted in a highly polysemic term or 'notion étonnamment labile' (Simonet-Tennant 2009: 40), employed figuratively and at times euphemistically. In his study of the phrase *je-ne-sais-quoi*, Richard Scholar (2005) states that it is the cap on multiple meanings which signals a word's crystallisation in cultural usage, yet intimacy arguably demonstrates its currency through the opposite process. Its polysemy partly explains its increased employment in the nineteenth century. Montémont's searches of the bibliographic database Frantext and the Bibliothèque nationale de France library catalogue reveal a marked surge in uses of the word *intime* between 1800 and 1900 in comparison with earlier and also later periods (2009: 24–25).[4] My own searches on titles and content in Frantext reveal 564 instances of the word *intime* in eighteenth-century texts and 2967 in the nineteenth century, which reveals an absolute increase of 426.06%; when the relative size of the corpus for each century is taken into account, the increase is 183.33%. A survey of *intimité* on Frantext reveals an even more significant rise. The occurrences are themselves markedly fewer, given the relative inflexibility of nouns compared to adjectives, yet an absolute increase of 680% between the eighteenth century and nineteenth century, and a relative increase of 328.13%, is nonetheless apparent, with a particularly marked surge in use from 1820 onwards.

It is thus easy to acquiesce when Diaz and Diaz ask: 'Le XIXe siècle est-il le siècle de l'intime? La réponse est oui, si l'on se fie ne serait-ce qu'au déploiement sans précédent du mot' (2009: 130). It is not simply the increased deployment of the vocabulary of intimacy which can be assessed, however; functions on Frantext also allow searches for nouns co-occurring with *intime* as an adjective, revealing the range of spheres which intersect with intimacy more precisely. Searches reveal that *ami* is the term most frequently paired with *intime* in the nineteenth century, yet the range of co-occurrents encompasses what Montémont defines as five main thematic and semantic fields besides that of affective and romantic relations: speech and verbal practices (*causerie intime, conversation intime*); secrecy and privacy (*confidence intime, secret intime*); structures of human relations (*union intime, société intime*); the conscience and intuition (*pensée intime, conviction intime*); and internal make-up (*nature intime, structure intime*) (2009: 28). Even more revealing, perhaps, my search of co-occurrents for the noun *intimité* on Frantext shows how the state of intimacy could be qualified and evaluated. Between 1830 and 1870, the adjectives associated with *intimité* are largely positive (Table 2). The adjective used most frequently to describe intimacy in this period is 'douce', followed by 'complète', 'fraternelle', 'grande', 'parfaite', 'forcée', 'profonde', and 'tendre'. The prominence of superlative, hyperbolic adjectives such as 'complète', 'parfaite', and, further down in the list of frequencies, 'divine', 'sacrée', 'sainte', or 'supérieure', suggests that intimacy is

TABLE 1.3. Terms co-occurring with *intimité* between 1830 and 1870 in order of frequency. Source: Frantext, Centre national de la recherche scientifique (CNRS). The search accounts for those terms appearing immediately (one word only) before or after the noun. Terms which I have evaluated as negative are asterisked.

13 occurrences
douce

6 occurrences
complète, fraternelle, grande

5 occurrences
parfaite

4 occurrences
*forcée, profonde, tendre

3 occurrences
affectueuse, chaste, croissante, domestique, mystérieuse, secrète

2 occurrences
agréable, aucune, auprès, bienveillante, bourgeoise, continuelle, *dangereuse, *décroissante, délicieuse, *étrange, étroite, extrême, intime, longue, momentanée, nouvelle, pareille, quotidienne, recueillie, subite

1 occurrence
adorable, ancienne, ardente, arriva, *atroce, auquel, autorisait, belle, bonne, certaine, composée, confidentielle, conjugale, consacrée, constante, cordiale, *cruelle, dernière, devenue, deviendra, divine, donna, délicate, *déplorable, échouent, entière, espiègle, exclusive, existe, familière, *féroce, glorieuse, hardie, humaine, idéale, innocente, intellectuelle, intelligente, involontaire, irait, journalière, *juvénile, libre, loyale, *lugubre, *malheureuse, marcha, moindre, morale, muette, nulle, paisible, parut, persévrante [sic], peuple, pleine, prolongée, propre, pure, quotidiennes, recélait, refaite, renouée, restreinte, récente, réciproque, réglée, *révoltante, sacrée, sainte, semblable, solennelle, soutenue, subsistante, supérieure, *triste, *trompeuse, troublerait, trouvaient, tutoyante, ursus, va, véritable, vraie

often conceptualised and represented in terms of an ideal. Intimacy might be this perfect state or a precondition for reaching it: in the context of romantic love, for example, Stendhal's *De l'amour* [1822] claims that 'l'intimité n'est pas tant le bonheur parfait que le dernier pas pour y arriver' (1980: 109); by way of analogy, 'le moment de l'intimité est comme ces belles journées du mois de mai, une époque délicate pour les belles fleurs' (1980: 110).[5] Yet the inclusion of 'forcée' in the above list draws attention to the parallel presence of forms of intimacy which fail to meet these ideal standards. Of the 118 co-occurrents revealed from the search, 14 adjectives might be construed as 'negative' (Table 1.3). These fall into three groups: one which emphasises the danger and violence potentially involved in intimacy ('dangereuse', 'atroce', 'cruelle', 'déplorable', 'féroce', and 'révoltante'); a second which articulates this suffering in more moderate, melancholic terms ('étrange', 'lugubre', 'malheureuse', 'triste'); and a third which describes types of intimacy which are in certain ways deficient or disingenuous ('forcée', 'décroissante', 'juvénile', 'trompeuse').

The results of this word search can, of course, only provide an initial suggestion of the way intimacy was evaluated in nineteenth-century France: terms are isolated from their original context, leaving room for interpretative error, and the Frantext corpus is representative rather than exhaustive. Nevertheless, the small but distinct cluster of negative adjectives extracted from the list draws attention to the mixed feelings surrounding *intimité* in the nineteenth century; these will emerge more fully in subsequent chapters. Certainly, intimacy was more frequently idealised: Littré's *Dictionnaire de la langue française*, for example, includes Germaine de Staël's reference to 'cette noble et touchante intimité' from *Corinne* [1807] in its definition of *intimité*, thus granting these connotations of social distinction and emotional solace the status of received opinion. Yet it is important to note that intimacy could also be demonised. The second part of this chapter will explore *why* intimacy took on such significance in the nineteenth century, and what was attractive but also in certain contexts repellent about it as a concept. I should make clear at this point that I am not attempting to suggest that the experience of intimacy did not occur in previous eras, but rather, in line with Taylor's argument relating to conjugal and familial affection, that more begins to be 'made of' intimacy in nineteenth-century culture (Taylor 1989: 292) as evidenced by its lexical proliferation. The following sections will suggest ways we might begin to explain the increased prominence of intimacy as a 'vogue-word' (Scholar 2005: 21) and, by extension, concept and practice in post-Revolutionary France. Focusing on a range of interrelated and historically specific phenomena, such as the long legacy of sensibility on French culture and the influence of bourgeois, nationalist, and Catholic ideologies, I argue that these factors combined to create a climate in which intimacy was increasingly *meaningful*, and increasingly — but not unreservedly — desirable.

II. Ideologies of Intimacy

The Influence of Sensibility

The increased employment and largely positive evaluation of intimacy in the nineteenth century can be traced first to the pan-European culture of sensibility. Certain scholars present sensibility as a specifically eighteenth-century phenomenon which died out with the French Revolution (Todd 1986: 130). However, if yoked to the late-eighteenth and early-nineteenth-century cultures of sentimentality and Romanticism, sensibility can be interpreted more broadly as the crystallisation of a major shift in values which persisted after 1789 and is, moreover, still in evidence today. Directions in recent criticism support this view. Ellison's expanded 'Age of Sensibility', for example, begins with the behaviour of male political elites at the time of the English Exclusion Crisis (1679–81) and ends with the Tripolitan War of 1815, but Ellison also reads the 'liberal masculine emotion' (1999: 1) in evidence in late-twentieth-century American political culture as an echo of this earlier age. Cohen (1999) charts the popularity of female-authored sentimental fiction in France in the early nineteenth century; Berlant (2008) considers sentimentality in relation to 'female-coded' American literature of the nineteenth and twentieth centuries.[6] Despite differences pertaining to period and country, sensibility and sentimentality are both outlooks which share a commitment to the importance of emotion. This commitment was made possible by changes in the moral evaluation of nature and so-called 'natural' feeling in the modern era.[7] In earlier cultural and theological frameworks, the natural world had been considered as at best insignificant and, at worst, morally reprehensible. Within orthodox Catholicism, for example, it was believed that humans' natural instincts testified to the presence of original sin which could only be alleviated through God's grace, via the mediation of Church authorities. Emotions, or passions, operating at the level of instinct, were what led humans to deviate from the right course of conduct promoted by religious instruction or, in a secular paradigm, reason; they were thus to be distrusted. However, shifts in the theological and scientific landscape were to alter assumptions regarding the ethical and epistemological advantages of emotion. Taylor (1989) traces these changes to the Reformation and the Protestant rejection of theological mediation, together with the emergence of the Deist thought of John Locke, Francis Hutcheson, and the third Earl of Shaftesbury. In Deist terms, for example, the natural world made visible the providential order of God's design; God's activity could thus be perceived through observation of the non-sacred, everyday environment.[8] Correspondingly, in the realm of the human, 'natural' or apparently spontaneous and unpremeditated movements of love and sympathy were now seen to link individuals directly to the divine. Even in the more overtly secular context which emerged with Enlightenment empiricism, scientific awareness of the importance of sensation and sense-perception for the human accumulation of knowledge was closely bound up with, and further contributed to, the positive evaluation of emotion.[9] Emotions, whether these were seen as physiological, psychological, or spiritual in nature, could provide agents with the means to knowledge, both human and divine.

Early artistic articulations of sensibility drew on both the materialist and religious discourses surrounding sensation and sentiment, on 'a new set of attitudes towards love and virtue, and more generally, the celebration of the ascendency of "nature", "instinct", and the emotions in moral life' (Lewis 2009: 15). Natural feeling now became 'the source of right impulse or sentiment' (Taylor 1989: 284): at least in theory, an individual's worth correlated with his or her capacity for feeling instead of his or her social, financial, or political status. The new literary aesthetic emerging in the mid eighteenth century reflected these ideas: popular epistolary fictions such as *Pamela, or Virtue Rewarded* [1740] by Samuel Richardson and *Julie, ou la nouvelle Héloïse* [1761] by Rousseau centred on sensitive and by extension virtuous protagonists, typically young and poor, in morally testing predicaments. These protagonists elicited sympathetic and often tearful responses from an increasingly literate bourgeois readership, which affirmed the moral worth of all concerned in the reading encounter.[10] Such responses relied on a universalist conception of humanity which valued sentiment for what it communicated of a natural character and shared moral code. As Hunt explains, eighteenth-century readers:

> Empathized across traditional social boundaries between nobles and commoners, masters and servants, men and women, perhaps even adults and children. As a consequence, they came to see others — people they did not know personally — as like them, as having the same kind of inner emotions. (Hunt 2007: 40)

The literature of sensibility was prized by readers for what the narrative and, crucially, their affective response to it, expressed and affirmed about human nature at large. Yet this literature was not valued by all. As Todd has demonstrated, the literature of sensibility was 'always on the defensive' (1986: 129), frequently criticised as 'anodyne, escapist and simplifying' (1986: 129), premised on vicariousness.[11] A misogynistic agenda was in operation in much anti-sentimentalist rhetoric, whether implicitly or explicitly: although the paradigmatic texts of sensibility were male-authored, the cultural attitude as a whole was seen to be beholden to the so-called 'feminine' qualities of excessive susceptibility to sensation, and physiological and moral weakness. These initially negative evaluations took on added urgency in the wake of the French Revolution and Terror, both in France (Reddy 2001) and Britain (Todd 1986: 130), the latter country highly attentive to and affected by developments across the Channel. Nineteenth-century critics interpreted these events as an outcome of the excessive attention paid to sentiment by the 'emasculated' literature and culture of the preceding century. In the nineteenth century, the ethics and aesthetics of eighteenth-century sensibility were thus a convenient explanation and scapegoat for the chaos of revolution.[12] However, despite the virulent strain of anti-sentimentalist rhetoric, the appeal of shared feelings in the literary sphere lived on, albeit in new guises.

Intimacy is not in itself an emotion. Yet, when considered as a state conducive to conceptualising and communicating emotions, it can be seen to participate in sensibility's moral economy. Lexical studies of Rousseau's œuvre, for example, treat *intimité* and *intime* as part of the wider semantics of sentiment evident in his writing.[13] While *intimité* does not recur with the same frequency as *amour* or *amitié*, Rousseau's use of the term shows it to be a quality of romantic love and friendship. It thus contrasts with and compensates for the majority of bonds experienced in society. In Rousseau's eyes, social conventions based on hierarchical systems and strict codes of *politesse* destroy the naivety of childhood and lead to inauthentic human relations in which natural inclinations and sentiments are restrained, disguised, and falsified. Intimacy, in contrast, emerges as 'un type de relation échappant aux contraintes' (Perrier 1980: 428): a relational mode which brings individuals into contact with the 'true' nature of themselves and others, and allows them to live in harmony. In Rousseau's lexicon, intimacy connotes transparency, authenticity, and sincerity. And by endowing his *Confessions* [1782] with the epigraph '*intus, et in Cute*' ('intérieurement et sous la peau' (1959: 5)), Rousseau signals — even if, ultimately, disingenuously — his intention to unveil his 'inner self' to the reader.[14] Prominent in Rousseau's vocabulary of sensibility and sentimentality, *intimité* thus profits from the ethical and aesthetic privileges attached to these cultural attitudes. Yet it also emerges as an obvious target for the critical hostility which has simultaneously dogged these paradigms since their first emergence in artistic culture (and which has also, of course, dogged Rousseau's work). While the following sub-sections continue to explore key aspects of the ideological *appeal* of intimacy in nineteenth-century France, the negative connotations of sensibility and the effect of these on evaluations of intimacy should nonetheless be kept in mind.

Intimité bourgeoise

One site where the 'authentic' intimacy prized by Rousseau might be seen to flourish in the eighteenth and nineteenth centuries was the home. Michelle Perrot has argued that, post-1789, the middle-class family emerged as the new 'cellule de base' (1999: 82) of modern French society: ensuring the pre-eminence and stability of the family unit over and above other collective allegiances would, it was hoped, ensure stability and, significantly, a reproducible social order at the national level. Etiquette manuals, produced and consumed primarily by the bourgeoisie, promoted the pleasures and privileges of the *foyer*.[15] These etiquette manuals reveal and thus perpetuate a marked distrust of the post-Revolutionary public sphere, populated by a sea of unknown and potentially threatening strangers; while Sennett (1993) suggests that distance provided a safe space for 'play' in eighteenth-century public life, it can appear closer to a strategy of self-defence in the nineteenth century, marked by political turmoil and a climate of paranoia and suspicion. In contrast, home life was seen to allow for the expression of natural affections and emotions, and thus, remaining within the sentimental paradigm, for an individual's inner self and moral worth to flourish. From Reddy's perspective (2001), the home thus becomes a form of private 'emotional refuge' from the 'emotional regimes' in operation in public life. In the language of the etiquette manuals, private life is often articulated as *intimité*. The *Nouveau manuel complet de la bonne compagnie, ou Guide de la politesse et de la bienséance* by Mme Celnart, the pseudonym of Élisabeth-Félicie Bayle-Mouillard, claims, for example, that 'l'intimité conjugale dispense, il est vrai, de l'étiquette établie par la politesse' (1839: 22). Discussing the practice of *tutoiement*, Jules Rostaing — gender-swapping under the pseudonym Mme J.-J. Lambert in the *Manuel de la politesse des usages du monde et du savoir-vivre* — affirms that husband and wife 'pourront bien se tutoyer dans l'intimité; mais jamais devant une tierce personne, et encore moins en public' ([18—]: 20). As this sentence suggests, the lines of intimacy in these normative texts are strictly drawn and demand constant care and attention. It is only in an 'intimité parfaite' (Bayle-Mouillard 1839: 242) that etiquette can be relaxed, and this relaxation does not preclude mutual 'égards' or respect (1839: 22).

If these manuals frequently use *intimité* to evoke the safe space of home, we have already seen that adjectives co-occurring with *intimité* in the Frantext corpus (*domestique*, *quotidienne*, *bourgeoise* and *conjugale*; see Table 1.3) present intimacy as a specifically middle-class and house-bound state. In this light, the appeal of intimacy inevitably takes on a gendered dimension. Conventional sex roles, particularly restrictive in the post-Napoleonic landscape, limited female participation in the public sphere while the emerging ideal of the *femme au foyer* effectively defined middle-class women in terms of domestic space.[16] Indeed, in Ernest Feydeau's *roman intime*, *Fanny*, it is, ironically, against the backdrop of 'une intimité si captivante' (1858: 50) that the narrator sets his adulterous fantasies:

> Je me représentais Fanny, le soir, seule avec lui [son mari], après le départ des enfants, dans la chambre close où le thé fumait dans les tasses, sous la lueur adoucie de la lampe, auprès du feu qui doucement bruissait dans les cendres chaudes. Alors, de ces mêmes yeux que j'aimais tant, elle le regardait. Elle causait avec lui, aimable, facile, parlant peu pour lui laisser le plaisir de parler, soumise comme il convient à la femme quand elle est belle et le maître est fort.
> (Feydeau 1858: 50)

In Feydeau's depiction, the idealised space of *intimité* is rendered both through and for the male gaze, manifest at the three-fold level of husband, lover, and author; the male is the creative force at the centre of this world, leaving no room for female fulfilment.[17] Likewise, the *intimité* of the etiquette book, whether male or female authored, appeals to a patriarchal social order in which wife is rendered subordinate to husband: the intimacy of the *foyer*, real or imagined, may be an 'emotional refuge' (Reddy 2001: 129) for the male, but is, arguably, another space of emotional and intellectual constraint for the female. As a bourgeois value, therefore, intimacy appears sanctified and safeguarded through representations in both normative and non-normative literature. Central to the 'affirmation of ordinary life' characteristic of Western modernity (Taylor 1989: 211), intimacy speaks of the cultural, political, and legal investment in private life responsible, in Sennett's narrative (1993), for the 'fall of public man', and of pervasive bourgeois ideology consigning women to the domestic sphere.[18]

'Ces foyers d'autrefois': Intimacy and *salon* Culture

However, as the excerpt from *Fanny* so neatly demonstrates, while intimacy might frequently evoke the material and emotional comforts of middle-class married life (steaming cups of tea, embers glowing in the fireplace), it can also connote extra-familial bonds — like those of adultery, or simply friendship — which threaten the autonomy of the bourgeois family unit. And in certain nineteenth-century contexts, intimacy can gesture also to an aristocratic value system articulated in *opposition* to the increasingly dominant bourgeois ethos. This might seem, at least, counter-intuitive and, at most, contradictory: in many cases, *intimité* is identified with the bourgeoisie *against* behavioural practices associated with the nobility as part of a conscious effort at self-definition on the part of the former. Returning to the question of *tutoiement*, for example, Pierre Boitard's *Guide-manuel de la bonne compagnie, du bon ton, et de la politesse* [1851] contrasts nature and affection with aristocratic codes of conduct: 'Devez-vous *tutoyer* votre père, votre mère, votre femme ou votre mari, et vos enfants? L'orgueil et l'aristocratie disent *non*! L'affection et la nature disent *oui*!' (1861: 18). Here, Boitard alludes to the 'aristocratic' virtue of reserve which can be seen to have developed across sixteenth- and seventeenth-century royal courts in a displacement of medieval warrior ethics.[19] Yet the dichotomy he draws in this instance is complicated by two factors: first, the paradoxical tendency of the nineteenth-century bourgeoisie to model their behaviour on aristocratic ideals as much as against them, and vice versa; and second, a pervasive nineteenth-century nostalgia for 'elite' modes of pre-Revolutionary or Restoration sociability seen to be threatened in post-1830 France. One of these modes was the *salon*, a regular and small-scale social gathering held at an individual's home which offered a particular kind of intimacy or, to use Reddy's terminology again, 'emotional refuge' (2001: 129).

Salons continued to be held in the July Monarchy and Second Empire, but these were widely considered to be pale imitations of the 'foyers d'autrefois' (Rostaing [18—]: 58): *foyers* associated not with the bourgeoisie but rather 'high-status' socialising in which intimacy extended comfortably beyond the family unit. A common complaint amongst nineteenth-century cultural commentators concerned what was felt to be the increasingly 'individualistic' society developing in France, and the concomitant loss of forums for collective sociability.[20] In the subsection 'Les Salons: jadis et aujourd'hui' of the *Manuel de la politesse*, a text with clear Royalist sympathies, Rostaing diagnoses France's perceived ills:

> Ce qui lui manque ce sont des centres de réunion, ces foyers d'autrefois où [l'esprit] venait se former, se polir au contact de l'intelligence, du génie et de la beauté, et où il rencontrait des modèles de perfection en tout genre. (Rostaing [18—]: 58)

The description that follows, slipping between the general and the anecdotal, elaborates this ideal vision of *ancien régime* sociability. The perfection of these exclusive communities is articulated at the level of tone, mood, and figurative aroma: it is the 'cachet particulier' and 'parfum de délicatesse' ([18—]: 58) which sets these forums apart from later, more democratic modes of socialising. In his 1831 study of Victor Hugo, Sainte-Beuve uses similar terms to describe the Romantic literary *salons* or *cénacles* of the Restoration era, recalled as spatial and sentimental refuges from the '*vulgarité* liberale' (*PC*: 340) of modern life, and critical indifference or hostility to Romanticism: 'C'était au premier abord dans ces retraites mondaines quelque chose de doux, de parfumé, de caressant et d'enchanteur'; 'Un écho de la *sentimentalité* de Mme de Staël y retentissait vaguement' (*PC*: 340). The Romantic *cénacles* of the 1820s, home to Hugo, Sainte-Beuve, Alphonse de Lamartine, and Alfred de Vigny amongst others, were predominantly spaces of male intimacy: 'Autour de Hugo, et dans l'abandon d'une intimité charmante, il s'en était formé un très-petit nombre de nouveaux' (*PC*: 342). Yet Sainte-Beuve's descriptions connect this homosociality to past literary communities which include, for example, the seventeenth-century *salons* of Mme de Rambouillet. They thus gender the *salon*, and intimacy, at the level of language and cultural memory by evoking images of the female-facilitated sociability characteristic of the *ancien régime*. In these descriptions, it seems, the 'feminised' intimacy of the *salon* is located in an idealised and essentially aristocratic past, to the extent that Rostaing, writing under a female pseudonym, can conclude that it is 'la démocratie [qui] a tué le règne des femmes et des salons' ([18—]: 72). Remaining *salons* were the mere vestiges of former glories. Rostaing describes attempts to resurrect *salon* culture under the Second Empire: 'Les lundis de madame de Blocqueville, les jeudis académiques de madame d'Haussonville, les raoûts intimes de madame de Janzé, [...] n'avaient pas d'autre but que de recueillir les épaves de ce qui fut autrefois le monde' ([18—]: 72).[21] However, even if *salons* were considered a thing of the past, this past had, nonetheless, been inimitably French: the ideal of the *salon* thus had continued leverage within a nineteenth-century nationalist discourse seeking to shape the identity — simultaneously past, present, and future — of the country.

National Ideology: Intimacy as French?

As used by Sainte-Beuve in the 1830s, the vocabulary of intimacy, and what appear to be cognate terms (*sentimentalité, délicatesse, douceur*), aligns with a nostalgic idealisation of the past. The *salon* and *cénacle* as intimate social spaces recall the manners of past elite groups, and thus function as antidotes to the behavioural norms prevailing in modern French society. It is this particular sense of intimacy as a social rather than a domestic phenomenon that becomes tied to notions of French self-definition in the period, and partakes in the prevalent nationalist and patriotic rhetoric. While Stendhal makes claims for Italy's superior gifts at romantic intimacy in *De l'amour*, the French appropriation of the value can be seen most evidently in cross-cultural comparisons with England, a nation which symbolised, perhaps more than any other, what was different about France, politically, socially, and psychologically.[22] England shared in the apotheosis of the home visible in France; indeed, for many, this phenomenon had itself spread from England, and the country thus stood as a warning for what French society might become if no action was taken against the rise of individualism. Thus rather than argue that domesticity was distinctively French, patriotic commentators detached intimacy from the home and used it to refer to a quality of sociability which, even if *salons* were in decline, was still considered characteristically 'French'. The English, it was held, were antisocial and reserved to the point of coldness; they were thus unsuited to the sort of interactions associated with 'intimate' gatherings.[23] Such stereotypes had long formed part of the French repertoire of Anglophobic discourse and persisted during the July Monarchy: even though this was a period of relative calm with regard to Franco-British relations, insistence on national identity and particularity was still considered necessary for political cohesion and stability.[24] As Horowitz (2008) shows, François Guizot identified *intimité* as a key point of difference between France and England during his time as the French ambassador to London. Writing in a letter to his mistress, Princess Lieven, in 1840, he describes how a dinner party one evening provided him with the perfect opportunity to air this observation:

> 'Mais nous avons un seul avantage, l'intimité; nous aimons l'intimité; nous avons l'intimité' Je me suis recrié 'C'est précisément ce que vous n'avez pas. Je ne sais pas comment vous êtes dans vos ménages; mais en sortant du ménage, de la famille, vous tombez tout de suite dans le *rout*. Il faut à l'intimité un laisser-aller, un besoin de communication, de sympathie, d'épanchement, que vous n'avez pas'.[25]

The English, Guizot suggests, socialise either with their immediate family or at large-scale gatherings which preclude any genuine communication or interpersonal intimacy: these are 'routs' *tout court* rather than the 'raoût intime' evoked by Rostaing ([18—]: 72) in relation to the France of the Second Empire. Lamartine shares this view of English forms of intimacy. In the account of his European and Middle Eastern travels from 1832–33, he provides a description of the English character:

> Les Anglais sont un grand peuple moral et politique; mais, en général, ils ne sont pas un peuple sociable. — Concentrés dans la sainte et douce intimité du foyer de famille, quand ils en sortent, ce n'est pas le plaisir, ce n'est pas le besoin de communiquer leur âme ou de répandre leur sympathie; c'est l'usage, c'est la vanité qui les conduit. (Lamartine 1845: 77)

Together, these two passages exemplify the semantic plasticity of intimacy and also its political and patriotic potential. For Lamartine, the *foyer*-based intimacy of the English might be *sainte* and *douce*, but this morality does not extend to the English attitude to social life more broadly, for which vanity is the overriding motivation. Yet when intimacy alludes to sociability, sensibility, and sympathy, and the moral superiority embedded in these terms, it is seen as the distinct property of the French, and a source of national pride.

Cœur à cœur avec Jésus: Intimacy and Religion

In addition to its role in nationalist discourse, intimacy was associated with religious faith and practice in nineteenth-century France. The relocation of the divine 'within' the individual rather than 'without', which Taylor dates to St Augustine, gradually wedded the 'vertical' axis of intimacy with God.[26] Over time, although the role of the priest as mediator varied between denominations, both Protestant and Catholic Christians felt increasingly able to access the divine through personal introspection.[27] As we have seen, the eighteenth-century move to conceptualise moral faculties, such as the conscience or soul, as *intime* attests to this shift in perspective. Yet the vocabulary of intimacy, love, and friendship was also employed by nineteenth-century theologians and religious writers as a model for an individual's affective relationship with the divine. Hubert Lebon's Catholic handbook *Cœur à cœur avec Jésus, ou Pieuses affections d'une âme aimante se plaçant en toute intimité avec son Dieu* (1857) suggests a personal and private way of relating to Jesus as a friend or an intimate to which, surprisingly, Ernest Renan's hugely popular secular biography of Jesus, *Vie de Jésus* [1863] (1873), gave further impetus.[28]

The 1872 English-language version of Lebon's work, translated by Samuel Cooke, bears the title *Heart to Heart with Jesus: or, Pious Affections of a Loving Soul Placing Herself in Tender Intimacy with Her God*. By maintaining the feminine pronoun, Cooke draws attention to the highly gendered emphasis of debates surrounding religion in both France and Britain in this period, and so implicitly signals a third function of intimacy semantics in religious discourse. The secularisation narrative proposed by theorists of western modernity such as Sennett (1993) has received significant challenges; as Robert Priest shows, work by historians including Thomas A. Kselman (1993), Ruth Harris (1999), and Sarah A. Curtis (2000) has suggested that 'religious belief was [still] a powerful and dynamic force in nineteenth-century politics and society, rather than a curious anachronism' (2014: 261). Religion was particularly important to women in the period, and anticlerics thus used gendered arguments to attack the Church and, simultaneously, the existence religion could give women outside the purely domestic sphere.[29] The largely but not exclusively Catholic practice of religious confession was subject to particular critique. Women were amongst the most regular penitents in nineteenth-century France, and anticlerics feared that the authority held by the confessor over the woman could, if unchecked, ultimately usurp that of father or husband.[30] Privy to a woman's thoughts and fears, the confessor could, in Anne Hartman's words, access the 'intimacy normally contained within the domestic sphere'.[31] It was held that the priest might also influence a woman's thoughts by focusing on and stimulating an interest in vice: in *Du prêtre, de la femme, de la famille*, for example, Jules Michelet claims that 'par la causerie intime, [le directeur de conscience] influe sur les pensées' (1845: 263). Moreover, much anticlerical writing of the mid-century sexualised the confessor, implying that what was at first a verbal betrayal of *confidence* during confession could easily become a physical act.[32] Michelet describes the confessional box in melodramatic terms, depicting a scene in which divine love becomes the pretext, and facilitator, for all-too-human desire:

> Mais comme si cette chapelle sombre n'était pas encore assez sombre, elle enferme dans un coin l'étroit réduit de chêne noir, où cet homme ému, cette femme tremblante, réunis si près l'un de l'autre, vont causer tout bas de l'amour de Dieu. (Michelet 1845: 244)

Confession between male priest and male penitent could be just as problematic. Often rendered effeminate in anticlerical literature, the priest, described by Michelet as someone 'né homme et fort, mais qui veut bien se faire faible, ressembler à la femme' (1845: 12), destabilised the norms of heterosexuality by entering into the gendered, sexualised dichotomy of confession with a masculine penitent. Consequently, Hartman writes:

> Many of the opponents of confession cited with horror the spectacle of a man revealing his inner thoughts to another man, thus effectively undermining the norm of autonomous, rational manliness. Rather than reproducing heterosexual power dynamics, then, confession threatened to expose instability in the cultural construction of heterosexuality. (Hartman 2005: 537)

Certain male interventions into the sphere of intimacy, in this case by way of the theological sacrament of confession, could thus trouble the dominant vision or 'regime' of manliness in operation in nineteenth-century France. Certainly, the norm Hartman singles out — that of 'autonomous, rational manliness' — existed alongside alternative styles of masculinity which did allow for emotional susceptibility. But, as we shall see in Chapter Two, even for men adopting these behavioural styles, practices and performances of intimacy were vulnerable to attack and needed to be navigated with care.

The ideological appeal of intimacy in the nineteenth century was complex and at times contradictory. At root, the increasing focus on intimacy was tied to the positive evaluation of nature and natural feeling which emerged in the eighteenth century and which the cultures of sensibility and sentimentality rendered widespread. However, its more specific appeal and application remained context-dependent. In certain cases, intimacy appealed to those who shared and identified with the values of family, domesticity, and privacy; in others, to those who privileged personal interactions or collective allegiances which operated independently of the *foyer*, at the level of personal affinity, patriotism, political persuasion, or religious faith. In whichever case, intimacy was often articulated in superlative and highly idealised terms, imbuing it with a strong rhetorical force which bespoke the ideological and emotional stakes at work in its representations. Evocations of intimacy in this period, often highly gendered, intersected with anxieties surrounding societal and political change and engaged, implicitly or explicitly, in debates concerning the value of interpersonal bonds and the source of well-being for both individual and collective. In the light of these ideological associations, the third and final part of this chapter focuses on the way intimacy operated in the literary culture of the July Monarchy; in particular, it considers the newly labelled genres of intimacy — the *roman intime* and *poésie intime* — and the reading practices associated with them. The discussion highlights the explicit connections between literature and the *intime* which materialised in this period, and demonstrates that literary and critical discourse actively produced and promoted new understandings and experiences of intimacy.

Part III: Intimacy and Literary Culture

The *roman intime*

The increasing prominence of the *intime* as a generic category in nineteenth-century France testifies to the ideological appeal and desirability of intimacy within the cultural imagination, and its corresponding marketability. As discussed, *intime* is imprecise as a literary category, given the semantic plasticity of the term and the tendency of nineteenth-century writers to 'prodiguer l'adjectif pour couvrir des marchandises diverses' (Madelénat 1989: 173). Nevertheless, the category offers a way to ground understandings of intimacy and its role in nineteenth-century literary culture within a concrete phenomenon. A 'vogue' for intimate literature flourished in France from the late years of the Restoration into the 1830s and 1840s, a period referred to by Madelénat in his chronology of literary intimacy as 'l'intimisme romantique' (1989). Whether or not the intimate literature of this period was cohesive enough to be considered a school is debatable, and largely a question of definition.[33] *Intime* was later used to characterise non-literary forms of personal writing: the term *journal intime* came into use in the mid nineteenth century, and the Third Republic witnessed a proliferation of journalistic features and biographies employing the formula 'proper name + adjective *intime*' in their title: *Victor Hugo intime* [1885], *Balzac intime* [1886], *Napoléon intime* [1898], and even, as we shall see, a *Charles Baudelaire intime* in 1911.[34] Initially, however, the term was principally applied to narrative fiction and to poetry. Cultural commentators were keen to stress the novelty of the generic category: although we do see references to *poésie intime* earlier in the century, the critic Jules A. David can still claim to be speaking a 'langue inventée d'hier' in his essay on 'la poésie intime' in 1834.[35] In his 1832 essay 'Du roman intime ou Mademoiselle de Liron', published in the fledgling *Revue des deux mondes*, Sainte-Beuve seeks to establish the cultural currency of the genre, and cast new light on it as an object of appreciation; indeed, in a footnote added retrospectively to 'Du roman intime', he claims to have been the first to use 'ce mot *Roman intime*' (PF: 60). The label's newness, however, was still at issue five years later: an editorial preface to Julie de Krüdener's *Valérie* asserts that 'le roman intime, dans le sens où nous entendons le mot, est presque né d'hier' (Anon 1837: x). The focus on the vocabulary of intimacy evident in these quotations ('la langue', 'le mot') points to a fundamental paradox of which those engaging with intimate literature, whether as writers or critics, were acutely aware: while the language of intimacy might be new, the genres it was used to describe were not, and formed part of a tradition dating back to the eighteenth century; *Valérie* itself was first published in 1803.[36] For some, the retrospective 'christening' of the *roman intime* chimed, ironically, with its swan song: in 1831, the critic Désiré Nisard employs the term to signal its demise in the face of the historical or fantastical novel, epitomised for him by Hugo's *Notre-Dame de Paris*: 'Adieu *Clarisse Harlowe*, adieu *René* et *Adolphe*, admirables modèles du roman intime' (Nisard 1891: 112). Yet for those committed to the genre, a literary heritage stretching back to the heyday of sensibility was necessary to establish its credibility. What, then, *was* the sense in which the *roman intime* was understood by these critics?

The term *roman intime* was far from being universally adopted at this time, and coexisted with a variety of other labels including the *roman d'analyse*, *roman d'observation*, and *roman de mœurs*, often applied to the same body of novels and thus testimony to what Cohen calls the 'discursive slippage' of nineteenth-century literary debate (1999: 121). Sainte-Beuve even complained about the indiscriminate and inaccurate use of the term in his review of George Sand's *Lélia* in 1833. However, there were efforts to elucidate the novel of intimacy as a particular genre: the editor of *Valérie* sketches a 'famille de livres intimes' (Anon 1837: ix), beginning with Johann Wolfgang von Goëthe's *Werther* [1774] and including *René* [1802] by François-René de Chateaubriand, *Adolphe* [1816] by Benjamin Constant, Claire de Duras's *Édouard* [1825], and Sainte-Beuve's novel *Volupté* [1835]. In his own critical survey of 1832, Sainte-Beuve aligns the third-person novel which is the central focus of his study, *Mademoiselle Justine de Liron* by Étienne-Jean Délécluze [1832], with Isabelle de Charrière's epistolary novel *Lettres écrites de Lausanne* [1785], and the correspondence of Charlotte-Élisabeth Aïssé, written in the early eighteenth century but first published in 1787. Later in the essay, he draws parallels between *Mademoiselle Justine de Liron*, the letters of Mme de Sévigné and Mademoiselle de Montpensier, and the writings of Denis Diderot and Rousseau (PF: 62–63). Nowadays, many of these works are considered in the context of 'sentimental fiction' or the *roman personnel*, a term introduced in the late nineteenth century: in his 'long-list' of novels representative of the *roman personnel*, Nigel Harkness includes *René*, *Valérie*, *Adolphe*, *Édouard*, and *Volupté* (2011: 441). Like the *roman idéaliste* excavated by Schor (1993), the *roman intime* is something of a forgotten or consciously disregarded category. Cohen's *Sentimental Education of the Novel* does not include specific discussion of the *roman intime*, but a footnoted reference to a review of 1837 which awards '"the prize for the novel of private life [*roman intime*] to women"' (1999: 79, n.3), shows that Cohen considers the *roman intime* to be synonymous with sentimental social fiction, and subsumes it under this broader category; the citation also, of course, highlights the gendered connotations of the genre. Yet, in the context of this book, referring to the works listed above as examples of sentimental fiction or the *roman personnel* is problematic. First, by ignoring the existence of the *intime* as a category it neglects a frame of reference determining nineteenth-century writers' and readers' expectations and experiences. Second, it impoverishes historical understandings of intimacy by obscuring those cultural artefacts which connected and contributed to a sense and appreciation of the concept in nineteenth-century France.

The label *roman intime* signalled a text with particular characteristics in terms of subject matter, narrative features, and tone. These characteristics can be seen to set it apart from the rival forms of historical or sentimental social novel. As Sainte-Beuve writes in his 1832 essay, the *roman intime* is typically concerned with the evocation and exploration of romantic love: 'C'est d'amour que se composent nécessairement ces trésors cachés' (PF: 60–61); these works are 'productions nées du cœur' (PF: 61).[37] His essay thus affirms the connection between intimacy and romantic love in the period, but proceeds to nuance it by suggesting that this love is frequently accompanied by suffering: similarly, in his notice to the 1837 edition of *Valérie*, the anonymous editor describes 'ces histoires du cœur, [...] ces confidences bien-aimées, qui sont le récit presque exclusif et isolé d'une souffrance ou d'une passion' (1837: x).[38] The shifts between *histoire*, *confidence*, and *récit* in this sentence exemplify the ambiguity surrounding the 'literary' or fictional status of the intimate novel, which derives from the apparent basis of the latter in lived experience. This is fiction with, it is held, a major non-fictional and often autobiographical element: authorial alterations for reasons of artistic effect or propriety cannot disguise, Sainte-Beuve writes, the 'vérité profonde' which animates the work (PF: 61).

Within this interpretative model, therefore, *roman* is perhaps best understood in terms of 'narrative' rather than 'novel'. As shown by Sainte-Beuve's article, the *roman intime* often takes the form of historical documents, be these real letters exchanged between lovers or a *confidence* prepared by one of them ('pour des temps où il ne sera plus, une confidence, une confession qu'il intitulerait volontiers, comme Pétrarque a fait d'un de ses livres, *son secret*' (PF: 61)). Ultimately, Sainte-Beuve concludes, the novel's formal properties are 'assez insignifiantes, pourvu qu'elles n'étouffent pas le fond et qu'elles laissent l'œil de l'âme y pénétrer au vif sous leur transparence' (PF: 61). Moving from description to prescription, Sainte-Beuve states that those intending to write a *roman intime* should, paradoxically, 'viser au roman le moins possible' (PF: 61). This way, a writer can produce 'livres qui ne ressemblent pas à des livres' (PF: 60), but which suggest, simply and clearly, the immediacy of lived experience:

the 'pure et naïf détail des choses éprouvées'; 'les traces de la réalité observée ou sentie' (*PF*: 61–62). Such aspirations denote the influence of eighteenth-century sensibility on nineteenth-century conceptualisations of the *intime*. Returning again to *De l'amour*, we see Stendhal suggest that, instead of attempting to dazzle with wit, a lover should 'détendre [son] âme de l'empesé du monde, jusqu'à ce degré d'intimité et de naturel d'exprimer naïvement ce qu'[il] sent dans le moment' (1980: 111–12). Literature *about* love, and about lovers, participates in this same value system in which intimacy, synonymous with spontaneity and truth, functions in opposition to the artificiality and derivative nature of society.[39] The moral value and particular emotional charge of the *roman intime* lies in its 'audience-orientated' intimacy (Habermas 1989: 159): the access it gives to inner, purportedly unmediated emotions. In this sense, the adjective *intime* alludes simultaneously to the self-orientated intimacy of the writer or narrator (in terms of introspection) as well as to other-orientated intimacy (both love and communication): the intimate novel looks 'inwards' to the *intime* and then transmits the *intime* outwards to the reader in an *épanchement* of feelings '*qui n'ont fait qu'un saut du cœur sur le papier*' (*PF*: 77).

A final factor in the appeal of the *roman intime* relates to the tone of the works, and their implied readership. As noted in the previous section in relation to literary sociability, Sainte-Beuve links intimacy with the delicate and discreet manners of social or cultural 'elites'. This association is reflected at the level of narrative style in the *roman intime*. Sainte-Beuve's essay refers to a number of female writers with ties to the nobility and thus reiterates the social and sentimental superiority of these 'cœurs de choix' (*PF*: 60) or 'âmes aimantes et polies' (*PF*: 63) with 'sentiments délicats' and 'simples et discrètes destinées' (*PF*: 60). Distinction at the level of character translates into delicacy at the level of style and tone. Attacking the apparently misplaced critical tendency to label Sand's *Lélia* [1833] a *roman intime*, Sainte-Beuve vehemently denies 'le moindre rapport entre le genre intime et le ton presque partout dithyrambique, grandiose, symbolique ainsi qu'on l'a dit, et même par moments apocalyptique de ce poème' (*PC*: 403). The *genre intime* is quiet where Sand's 'poème' is dithyrambic, simple where her writing is grand, literal rather than symbolic, and calm rather than cataclysmic. And Sainte-Beuve suggests that the *genre intime* can, in turn, be calming for the reader, 'quelque agités que soient les temps' (*PF*: 60). Intimate novels are, in Sainte-Beuve's extended floral metaphor, wild flowers ('fleurs toutes naturelles, dont on croyait l'espèce disparue') growing along country lanes far from the 'grand chemin poudreux' (*PF*: 60) of modern urban life. The primary focus of Sainte-Beuve's essay is the fictional, male-authored, Justine de Liron, the daughter of a nineteenth-century provincial landowner living near Clermont-Ferrand. Despite her rustic qualities, Sainte-Beuve concludes that Justine shares an 'air de famille' (*PF*: 69) with her pre-Revolutionary predecessors or 'sœurs' (*PF*: 63). Consumers of intimate literature can also partake in this family likeness. In the sentimental and, by extension, intimate paradigm, reading and being affected by such 'noble' literature testifies to the reader's noble nature, too; the 1837 preface to *Valérie* cites a sentence from an earlier 1804 preface: '"Vous aimerez les larmes que vous répandrez en lisant ce livre; elles vous seront un sûr garant de votre propre valeur"' (Anon 1837: vii).[40] Intimate literature demands appropriately sentimental responses from its readers, but Sainte-Beuve's emphasis on the rarity of the genre in modern-day France suggests that such responses may indeed themselves be rare. The *roman intime* does not target an 'elite' readership deliberately, but Sainte-Beuve's essay implies that the number of readers able to appreciate its discreet, delicate tonalites is small. While Sainte-Beuve damned Stendhal with notoriously faint praise,[41] the latter's well-known formulation of the 'happy few' — his 'hypothesis of a small, understanding readership' for his work[42] — resonates with Sainte-Beuve's vision of the *roman intime* as a genre which generates a (pleasingly) exclusive reading community brought together through the shared bonds of sensibility and taste.[43]

Poésie intime

As with the *roman intime*, Sainte-Beuve's work is central to a discussion of *poésie intime*. His collections of poetry, published between 1829 and 1837, made significant contributions to the popularity of 'intimate poetry', which was one of the many literary 'postures' to proliferate in France in the 'foisonnante période d'après 1830' (Diaz 2007: 94). This is evident both in the work of poets well-known today (Hugo's *Les Feuilles d'automne* [1831] or *Les Voix intérieures* [1837], for example, or Lamartine's *Jocelyn* [1836]), as well as those less well known: Maurice de Guérin, Hippolyte de La Morvonnais, Delphine de Girardin, Anaïs Ségalas, Nicolas Martin, and Charles Magnin, many of whom express a specific debt to Sainte-Beuve in their work.[44] Precise definitions of the genre are as difficult to achieve as those of the *roman intime*. To an extent, intimacy appears to be what defines poetry *tout court* in the Romantic period, rendering the adjectival qualification of *intime* somewhat tautological and unnecessary. Hugo's statement that 'la poésie, c'est tout ce qu'il y a d'intime dans tout' (1867: 2) in his 1822 preface to *Odes et ballades* resonates throughout the Restoration and into the July Monarchy, to be reworked by Baudelaire in 1846 in relation to visual art: 'Qui dit romantisme dit art moderne, — c'est-à-dire intimité, spiritualité, couleur, aspiration vers l'infini' (*OC* II: 421). Intimacy in this sense alludes to a mode of seeing or relating which enables the ultimate 'essence' of an object to be grasped, whether this is God or an analogous conception of the infinite. The subject matter of intimate poetry is, in this sense, immaterial, and boundless: the intimate, like God, is 'dans tout' (Hugo 1867: 2). Nevertheless, a more precise body of associations did grow up around *poésie intime*. The literary critic Alexandre de Saint-Chéron's observations on the state of the literary field in 1831 outline certain key characteristics: he writes, with palpably mixed feelings, that 'aujourd'hui [...] le poète doit exprimer avec le plus de sentiment les détails intimes de sa vie et se chanter lui-même; et, comme il souffre, la forme poétique qu'il adopte, c'est l'élégie'.[45] As this statement suggests, *poésie intime* and the *roman intime* share similar themes, moods, and interpretive paradigms: in both cases, the narrative or poetic voice is closely identified with that of the writer. There are differences, however, which amplify the meanings and associations attached to the idea of intimacy in this period. In addition to romantic love, for example, a source of the intimate poet's 'inward' suffering can be found in religious or spiritual anxiety. Sainte-Beuve's second collection of poetry, *Les Consolations*, published in 1830, epitomises this tendency, charting the poet's *état de l'âme* and the confused 'mélange de sentiments tendres, fragiles, chrétiens' which accompany his tentative conversion (1879: 163). This, we can add, represents a further association between intimacy and the religious in French culture of the period.

While the appeal of the *roman intime* gestures to a collective nostalgia for pre-Revolutionary eras, critical commentary surrounding *poésie intime* actively highlights and praises its middle-class qualities. *Les Consolations*, for example, depicts scenes pertaining to family, friendship, and the everyday, domestic life of the *foyer*; in his preface, Sainte-Beuve claims that 'c'est presque toujours de la vie privée, c'est-à-dire d'un incident domestique, d'une conversation, d'une promenade, d'une lecture, que je pars' (1879: 21). Detail is particularly important: in the preface to an edited volume of Sainte-Beuve's poetry, Anatole France suggests that the originality of the *poète intime* lies in 'le menu paysage, [...] l'élégie détaillée qu'il apporte' (1879: xiv), and it is here that the specific influence of the English Romantics or 'Lakistes' on Sainte-Beuve's conception of poetry is most obvious.[46] The politician and journalist Prosper Duvergier de Hauranne, writing in *Le Globe* in 1830, praises the 'modesty' of Sainte-Beuve's intimate poetics through the means of a conventionally feminised muse:

> Il ne lui faut ni grandes catastrophes, ni sublimes spectacles. Plus modeste et plus bourgeois, [la muse] loge en garni, dîne à table d'hôte, se promène sur les quais ou les boulevards, et partout s'inspire par ce qui l'entoure. (Duvergier de Hauranne 1879: 138)

Akin to the *roman intime*, meanwhile, *poésie intime* also aspires to transparency. Poets typically encouraged autobiographical interpretations of their work through prefatory material and dedications which readers and critics were keen to accept: Duvergier de Hauranne agrees that, in the case of *Les Consolations*, 'l'auteur et le livre sont tellement identifiés, que, raconter l'histoire de l'un, c'est presque rendre compte de l'autre' (1879: 137). At the level of language, intimate poetry employed informal, conversational lexicon and syntax, appropriate for the expression of idiosyncratic thoughts and feelings not traditionally treated to poetic renderings. Strict adherence to the rules of versification and the consistent use of elevated language were seen as unnecessary for, and even damaging to, the intimate aesthetic: Duvergier de Hauranne notes that 'par un travers assez rare dans notre vieille école poétique, l'auteur sent à sa manière et écrit comme il sent; de plus, le mètre n'est pour lui que le moyen, non le but' (1879: 133).

Not surprisingly, while there was praise for this new form of poetry, criticism abounded in equal measure. The 1842 *Physiologie du poëte*, written by Edmond Texier under the pseudonym Sylvius and illustrated by Honoré Daumier, includes a playful satire of the genre (1842: 44–47), exploiting and simultaneously reinforcing the stereotypes attached to *poésie intime*. While Duvergier de Hauranne stressed the modesty of the intimate poet and his muse, Texier emphasises his immodesty, impudence, and over-familiarity; his egotism, and lack of inspiration or originality (he resorts to writing about 'sa femme, [...] son chien, [...] sa maîtresse, [...] sa dernière digestion' (1842: 45)); his childlike and derivative style; and, perhaps most damningly of all, his apparent deficit of readers combined with an overly inflated sense of self-importance. Less light-hearted criticisms of the poetic practice resuscitated conventional attacks on the eighteenth-century culture of sensibility. Not only was this style of poetry essentially 'modish', a criticism long levelled at the literature of sensibility (Lewis 2009: 15), but it testified to a worrying level of solipsism amongst writers which was leading them to eschew more elevated themes, whether classical, biblical, or historical, and urgent political and humanitarian concerns.[47] Intimate poetry was a sign of artistic weakness or prostration, often gendered as feminine in male-authored criticism. In 1834, for example, Jules A. David bemoans the lack of 'great' poetry in France, connecting this to the underlying and fundamentally damaging democratisation and 'feminisation' of literary *mœurs*:

> La grande et vraie poésie s'enfuit et nous délaisse. [...] La poésie n'est point cette médiocre sensibilité qui vient à toute espèce de gens à propos des moindres affections. À ce compte, quelle jeune fille ne serait poète?[48]

An analysis of the conventions associated with the *roman intime* and *poésie intime* enhances an understanding of what intimacy signified in nineteenth-century France. The content and narrative features of these genres confirm that intimacy was associated with certain affective bonds and encounters (between lovers, family, and friends, or with the self or God), moods (melancholy), tones (delicacy), social groups (both the nobility and bourgeoisie), and questions of gender (female or figuratively 'feminised' writers or protagonists); whether these associations were a cause for praise or blame was context-dependent. This focus on content and narrative, however, might imply that intimacy refers predominantly to modes of writing. Yet intimate literature existed in the public literary sphere and thus took on an inevitably communicative function in relation to the readership it aimed to attract. The 'lateral' axis of intimacy as a relation between self and other was thus a key component of intimate literature. Thematically evident through the centrality of romantic love and friendship to the narratives of both intimate prose and poetry (*Les Consolations* is prefaced, for example, by an extended homage to friendship and its virtues), intimacy became structurally significant through the relationship it implied and encouraged between writer and reader. In her discussion of the terms *sentimental* and *sensible* in the eighteenth century, Lewis writes that 'these terms were applied not only to authors, characters, and readers but also to the trigger objects stimulating them (spectacles, signs, texts)' (2009: 27). The same phenomenon occurred with the *intime*. How might intimate literature, as a cultural product, be seen to 'trigger' intimacy in this period? The final part of the chapter will propose that intimate writing practices in turn created intimate reading practices, both product and producer of what Mole (2007) has called, in relation to Victorian literature, the emerging 'hermeneutic of intimacy'. Not only did literature shape collective conceptions of intimacy, but conceptions of intimacy in turn shaped views about literature, and the interpersonal bonds that reading could, and *should*, create.

Intimate Reading

Intimate reading practices were constructed in a variety of ways in nineteenth-century France. Work on sentimental literature has concentrated on the formal and rhetorical strategies within the primary texts themselves; these are seen to position the reader, implicitly, in a relationship of proximity with the narrative voice or protagonist. Discussing Sophie Cottin's *Claire d'Albe* [1799], for example, Cohen cites intimacy as a 'text-effect' of epistolary and first-person narratives; these 'join reader and protagonist in an I-you intimacy' (2002a: xi). However, text-effects operated alongside, and in symbiosis with, paratextual material and secondary criticism able to reflect and encourage certain reading modes more explicitly. The reading practices promoted for intimate literature can be seen to hinge on the question of reciprocity. This emerges in three separate but interrelated reading scenarios: the reader figured as the 'friend' of the writer or protagonist; identification between the reader and writer (the reader becomes the writer); and a reading experience which mirrors the writing experience. While I associate these reading scenarios with nineteenth-century literary culture, it is important to note that they are, at least in part, refashionings of the eighteenth-century modes of sympathetic reading theorised, for example, by Adam Smith and Diderot, and still highly influential for post-Revolutionary writers like Stendhal.[49]

Sainte-Beuve's 'Du roman intime' encourages readers to approach intimate literature as a predominantly interpersonal rather than textual encounter which, mediated through but ultimately surpassing the literary work, can impact on emotional and social life. The work in question is, he writes, 'littérature aimable et intime' (*PF*: 62): in a correlation far removed from, — moreover, anathema to — twentieth- and twenty-first-century interpretive models (Barthes's 'texte lisible' and 'texte scriptible', for example), the 'likeability' of the literature is dependent on the likeability of the narrator or character. Sainte-Beuve's essay encourages readers to evaluate intimate literature on the basis of their affinity with and sympathy for the novel's protagonists, and to conceive of their relationship with these protagonists in terms of 'para-social' friendship: a feature of what Mole identifies as the nineteenth-century 'hermeneutic of intimacy' (2007: 24). In discussing the eponymous protagonist of *Mademoiselle Justine de Liron*, Sainte-Beuve alludes to but wilfully sidesteps the question of literary construction, presenting Justine as much more than a 'charmante composition littéraire' or sum of formal parts; rather, she is read about and loved 'comme une personne que nous aurions connue' (*PF*: 75), a textual phenomenon whose extra-textual reality the reader can both believe and take pleasure in.[50] In this reading model, love and affection play a crucial role as both cause and effect of the amiable encounter between reader and protagonist. Sainte-Beuve, and the community of like-minded readers implied by his use of the collective pronoun, is shown to elect his affinities on the basis of moral worth. An individual can demonstrate this worth most persuasively by his or her capacity to love. Justine, for example, 'aime comme il faut aimer' (*PF*: 64), and for the reader who:

> Cherche contre le fracas et la pesanteur de nos jours un rafraîchissement, un refuge passager auprès de *ces âmes aimantes* et polies des anciennes générations

> [...]; pour celui-là, Mlle de Liron n'a qu'à se montrer; elle est la bienvenue: on la comprendra, *on l'aimera*. (*PF*: 63, my emphasis)

In an imitative and thus mutually reinforcing process, the reader comes to love the protagonist for her own ability to love: affectionate, loving protagonists ('ces âmes aimantes') breed affectionate, loving readers ('on l'aimera'); romantic love slides, imperceptibly, into platonic love. This mimetic reading encounter is seen as more than a by-product of the intimate reading experience and emerges as a key and justifiable motivation for it: reading as the search for solace and affection, and the trigger for a morally enhancing intimacy.

Intimate reading involves more than the transfer of emotions between writer and reader, however. As will be explored further in Chapter Six in relation to Sainte-Beuve's literary criticism, it is also presented as a process of transformation, or becoming-the-other. Duvergier de Hauranne suggests that the pleasure found in reading Sainte-Beuve's poetry derives from the special access it gives to the poet's mind: 'On aime à suivre cette pensée unique à travers tous ses détours et sous toutes ses transformations' (1879: 135). Here, the two subjectivities, those of writer and reader, remain separate. A later description, however, developing the figurative articulation of thought as movement, suggests the co-mingling of identity brought about by reading. Initially likened to a companionable stroll *à deux,* the reading process gradually divests the reader of his (or her) status as proximate friend and elides him (or her) with the writer, and his thoughts: 'Il semble que nous marchions côte à côte avec l'auteur, et que le long de ce quai désert notre pensée erre avec la sienne et se prenne machinalement aux mêmes vieux souvenirs, s'abandonne aux mêmes réflexions' (1879: 138).

In these examples, critics use the language of friendship, love, and identification to illuminate and heighten the effects of reading intimate literature. Yet evidence that intimate literature was indeed read in this way is provided by documentation of readers' responses at the time. The preface to Krüdener's *Valérie*, for example, alludes to the extra-textual fashion for naming children after the novel's protagonist, Gustave (Anon 1837: vii–viii), suggestive of a desired identification between offspring and literary character, and testament to the deliberate merging of real and imaginary, non-literary and literary, sympathies. Moreover, the rise of literary celebrity and 'fan mail' indicates that readers genuinely conceived of writers, and the narrators or protagonists behind which they were seen to hide, as potential intimates.[51] In the 1840 preface to his 'épopée intime' *Jocelyn* (1954: xxi), Lamartine provides an extensive account of the letters he has received from readers across Europe. Here, reader and writer switch roles: the writer of intimate literature (this poem 'n'est point une invention, c'est presque un récit', claims Lamartine in 1836 (1954: xxi)) finds himself confronted with the personal accounts of his own readers. He explains:

> *Jocelyn* est celui de tous mes ouvrages qui m'a valu les communications les plus intimes et les plus multipliées avec des inconnus de tout âge et de tout pays. Combien d'âmes que je n'aurais jamais devinées se sont ouvertes à moi depuis ce livre. (Lamartine 1954: xxvi)

> Je lis celles [les communications] qui sont des émanations du cœur et de l'âme, et qui ne sont écrites que pour être lues. Quelles charmantes choses! que de trésors cachés! quel abîme de sensibilités et d'émotions intimes! (Lamartine 1954: xxviii)

This phenomenon reveals a desire on the part of readers to 'befriend' and share experiences with the writer (interpersonal intimacy), yet it also testifies to a transfer of practice: that is, the process by which intimate reading leads to intimate writing (introspective intimacy). Lamartine discusses these letters using much the same vocabulary as that employed by Sainte-Beuve in his evaluation of the *roman intime*: in terms of charm, sensibility, and 'audience-orientated' intimacy. Reading intimately thus involves an internalisation and subsequent imitative reproduction of intimate writing practices. This bears comparison with what Martyn Lyons has identified as the 'improvised reading' practices of note-taking and copying widespread in nineteenth-century France, particularly popular amongst 'autodidacts' or self-taught readers. As he writes: 'The private memo-book or notebook was another intimate method of appropriating a literary culture and conducting a personal dialogue with the text' (1999: 342). Yet heightened 'exemplarity' can be considered a specific quality of intimate writing; Diaz and Diaz (2009: 126–29), for instance, date such exemplarity to Rousseau's challenge to the reader of the *Confessions* to 'découvr[ir] à son tour son cœur [...] avec la même sincérité' (1959: 5); a challenge which, as we shall see, was to resonate even with Baudelaire.

A final example of the reciprocity associated with reading intimate literature centres on the establishment of the appropriate environment for the reading moment. Here, the ethical stakes of intimate writing and reading emerge more fully. If intimate writing demands a particular environment then, critics suggest, the intimate reader should in turn adapt his or her reading techniques accordingly:

> Une poésie un peu intime a besoin, *même chez le lecteur*, de solitude et de méditation. Jetée comme délassement au milieu des préoccupations politique, ou prise après dîner pour stimuler la longueur d'une conversation qui ennuie, comment pourrait-elle être sentie? (Duvergier de Hauranne 1879: 135, my emphasis)

The allusion to 'préoccupations politiques' is telling. As we have seen, the ambivalence surrounding intimate literature at this time derived in part from its apparent ability to distract readers from pressing political matters, but in a letter to Sainte-Beuve of 27 June 1830, Lamartine formulates his *pleasure* in reading Sainte-Beuve's *Les Consolations* in these very terms. In a mutually gratifying evocation of both writerly and readerly sensibility, Lamartine alludes to the political unrest of the period:

> Hier j'ai relu *Les Consolations*, pour me consoler de ce que j'entrevois; elles sont ravissantes. Je le dis et je le répète: c'est ce que je préfère dans la poésie française intime. Que de vérité, d'âme, d'onction et de poésie! J'en ai pleuré, moi qui oncques ne pleure. (Lamartine 1879: 148)

Both Lamartine and Duvergier de Hauranne acknowledge a space between intimate literature and politics, yet while Lamartine suggests a relationship of symbiosis and interdependence, Duvergier de Hauranne posits one of absolute separation.[52] For Lamartine, the sentimental pleasures of intimate literature are accentuated by an awareness of the painful political context, hence their therapeutic effect. For Duvergier de Hauranne, the intimate writer is necessarily depoliticised, entirely removed from collective concerns and focused on the self: the reader must adopt similar characteristics in order to fully appreciate his or her work. This advice is reiterated over twenty years later in Baudelaire's 1859 review of his friend Charles Asselineau's collection of short stories *La Double Vie*, which is a work akin, Baudelaire writes, to a 'lettre intime' (*OC* II: 91). Here, Baudelaire proposes a material setting for the reading experience which mirrors that of the writing experience: 'Ce charmant petit livre, personnel, excessivement personnel, est comme un monologue d'hiver, murmuré par l'auteur, les pieds sur les chenets' (*OC* II: 91). The book, therefore, 'veut être lu comme il a été fait, en robe de chambre et les pieds sur les chenets' (*OC* II: 91). This *mise en scène* positions both writer and reader, virtually, in the same private scene, feet warming before the same fire: monologue has become dialogue. The repeated image of the firedogs contributes to what Diaz and Diaz have theorised as the *effet d'intime*: it locates the writing and, by extension, reading experience within a comfortable domestic interior, associating intimate literature with a relatively affluent and leisured class of writer and reader, removed, at least momentarily, from the public sphere.[53]

While his review undoubtedly carries a veiled critique, which will be explored further in Chapter Two, Baudelaire's insistence on mimetic reading simultaneously connects to a broader attempt amongst critics to encourage a sympathetic readership for intimate literature. This can be understood as a response to the anxiety surrounding the vulnerability of the intimate writer, fashioned here by Baudelaire in a state of relative undress ('en robe de chambre'). The extra-textual reality of the narrative voice or protagonist, needed to trigger the particular affective charge and emotional resonance of the *genre intime*, turns reading into a form of interpersonal interaction with ramifications beyond the text. Reading intimate literature means engaging with the emotional life of others, who may be sensitive or suffering: it thus needs to be conducted with care and respect. For Sainte-Beuve, writing in 'Des soirées littéraires ou Les poètes entre eux' [1832], literary *salons* and *cénacles* can provide young writers with this much-needed 'appréciation réciproque, attentive et complaisante' (*PL*: 295), and attentive and indulgent appreciation is figured as an ethical imperative for readers of intimate literature, too. Yet sympathy towards intimate writing was in reality far from universal in the period, and reading scenarios envisaged in terms of reciprocity take on enhanced significance as an ideal, an aspiration, even a plea. As this chapter has discussed, writing practices aligned with intimacy were subject to intense criticism in the period, born from long-standing associations between sensibility, women, and the conventionally 'feminised' characteristics of physical weakness and emotional susceptibility. Under the Napoleonic Empire, sex differences came to underpin the social structure with particular force and with particularly restrictive consequences for women; the charge and insult of 'femininity' thus took on added symbolic weight which was to resonate throughout the century. As the following chapters will show, male writers continued to engage with the literary construction and representation of intimacy but, given this negative stereotyping, developed specific textual strategies in order to do so.

Notes to Chapter 1

1. <http://www.crisco.unicaen.fr/des/> [accessed 26 May 2017].
2. The following paragraphs are indebted to etymological research carried out by Montémont (2009). My survey follows the chronology she establishes but includes new examples and interpretations where appropriate. The historical dictionaries I refer to have all been accessed online; see the bibliography for details.
3. Cited in Montémont (2009: 17).
4. Frantext is an online database of French-language texts (literary and philosophical principally, but also scientific and technical) run by researchers affiliated with the ATILF-CNRS. It currently includes some 4516 references. As the site itself explains: 'Frantext est une base de données de taille moyenne, qui n'a pas l'ambition d'être exhaustive. Son ambition est de proposer un échantillon le plus pertinent possible de la langue française, et de sélectionner le corpus pour lui assurer une certaine représentativité: types de textes, siècles, genres différents'. For further information, consult the database itself: <http://www.frantext.fr> [accessed 26 May 2017].
5. For analyses of *De l'amour*, consult Ann Jefferson (1988) and Miranda Gill (2015).
6. I am arguing that sensibility and sentimentality are broadly similar outlooks. However, for purposes of precision, and given sensibility's long-held associations with the eighteenth century, I tend to use 'sensibility' to refer to eighteenth-century texts and 'sentimentality' when referring to later periods. Ultimately, however, I mean to stress the continuity between these periods, rather than the changes. For discussion of the problems relating to the terminology of sensibility, see Ann Lewis (2009: 27–29).
7. Today, the question of 'natural' feeling is heavily debated. Historians of emotion suggest that our emotional responses are to a great extent culturally conditioned. Certain schools of psychology hold, however, that while emotions may be articulated variously across cultures, they can be seen to stem from the same universal range of affects. For a brief discussion, see Tiffany Watt-Smith (2014: 3–10); for additional texts to consult on these questions, see Introduction, n. 19.
8. See Taylor (1989), Chapter 16.
9. See Jessica Riskin (2002).
10. Cf. Habermas (1989: 48–51).
11. For discussion of the negative connotations of the 'vicarious' and its relation to the sentimental, see Eve Kosofsky Sedgwick (1990: 150–52).
12. Cf. Lewis (2009: 43–44, n. 2).
13. See Louis Perrier (1980).
14. Cf. Jean Starobinski (1957).
15. For further discussion of the etiquette manual as a historical source, see Chapter Four.
16. See James F. McMillan (2000), in particular Chapter Four; also Catherine Hall (1999: 62–64).
17. For a study of voyeurism and jealousy in nineteenth-century France, with reference to *Fanny*, see Masha Belenky (2008).
18. The history of privacy laws in France is highly relevant to the topic of intimacy; readers are referred to François Rigaux (1990), André Bertrand (1999), and Micheline Decker (2001).
19. Cf. Norbert Elias (1994).
20. 'Individualisme' first appears in the *Dictionnaire de l'Académie française* in 1836; see discussion in Koenraad W. Swart (1962), Steven Lukes (1971), and 'Individualism' in Williams (1976).
21. See Pierre Bourdieu (1992: 76–84) on the politics of the Second Empire literary *salon*. A 'raoût' is a nineteenth-century term for a party ('rout' in English). The spelling varies in both languages.
22. Stendhal holds that 'le charme de l'intimité' is particularly strong in Italy (1980: 155) given the

frankness particular to the nation: 'En Italie, [...] il faut exactement penser tout haut. Il y a un certain effet nerveux de l'intimité et de la franchise provoquant la franchise, que l'on ne peut attraper que par là' (1980: 180–81). See, again, Gill (2015: 463) for a discussion of Stendhal as the inaugurator of cross-cultural psychology.
23. On historical stereotypes concerning the English, including their limited capacity for socialising, see Paul Langford (2000). The reserved character of Ralph in George Sand's *Indiana* [1832] exemplifies the way these stereotypes permeated the French literary imagination.
24. On French perceptions of the British during the July Monarchy, see Isabelle Tombs and Robert Tombs (2008), Chapter Seven.
25. François Guizot, letter of 23 September 1840, quoted in Horowitz (2008: 1–2).
26. See Taylor (1989), Chapter Seven.
27. For a discussion of the history of Catholicism in nineteenth-century France, see James F. McMillan (2005).
28. On the popular reception of the *Vie de Jésus* in France, see Robert D. Priest (2014). Priest argues that whilst Renan was concerned with Jesus as a human being rather than the son of God, many readers felt that his work had the potential to 'rejuvenate the Christian heritage' (2014: 259).
29. See Caroline C. Ford (2005).
30. See Corbin (1999: 464–65).
31. Anne Hartman (2005: 536).
32. Consider also Baudelaire's gendering and sexualisation of the confessional in *La Belgique déshabillée*, e.g. 'Charmants confessionaux. Coquetterie religieuse' (*BD*: 265).
33. For a discussion of the controversy surrounding Sainte-Beuve's perceived attempt to establish an 'école intime', interpreted by some as an act of disloyalty towards Hugo, see A. G. Lehmann (1962: 174).
34. Cf. Diaz and Diaz (2009: 131) and Elizabeth Emery (2015).
35. Jules A. David, 'De la poésie intime', published in *La France littéraire* in 1834, cited by Madelénat (1989: 173).
36. On the publication history of *Valérie*, see Stephanie M. Hilger (2006).
37. By 1858, the critic Émile Montégut can label *Fanny* 'le roman intime de la littérature réaliste', explaining that 'les confidences du héros au lecteur se partagent entre sa passion et son mobilier' (1858: 201). While Montégut's essay does fuse intimate and realist literature, it simultaneously implies that the *roman intime* is normally concerned only with passion, not the trivial details of material life considered the hallmark of realist fiction.
38. The narratives Sainte-Beuve refers to frequently feature ill-fated love affairs. On the appetite of French readers for tragedy over melodrama, preferred by the English public, see Margaret Cohen (2002b: 119).
39. Jefferson, likewise, identifies in Stendhal's *De l'amour* a parallel between the lover and the writer: both struggle to express something original and authentic using overdetermined forms which lend themselves more readily to cliché (1988: 45–46).
40. On the changing historical significance of tears and crying, see Vincent-Buffault (1986), Coudreuse (1999), and, in the British context, Thomas Dixon (2015).
41. Sainte-Beuve's neglect of Stendhal is one of the many faults levelled at Sainte-Beuve by Proust in *Contre Sainte-Beuve* (1971: 222–23).
42. Roger Pearson (1988: 38).
43. For detailed discussion of the concept of the 'happy few', and its implications for a Stendhalian theory of reading, see Pearson (1988: 3–18). Baudelaire references Stendhal's 'happy few' motif in an early, undated letter to Sainte-Beuve: 'Stendhal a dit quelque part — ceci ou à peu près — J'écris pour une dizaine d'âmes que je ne verrai peut-être jamais, mais qui j'adore sans les avoir vues' (*BC* 1: 116).
44. For further references, see Madelénat (1989: 172–86).
45. *Revue encyclopédique*, LII, 495, cited by Madelénat (1989: 172).
46. On the influence of the English Romantics on Sainte-Beuve's poetics, see Madelénat (1989: 170). See also the dated but informative Maxwell A. Smith (1920). On variations between the French and English Romantic traditions, see Margery Sabin (1976).

47. See Madelénat (1989: 172–76) for further discussion of the attack on intimate literature.
48. David, 'De la poésie intime', cited by Madelénat (1989: 173).
49. For discussion of eighteenth-century theories of artistic reception, and, in particular, their continued impact on nineteenth-century novelistic practice, see Pearson (1988), Jefferson (1988), and Sotirios Paraschas (2013). Jefferson (1988), for example, argues that whilst twentieth-century criticism has tended to focus on the question of representation and mimesis in Stendhal's *œuvre*, Stendhal is just as concerned with the *effect* of his work on his readers: a legacy of eighteenth-century reading models.
50. This language surfaces again in Montégut's discussion of the 'bourgeois' Werther in the *Revue des deux mondes*: 'Toutes les fois que je reprends le récit de sa lamentable destinée, je sens renaître mon affection pour lui. J'éprouve même une recrudescence d'affection pareille à celle que l'on ressent au retour d'un ami absent depuis longues années' (1855: 333); 'Quant à Werther, nous l'avons connu, celui-là; il est du même sang que nous, il appartient à la même classe sociale. Son père était un honnête bourgeois de notre voisinage; sa mère et la nôtre étaient amies. Enfans [*sic*], nous avons joué ensemble' (1855: 335).
51. See José-Luis Diaz (1994) on the rise of literary fan mail in France, a phenomenon he dates to Rousseau. Jann Matlock (1994: 88) cites an anecdote claiming that Balzac received some 12,000 letters from readers during the July Monarchy period.
52. For a discussion of the ways in which the private and political functions of poetry could nonetheless come together in post-Revolutionary France, see Pearson (2016).
53. For an extensive discussion of the history of reading in nineteenth-century France in its institutional, social, and material contexts, see James Smith Allen (1987, 1991). Allen remarks that, over the course of the nineteenth century, 'individuals increasingly sought the meaning of more freely available texts in deeply personal, isolated acts' (1987: 266), moving away from the communal reading experiences of previous centuries. Yet, as we have seen, the hermeneutic of intimacy meant that solitary, silent reading could still be conceived of as an interpersonal activity. A more detailed discussion of the points of intersection between the history of reading and the history of intimacy would undoubtedly be productive. See also Mikkel Bogh (2016), Chapter Three, on reading as an exemplary motif of immersion and absorption in visual art.

CHAPTER 2

The Embarrassments of Intimacy

> With hard men, intimacy is a thing of a shame, and something precious.
> FRIEDRICH NIETZSCHE, *Beyond Good and Evil*[1]

Nietzsche's aphorism, in its beguiling simplicity, identifies intimacy (*Innigkeit*) as a point of contact, and potential resistance, between two powerful impulses: one which is seduced by and seeks out the gratification of interpersonal bonds, and one which shrinks from the social stigmatisation that these bonds can engender. Nietzsche is careful not to grant these impulses the neat symmetry of opposition; instead, they exist in a relationship of uneasy overlap which hints at a causal link between them, and gestures to a possible reconciliation in the future. The fragment speaks, of course, of men. In doing so, it makes light of a weighty historical accumulation of received opinion regarding sex differences, gender norms, and love. Yet in the context of this chapter, it also functions to crystallise a particular double-bind characteristic of male-authored intimate literature in nineteenth-century France.[2] Male-authored representations of, and engagements with, intimacy in this period are often evoked in terms of shame or embarrassment. This chapter explores why intimacy was considered embarrassing in the literary field and demonstrates how two late-comers to intimate literature, Baudelaire and Fromentin, attempt to cope with and indeed exploit this literary and social predicament. It concentrates in particular on the representations of confessing and confiding embedded in their work: moments of heightened and highly charged interpersonal intimacy which function as self-reflexive *mises en abyme* for the confessional narrative itself.

The first part of this chapter explores problems of self-presentation affecting male writers in the post-Revolutionary era in France, focusing in particular on models of masculinity foregrounding honour, modesty, and emotional restraint in place of sentimental susceptibility. These models make intimacy, whether as a social or literary practice, a trigger for embarrassment. In light of this discussion, the second and third parts of the chapter analyse two Second Empire examples of intimate literature by Baudelaire and Fromentin: Baudelaire's verse poem 'Confession' (first sent by letter to Apollonie Sabatier in 1853, then published in the *Revue des deux mondes* in 1855, before appearing in *Les Fleurs du Mal* two years later) and Fromentin's *roman intime*, *Dominique* (first published in 1862 in the *Revue des deux mondes* and in book form in 1863). Literary history has treated these two authors very differently. This is in large part due to twentieth-century critical tendencies to evaluate writers in terms of their 'proto-modern' potential, resulting in a celebration of Baudelaire's poetics and a concomitant neglect of that of Fromentin. However, if both writers are resituated in their literary-historical context, we see that they share similarly mixed feelings towards the implications of intimacy in the literary field, and that both employ similar strategies in an effort to attenuate the potential embarrassments of the intimate mode. By thematising embarrassment, Baudelaire and Fromentin seek to anticipate and alleviate the potential damage an engagement with intimacy might do to their personal and professional reputation.

I. Models of Masculinity

Recent work on 'masculinities' in the nineteenth century has stressed the plurality and often incompatibility of behavioural ideals for men.[3] As R. W. Connell argues, we cannot speak of masculinity as an autonomous category or system operating independently of the gender order as a whole:[4] certainly, in France, concerns surrounding legitimate styles of masculinity can be linked to the broader Napoleonic desire to accentuate and cement sex differences as a means of controlling both the legacy of the Revolution and the new social and political order of the Empire. Differentiations on the basis of sex are to be found in most cultures, of course, and are in no way unique to nineteenth-century France. Yet, citing Denise Riley (1988), Reddy argues that the post-Revolutionary period was one 'when the assignment of gender differences to the natural order was pushed to an unprecedented extreme' (1997: 63). Post-Revolutionary politics sought to establish the incontestability of male authority and autonomy by relegating women to the childlike status of minors and dependents. The Code Civil of 1804 introduced severely restrictive legislation surrounding marriage which ordered wives to demonstrate obedience to husbands. Access to divorce was rendered difficult and by 1816 was entirely outlawed.[5] The distinct treatment of men and women in a legislative context was reliant on a world view which saw, as Robert Nye writes, 'biological sex as a primordial category of being' (1998: 5) and in which legal difference was a correlative of anatomical and thus ontological difference. While such essentialist beliefs were current in nineteenth-century France, they appeared to need bolstering by the promotion of behavioural styles which firmly demonstrated the difference between men and women. Unsurprisingly, emotional discipline (for men) and the lack of it (for women) emerged as one of the key points of difference. The eighteenth-century 'man of feeling' could no longer be condoned as a behavioural model for men: not only was the culture of sensibility blamed for the political volatility of the eighteenth century, but this style of masculinity did not sufficiently allow for displays of sexual difference. Indeed, sensibility and sentimentality in their historical formulations were qualities in which men, women, and children could share. Post-Revolutionary politics sought to redefine sentimentality as a weak function of the female body while the apparent opposite of sentimentality — emotional reserve and control — was aligned with the male.

Questions of sentimental discipline were frequently articulated in terms of male honour and, perhaps more surprisingly, modesty. Honour became central to post-Revolutionary society during what has been defined as the 'democratisation' of the aristocratic male honour code under Napoleon.[6] As Nye has shown, the concept of honour was associated in feudal times with the 'martial virtues of strength and courage' (1998: 17), testament to the original military vocation of the French nobility. Yet by the seventeenth century, the bellicosity of the aristocracy had become problematic for the monarchy; in turn, the latter effected a strategic transformation of the old honour code in order to privilege discipline rather than unrestrained physical prowess.[7] Honour was gained and maintained through calm civility; shame, and potential sanctions, through volatile, uncivil comportment. Honour and shame thus enacted a regulatory function which controlled the physical and emotional behaviour of the aristocracy, and lessened political conflict. The appropriation of the aristocratic honour ethic for a new bourgeois public under Napoleon reflects a similar strategic effort to regulate the socially mobile and self-directing patriarchy of early-nineteenth-century France and to mark a break with the elision of sentiment and virtue constitutive of eighteenth-century sensibility. 'Real' means (legislative and institutional) were now combined with symbolic means (systems of reward including the *légion d'honneur*) to create, in Reddy's words:

> An order in which the pursuit of honor, not virtue, was enshrined as the normative motive for action in the public service (military, administrative, and political) as well as in the private realm of the family [...]. Sentiment was set aside, a private issue, purely a matter of individual inclination and consumer preference, implicitly feminine. (Reddy 2001: 203–04)

In this context, public demonstrations of sentiment could symbolically emasculate and dishonour a man, resulting in what, according to Stendhal, was one of the states most feared in post-Revolutionary France: ridicule.[8] Under the July Monarchy, the honour code may have become less visible, but, together with the on-going practice of duelling (Nye 1998), the prevalence of references to honour in written documents (literary, journalistic, and legal) indicates that it retained its resonance, passed on, as Reddy suggests, through schooling, reading, and 'the rhythms of everyday life' (1997: 24).

The shameful potential of male sentimental display was also linked to the importance of *pudeur*, a complex emotional disposition encompassing aspects of modesty, shyness, decency, humility, and shame. As with modern definitions of *intimité*, *pudeur* is nowadays predominantly associated with sexuality and the body: Jean-Claude Bologne's *Histoire de la pudeur* (1986) deliberately limits itself to attitudes towards nudity, while Marcela Iacub's *Par le trou de la serrure* (2008) is concerned with legislative attitudes towards sexual conduct. Yet the nineteenth century understood *pudeur* in a wider and more pervasive sense, even if bodily modesty remained a touchstone and common analogy for other forms. The Catholic writer Alexandre de Saint-Albin, for example, asserts that 'l'âme a sa pudeur aussi bien que le corps' (1851: 3). *Pudeur* was the awareness of what decent behaviour should be in the field of sentiment as well as sex, and of the appropriate sense, or at least sign, of embarrassment when 'indecent' behaviour was exhibited. Discussion of *pudeur* was frequently associated with children and women, but this was far from absolute: nineteenth-century etiquette manuals, educational texts, and much theological and medical discourse rendered *pudeur* a desirable value for men and women alike.[9] Stéphane Gerson (2006) has shown that modesty rhetoric gained particular resonance in male-dominated nineteenth-century public and professional realms, employed to temper the egotism and ambition which many feared would fracture French society and its sense of collective identity.[10] Much as the honour code made displays of emotion dishonourable and degrading for men, the language of *pudeur* ensured that 'excessive' self-display retained its potential to shame, complicating and somewhat attenuating the growing appeal of success, renown, and celebrity. Certainly, modesty could seem effeminate, childish, or perhaps old-fashioned for some; Baudelaire writes that 's'il est un sentiment vulgaire, usé, à la portée de toutes les femmes, certes, c'est la pudeur' (*OC* II: 122). Yet Gerson argues that many behavioural models explicitly 'linked masculinity with modesty, cordiality, [and] self-control' (2006: 194). Young men were schooled in self-effacement as much as girls, albeit a self-effacement cast in a specifically masculine idiom: modesty was less a natural state of sexual being for men than a desirable quality to aspire to, evidence of honesty, maturity, and self-discipline (Gerson 2006: 196). Modesty also had an aristocratic heritage, incorporated into the rules of *honnêteté* associated with the French court, entwined with the honour ethic already discussed. This complex heritage suggests that, for the nineteenth century, *pudeur* was as much an aristocratic virtue as it was bourgeois, as exclusive as it was egalitarian, and as 'manly' as it was 'effeminate'. Therefore, Baudelaire can also speak of a somewhat oxymoronic 'pudeur majestueuse' (*OC* II: 104) in relation to Théophile Gautier, whose heroic, age-old modesty contrasts with that vulgar sense known to women. In Gautier's writing, 'la pudeur a un caractère superlatif qui la fait ressembler à une religion; [...] c'est une pudeur archaïque' (*OC* II: 122).

Honourability and modesty were significant styles of masculinity in post-Revolutionary France. They should not, however, be regarded as the only ones. Reddy (2001) might speak of a systematic attempt to 'erase' the legacy of eighteenth-century sensibility in the nineteenth century, but while the attempt is evident, its success is less certain. It is perhaps more accurate to say that styles of masculinity inevitably ebb and flow; that earlier behavioural ideals and codes of conduct survive into later periods, coexisting, perhaps uncomfortably, with new ones. In this light, then, it is again more accurate to say that there was a repertoire of behavioural styles available to men in post-Revolutionary France: honour and modesty were important, but not absolute or sole principles. As Chapter One has shown, sentimentality in its nineteenth-century articulation was still a possible option for men seeking to align themselves with historically privileged behaviours, albeit ones which could also elicit intense criticism or ridicule in certain contexts. An awareness of these competing paradigms and their implications is evident in the writing of male authors for whom the navigation of masculine postures was particularly urgent: distinctions and honours, humiliations and penalties, were to take place, for them, in the public domain. In an effort to reconcile these postures,

Sainte-Beuve's early critical discussions of intimacy propose a literary mode in which sentiment is present, but muted and discreet. Yet intimate literature was, for many, immodest and emasculating in its very essence. The following parts of this chapter will argue that Baudelaire and Fromentin certainly adopt intimate genres, and explicitly acknowledge their debt to Sainte-Beuve. Yet their shared awareness of the embarrassments of intimacy motivates the rhetorical manoeuvres they proceed to make in their texts.

II. Baudelaire's *confessions*

Baudelaire's 1859 review of Asselineau's short-story collection *La Double Vie*, already discussed in Chapter One, alludes to a specifically masculine horror of 'effeminate' intimacy and the related values of candour and sincerity. For Baudelaire as literary critic, Asselineau's writing shares in the qualities of intimate literature: 'Ce livre exquis, par son abandon, son négligé de bonne compagnie et sa sincérité suggestive, participe du monologue et de la lettre intime confiée à la boîte pour les contrées lointaines' (*OC* II: 87).[11] The language of neglect is reiterated in the closing paragraph: 'Il [le livre] a tous les charmes du monologue, l'air de confidence, la sincérité de la confidence, et jusqu'à cette négligence féminine qui fait partie de la sincérité' (*OC* II: 91). The critic admits that *abandon* and lack of *pudeur* have the potential to be charming, even exquisite; within the sentimental paradigm, common to intimate literature, neglect — both personal and stylistic — equates with what is natural and good. Yet Baudelaire instantly attenuates and undermines this charm by gendering it as feminine. Indulging in it as a male writer or reader testifies to a lack of emotional discipline and renders one open to symbolic emasculation and thus ridicule on grounds of effeminacy. For the male writer and reader, the pleasures that neglect or *abandon* might offer are compromised. Baudelaire invokes Asselineau, however, as an exception:

> Heureux l'auteur qui ne craint pas de se montrer en négligé! Et malgré l'humiliation éternelle que l'homme éprouve à se sentir confessé, heureux le lecteur pensif, l'*homo duplex*, qui, sachant reconnaître dans l'auteur son miroir, ne craint pas de s'écrier: *Thou art the man!* Voilà mon confesseur! (*OC* II: 91)

In the wake of Rousseau, the secular, autobiographical *confession* had become a highly popular cultural form, associated with literary intimacy.[12] The above passage can thus be read in two ways. It can be read as an acknowledgement of genuine admiration for and, potentially, envy of male writers like Asselineau, or indeed Rousseau, who live happily with both the pleasures and penalties of the confessional encounter. Alternatively, this admiration can be read ironically and interpreted as an indictment of those writers who, by revealing themselves immodestly 'en négligé', force readers into the humiliating position of both confessor and penitent. When considered alongside Baudelaire's appraisal of Gautier and his 'pudeur majestueuse du vrai homme de lettres' (*OC* II: 104), the latter option seems most plausible: an eternity of humiliation weighs more heavily, surely, than an instant of pleasure.

Indeed, Bernard Howells has rightly pointed out that modesty is of the utmost importance for Baudelaire: 'Despite his obscenity, real and alleged, *pudeur* remains a fundamental value for Baudelaire at all levels, aesthetic, moral and intellectual' (1996: 82). This second, and more immediately seductive, interpretation is, however, complicated by the existence of Baudelaire's own attempts at confessional writing. Baudelaire's plan to rival Rousseau's *Confessions*, articulated in a letter to his mother of 1 April 1861, is well known.[13] While the fragments constituting this project were to remain unpublished during Baudelaire's lifetime, a verse poem entitled 'Confession' *was* published, in 1857, in the 'Spleen et Idéal' section of *Les Fleurs du Mal*. What motivated this apparently perverse desire on the part of Baudelaire to align himself with a literary and theological practice which, elsewhere in his vocabulary, and in French culture more widely, suggested negligence and effeminacy?[14] Why cast doubt on his own status as a 'vrai homme de lettres' (*OC* II: 104) in this way?

The ambiguity, and inscrutability, of Baudelaire's review of Asselineau's *La Double Vie* points to a fundamental ambivalence on the part of the writer when faced with the intimate paradigm. Baudelaire offers his own explanation for this ambivalence in his 1861 study of the female poet Marceline Desbordes-Valmore, whose work he characterises using the same letter analogy found in his review of Asselineau's text: 'Elle [Desbordes-Valmore] trace des merveilles avec l'insouciance qui préside aux billets destinés à la boîte aux lettres' (*OC* II: 147). Positing a total discord between the 'carefree' aesthetic of Desbordes-Valmore and his own, Baudelaire suggests that his appreciation of Desbordes-Valmore's writing is a result of the age-old 'attraction of opposites'; in dialogue with the voice of an interlocutor-friend, the critic explains: '"J'aime cela; je l'aime, probablement à cause même de la violente contradiction qu'y trouve tout mon être"' (*OC* II: 146). The critic's horror at Desbordes-Valmore's 'natural' style is countered by an uneasy awareness of the power that this style can have over the reader (himself, it seems, included). But Baudelaire's decision to position himself in *absolute* opposition to the cultural and literary tendencies embodied in the writing of Asselineau and Desbordes-Valmore is misleading. Baudelaire's guarded appreciation of their aesthetic relates, I argue, to the early influence of intimate literature on his own poetic practice and, in particular, that of Sainte-Beuve: the principal practitioner and promoter of the *intime* in the first half of the nineteenth century.

Sainte-Beuve and Baudelaire

While Baudelaire's posthumous reputation grew steadily throughout the twentieth century, Sainte-Beuve's reputation, as both poet and critic, was suffering a reverse and not unrelated decline. In his *Contre Sainte-Beuve*, Marcel Proust attacked Sainte-Beuve's method of biographical criticism with vitriol, stating, provocatively, that: 'Je me demande par moments si ce qu'il y a encore de mieux dans l'œuvre de Sainte-Beuve, ce ne sont pas ses vers' (1971: 231). Sainte-Beuve's poetry was, as we have seen, highly acclaimed on first publication. For Proust, however, Sainte-Beuve's poetry is worthy of praise only in comparison with the utter triviality of his prose: 'Mais ce peu de chose, ce peu de chose charmant et sincère d'ailleurs qu'est sa poésie

[...] montre — parce qu'on sent que c'est la seule chose réelle en lui — l'absence de signification de toute une œuvre critique' (1971: 232). And while nineteenth-century critics were quick to identify affiliations between Sainte-Beuve's and Baudelaire's writing, such narratives became less common in the twentieth century. In 1939, Georges Blin *does* invoke a possible connection between the two writers' 'poésie "d'intimité"': 'On prétextera que [...] Baudelaire doit à l'oncle Beuve son art d'intimité' (1939: 26). Yet he immediately rejects this genealogy, arguing that the audience-orientated intimacy of Sainte-Beuve, 'le servile sans dignité qui mendie des prix des *Consolations*', is far removed from Baudelaire's aesthetic of intimacy 'qui ne s'adresse à personne' (1939: 26). We shall have reason to come back to Blin's interpretation shortly. For the moment, however, I want to emphasise that such crude representations of Sainte-Beuve, combined with the recent renewal of interest in his literary criticism *alone*, continue to obscure the impact of Sainte-Beuve's poetry on a generation of writers.[15] Baudelaire's admiration for Sainte-Beuve's intimate literature is a recurring motif throughout his correspondence. In a poem sent to Sainte-Beuve in the mid-1840s, by way of introduction, Baudelaire evokes the formative and transformative influence of Sainte-Beuve's *œuvre* on the mind and body of the young poet:

> Ce fut dans ce conflit de molles circonstances,
> Mûri par vos sonnets, préparé par vos stances,
> Qu'un soir, ayant flairé le livre et son esprit,
> J'emportai sur mon cœur l'histoire d'Amaury.[16]
> Tout abîme mystique est à deux pas du Doute —
> — Le breuvage infiltré, lentement, goutte à goutte,
> En moi qui dès quinze ans vers le gouffre entraîné,
> Déchiffrais couramment les soupirs de René,
> Et que de l'inconnu la soif bizarre altère,
> — A travaillé le fond de la plus mince artère. (*BC* I: 117–18)

Some twenty years later, a letter to Sainte-Beuve of 15 January 1866 repeats, but with greater detail and historical distance, Baudelaire's appreciation of Sainte-Beuve's poetry, particularly *Vie, poésies et pensées de Joseph Delorme* [1829], *Les Consolations* [1830], and *Les Pensées d'août* [1837]:

> J'ai repris la lecture de vos poësies *ab ovo*. J'ai vu avec plaisir qu'à chaque tournant de page je reconnaissais des vers qui étaient d'anciens amis. Il paraît que, quand j'étais un gamin, je n'avais pas de si mauvais goût. (*BC* II: 583)

The complexities of the two writers' relationship, and the evident imbalance of power between them, mean that their correspondence must be read with caution: Baudelaire's profession of affection for Sainte-Beuve's poetry can easily be read as a strategic attempt at flattery and recognition. Yet ample textual, and intertextual, evidence does exist to support the influence of Sainte-Beuve's brand of literary intimacy on Baudelaire's verse poetics. Indeed, what Madelénat calls the 'arsenal' (1989: 176) of poetic tropes associated with literary intimacy surface throughout *Les Fleurs du Mal*. Most evident in this regard are the recurring themes of romantic love and home life. The formal repetitions of 'Le Balcon', for example, build up a soothing, richly layered scene of domesticity ('La douceur du foyer et le charme des soirs'; 'Les soirs illuminés par l'ardeur du charbon' (*OC* I: 36–37)), the anecdotal and the everyday imbued by the poet with the qualities of the eternal: 'Nous avons dit souvent d'impérissables choses | Les soirs illuminés par l'ardeur du charbon' (*OC* I: 36–37). The home is the subject of 'Je n'ai pas oublié, voisine de la ville', with its 'dîners longs et silencieux' (*OC* I: 99), while the abstract 'luxe, calme et volupté' of which the poet dreams in 'L'Invitation au voyage' is conveyed, materially, through the extravagant list of furnishings in the second stanza:

> Des meubles luisants,
> Polis par les ans,
> Décoraraient notre chambre;
> [...]
> Les riches plafondes,
> Les miroirs profonds. (*OC* I: 53)

The poet who 'sai[t] l'art d'évoquer les minutes heureuses' ('Le Balcon' (*OC* I: 37)) recurs in 'La Cloche fêlée', where the fireside is the setting for the narrator's bittersweet reveries; the influence of Sainte-Beuve is particularly manifest in this sonnet which bears striking and, to my knowledge, unexamined traces of 'Sonnet VII' from *Les Consolations* ('L'autre nuit, je veillais dans mon lit sans lumière' (1863a: 35)). Moreover, while Felix Leakey suggests that Baudelaire inaugurated the poetic 'conversation piece' with verse like 'Causerie', 'Semper eadem', or 'Sonnet d'automne' (1998: 137), such poems can in fact be seen to speak more of Sainte-Beuve's poetic legacy than Baudelaire's originality: Sainte-Beuve's 'Causerie au bal' from *Vie, poésies et pensées de Joseph Delorme* (1863b: 65–66), for example, proves that this formal structure was already established by the time Baudelaire came to write his 'Causerie'. Representations of *confidences* and *confessions*, often with the intermittent use of *tutoiement*, further add to the repertoire of intimate tropes in *Les Fleurs du Mal*. A reference by the critic Armand Fraisse in 1860 to the collection as as a 'recueil de poésie intime' (1973: 41) indicates that it was certainly received by nineteenth-century readers in the context of literary intimacy, undoubtedly due to these shared thematic and formal concerns.

How have twentieth-century critics made sense of Baudelaire's *intimisme*? For Blin, as we have seen, Baudelaire's poetry '"d'intimité" [...] ne s'adresse à personne' (1939: 26), a function of his cultivated isolation and rejection of the public. Madelénat argues that Baudelaire 'caricature, ironise et extrémise l'intimité' (1989: 188), infusing its literary conventions with sarcasm and 'dérision' (1989: 190). More recently, it has become commonplace to consider the poet of *Les Fleurs du Mal* as one of many '*dramatis personae*' played by Baudelaire '*comédien*' (Dupont 1991: 33): any kind of intimacy or shared sentiment between writer and reader is, in this context, purely performative. *Les Fleurs du Mal* certainly attests to a renegotiation of intimate aesthetics, and it is not my intention to refute these arguments. They can, however, be nuanced. Baudelaire's feelings towards intimate literature were decidedly mixed. Writing some twenty years after the publication of Sainte-Beuve's major poetry collections, he was undoubtedly aware of Sainte-Beuve's own recognition, and partial endorsement, of the negative stereotypes surrounding the intimate mode, articulated in the conflation of intimacy with immaturity in the preface to his *Pensées d'août*: 'On ne peut toujours se distribuer soi-même au public dans sa chair et dans son sang, et après l'indiscrétion naïve des premiers aveux, après l'effusion encore permise des seconds, il vient un âge où la pudeur redouble' (1879: 169). Sainte-Beuve's maturational narrative can be read at both an individual and a collective level, spoken on behalf of a generation of male writers for whom intimacy in the literary field was still, and indeed increasingly, problematic. However, to sever all contact or continuity between Sainte-Beuve's verse and that of Baudelaire, as Blin does, or to consider Baudelaire's poetry as simply a caricature of the intimate mode, suggests a partial reading of the verse which fails to take into account the way the poems of *Les Fleurs du Mal* operated within quite different communicative contexts before their publication in a volume. Baudelaire's 'superstition de la différence' (Blin 1939) might mean that, in book form, he 'interpose entre la foule et lui une poésie d'"intimité" qui ne s'adresse à personne' (1939: 26). But if we consider the poems' 'private lives' prior to their commercial publication, it is possible to see in Baudelaire's writing a vision of the poetic gesture as a form of 'other-orientated' intimacy, very much addressed to *someone*. In the following pages, I focus in detail on one verse poem, 'Confession'. By tracing this poem's evolution through its shifting communicative contexts, from letter to newspaper to book, I seek to identify, more subtly, the awareness on Baudelaire's part of the therapeutic effects the intimate paradigm can offer the author in private, as well as the penalties and humiliations it can incur in public.

The 'confessionnal du cœur'

In an article on Baudelaire and the press, Alain Vaillant makes the passing, but highly pertinent, comment that 'les poèmes font presque toujours l'objet de lectures privées, [...] notamment par le biais de la correspondance épistolaire. Il reste encore à écrire une histoire moderne de la communication littéraire privée' (2009: 43, n. 2). As exemplified by the verse addressed to Sainte-Beuve in the 1840s (*BC* I: 116–18), it was a common practice for Baudelaire to send poems by post. In the case of 'Confession', he first included the poem in a personal, but anonymous, letter of 9 May 1853 to the *salonnière* and 'muse' Apollonie Sabatier. Baudelaire was soon identified as the author of this letter, as well as several others.[17] Nevertheless, his attempt at anonymity is significant: in an earlier letter to Sabatier of 9 December 1852, Baudelaire explains his decision to remain anonymous in terms of *pudeur*, an explanation which allows him to highlight his profound sensibility while maintaining a crucial, and playful, element of mystery: 'Les sentiments profonds ont une pudeur qui ne veut pas être violée. L'absence de signature n'est-elle pas un symptôme de cette invincible pudeur?' (*BC* I: 205). In its function as a private literary communication, and as a textual means of flattery and (indirect) seduction, the poem of 1853 hints at a memory of past intimacy between writer and recipient.[18] The poem recalls a highly charged and unsettling encounter in which a confession is made by the female recipient-repentant ('vous') not to a priest, but rather the poet, 'au milieu de l'intimité libre' and 'au confessionnal du cœur' (*BC* I: 226). Baudelaire employs a variety of techniques in the text to establish what Diaz and Diaz (2009) have theorised as the *effet d'intime*: repeated references are made to a specific time and place ('Une fois, une seule', 'Il était tard' (*BC* I: 225)); a sense of seclusion, security, and sanctity, even in public — the couple walk through the streets alone while 'la solennité de la nuit, comme un fleuve | Sur Paris dormant ruisselait' (*BC* I: 225); and an exceptional, entrancing atmosphere — 'la pleine lune' (*BC* I: 225) and 'cette lune enchantée' (*BC* I: 226). Following the extended scene-setting of the first six quatrains, the confession finally occurs in the seventh stanza. Despite her outwardly sunny disposition, the repentant admits, she is all too aware of the futility of human, and specifically female, existence:

> '— Que bâtir sur les cœurs est une chose sotte,
> — Que tout craque, — amour et beauté,
> Jusqu'à ce que l'Oubli les jette dans sa hotte
> Pour les rendre à l'éternité!' (*BC* I: 226)

The tone of despondency which this confession introduces, while abrupt ('tout à coup') and 'étrange' (*BC* I: 226) in terms of the poetic narrative, can be seen as a common device of *poésie intime*. While the *mal du siècle* is often perceived as a specifically male malady, intimate literature also featured melancholic female protagonists. The opening poem of Sainte-Beuve's *Les Consolations*, for example, constructs a similar confession in the voice of its female addressee, Hugo's wife, Adèle:

> 'Hélas! non il n'est point ici-bas de mortelle
> Qui se puisse avouer plus heureuse que moi;
> Mais à certains moments, et sans savoir pourquoi,
> Il me prend des accès de soupirs et de larmes.'
>   (Sainte-Beuve 1863a: 16)

Like Sainte-Beuve's verse, then, Baudelaire's poem *seems* to be concerned with the representation of somebody else's confession. It is the woman's avowal which engenders vicarious, red-faced embarrassment in the fifth and sixth quatrains, where an analogy is established between the confessing woman and an:

> Enfant chétive, horrible, sombre, immonde,
> Dont sa famille rougirait, et qu'elle aurait longtemps
> pour la cacher au monde, dans un caveau mise au secret. (*BC* I: 226)

Yet, as we shall see, in the context of its private epistolary communication, the woman's shamefacedness is overshadowed by that of the poet.

In the letter to Sabatier, the poem succeeds a series of paragraphs dominated by the first-person singular in which the writer explores the sense of embarrassment he professes to feel about the work in question. Indeed, while the reference to the 'confessionnal du cœur' (*BC* I: 226) in the final line of the poem embeds it in the confessional tradition, the poem does not bear the title 'Confession' at this stage: instead, these introductory paragraphs function as the sole paratext. In them, the poet undertakes an extensive apology for his verse: a confession in prose which anticipates and eclipses the verse confession of the female which follows. Baudelaire's letter opens with a disclaimer, in self-deprecating fashion: 'Vraiment, Madame, je vous demande mille pardons de cette imbécile rimaillerie anonyme qui sent horriblement l'enfantillage; mais qu'y faire? Je suis égoïste comme les enfants et les malades' (*BC* I: 225). Despite his insistence ('Vraiment, Madame'), the regret the poet professes to feel at his own poem is not unqualified and is, rather, indicative of an ambivalent attitude towards the opportunities and limitations of the intimate mode for the male writer. For there *are* opportunities: the immaturity and sickliness of the verse may be what the poet appears to bemoan, but it is also possible to see this apology as a rhetorical device used to draw attention to the vulnerability embodied in these traits.[19] As Margaret Waller (1993) has shown, fictions of 'disablement' were frequently adopted by men as oppositional styles of masculinity in post-Revolutionary France; these Romantic fictions made weak, sensitive, or suffering males attractive by virtue of their very difference from dominant modes of manliness premised on power or vigour. In keeping with Waller's thesis, the poet actively seeks to highlight his suffering in these introductory paragraphs; the genesis of the poem is explained in terms of the affective consolations that memories of intimacy with a loved one provide for the person suffering: 'Je pense aux personnes aimées quand je souffre. Généralement, je pense à vous en vers, et quand les vers sont faits, je ne sais pas résister à l'envie de les faire voir à la personne qui en est l'objet' (*BC* I: 225).

These prose paragraphs and the verse poem itself amount, then, to an avowal of weakness on the part of the poet which is paradoxically gratifying, and also flattering for Sabatier. But this avowal is not, as the rhetorical contortions of the disclaimer suggest, without its complications. Poetic creation is figured as an act of self-exposure and imagined intimacy with a reader which is therapeutic, but never entirely free from the threat of humiliation. The poet, caught between the two competing behavioural styles of emotional susceptibility and emotional reserve, can only ever expose himself *to a certain point*: ' — En même temps, je me cache, comme quelqu'un qui a une peur extrême du ridicule. [...] Mais je vous jure que c'est bien la dernière fois que je m'expose' (*BC* I: 225). When the poem is finally reached, the reader sees the poet's cautious attitude to self-display wrought into the verse through the foregrounding of the female voice rather than the male. In the poem itself, dominated by the woman's confession, the first-person pronoun of the male is employed only once, along with two fleeting uses of the first-person possessive ('mon bras', 'mon âme'). Yet the ample, and defensive, commentary which precedes the poem in the letter suggests that, as a private communication between poet and recipient, it represents a confession on the part of the poet. The poetic gesture is conceived of as a facilitator of intimacy between male writer and female reader and the emphasis placed on his, not her, *pudeur*.

'Confession' in Public

The question of whose confession, and whose modesty, is at stake is further nuanced when the poem migrates into the public domain on 1 June 1855. The poem is the fourth in a group of eighteen poems by Baudelaire which appeared, under his name, in the *Revue des deux mondes*; it was later to feature in the 1857 *Les Fleurs du Mal* and all subsequent editions.[20] Alongside certain alterations in punctuation and vocabulary — including, most significantly, the new qualification of the woman's *confidence* as 'horrible' (*OC* I: 46) rather than 'étrange' (*BC* I: 226) — a major difference between the poem in its published and epistolary form is the addition of the title, 'Confession', in place of the justificatory paragraphs penned for Sabatier. If the private communication of this poem to just one individual places Baudelaire in a compromised position vis-à-vis its recipient, its commercial publication is likely to create further anxieties. How can the public rendering of 'Confession' be reconciled with Baudelaire's assertion in 1853 that the poem sent to Sabatier is 'bien la dernière fois que [il s]'expose' (*BC* I: 225)? It is, I suggest, the removal of the first-person dominated paragraphs and the Baudelairean cogito contained within them ('je suis', 'je pense', 'je souffre') that further screens the poet and transforms what was presented and, arguably, received as the male poet's confession into that of its female recipient. In the original letter form, I argued, the poet's embarrassment framed the poem, overshadowing the woman's shame evoked in stanzas five and six. Yet without the communicative context of the letter, the reader of the *Revue des deux mondes*, and later *Les Fleurs du Mal*, is aware *only* of the shame associated with the female repentant, figured as a sickly, undignified, 'impure' child. The poet veils his shame behind that of the woman, his emotional restraint implicitly heightened by her very lack of it. Embarrassment is no longer explored as an emotion experienced by the male poet in relation to his work, but attributed solely to the female protagonist of the poem, 'naturally' prone to the 'négligence féminine' (*OC* II: 91) of confession.

The implications of this shift in emphasis, first in the *Revue des deux mondes* and subsequently in *Les Fleurs du Mal*, were to unsettle readers and critics of the period invested in the hermeneutic of intimacy.[21] The very title, and the poem's tantalising uses of the first-person, clearly beg autobiographical interpretations and gesture to the intimate tradition. In his discussion of *Les Fleurs du Mal* in 1860, Fraisse asks: 'Dans un recueil de poésie intime, où l'auteur emploie toujours la formule personnelle, le "moi", le "je", à quel signe pouvons-nous reconnaître que tantôt il parle en son nom, tantôt au nom des divers personnages?' (1973: 41–42) Twenty-first-century critics continue to make similar observations: E. S. Burt, for example, acknowledges, with some irony, that 'the enterprising reader who heads to a poem like "Confession" in search of a genuine autobiographical moment will be disappointed to discover that the confession consists of a discourse overheard in the false note of somebody else's voice' (2009: 83). The perplexed response of critics and readers results from Baudelaire's consciously guarded approach to the intimate paradigm in general, and the literary confession in particular. The comfort he gleans, or shows himself to glean, from indulging in it in private with a sympathetic audience ('Je pense aux personnes aimées quand je souffre. Généralement, je pense à vous en vers' (*BC* I: 225)) conflicts with the potential dangers of doing so in public. In a private letter to Fraisse of 12 August 1860, concerning *Les Paradis artificiels*, Baudelaire explains his reluctance to 'faire servir l'imprimerie à des confidences' (1980: 6): 'J'ai une très profonde horreur de la candeur dans l'exercice du métier littéraire, parce que le genre humain n'est pas un confesseur, et qu'infailliblement l'homme de lettres candide en sera dupe' (1980: 5). Assuring Fraisse of his *abandon* while simultaneously, and playfully, warning against such self-surrender, he adds:

> Je vous écris, comme vous voyez, avec un parfait abandon. Je compte que vous voudrez bien ne pas faire confidence de mes confidences. Il ne faut jamais rien livrer de personnelle à la canaille. Je comprends parfaitement bien les besoins de dignité qu'éprouvent tous les bouffons de profession. (Baudelaire 1980: 6)

The evocation of the 'canaille' indicates that an additional reason for Baudelaire's mistrust of confessional writing, aside from its potential affront to professional dignity and the ideals of manliness explored earlier, is a fundamental lack of affinity with his reading public; here, we can realign ourselves with Blin's arguments.[22] During the Second Empire, a period in which censorship became increasingly repressive, the reception of the poetic text would not occur in the 'intimité libre' evoked in 'Confession' (*BC* I: 226), and perhaps possible in the private form of the letter, but rather in an atmosphere of hostility and suspicion, to which Baudelaire's experience of publishing *Les Fleurs du Mal* and the subsequent obscenity trial would attest. Even before this experience, however, what Ross Chambers has succinctly described as the 'loneliness of the writing gesture' (1988: 13) particular to the nineteenth-century French literary field explains the need for a strategy on the part of Baudelaire. The historical situation of loneliness to which Chambers refers is 'one in which artists have ceased to be attached to some nobleman's entourage and now form a "class" of their own, a group apart' (1988: 13). The shifting communicative contexts of 'Confession' provide an insight into the sort of literary mechanisms established to cope with this historically specific form of isolation and alienation. The act of confession provides Baudelaire with imaginative and emotional consolations in private, particularly while he can benefit from the temporary smoke-screen of anonymity. Yet, once explicitly attached to Baudelaire's name on publication, the poem is reused, recycled, and transformed. Without the persistent first-person allusions of the letter, the poem is distanced from its poet: embarrassment is associated solely with the female protagonist and becomes the subject, rather than the side-effect, of the literary confession.

III. Timid Intimacy in Fromentin's *Dominique*

Fromentin's *roman intime*

Since the early twentieth century, the 'myth' of a 'Baudelaire moderne', 'l'inventeur de la *modernité*' (Compagnon 2003: 24), has presided over literary history. In contrast, the writing of Fromentin has, like that of Sainte-Beuve, received relatively little attention and is often dismissed as reactionary and backward-looking. For Barthes, writing in his 1971 essay on *Dominique*, Fromentin is 'indéfectiblement sage, conformiste, pusillanime même (si l'on songe à tout ce que la modernité a libéré depuis)' (1972: 157). Meanwhile, Naomi Segal (1988) provides a lucid, and damning, account of the misogynistic gender politics on display in the work.[23] There have, however, been attempts to 'redeem' Fromentin, and *Dominique* in particular, by mining the ambiguities which exist in the text for proto-modern meaning. Barthes, for example, admits that 'ce texte idéologique comporte-t-il des interstices; [...] tirons au moins toute la polysémie qu'il peut nous livrer' (1972: 157–58). Pierre Barbéris reads *Dominique* as a deeply political novel (1987), while Alain Clerval (1984) sees in the uncomfortable position of Dominique, a member of the landed gentry grappling with an aggressively industrialising and urban society, a symbol of Fromentin's 'antiromantisme'. For Clerval, *Dominique* works to undermine Romantic ideology, and can thus be placed alongside Baudelaire's early 'modernist' project.

There are many reasons to compare the work of Baudelaire and Fromentin, born less than a year apart, and well known to each other: Fromentin was a visual artist as well as writer, and Baudelaire praised his paintings highly in his *Salons*. Baudelaire is, moreover, known to have read Fromentin's travel writing and literary fiction. His reaction to these texts is, however, more ambivalent: he describes Fromentin's travel books as 'charmants', his 'esprit [...] tient un peu de la femme' (*OC* II: 650), and his cryptic comments on a private proof copy of *Dominique* signed by Fromentin suggest certain reservations about his writing: 'Pas de drame. Toujours la même délicatesse dans la peinture du décor' (*OC* II: 245). Unsurprisingly, critics are divided over whether to focus on the points of similarity or difference between Baudelaire and Fromentin, and this division typically hinges on the question of their respective modernity. However, rather than evaluate these two writers in terms of their status as precursors to and enablers of future revolutions, another way of comprehending the points of contact (generational, social, and intertextual) which clearly exist between them is to consider them both as late-comers to the intimate paradigm, still operating, albeit uncomfortably, within it. I suggest that much as Baudelaire's verse poetry was received in the tradition of *poésie intime*, Fromentin's novel of unrealised and impossible love was considered a somewhat belated *roman intime*. Sainte-Beuve makes this generic position explicit when, in a *causerie* of 8 February 1864, he refers to Fromentin's publication as a 'roman du genre intime, [...] dont tout le charme est dans le développement et les nuances' (*NL* VII: 145).[24] In this review, Sainte-Beuve applies the semantics and hermeneutic of intimacy to *Dominique*, describing it as 'l'histoire de l'enfance, [...] du personnage qui porte ce nom [Dominique]; lui-même raconte à un ami cette histoire toute simple, tout intérieure, en partie délicieuse, en partie douloureuse, et lui fait de vive voix sa confession' (*NL* VII: 129); 'et cet ami, à son tour, nous fait part de la confidence' (*NL* VII: 134). Moreover: 'Il est évident, à lire ces pages de description détaillée et comme attendrie, que l'enfance de Dominique n'est pas une fiction de l'auteur, et qu'il y a là-dessous une réalité vive et sensible' (*NL* VII: 135): 'son roman est une autobiographie' (*NL* VII: 134).[25]

Given the continued persistence of the intimate hermeneutic, such autobiographical interpretations would have been expected at this time. The following section of this chapter discusses how Fromentin seeks to reconcile the inevitability of these interpretations, and the pleasures — or, to use Sainte-Beuve's lexicon, delicacies — of the confessional moment with his authorial sense of *pudeur*: a value as important for Fromentin as for Baudelaire. As early as 1842, in a preparatory note for his study of Gustave Drouineau, the author of the *Confessions poétiques* [1834], Fromentin theorises the form of the discreet, 'indirect' confession:[26]

> Il est d'autres livres qui, sans affecter la forme directe de la confidence avec le public, — lui laissent entrevoir sous le masque de certains personnages, ou sous le fiction du conte, la physionomie morale, et les faits que l'auteur a par discrétion, par pudeur, ou par faux orgueil hésité à mettre à découvert. (Fromentin 1969: 103)

Dominique can be seen as one such indirect confession. By using the device of the frame-narrator, for instance, Fromentin seeks to distance the central protagonist from his own confession: as Sainte-Beuve outlines above, the first two chapters of the novel are told from the first-person perspective of Dominique's unnamed, 'hyper-indulgent' friend, as described by Trevor A. Le V. Harris (1993: 8), who then relays the 'confidence' made by the middle-aged Dominique to the reading public. Yet the very expectation, confirmed by Sainte-Beuve's *causerie*, that the reading public will nonetheless take pleasure in identifying a living, feeling 'reality' beneath — and despite — these fictional devices calls, I suggest, for additional strategies on the part of the writer. While, in 'Confession', Baudelaire transfers his avowal, and concomitant embarrassment, to his female confessor, I argue that Fromentin uses the extended form of the prose narrative, and the frequent opportunities it offers for the production of *mise en abyme*, to expand on the problem of intimacy and embarrassment in the novel.[27] This problem is especially urgent in what, as Segal (1988) rightly points out, is an androcentric text in which, despite the real and fantasised presence of Dominique's love-object, Madeleine, homosocial relations dominate. By insisting on the embarrassments of intimacy, Fromentin is able to promote masculine *pudeur* as an aspirational value. Yet, paradoxically, and chiming with the aphorism by Nietzsche which opened this chapter, he is also able to foreground the privilege implicit in momentary and strictly delimited lapses from it. By highlighting these concerns explicitly, Fromentin worries about *pudeur* on behalf of his readers; he thus frees the reader to enjoy the *confidence* staged between Dominique and frame-narrator, frame-narrator and reader, and ultimately and extradiegetically, Fromentin and reader, without feeling vicariously ashamed or offended. The success of Fromentin's enterprise can be read, between the lines, in Sainte-Beuve's overwhelmingly positive evaluation of *Dominique*'s 'douce lecture' (*NL* VII: 128). Sainte-Beuve praises its soothing, consolatory effects which hark back to the earliest examples of the *roman intime*, and contrast with the harshness of the modern novel:[28]

> Enfin, j'ai rencontré un roman qui m'émeut doucement et qui me touche. Autrefois, quand on ouvrait un livre de ce genre, un roman nouveau, on voulait être touché, ému, intéressé: maintenant, et depuis longtemps, on veut être *empoigné,* c'est le mot, — violent et dur comme la chose. [...] Mais enfin je retrouve quelqu'un qui laisse la note dans son naturel, et qui me prend par mes fibres délicates, sans me heurter, sans m'offenser et me faire souffrir. (*NL* VII: 128)

Intimacy and Inhibition

Fromentin's concern with the potential embarrassments of intimacy is first voiced in his early lyric poetry of the 1840s. While Guy Sagnes maintains that the poems 'n'ajoutent rien à la gloire d'Eugène Fromentin' (*OCF*: 1643), these early works nevertheless introduce topics which reappear in Fromentin's *œuvre* and reverberate through the century. Sagnes links the form and tone of many of Fromentin's poems ('la forme des strophes, le ton de la causerie, la façon de rattacher un poème à une heure de la journée ou à quelque propos entendu' (*OCF*: 1643)) to the influence of Sainte-Beuve's *poésie intime*. Indeed, explicit references to Sainte-Beuve in Fromentin's poetry, along with the recurring trope of friendship and a preoccupation with modesty, also indicate his influence.[29] 'À de nouveaux amis', written in 1841 but unpublished in Fromentin's lifetime, evokes an idyllic picture of youthful male friendship in which candour and easy familiarity alleviate the pain caused by loneliness and isolation. Employing a strategy similar to that found in the private communication of Baudelaire's 'Confession', the poet flatters his new-found friends by presenting them with a shared memory of intimacy:

> Et, depuis l'autre soir, je garde en ma pensée
> L'impression d'une heure en un cercle passé,
> Un petit cercle intime, où par hasard admis,
> Moi, jeune homme inconnu, j'ai trouvé des amis.
> Des amis! ... les liens, mon Dieu, se forment vite
> Quand à tendre la vôtre une main vous invite,
> Quand parole, regard, geste amical et doux,
> Tout est franc, tout captive, et tout dit: aimez-nous!
> Un mot vous met à l'aise, on s'égaie, on s'épanche,
> Pour causer librement, sur son siège on se penche;
> On dirait que de longs entretiens familiers
> Vous ont en d'autres lieux à votre insu liés. (*OCF*: 828)

This idealisation of emotional expansiveness is, however, in constant tension with a parallel impulse on the part of the 'jeune homme inconnu' towards emotional reserve and restraint. The poet has, he admits, always been 'taciturne' and 'timide':

> J'avais si peu connu dans mes temps de collège
> Ces soucis partagés qu'un tête-à-tête allège,
> Cet échange empressé de soupirs et d'aveux,
> Ce bonheur de penser, d'aimer, de vivre à deux. (*OCF*: 828)

Consequently:

> [...] lorsqu'enfin je voulus
> Rompre l'anneau d'airain qui scellait ma pensée,
> Ma main trembla, j'eus peur, ma langue embarrassée,
> Hésita, le mot vint à mes lèvres, et ma voix
> Au milieu d'un élan se tut plus d'une fois. (*OCF*: 829)

The poet's self-confessed shyness, embodied in the psychological and physiological impossibility of enunciation, renders his recent and unexpected experience of friendship all the more valuable. Yet it also inhibits any straightforward assimilation or imitation of his new friends' practices of sociability. The fifth verse admits some reservations: 'Pour un rêveur timide et toujours pris de honte, | Je trouve, en y songeant, ma franchise un peu prompte' (*OCF*: 830). A subsequent figure of infantilisation ('Je rêve tout haut, causeur comme un enfant' (*OCF*: 830)) indicates an adoption of certain stereotypes associated with self-disclosure — in this case, its childishness — and a concern with self-presentation which renders intimacy problematic.

Some twenty years later, we see the same tensions explored by Fromentin in *Dominique*, but this time in more sustained fashion. The figure of Dominique is first introduced to the reader as a paragon of humility: a value, and indeed virtue, which the frame-narrator immediately appropriates and emphasises in relation to his own narrative. The narrator, and the novel, begin by recalling Dominique's own words:

> Certainement je n'ai pas à me plaindre — me disait celui dont je rapporterai les confidences dans le récit très simple et trop peu romanesque qu'on lira tout-à-l'heure — car, Dieu merci, je ne suis plus rien, à supposer que j'ai jamais été quelque chose, et je souhaite à beaucoup d'ambitieux de finir ainsi. (*OCF*: 369)

This double-dose of self-negation on the part of Dominique and the frame-narrator (neither individual is named at this stage) introduces a dichotomy between modesty and ambition which runs throughout *Dominique*. Despite suggestions made by Dominique that this dichotomy might ultimately be false ('"Vous me pardonnerez de ne plus distinguer la modestie de l'orgueil, quand vous saurez à quel point il m'est permis de les confondre"' (*OCF*: 391)), the frame-narrator continues to insist on the admirable sense of 'embarrassability' or *pudeur* which motivates many of Dominique's life-choices: Dominique's decision to move back from Paris to his country estate, Les Trembles, for example, is presented as an 'acte de modestie, de prudence et de raison' (*OCF*: 369). In his 1864 review, moreover, Sainte-Beuve suggests that it is his 'timidité naturelle' (*NL* VII: 147) which ultimately prevents Dominique pursuing and consummating his relationship with Madeleine. In addition to this 'natural' shyness, and his aversion to celebrity and self-promotion, Dominique, as an adult, is shown to suffer from a more particular sense of embarrassment triggered by exposure to, or employment of, sentimental topoi. The narrator elucidates:

> Il y avait certains mots qui ne sortaient jamais de sa bouche, parce que, plus qu'aucun autre homme que j'aie connu, il avait la pudeur de certaines idées, et l'aveu des sentiments dits poétiques était un supplice au-dessus de ses forces. (OCF: 392)

Yet this passage, both through its echo of certain images from 'À de nouveaux amis' (the word on the tip of the tongue) and its relation to the American psychologist Silvan Tomkins's theories of shame, is suggestive of a relationship between Dominique and 'so-called poetic sentiments' which is less straightforward than the narrator appears to acknowledge, and which provides us with a way to conceptualise the workings of the novel as a whole. If we consider Tomkins's theory that shame can only operate once interest or enjoyment has been activated (see Elspeth Probyn (2005: ix)) and recognise that the painful inhibition expressed in 'À de nouveaux amis' is in tension with, and to a large extent caused by, a powerful desire for intimacy, 'poetic' sentiment emerges as deeply repellent, but simultaneously deeply appealing, for Dominique. The cultural association of sentimental susceptibility with weakness can be identified as the nexus for Dominique's less-than-humble fear of humiliation. Dominique explains:

> 'J'ai fait l'impossible pour n'être point un mélancolique, car rien n'est plus ridicule à tout âge et surtout au mien; mais il y a dans l'esprit de certains hommes je ne sais quelle brume élégiaque toujours prête à se répandre en pluie sur leurs idées. Tant pis pour ceux qui sont nés dans les brouillards d'octobre!' ajoutait-il en souriant à la fois et de sa métaphore prétentieuse et de cette infirmité de nature dont il était au fond très humilié. (OCF: 371)

Acutely aware of the ridicule surrounding male emotionality in the post-Revolutionary social and cultural order, Fromentin chooses to present Dominique as suffering *despite himself* from an innate but unwanted melancholy which finds a necessary release in elegiac outpourings. Dominique's 'métaphore prétentieuse', emerging irrepressibly in the course of the discussion, demonstrates a deep-rooted inability on his part to resist such language. Fromentin presents this temperamental predisposition as natural, but it can also be seen to have a significant cultural dimension. Dominique is symbolic of a generation raised, like Baudelaire and Fromentin, on a diet of Romantic and, in the context of this discussion, intimate literature: we have already seen the critic Saint-Chéron align *poésie intime* with the elegy. Melancholic sentimentality therefore retains its appeal as a style of 'elite' manliness, attractive to readers of a similar generation or *esprit*, such as Saint-Beuve. Yet the awareness of a body of readers beholden to other, and opposing, models of masculinity explains Fromentin's need to excuse his protagonist's weakness for such old-fashioned, even clichéd, behavioural styles, and, in doing so, excuse his own adoption of a genre with echoes of 'autrefois' (NL VII: 128).

The Limits of Intimacy

Dominique's need for intimacy, a constant theme of the narrative, is thus necessarily bound up with melancholy, and embarrassment. His desire for intimacy is first verbalised in relation to a youthful moment or 'crise' (*OCF*: 421), linked to sexual awakening:

> J'aurai souhaité que quelqu'un fût là; mais pourquoi? Je n'aurais pu le dire. Et qui? Je le savais encore moins. S'il m'avait fallu choisir à l'heure même un confident parmi tous les êtres qui m'étaient alors les plus chers, il m'eût été impossible de nommer personne. (*OCF*: 423)

Dominique's attempt to find this desired *confident* remains for the most part unfulfilled in his youth. Interactions with Madeleine are complicated by the romantic and erotic agenda. Moments of intimacy with a childhood friend, Olivier, are described as painful rather than comforting: a sudden *confidence* from Olivier is 'brusque' and 'trop forte'; Dominique's reaction to it comes in the form of 'des effrois et des éblouissements' (*OCF*: 432–33). This does not rid Dominique of his desire for a confident. Rather, it can be seen to motivate the search for a gentle, discreet intimacy which is finally, and formally, realised in the friendship between Dominique and the frame-narrator which is necessary for the 'indirect' confession to take place. Fromentin's construction of this relationship exemplifies his ideal of an intimacy which is constantly aware of its limits. The dose of metaphorical 'distance' demanded by this ideal is initially represented in the narrative in terms of space. The frame-narrator's first sighting of Dominique occurs at a remove, during a hunting trip undertaken with another friend, an unnamed doctor: 'Au moment où nous sortions du village, un chasseur [Dominique] parut en même temps que nous' (*OCF*: 371); 'Pendant le reste de la journée, nous l'eûmes en vue, et, quoique séparés par plusieurs cents mètres d'intervalle, nous pouvions suivre sa chasse comme il aurait pu suivre la nôtre' (*OCF*: 372). It is, the narrative suggests, Dominique's characteristic 'discrétion' (*OCF*: 372) which prevents him approaching the frame-narrator at this point. While Sainte-Beuve may allude to the unnecessary 'lenteur' of this 'préambule' (*NL* VII: 131) in his review, the extended hunting scene clearly functions to prefigure the cautious way in which the friendship between the two men will later develop. And in order for discretion to remain intact, this rapprochement occurs, curiously and yet logically, whilst both individuals are apart.

The frame-narrator begins Chapter Two with an analysis of the nature of absence:

> L'absence a des effets singuliers. J'en fis l'épreuve pendant cette première année d'éloignement qui me sépara de M. Dominique, sans qu'aucun souvenir direct parût nous rappeler l'un à l'autre. [...] Une année se passe. On s'est quitté sans se dire au revoir; on se retrouve, et pendant ce temps l'amitié a fait en nous de tels progrès que toutes les barrières sont tombées, toutes les précautions ont disparu. Ce long intervalle de douze mois, grand espace de vie et d'oubli, n'a pas contenu un seul jour inutile, et ces douze mois de silence vous ont donné tout à coup le besoin mutuel des confidences, avec le droit plus surprenant encore de vous confier. (*OCF*: 379–80)

The interval conceptualised in terms of space in the narrator's first encounter with Dominique ('plusieurs cents mètres d'intervalle') has here become one of time: 'ce long intervalle de douze mois'. Fromentin is thus able to leave to 'l'ingénieuse absence' (*OCF*: 380) the task of uniting the friends. This narrative device is itself ingenious: Fromentin can avoid entering into the details, and potential ambiguities, of homosociality by endowing the relationship with a magical or divine quality which absolves the participants of conscious agency or responsibility: 'Cette intimité qui commençait à peine était-elle ancienne ou nouvelle? C'était à ne plus savoir' (*OCF*: 381). The friendship is intimate: 'toutes les barrières sont tombées' (*OCF*: 380). Yet despite this hyperbole, the narrator suggests that certain, crucial boundaries *do* still exist. The narrator's interactions with Dominique and his family, for example, suggest that formality is only set aside gradually: 'Plus tard on m'appela par mon nom, sans supprimer tout à fait la formule de *monsieur*, mais en la négligeant fréquemment' (*OCF*: 381). Moreover, the return to the voice of the frame-narrator in Chapter 18, following Dominique's confession of love for the married Madeleine, confirms that the 'existence intime' (*OCF*: 392) established between the two men is bound by conventions whose violation, whilst necessary for the narrative to occur, comes at the cost of unpleasant feelings of awkwardness and embarrassment. The frame-narrator describes the end of Dominique's confession:

> Il s'arrêta sur ces dernières paroles dites avec la voix précipitée d'un homme qui se hâte et de pudeur attristée qui suit ordinairement des épanchements trop intimes. Ce que de pareilles confidences avaient dû coûter à une conscience ombrageuse et si longtemps fermée, je le devinais, et le remerciai d'un geste attendri auquel il ne répondit que par un mouvement de tête. [...] Il demeura ainsi pendant quelque temps dans un silence embarrassé que je ne voulus pas rompre. (*OCF*: 560)

The evocation of discomfort and sadness at this stage is crucial for Fromentin for two reasons. First, it ensures that the reader's sympathy is maintained for Dominique at the narrative's close. Embarrassment appears as the correct response to the painful predicaments presented in the account: it thus operates as a marker of Dominique's common humanity ('ordinairement') and, at the same time, his special and exemplary sense of *pudeur* ('une conscience [...] si longtemps fermée') which increases the cost, and value, of the confession. Second, it signals to the reader an awareness on Fromentin's part that his *roman intime* ('trop peu romanesque' (*OCF*: 369)) may indeed constitute an affront to certain ideals of masculine reserve: his vicarious acknowledgement of this, by way of Dominique, enables him to preempt and dispel potential criticism. Dominique's embarrassed response to this too-intimate intimacy ('des épanchements trop intimes') thus exemplifies the writer's struggle to reconcile the personal, and public, desire for the *intime* with contradictory behavioural codes. Much as it can enact a useful function in social life, embarrassment is a useful literary device in the *roman intime*, allowing for the momentary transgression, but also reinforcement, of the value of *pudeur*.

Baudelaire's and Fromentin's writings testify to a concern with the embarrassments of intimate literature for the Second Empire male writer. While criticism frequently opposes their artistic endeavours, their shared literary inheritance places them in a similar position in relation to the genres and the representation of intimacy. Both writers seek to reconcile certain conventions of intimate fiction with the simultaneous pull of emotional discipline and dignity in the public sphere. In their work, intimacy and, in particular, moments of confessing or confiding, appear as both pleasurable and problematic: the language of embarrassment emerges as a way for these writers to articulate and exploit this predicament. For Fromentin, the construction of the embarrassed 'man of feeling' epitomised in the figure of Dominique is an attempt to preserve the historical privileges of sentimentality while adapting to the mid-century demands of masculine modesty. For Baudelaire, the model of the shameful sentimental male is employed in private epistolary correspondence. In public, however, emotional disclosure is gendered in line with prevailing cultural norms, and attributed to the female. The rhetoric of embarrassment surrounding both 'Confession' and *Dominique* points to the guarded appreciation of intimacy in the literary culture of nineteenth-century France. It is not the only device to do so, however. The following chapter considers the ways in which irony, as both textual figure and contextual effect, permeates, and complicates, the third genre of intimacy to flourish in nineteenth-century France: the diary, or *journal intime*.

Notes to Chapter 2

1. Nietzsche (1990: 105).
2. By 'double-bind', I refer to a situation in which an individual is confronted with two simultaneous, but contradictory, demands or behavioural cues.
3. See Orr (2000), and, in the Victorian context, James Eli Adams (1995) and Herbert Sussman (1995). Sussman writes that nineteenth-century 'masculinity' was not a 'consensual or unitary formation, but rather [...] fluid and shifting, a set of contradictions and anxieties' (1995: 2–3). On twentieth-century theories of plural masculinity, see R. W. Connell (1995); for a discussion of more recent directions in Masculinity Studies, and in particular the 'crisis trope' so prevalent in this body of scholarship, see Catherine O'Rawe (2014: 3–10).
4. See Tim Edwards (2006: 17).
5. On the history of divorce in France, see Nicholas White (2013), Chapter One.
6. On this process, see Reddy (1997) and Nye (1998).
7. See Elias (1994) and Kristen B. Neuschel (1989).
8. 'Un Français craint moins d'avoir tort que d'être ridicule', letter from Stendhal to his sister Pauline, cited in Ansel and others (2003: 611). For discussion of the concepts of ridicule and vanity in Stendhal's *œuvre*, see Georges Blin (1958) and Ansel and others (2003: 611, 725–26).
9. Indeed, in certain contexts emotional restraint could be associated with femininity as well as masculinity; see the discussion by Anderson in relation to Charlotte Brontë's *Villette*: 'It would be misleading to assume or to insist that women are simply excluded from those forms of detachment seen as intellectually or morally heroic in the culture' (2001: 35). For discussion of female self-control in the context of romantic and erotic love in nineteenth-century France, see Gill (2015: 472–74).
10. On the ambivalence surrounding the quality of ambition in post-Revolutionary France, see Kathleen Kete (2012).
11. For a study of Baudelaire's literary criticism, see Rosemary Lloyd (1981); Lloyd discusses Baudelaire's review of *La Double Vie* in Chapter Three (1981: 101–12).
12. For Sainte-Beuve, the *roman intime* often takes the form of 'une confidence, une confession'

(1832: 239), the latter characterised by the Littré dictionary in terms of 'ouvrages de différents auteurs qui y font l'aveu des erreurs de leur vie. Les Confessions de St. Augustin. Les Confessions de J. J. Rousseau'. Consider for example Thomas De Quincey's *Confessions of an English Opium Eater* [1821], Alfred de Musset's *La Confession d'un enfant du siècle* [1836], or George Sand's *Confession d'une jeune fille* [1865].

13. In this letter, Baudelaire writes of his plan for 'un grand livre auquel je rêve depuis deux ans: *Mon cœur mis à nu*, et où j'entasserai toutes mes colères. Ah! Si jamais celui-là voit le jour, les *Confessions de J-J* paraîtront pâles' (*BC* II: 141); he later refers back to this dream of 'un grand livre sur *moi-même*, mes *Confessions*' (*BC* II: 182). The preparatory notes Baudelaire produced are often, but not unproblematically, referred to as the *Journaux intimes* (see Chapter 3, n. 42); see Howells (1996), Chapter Three, for an excellent analysis of these notes in their philosophical context.
14. Baudelaire also had theological objections to confession, linked to his belief in original sin; see Howells (1996: 67–68).
15. See Norman H. Barlow (1964) for one of the few twentieth-century studies tracing the poetic relationship between Sainte-Beuve and Baudelaire. For a discussion of the rehabilitation of Sainte-Beuve's literary criticism in the late twentieth century, see Christopher Prendergast (2007), Chapter One.
16. A reference to Sainte-Beuve's *roman intime*, *Volupté* (*BC* I: 761).
17. In a letter of 18 August 1857, Baudelaire admits to Sabatier: 'J'ai compris d'abord que quand je voulais me cacher, je me cachais fort mal' (*BC* I: 421). Little is known for certain about the relationship between Baudelaire and Sabatier. It is thought the two became acquainted at the Sunday evening *salons* Sabatier held in the rue Frochet in Paris in the 1850s. From their incomplete correspondence, there are suggestions that their relationship became sexual, but this is not certain. For further discussion of their relationship and correspondence, see Claude Pichois and Jean Ziegler (1987: 318–23) and Virginia Rounding (2003); the latter also includes a more wide-ranging discussion of Sabatier's life.
18. Although Baudelaire's letter to Sabatier suggests otherwise, the composition of the poem may in reality predate their first meeting; see Pichois and Ziegler (1987: 323).
19. Indeed, Baudelaire was attacked on grounds of 'childishness' by many Second Empire critics; Sartre was also to conclude that Baudelaire 'n'a jamais dépassé le stade de l'enfance' (1975: 50).
20. For discussion of the placement of these poems in the *Revue des deux mondes*, see Vaillant (2009: 53–54).
21. See Maria Scott (2005: 203–08) for further discussion of the mystified, often hostile, response of nineteenth-century critics to *Les Fleurs du Mal*.
22. Cf. a letter from Baudelaire to his mother of 20 January 1858: 'Et puis comment me connaissez-vous si peu que vous ne sachiez pas que j'éprouve naturellement le besoin de cacher presque tout ce que je pense? *Appelez cela dandysme, amour absurde de la Dignité*' (*BC* I: 448).
23. See also the feminist rewriting of *Dominique* by Jacqueline Harpman, *Ce que Dominique n'a pas su* (2008).
24. Nowadays, *Dominique* is typically classed as a *roman personnel* as in Véronique Dufief-Sanchez (2010).
25. The word 'biographie' emerges in the eighteenth century; 'autobiographie' enters French dictionaries in 1836.
26. See Barbara Wright (2000: 85) for further discussion of Fromentin's *Gustave Drouineau*, co-authored with his friend Émile Beltrémieux.
27. In this way, my interpretation complements Robert Lethbridge's reading of *Dominique* as a novel concerned above all with 'a dynamic exploration of its own genesis' and which adopts not only a confessional form, but the 'theme of confiding in its own right' (1979: 47).
28. It should be pointed out that in the radically different critical context of the twentieth century, however, Barthes is to find this 'autobiographie discrète' (1972: 156) highly objectionable.
29. Fromentin's 1841 poem 'À Madame Thérèse Bataillard' features an epigraph from Sainte-Beuve; *Les Consolations* are explicitly referred to in l. 50 (*OCF*: 830–31).

CHAPTER 3

Intimacy and Irony in the *journal intime*

The consolidation of intimacy as a literary concept occurred in France in the 1830s with the establishment of the *roman intime* and *poésie intime* as culturally recognised, albeit controversial, categories. Literary intimacy emphasises the pre-textual and non-fictional reality of its practitioners and protagonists, but is nonetheless supported and maintained through the means of fiction. This paradox persists in the case of the *journal intime*. More so than the *roman intime* and *poésie intime*, the diary as *journal intime* has preserved its generic affiliation with intimacy into the twenty-first century. It is often seen, moreover, as a resolutely non-fictional and 'non-figurative' genre. John Sturrock encapsulates what makes the diary problematic for many literary theorists:

> With the diary or journal, written intermittently and published without any attempt at its later integration into a narrative, we could argue that a past life is represented in a 'literal' form, or in a form as close to literalism as any writer can come. (Sturrock 1993: 30)

However, a study of the *journal intime* in its nineteenth-century guises shows that it had a more complex relationship with the tools of fiction than such comments might suggest. This chapter analyses three forms of diary-writing which exemplify the tension between the popular image of diary-writing and reading as a private and highly personal encounter and the realities of a practice born of and thus inevitably engaged with the public appetite for fictions of intimacy. I argue that this tension is embodied in the multiple forms of irony associated with, and generated, by the nineteenth-century diary. Intimacy and irony *can* be opposed as incompatible impulses or literary modes: while intimacy facilitates and depends on the exchange of emotions, irony is often theorised as a reprehensible form of emotional detachment.[1] In the reading of the diary-writing projects that follows, however, I see both intimacy and irony as inextricably linked. Irony, like embarrassment, can be seen to mediate sentimental susceptibility while simultaneously emphasising it, and thus contributes to the particular affective texture of these works.

Following a survey of the nineteenth-century *journal intime* as both an everyday writing practice and a mode of literary fiction, the chapter turns to the diary of Eugénie de Guérin. This journal was written between 1834 and 1841 and published in 1862, after Guérin's death, by François-Guillaume-Stanislas Trebutien, a friend and collaborator of Barbey d'Aurevilly. Guérin's *Journal* has traditionally been treated as an exemplary model of diary-writing in which the young, female diarist aspires to the values of sincerity, spontaneity, and transparency, and sees in the diary an aid to self-improvement, a means of consolation, and a vehicle for intimate communication with a loved one. Yet a closer examination of Guérin's writing reveals a simultaneous problematisation of the diary project and thus the possibility and even desirability of textually mediated intimacy. I conceptualise this split in the text, testimony of ambivalence on the part of Guérin towards her diary, as a form of irony in the sense of duplicity or 'being double'.[2] The chapter then turns to Barbey d'Aurevilly's own contemporaneous diaries, the *Memoranda* of 1836 to 1839, which stage a more explicit encounter between intimacy and irony. In the *Memoranda*, Barbey indulges in and experiments with the consolations of diary-writing. Yet his active engagement with irony as a tone and indeed subject matter suggests unease with the cultural connotations of intimacy. Irony emerges as a defensive strategy and means of mystification through which Barbey can resist total transparency and maintain an authorial power otherwise threatened by the vulnerability of intimate communication. Building on this discussion, the fourth and final part of the chapter returns to Baudelaire and focuses on the prose poem 'À une heure du matin'. This poem was first published on the front page of *La Presse* in 1862: the same year that Guérin's *Journal* had its first commercial publication. Building on this chronological coincidence, my reading draws out the formal, rhetorical, and affective affinities which Baudelaire's poem shares with the diary genre. Yet it also highlights the incongruities crafted into the text and further generated by the poem's highly visible and, at least in part, commercially motivated placement in the press. Many readers respond to this poem as a sincere piece of life-writing on the part of Baudelaire. I pay attention to this impulse, but argue that its textual and contextual ironies inevitably complicate these responses, creating an opaque and unstable work of fiction which is implicated in, but which also eludes, the increasing 'industrialisation' of intimacy.

I. The *journal intime* in Nineteenth-Century France

The legitimacy of the diary as a subject for academic study has long been a controversial issue. Philippe Lejeune's work over the last twenty years has done much to counter polemical writings by, amongst others, Maurice Blanchot and Roland Barthes, which deny the diary the status of literature.[3] Nowadays, the need to determine the 'literary' status of a text is itself increasingly questionable, at least in the field of cultural history: whether we regard a text as literary or not does not affect its ability to testify to cultural phenomena. Yet distinctions between literature and non-literature *did* have relevance in nineteenth-century France, and research into diary-writing in this period reveals two separate but interrelated facets of the activity: on the one hand, the diary as a social practice or form of everyday writing (positively seen as 'non-literature') and, on the other, the nineteenth-century *roman-diaristique*, the diary as fiction.[4] Despite this distinction, however, there were numerous points of contact between these two modes which mutually and symbiotically influenced each other. 'Ordinary' diaries were, and still are, highly idiosyncratic, but they developed in relation to a range of public models, both fictional and educational. Moreover, as the century progressed and contemporaneous diaries began to be published — and indeed to be written for publication — they became progressively fictionalised themselves, blurring boundaries between 'figurative' and 'non-figurative' work still further.

Critics agree that the diary in a recognisably modern form began to take shape in France in the eighteenth century and flourished in the post-Revolutionary period. Daily self-analysis and note-taking have many possible antecedents dating back to Antiquity, and later given a Christian emphasis in the form of the oral and written *examen de conscience*.[5] Yet for Alain Girard, the nineteenth-century articulation of the practice was the precise result of the scientific move towards empirical observation combined with the legacy of the eighteenth-century culture of sensibility which, as we have seen, privileged the cultivation and communication of feeling (1963: ix). These twin currents contributed to the emergence of a diary focused on the daily and detailed description of emotional life rather than, as was the case in previous epochs, something akin to a public register or account book. Education was also a factor in the emergence of the 'modern' diary: despite the prominence of male diarists including Stendhal, Constant, Henri-Frédéric Amiel, and, as will be discussed, Barbey d'Aurevilly, research suggests that diary-writing was very much a female pursuit in the nineteenth century.[6] The Catholic Church, which took charge of much education post-1814, used the diary as a key educational tool for girls and young women: it was seen as a way for them to practise their writing skills, and record, reflect on, and improve their moral comportment; the diary was thus also a means for educators to surveil and regulate female behaviour.[7] Having left school, a woman might continue to write a more secular form of journal. Diaries were thus increasingly common amongst educated women. Alix de Lamartine, for example, wrote a diary from childhood, a phenomenon which Lamartine connects to her Roman Catholic education in the preface to his 1849 *Confidences*:

> Ma mère avait l'habitude, prise de bonne heure, dans l'éducation un peu roumaine qu'elle avait reçue à Saint-Cloud, de mettre un intervalle de recueillement entre le jour et le sommeil, comme les sages cherchent à en mettre entre la vie et la mort. Quand tout le monde était couché, [...] elle tirait d'un tiroir de petits cahiers reliés en carton gris comme des livres de compte. Elle écrivait sur ces feuilles pendant une ou deux heures sans relever la tête et sans que la plume suspendît une seule fois sur le papier pour attendre la chute du mot à sa place. C'était l'histoire domestique de la journée, les annales de l'heure, le souvenir fugitif des choses et des impressions, saisi au vol et arrêté dans sa course, avant que la nuit l'eût fait envoler; les dates heureuses ou tristes, les événements intérieurs, les épanchements d'inquiétude et de mélancolie, les élans de reconnaissance et de joie, les prières toutes chaudes jaillies du cœur à Dieu, toutes les notes sensibles d'une nature qui vit, qui aime, qui jouit, qui souffre, qui bénit, qui invoque, qui adore, une âme écrite enfin! (Lamartine 1849: 3–4)

Writing with an eloquence which mirrors that of his mother, Lamartine idealistically evokes diary-writing as a spontaneous, although simultaneously ritualised, record of domestic, emotional, and religious life ('les événements intérieurs') and thus highlights its affiliations with the literature of intimacy. At the time, this mode of diary-writing was not regarded as a literary act suitable for public consumption; indeed, in a letter to Trebutien of 29 July 1851, Barbey d'Aurevilly discusses his own diaries and claims that 'ce qui m'en plaît surtout, à moi, c'est que ce n'est pas là de la littérature' (*LT*: 452). Nonetheless, diaries already intersected with the public literary sphere in a number of ways, and were a feature of the collective cultural imagination even while thoughts of publishing contemporary journals were still taboo.[8] First, ordinary diaries were not always the 'private' affair they have since come to be seen as: they might be monitored by an educational practitioner or spiritual director, or shared between family and friends.[9] Second, anecdotes like Lamartine's, evoking the practice and content of his mother's diary-writing in a published document, inevitably contributed to the public-private intersection and provided models for aspiring diary-writers.[10] Third, novels in diary form were highly popular from the July Monarchy onwards, as a formal adaptation of the eighteenth-century epistolary genre.[11] These *romans-diaristiques* were generally marketed at young women, further evidence of the gendering and age associations of the diary. Marie Tourte-Cherbuliez's *Le Journal d'Amélie* [1834] was one of the first in a line of edifying diary-novels which reached a peak in 1858 with Victorine Monniot's *Le Journal de Marguerite*, the first-person diaristic narrative of the eponymous young heroine, Marguerite, as she prepares for her first communion. Mathilde Kang writes: 'À l'émergence du genre [du roman-diaristique] entre les années 1830 et 1850, succède un véritable engouement qui fait du journal intime le genre privilégié de la jeune fille' (2009: 19–20).

Significantly, while Kang qualifies the journal as 'intime', the July Monarchy and Second Empire diary-novels to which she refers did not. Until the second half of the nineteenth century, writers tended to rely on the traditional term *journal*, with its links to the accounts book or public register, although other expressions might also be used: *mémorandum*, *cahier*, or *carnet*.[12] While in the domain of the novel and poetry, the *intime* had been a recognisable generic qualification since at least the 1830s, the expression *journal intime* and its use as a title was slower to develop. Diaz and Diaz (2009: 132) date the first titular uses of the term *journal intime* to the latter years of the Second Empire, although the expression was employed earlier in the body of texts (Montémont 2009: 34). The development of the notion of the *journal intime* can be seen to respond to a gradual need to distinguish this type of text, the specificity of which was emerging in the collective consciousness, from the daily newspaper — also referred to as a *journal* — and alternative forms of diary: the eighteenth-century mode of diary, for example, or the *journal de voyage* (discussed in Chapter Four). The move to define this kind of daily writing in terms of the *intime* reflects the continued relevance and appeal of intimacy in nineteenth-century French culture. It coincided with, and most likely resulted from, the emerging trend of publishing contemporary diaries, and the need to attract a readership for these.[13] Yet the step was also a logical extension of the idiom of intimacy already employed in the text and paratext of these nineteenth-century diaries, both fictional and non-fictional. In the preface to the *Journal de Marguerite*, for example, Monniot explains to her young readers:

> J'aime à croire que vous recevrez avec intérêt et indulgence le *Journal de Marguerite*, [...] car les confidences intimes de la vie réelle savent toujours trouver le chemin du cœur, et le vôtre répandra par de la sympathie à ces épanchements du cœur et de l'âme d'une enfant comme vous. (Monniot 1867: v–vi)

Guérin's *Journal* also uses and indeed innovates with the language of intimacy: Montémont (2009: 30) identifies Guérin as one of the earliest writers to employ *intime* in its substantive form to refer to a state of intimacy rather than to a friend. The next part of the chapter will turn to Guérin's diary as an example of one of the first nineteenth-century diaries to be published in the nineteenth century. I shall explore the *situational* irony created by the act of publishing the text so soon after its composition; however, I shall also suggest that this situational irony highlights certain contradictions already present in Guérin's diary-writing practice which question the possibility and moral worth of textually mediated intimacy.

II. Guérin and the Ethics of Diary-Writing

God and Friendship

Guérin started to write her diary at the age of twenty-nine and, over a period of seven years, filled at least twelve notebooks. From its beginnings, the diary was conceived and conceptualised as a vehicle for enhanced intimacy between siblings: between Guérin, living a solitary life at the family home of Le Cayla in Tarn, and her brother, Maurice, in Paris.[14] Indeed, Guérin appears to begin writing her diary at her brother's request, as a means of connecting him to life at home: 'Puisque tu le veux, mon cher Maurice, je vais donc continuer ce petit Journal que tu aimes tant' (*GJ*: 3);[15] 'C'est ici, mon ami, que je veux reprendre cette correspondance intime qui nous plaît et qui nous est nécessaire, à toi dans le monde, à moi dans ma solitude' (*GJ*: 119). As the reference to 'correspondance' implies, each notebook was posted to Maurice on completion, immediately inscribing Guérin's diary-writing project in what was described in Chapter One as a 'lateral' (other-orientated, intersubjective) form of intimacy as much as a 'vertical' (self-orientated, introspective) one. The 'privacy' which this diary assumes is one which is not absolute, then, but rather limited to and, moreover, dependent on a chosen few: following her brother's death in July 1839, Guérin at first continued to address her diary to 'Maurice au ciel' (*GJ*: 275) but later selected Barbey d'Aurevilly, a close friend of Maurice, as her *confident*:

> Vous voulez que j'écrive mes impressions, que je revienne à l'habitude de retracer mes journées [...]. Le voilà ce mémorandum désiré, ce de moi à vous dans ce monde, comme vous l'avez eu au Cayla: charmante ligne d'intimité, sentier des bois, mené jusque dans Paris. (*GJ*: 437)

The 'ligne d'intimité', emphasising the aforementioned lateral nature of the bond, conceptualises intimacy as a path which can overcome spatial distance by way of emotional proximity. And it also conceptualises the link between Guérin and Barbey: a line not of blood or marriage but rather, via Maurice, friendship.

Lejeune's analysis of female diary-writing in the nineteenth century identifies three main phases post-1830: the Romantic phase (1830–48) in which writing practices were largely uncodified; the 'ordre moral' between 1850 and 1880 in which the diary was associated primarily with institutionalised education; and the post-1880 generation of defiantly secular diary-writers exemplified by Marie Bashkirtseff.[16] These periodisations can only ever be schematic, however: Alix de Lamartine, although writing between 1800 and 1829, sees the practice as morally edifying, and Guérin's diary also appears to hover between the Romantic and 'moral' phases. Guérin was significantly older than the fictitious Marguerite when she began her diary, and her writing is thus free from any of the explicitly educational constraints associated with the institutionalised practice: while she shared the notebooks with her brother, she did not need to show them to a teacher or priest. Despite this relative liberty, however, Guérin as a devout Catholic was committed to beliefs and values which imbue the journal with a moral agenda. Diary-writing becomes a means for Guérin to conduct the essential process of what she calls 'recueillement' or 'contemplation intérieure' (*GJ*: 33). Yet it is also a way for her to spread the results of this self-examination 'outwards' in the form of an 'épanchement de mon âme au dehors, [...] devant Dieu et devant quelqu'un' (*GJ*: 65). Communication, simultaneously self, other, and God-orientated, frequently takes on a divine quality in Guérin's diary as she explains her desire for intimacy in religious terms. Like faith, friendship is sacred: inspired by readings of Saint Augustine and the seventeenth-century Bishop of Geneva, François de Sales, on friendship (*GJ*: 144), Guérin can talk of 'cette amitié céleste' and 'la sympathie [qui] naît des rapports de l'âme' (*GJ*: 52); 'l'amitié sainte [...] un écoulement de la charité qui ne meurt pas' (*GJ*: 208).[17] Unlike what Guérin identifies as the nature of the 'affections éphémères' which often occur between women, but which can be undone like loose 'nœuds de ruban' (*GJ*: 177), genuine and holy friendship depends on a sympathy and union of souls which is constantly strengthened through the *intime*. 'C'est de l'intime qu'il me faut. L'amitié se nourrit de cela', she writes on 15 May 1838 (*GJ*: 204). Letters, exchanges, or conversations 'sans intime' (*GJ*: 267) are recorded without interest or with disappointment: describing a visit to a friend, Louise, Guérin notes: 'Encore l'ai-je très-peu vue et si occupée, si entourée, que nous n'avons pu faire de l'intime' (*GJ*: 168). When it is attained, however, intimacy is shown to help others. Alluding to a friend, Marie, who has been ill, and establishing a form of *mise-en-abyme* in the process, Guérin explains to Maurice:

> Si je n'ai rien mis ici depuis huit jours, c'est que je n'ai fait qu'écrire à Marie, écrire un journal intime, feuilles volantes d'amitié qui iront joncher son lit un beau moment à sa surprise, et la pauvre malade aura plaisir à cela. Ce sont des riens, mais les riens du cœur ont du charme. (*GJ*: 372)

As well as helping others, however, intimacy also helps the self: in the *Journal*, it emerges as an essential, even addictive, life-force on which the health of the body depends. An enforced break from diary-writing due to a lack of ink amounts to figurative death for the diarist: 'De l'encre, enfin! Je peux écrire; de l'encre! bonheur et vie. J'étais morte depuis trois jours que la circulation de ce sang me manquait, morte pour mon cahier, pour toi, pour l'intime' (*GJ*: 232).[18] Guérin's use of corporeal metaphors to evoke the concrete effects that writing has on her recurs throughout the diary. Responding to a letter from Maurice, for example, she articulates her need for intimacy as a meeting of bodies, not minds:

> Je t'ai vu; mais je te connais pas; tu ne m'ouvres que la tête: c'est le cœur, c'est l'âme, c'est l'intime, ce qui fait ta vie, que je croyais voir. Tu ne montres que ta façon de penser; tu me fais monter et moi je voudrais descendre, te connaître à fond dans tes goûts, tes humeurs, tes principes, en un mot faire un tour dans les coins et les recoins de toi-même. (*GJ*: 83)

For Guérin, the physical, fleshy opening out of the inner depths evoked in this visceral presentation of self seems to demand an equally 'open' use of language. If social visits or letters are sometimes disappointing in this regard, Guérin depicts the diary as a vehicle perfectly suited to the transparent communication of interiority. It is through a process of *abandon* and negligence that the *intime* is to be reached: 'Pour moi, je me sens mieux après que je me suis laissée couler ici. Je dis ici, parce que j'y laisse l'intime, sans trop regarder ce que c'est, sans le savoir quelquefois' (*GJ*: 126–27). Resorting frequently to a lexicon of liquidity, Guérin presents language as a spontaneous extension or 'overflow' of herself, as clear as water: 'Le trop-plein fait torrent parfois, il vaut mieux lui ouvrir passage' (*GJ*: 208). At other points, language is a spontaneous extension of the divine: 'D'où peut venir, en effet, tant de choses tendres, élevées, douces, vraies, pures dont mon cœur s'emplit quand je te parle! Oui, Dieu me les donne, et je te les envoie' (*GJ*: 76). In part a commonplace rhetorical device used to preserve the humility of the Christian female, these expressions foreground a vision of univocal language as a conduit which channels the essence of the divine between friends or, in this case, sister and brother. There is no room for duplicity or dishonesty here, Guérin assures Maurice: 'Je ne dissimule pas avec toi et laisse tomber sur le papier tout ce qui me vient, même des larmes' (*GJ*: 22).

In this way, Guérin insists on the continuity between language, paper, and self, and imagines the diary as a form of embodied intimacy with Maurice, her tears soaking into the pages of the diary he will later touch.[19] For this interchangeability to be achieved, however, any sense of premeditated linguistic craft on the part of Guérin has to be denied. As the previous discussion has shown, this denial fulfils three principal functions: it allows Guérin to conceptualise diary-writing as the much desired physical rapprochement with Maurice, envisaged at the level of 'natural' feeling rather than calculated thought; it enables her to claim divine inspiration for her diary; and it places her writing within the sphere of literary intimacy which, through its emphasis on sentiment, spontaneity, and sincerity was one of the few socially acceptable modes of writing open to women in the period. To talk of irony in relation to Guérin's diary-writing might, then, seem at best incongruous and at worst inaccurate. Nineteenth-century Christian guides to moral behaviour, such as the *Nouvelle civilité chrétienne*, actively prohibited the use of words 'à double sens' and promoted univocality in all linguistic exchanges, going so far as to claim that 'les équivoques sont des mensonges formels'.[20] In its capacity as a communication with Maurice, therefore, it is unlikely that Guérin's diary would actively seek to utilise irony as a rhetorical device. Yet I suggest that for subsequent *readers* of the published *Journal*, it is difficult to receive the text without the activation of irony. This is, most palpably, a situational irony. But there is also evidence of an internal irony, understood as a contradiction or discrepancy rooted within the text, which, I shall argue, is highlighted by Trebutien's editorial decision to overlook it.

The Diary and Dissimulation

Guérin's diary was first published commercially in 1862 under the full title *Eugénie de Guérin, journal et lettres, publiés avec l'assentiment de sa famille, par G.-S. Trebutien*. The publication was an extension of the *Reliquiae*, a collection of Guérin's writings circulated privately amongst friends and acquaintances in 1855. While Barbey d'Aurevilly had been involved in work on the *Reliquiae*, Trebutien was responsible for the diary's commercial publication. As Raoul suggests, building on Béatrice Didier's arguments, the nineteenth-century move to publish diaries commercially can be seen to correspond to a burgeoning capitalist desire to 'let nothing go to waste' (2001: 142). While this may have been a factor in the decision to publish Guérin's diary, it coexisted with a genuine appreciation of her writing and a parallel desire to promote the work of her brother, whose own *Journal, lettres et poèmes* was also published posthumously in 1862.[21] Although it is little-known today, Guérin's *Journal* was an immense success on publication both in France and abroad, going through numerous editions and translations, and winning a prize from the Académie française (Raoul 2001: 145–46). However, twentieth- and twenty-first-century research has illuminated the extent to which the initial editorial work on the diary falsified the text, and promoted a distorted vision of the writer:

> La consécration du *Journal* par l'Académie française comme chef-d'œuvre d'édification chrétienne confère à l'œuvre et à son auteure une figure de l'"idéal féminin". Inlassablement exploitée, cette image constitue tout au long du XIXe siècle le principal leitmotive [*sic*] de la promotion guérinienne en France. [...] Rien que la sainte Eugénie, vierge, maternelle et chrétienne. (Kang 2009: 41–42)

Kang evokes the attempted erasure of 'toute voix discordante' from the text, namely, any evidence of Guérin's sensuality, moodiness, or melancholy (2009: 27). Yet a further discordance which Trebutien obscures in his preface emerges in relation to the question of diary-writing as a morally or ethically sound pursuit in itself; particularly intriguing given the subsequent uses to which the diary was put for purposes of Christian instruction. While Guérin states early on in the *Journal* that she *does* see diary-writing as an innocent pleasure, her formulation simultaneously introduces an element of doubt, and the possibility of an error on her part:

'Ce plaisir donc, je me le donne. Je crois qu'il est innocent. Si le scrupule me revient, je le laisserai tout de suite' (*GJ*: 36).[22] Alongside allusions to the divine nature of diary-writing is a parallel anxiety surrounding the practice, manifest in the need for Guérin to keep the activity secret from anyone other than Maurice. This need results in the kind of practical double-dealing or duplicity which, at the linguistic level, we find in the figure of irony. Guérin's anxiety stems from a number of causes. First, although written for someone else, the diary in its nineteenth-century guise involves an intensive focus on the (fallen) self which, within a Catholic perspective, can be considered morally wrong.[23] Guérin admits that the diary is a shameful form of vanity, but claims that it is the only form of writing of which she is capable:

> Mais je m'aperçois que je ne parle guère de qui que ce soit, et que mon égoïsme se met toujours en scène; je dis: 'J'ai fait ceci, j'ai vu cela, j'ai pensé telle chose,' [...]. Le petit peintre ne sait donner que son portrait à son ami, le grand peintre offre des tableaux. (*GJ*: 68–69)

Here, Guérin perpetuates a common critique of the literature and, in this analogy, visual art of intimacy by claiming that much as the portrait is inferior to history or religious painting, so the diary is inferior to genres treating subjects exterior to the self. The diary as a verbal self-portrait is a sign of small-mindedness, and, as such, Guérin intermittently doubts the benefits that either she or Maurice will glean from it: 'Mon ami, me liras-tu jamais? Sera-ce bon pour toi de me voir ainsi jusqu'au fond de l'âme?' (*GJ*: 97); 'Nous devons compte à Dieu de nos minutes, et n'est-ce pas les mal employer que de tracer ici les jours qui s'en vont?' (*GJ*: 35); 'Est-ce la peine de marquer mon temps? C'est écrire sur la poussière. Je ne sais pourquoi je me figure que cela te fera plaisir, ce fatras de choses, de jours et de papiers' (*GJ*: 82). At other points, Guérin consciously limits the extent of her personal disclosures: 'Je ne veux pas me confesser' (*GJ*: 23), or:

> Je parle quand je veux à ce petit cahier; je lui dis tout enfin, pensées, peines, plaisirs, émotions, tout enfin, hormis ce qui ne peut se dire qu'à Dieu [...]. Mais cela, je ferais mal, je crois, de le produire, et la conscience se met entre la plume et mon papier. Alors je me tais. (*GJ*: 112)

Alongside the myriad lacunae in the diary (weeks can go by between entries), this gap between pen and paper is a way of conceptualising the intermittent lack of that very 'proximity' referred to earlier: Guérin's pen hovers over the paper in an act of suspension and deliberation which troubles the supposed spontaneity and immediacy of her diary-writing.

Premeditation is further demanded of Guérin by the need to 'écrire en cachette', deriving from both the questionable moral worth of the diary and, more generally, the anxiety produced by the figure of the woman writing in nineteenth-century France.[24] Guerin recounts her strategies of concealment to Maurice, forms of dissimulation which include hiding the diary in her desk or under the carpet, and writing it alongside, and in between, her habitual letter-writing: 'Je vais commencer ma double lettre et parler à deux voix' (*GJ*: 83); 'Tu as raison quand tu dis que je ruse un peu pour écrire mes cahiers' (*GJ*: 119). In a later entry she explains how a day spent copying out poetry for her father is interspersed with snatches of illicit diary-writing: 'Ce n'est pas mentir; seulement, j'en fais deux, et l'un m'attache plus qu'un autre' (*GJ*: 179). While Guérin's diary-writing is often talked about in terms of letter-writing and should thus, logically, be no more shameful than the latter, we can hypothesise that the immediate transmission of the letter to its recipient would render epistolary writing less problematic in the eyes of others. Moreover, the honesty with which Guérin feels able to write to Maurice encourages the avowal of emotions and ideas which, if seen by her father, might disturb and upset him (*GJ*: 119–20). Such worries about the propriety and moral worth of diary-writing, and the deceit it entails, do not seem to destroy its pleasures and affective consolations for Guérin. Yet the double-voiced and, in this sense, ironic nature of the text, symbolically inscribed in Guérin's duplicitous writing practices (she writes a 'double lettre [...] à double voix' (*GJ*: 83)) is, I suggest, symptomatic of the mixed feelings surrounding the diary and literary intimacy more widely in this period. Sensitivity to Guérin's reservations thus allows for a greater appreciation of the situational ironies engendered for the reader by the publication of a text which Guérin had, in her eyes, good reasons to keep hidden.

'*Ceci n'est pas pour le public, c'est de l'intime, c'est de l'âme,* C'EST POUR UN' (*GJ*: 91). Trebutien as the editor of Guérin's diaries is clearly aware of the irony activated by reading this phrase, uncharacteristically emphasised by Guérin through the use of italics and capital letters, in a published volume.[25] The full title of the journal itself, with its reassuring qualification that both diary and letters are published with the permission of the family, is indicative of this; more explicitly, Trebutien alludes in the preface to the 'sorte d'anxiété' (1862: ii) produced in him by contradicting Guérin's will. He proceeds to justify the act of publication by referring to the hypothetical happiness Guérin would surely feel to know her diary had reached, and helped, a wider public. This approach relies on underplaying, if not omitting, Guérin's own intermittent doubts as to the moral worth of her diary. Trebutien's preface seeks to align Guérin with Lamartine's vision of his mother who, bending over her journal, 'écrivait sur ces feuilles pendant une ou deux heures sans relever la tête et sans que la plume suspendît une seule fois sur le papier pour attendre la chute du mot à sa place' (Lamartine 1849: 4), the unbroken line between paper and pen emblematic of her abundant and unproblematic inspiration. For Trebutien, likewise, Guérin consigns 'tout ce qu'elle sent, tout ce qu'elle pense, tout ce qui se passe autour d'elle' (1862: vi) to the diary; her writing is a 'joie' (1862: vii), a 'libre jet' (1862: ix) which expresses 'les épanchements intimes' (1862: iv) and 'tous les élans spontanés de son esprit, tous les battements involontaires de son cœur' (1862: iii). Trebutien borrows from Guérin's own lexicon when he writes this, but, as we have seen, his borrowing is selective. The gaps or absences which exist in the diary, referred to above, cause us to read the language which *is* present differently. Guérin's assertions of faith and pleasure in the diary as an ideal vehicle for intimacy are countered by the parallel language of hesitation and doubt which runs throughout it; this 'counter-language' of resistance to the diary-writing project creates an unsaid evaluative space around the pre-existing language of intimacy which is emblematic of how irony functions. The diary is thus beholden to two imperatives — to tell all, and to withhold — which exemplifies cultural anxieties surrounding the *journal intime* in the nineteenth century, both in relation to what it can suggest in principle (egotism) and involve in practice (secrecy and dissimulation). Moreover, the discrepancy between the doubts voiced in the diary and the way in which varying contexts of reception demand a waiving or contradiction of these doubts highlights a paradox: the idealisation of intimacy in the nineteenth-century public domain demands a 'fictionalisation' of it which arguably undermines much of what it is supposed to represent.[26] Guérin's *Journal*, and its publication history, thus enacts this paradoxical performance of intimacy which other examples of the diary deliberately exploit, as we shall see, for ironic effect.

III. Barbey d'Aurevilly's *Memoranda*: The Diaries of a Dandy

Revelations 'à la Rousseau'?

Barbey d'Aurevilly's first two *Memoranda* are products of the same metaphorical 'foyer d'intimisme' (Girard 1963: 70) as Guérin's *Journal*. Barbey began to write these diaries in Paris at the age of twenty-seven: the first *Memorandum* covers the period from 13 August 1836 to 6 April 1838, and the second from 13 June 1838 to 22 January 1839.[27] This was a difficult period in Barbey's life, in part due to a romantic rupture with his cousin, Louise Cantru des Costils; he later describes the diaries in a letter to Trebutien as 'deux espèces de *vomitoria* à la Romaine, ou une âme, accablée souvent, versait journellement ses ennuis et trouvait à cela je ne sais quel fougueux et voluptueux soulagement' (*LT*: 451–52).[28] Like Guérin, Barbey wrote his diaries for Maurice, and was well aware of Guérin's own, contemporaneous diary: Maurice is known to have read excerpts from her notebooks aloud to Barbey, doubtless sowing the seeds of his editorial interest in them. Maurice de Guérin thus emerges as the shadowy centre of a complex diaristic network; as Rainer Maria Rilke writes:

> On obtient une mesure de l'étendue intérieure de [Maurice de] Guérin, si l'on songe que pour lui, Eugénie, dans sa chambre inchangée du petit château de Cayla et Jules Barbey d'Aurevilly, ce projecteur de vanité, ont tous deux écrit leurs journées.[29]

Rilke's comment highlights the points of convergence yet also divergence evident in Guérin's and Barbey's diary-writing projects. His allusion to Barbey's well-documented vanity points to one underlying reason for the marked presence of irony in the *Memoranda*, both as a trope and a topic of discussion. While the internal inconsistencies in Guérin's *Journal* emerged partly from a deep-rooted suspicion of egotism, I shall argue that Barbey d'Aurevilly employs irony in his diary to bolster his *amour-propre*. Barbey may subscribe to the moral and consolatory qualities of intimate writing, but he is simultaneously deeply aware of what he as a male writer risks by practising it. Not only does the diary carry connotations of 'feminine' and childish writing practices, but to *tout dire* in the *Memoranda* would be to entail a loss of the 'mystère' (*OCB* II: 694) which is an essential component of Barbey's preferred styles of masculinity: those of the dandy and the Byronic 'fatal man'.[30] As discussed in Chapter Two, an emphasis on embarrassment is one strategy employed by male writers seeking to indulge in *poésie intime* and the *roman intime*. The explicit discussions of irony as a device in the *Memoranda* are, it will be argued, similarly strategic: by pointing to the potential duplicity of language they thus prevent readers from taking Barbey's *confidences* altogether literally.

On publication in the *Renaissance latine* in 1903, Barbey d'Aurevilly's second *Memorandum* was announced as an 'extraordinaire confession' (Anon 1903: 340). Perpetuating this language of confession, central to nineteenth-century literary intimacy, twenty-first-century critics have sought to reinstate Barbey d'Aurevilly as a writer of the *intime* who challenged the nineteenth-century hierarchy of genres by demonstrating a 'préférence dédaigneuse pour cette littérature virtuelle, intime, à peine littéraire, qui s'épanouit dans ces genres dits mineurs'.[31] Barbey's reputation still rests primarily on his novels and short stories yet evidence suggests that he did draw significant and, moreover, qualitative distinctions between his published and non-published writing. Work written for publication, he writes in a letter of 14 March 1855 to Trebutien, is equivalent to 'une toilette faite, un système d'épingles et de draperies; on ne touche pas les ganglions et les artères à travers cela' (*LT*: 821). Discussing his epistolary correspondence in 1856 he clarifies, emphatically: 'Le *meilleur de moi* est dans ces lettres où je parle ma vraie langue en me *fichant* de tous les publics!' (*OCB* II: 1048). Veiling, pinning, and covering appear as necessary correlatives of the publishing process, while the 'non-literary' allows for the flourishing of unclothed truth within and between subjects. Barbey displays clear antipathy for the public unveiling of self, constitutive of Rousseau's autobiographical project, yet the communication of one's inner life to a known other is, it seems, of a different order. In a letter of March 1854 to Trebutien, he writes:

> Faire une confidence à un ami comme vous, — un autre soi-même, — le mettre au courant des choses intimes de sa vie n'est pas une Révélation à la Rousseau, dans un livre destiné à tout le monde. J'ai toujours méprisé Rousseau et ses façons de dire et de faire. (*LT*: 684)

Like Guérin, Barbey's passion for intimate literature appears tied to the real and symbolic importance of friendship, and he can certainly be seen to take pleasure in the *Memoranda* as a written extension, and function, of his relationship with Maurice.[32] But while Guérin worries about the egotism involved in diary-writing, being the centre of another's attention is a major part of the diary's attraction for Barbey. Discussing his decision to begin the *Memorandum* again after a break of a month, he admits:

> [Maurice de] G[uérin] souhaite que je le continue, et je le ferai si cela peut lui faire plaisir. Quand on intéresse quelqu'un en agissant de la manière la plus insignifiante, voici que cette manière insignifiante signifie et que l'on s'intéresse d'intéresser. Diable de vanité! (*OCB* II: 826)

Barbey's sense of vanity can thus in part explain the existence of the *Memoranda*, and it can also in part explain the diary's recourse to irony.[33] Guérin's observation that the diary effects a *mise en scène* of the self ('Mon égoïsme se met toujours en scène' (*GJ*: 68)), is further heightened in the case of Barbey, self-confessed 'comédien [...] involontaire' (*OCB* II: 933). The explicit focus on irony in the *Memoranda* draws the reader's attention to the possibility of linguistic manipulation from which the diaries are not entirely immune.[34] Barbey may claim that his diaries are marked by 'un *je m'en f...* ! de la phrase' (*LT*: 451), yet writing with a constant awareness of the text's reception by known others (Maurice, and, during his lifetime, other friends including Trebutien and Paul de Saint-Victor), his 'vraie langue' (*OCB* II: 1048) is one which is, consciously or unconsciously, tailored to impress.

'Une éternelle ironie'

Irony features explicitly in the *Memoranda* in reference to Barbey's journalistic, epistolary, and conversational practice. 'J'admire cette puissance un peu fourbe du langage,' he writes in an early entry of 21 September 1836 (*OCB* II: 748), and it is the double-dealing, shape-shifting nature of language which enables Barbey to use words to express opinions he does not hold. In the volatile world of July Monarchy journalism, varying levels of censorship meant that even articles written in good faith might become divorced from their authors' original intentions, received by readers in an alien form. In this context, writing self-censored articles devoid of sincerity emerges as a logical anticipation of the external censor. Writing for newspapers and journals which do not correspond to his political allegiances, Barbey admits to a number of these duplicitous strategies: 'Corrigé mon article sur le *droit des gens* qui a paru aujourd'hui. — Quand je ne mens pas tout à fait, je ne dis vrai qu'à moitié. Morale chose!' (*OCB* II: 938); 'Me suis dépouillé de ma souquenille couleur de muraille de journaliste anonyme et libérale [...] et ai retrouvé un peu de *mon moi* en finissant le second volume des *Soirées de Saint-Pétersbourg* de de Maistre' (*OCB* II: 970); 'Penser à revêtir tous mes articles d'une éternelle ironie' (*OCB* II: 870). Irony as a rhetorical figure is not only deployed in Barbey's journalism, however, but surfaces in personal documents and interpersonal encounters. In the *Memoranda*, for example, Barbey notes a conversation with an acquaintance, Le F...: 'Lui ai sanglé au visage deux ou trois ironies qu'il a pris pour argent comptant' (*OCB* II: 941). As much as the rare and rarefied July Monarchy *salon* might appeal to Barbey for its idyllic mixture of 'intimacy and sociability' divorced from economic interest or personal gain, it also emerges as an environment in which Barbey can symbolically enrich himself at the expense of others.[35] Barbey's use of irony in social situations subtly destabilises the supposed harmony of this 'high-status' sociability. Another diary entry details the mechanics of irony in relation to an encounter with a relative, the Marquise de Héricy: 'J'ai imprégné le peu de paroles adressées à elle d'une fort dose d'ironie, reprenant en sous-œuvre ce qu'elle disait et l'exagérant jusqu'à l'absurde' (*OCB* II: 64); at another *salon*: '[J'ai] *ironisé* tout le temps' (*OCB* II: 876). Conversational irony also extends into correspondence, particularly letters written to family members: 'Remué divers papiers et commencé une lettre de sanglantes ironies à ma tante' (*OCB* II: 1012).

Barbey's tendency to employ irony in social situations is indicative of the cultural prestige it held, in certain circles, at this time. Elite styles of masculinity modelled on Byronism or dandyism placed emphasis on physical appearance, dress, and toilette, but they also relied on linguistic means, tropes, and tones to cultivate a seductive sense of latent mystery, and even danger.[36] By employing irony — 'slippery' (Hutcheon 1994: 140) and enigmatic — the speaker seeks to incite curiosity in his or her interlocutor: in Barthesian terms, we might say that irony activates the 'hermeneutic code' and maintains a form of narrative suspense.[37] This phenomenon is explicitly formulated in Barbey's 1845 essay *Du dandysme et de G. Brummell*:

> L'Ironie est un génie qui dispense de tous les autres. Elle jette sur un homme l'air de sphinx qui préoccupe comme un mystère et qui inquiète comme un danger. Or, Brummell le possédait, et s'en servait de manière à transir tous les amours-propres, même en les caressant, [...]. C'est le génie de l'ironie qui le rendit le plus grand mystificateur que l'Angleterre ait jamais eu. (*OCB* II: 694)

Yet Barbey is already formulating these opinions in the *Memoranda*: in an entry of 27 March 1838, he personifies irony as 'un génie qui dispense de tous les autres et même de ce dont tous les autres ne sont pas dispensés, c'est-à-dire de cœur et de bon sens' (*OCB* II: 886). By employing as well as analysing this 'ingenious' device in his diaries, Barbey can be seen to highlight his own genius, and seek out the attention and admiration of his peers.

Intimacy in Italics

Through allusions to Barbey's journalistic, conversational, and epistolary practice, irony migrates into the diary and comes into contact with the *cœur*. This interference is emblematic of the complex attitude displayed by Barbey towards the diary as a vehicle for intimacy. There are several points at which *intimité* is referred to positively in the *Memoranda*, typically to qualify a conversation: '[Je] aimerais mieux causer d'intimité avec lui [Maurice de Guérin] sur ce canapé' (*OCB* II: 944); 'Allé souper au Café Anglais avec G[uérin] — Causé d'intimité et n'avons vu personne' (*OCB* II: 977); 'Allé chez Mme de La R[enaudière], avec laquelle j'ai causé intimement et de manière à m'alléger l'infâme poids d'ennui et de tristesse que je sentais sur le cœur' (*OCB* II: 1021). These assertions align with the positive evaluation of the diary as a mode of emotional release and consolation: intimacy as a means of alleviating the heaviness of the heart. Yet intimacy can, it seems, also provoke and exacerbate suffering, chiming with the associations between intimacy and melancholy we saw articulated in the *roman intime* and *poésie intime*. In an entry of 1 April 1838, for example, the diarist recounts an evening spent with a friend, Victor Gaudin de Villaine:

> De là chez G[audin] où j'ai dîné. — Nous sommes restés à causer *intimement* et *tristement* (l'un suit toujours l'autre) au coin du feu mourant et aux approches de la nuit. — Ordinairement (quoiqu'il soit un ami pour le temps et pour l'éternité) j'ai peu d'ouverture avec lui sur de certains sentiments qui le maîtrisent moins que moi, mais ce soir, c'est lui qui, à propos de son *veuvage*, a pris cette pente. — L'ai étonné par ce que je lui ai dévoilé. [...] Pourtant je ne lui ai pas tout dit. (*OCB* II: 890–91)

This passage epitomises the role of mystification in the *Memoranda* and its use as a means for Barbey to compensate for what he loses through his otherwise rewarding interventions into the sphere of intimacy. By evoking a secluded setting, at nightfall, Barbey exploits the *effet d'intime* identified by Diaz and Diaz and stages a scene of intimacy for Maurice, his reader, casting himself in the starring role. Yet rather than promote an unequivocal celebration of transparent communion, Barbey emphasises intimacy's apparently inevitable association with, and generation of, sadness, and — we can see a causal link here — his self-protective reluctance to *tout dire*. Indulging in what he refers to elsewhere as a 'caprice de silence' (*OCB* II: 845), he introduces the spectre of the non-said into the space of the said. *Mise en scène* becomes *mise en abyme*, and, ironically, Maurice as reader is granted even less access to 'Barbey *intime*' through the *journal* than Gaudin ('étonné') appears to be during their fireside conversation.

In this way, the above passage amounts to a series of hints and an accumulation of literary motifs and devices (irony, suggestion, ellipses, and the *effet d'intime*), which bring it closer to Barbey's definition of literature as 'une toilette faite, un système d'épingles et de draperies' (*LT*: 821) than the 'naturel' of the non-literary ideal.[38] As a biographer of Barbey d'Aurevilly, Avrane notes that while readers of the *Memoranda* know that Barbey suffers, we never fully know the reasons for this suffering without turning to extra-textual material (2005: 15). For Baudelaire, a fellow theorist of the dandy, the dandy 'peut être un homme souffrant; mais, dans ce dernier cas, il sourira comme le Lacédémonien sous la morsure du renard' (*OC* II: 710). Barbey does not suffer in such complete, stoical silence yet his limited confidences consciously frustrate the transparency and legibility implicit in the ideal of intimacy, whether between two friends in fireside conversation or between the writer and reader of the *journal intime*. The irony implicit in this act of veiling is further heightened by the italicisation of intimacy in the above passage: '*intimement et tristement*'. Elsewhere, we read references to conversations '*d'abandon intime*' (*OCB* II: 880), and adjectives of sensibility are often italicised by Barbey, as are those explicitly referring to gender: Barbey expresses '[une] envie *féminine* de sortir' (*OCB* II: 749) and refers to a 'causerie *molle et dénouée*' (*OCB* II: 907) amongst women.[39] Italicisation can be employed for straightforward emphasis, but in Barbey's *Memoranda* — as in the writing of Stendhal or Baudelaire — it frequently imparts an ironic inflection to the word in question, highlighting its overdetermined status, for example, or the writer's disingenuous use of it. Barbey also uses italics to single out foreign words (the '*Marchesa*', for instance): italicising terms of intimacy and sensibility thus creates a visual equivalence with words of foreign origin. The italicised words remain as lexical intrusions, quotations, or imports from an alien vocabulary which do not embed fully in Barbey's own script: in Bakhtinian terms, his diary becomes dialogic or polyphonic.[40] In the process, the *Memoranda* develop an ambiguous textual surface which at times appropriates the language of intimacy and, at others, engages in a strategy of defamiliarisation or distancing which makes the *intime* appear strange and insincere.

Barbey does not present intimacy and irony as mutually exclusive literary modes or impulses in the *Memoranda*, but instead weaves them together: they exist as two unresolved aspirations which are heightened, but complicated, by the presence of the other. I have argued that the ironic mode works primarily to maintain enigma in the *Memoranda*, offsetting the parallel impulse towards intimacy. However, developing certain points raised above, it is also possible to see the diary's enigmatic tone as something which can *itself* generate a form of extra-textual intimacy between writer and reader. Barbey's diary entries evoke the way the ironiser can alienate his, or her, audience if irony is misunderstood ('Lui ai sanglé au visage [à Le F...] deux ou trois ironies qu'il a pris pour argent comptant' (*OCB* II: 941)). Yet, by extension, the shared comprehension of irony — and, we might add, the shared comprehension of the very desire, or even *need*, to ironise — might be seen to foster complicity between writer and reader.[41] Discussing German Romantic theories of irony, Paraschas has referred to August Schlegel's view that irony amounts to a 'wink', aimed at a '"select circle"' of readers (2013: 44). Although irony does not always function in this manner in the *Memoranda*, the pleasure Barbey takes in detailing his uses of irony to his chosen readers indicates a shared appreciation of the ironic mode which could be seen to strengthen, rather than frustrate, their bonds of friendship. The potential of irony to generate intimacy, but also its tendency to confuse communication, pertains to Baudelaire's prose poem 'À une heure du matin' and its critical reception, to which the final section of this chapter will turn. The highly divergent responses to this poem bear witness to a text which, while appearing to be, in Sonya Stephens's words 'a genuine *journal intime*, [...] more akin to a diary than any passage in the *Journaux intimes*', is simultaneously deeply critical of the writing practice it so persuasively replicates.[42]

IV. Baudelaire and the Diary *en trompe-l'œil*

In recent years, irony has come to be seen as the defining feature of Baudelaire's prose poetry collection, *Le Spleen de Paris*, and one of the elements distinguishing it most decisively from *Les Fleurs du Mal*.[43] While the first-person pronoun was, as we have seen, subject to strategic manoeuvring in *Les Fleurs du Mal*, *Le Spleen de Paris* is seen to mobilise a more coherent system of self-effacement, central to which is the consistent employment of irony. According to Steve Murphy, the existence of multiple, competing voices advocating subversive philosophies and displaying cruel or illogical behaviour (for example, in 'Assommons les pauvres!' or 'Le Mauvais Vitrier') is intended, ultimately, to provoke moral and ethical reflection on the part of the reader. Any literal conflation of the first-person pronoun with Baudelaire as author is, within this interpretive paradigm, mistaken:

> L'emploi de la première personne est souvent un leurre — un piège dans lequel le lecteur doit tomber avant de s'en extraire en s'apercevant que les locateurs des poèmes sont soumis à des ironies qui montrent que Baudelaire ne partage ni leurs perceptions, ni leurs valeurs morales. (Murphy 2003: 28)

Maria Scott concurs, arguing that the prose poems are 'textual snares' (2005: 7) which 'function actively to deceive us' (2005: 1); she connects this deliberate deception to Baudelaire's desire for revenge on the reading public following its spectacular misunderstanding of *Les Fleurs du Mal* (2005: 203–08). Whether the ironic inconsistences of *Le Spleen de Paris* were intended to be noted and appreciated — a wink at the 'happy few' — or to remain undetected is open to debate; nonetheless, Murphy and Scott contend that the more productive readings of the poems approach them through a 'herméneutique du soupçon' (Murphy 2003: 26).[44] They identify a number of scholars who fail to adopt this interpretive attitude and who thus fall victim to the Baudelairean 'ruse' (Scott 2005: 14): as Murphy states, 'beaucoup de commentateurs de ces poèmes sont restés pris dans le piège' (2003: 28). In the first part of this section, I align myself with Murphy and Scott's approach by offering a reading of 'À une heure du matin' which interprets the poem as an ironic take on the rhetoric of moral improvement surrounding diary-writing in the nineteenth century and, more broadly, as a subversion of the writing, reading, and publication practices associated with the expanding culture of intimacy. Yet, in the second part, I also take seriously certain critical responses to the poem founded on its perceived sincerity. Rather than suggest that such readings are necessarily facile or unproductive, I ask what the impulse to interpret this poem as a genuine piece of life-writing might tell us about the continued persistence of the intimate hermeneutic and the particular affective charge produced when intimacy and irony meet.

A Mock Diary?

As Murphy points out, 'Baudelaire recourt peu aux accents intimistes dans *Le Spleen de Paris*' (2003: 183); a shift in emphasis which might be read as a reaction to the hostile reception of *Les Fleurs du Mal* alluded to above. 'À une heure du matin' thus provides us with a rare opportunity to examine how Baudelaire uses the emerging genre of prose poetry to respond to the mid-century culture of intimacy and its own evolving writing and publishing practices. The following section argues that the poem can be read as a dramatisation of diary-writing which functions to critique the practice. Two factors in particular, one intertextual and one contextual, support this interpretation: the existence of Baudelaire's contemporaneous verse poem, 'L'Examen de minuit', and the initial publication of the prose poem in the newspaper *La Presse*.

'À une heure du matin' itself makes no explicit reference to irony yet the verse poem with which it is frequently paired, 'L'Examen de minuit', does. Dating from 1863, and first included in the 1868 edition of *Les Fleurs du Mal*, 'L'Examen de minuit' evokes the examination of conscience which the end of the day encourages for writer and reader alike ('nous'). The anticipation of the daily *examen de conscience* should, of course, motivate moral behaviour amongst committed Christians: in the fictitious *Journal de Marguerite*, Marguerite's exemplary comportment allows her to admit in her entry of Thursday 9 October that she is 'pas trop mécontente de ma journée hier parce que je n'ai pas fait de grandes fautes' (Monniot 1867: 5), her humility underscored by the use of litotes. The examination activated by the twelve chimes of the clock in 'L'Examen de minuit', however, occurs on Friday the thirteenth. The dissonance created by this numerical disunity, and deliberate bad luck, sets the tone for the extended array of sins which emerge in the course of the four stanzas, echoing 'Au Lecteur' of *Les Fleurs du Mal*: blasphemy, dishonesty, greed, cowardice, and pride. Stretching out in adverbial form, irony dominates the first octave, taunting the subject, and linking itself explicitly to the (self-destructive) project of self-examination:

> La pendule, sonnant minuit,
> Ironiquement nous engage
> À nous rappeler quel usage
> Nous fîmes du jour qui s'enfuit:
> Aujourd'hui, date fatidique,
> Vendredi, treize, nous avons,
> Malgré tout ce que nous savons,
> Mené le train d'un hérétique. (OC I: 144)

In 'À une heure du matin', it is a single chime, rather than twelve, which instigates the process of recapitulation. The mention of irony is missing but its effect is nevertheless created through the discrepancy between self-improvement and self-abasement, and the accumulation of neat pairs of perverse actions verging on the absurd. The poet cries:

> Horrible vie! Horrible ville! Récapitulons la journée: [...] M'être vanté (pourquoi?) de plusieurs vilaines actions que je n'ai jamais commises, et avoir lâchement nié quelques autres méfaits que j'ai accomplis avec joie, délit de fanfaronnade, crime de respect humain; avoir refusé à un ami un service facile, et donné une recommandation écrite à un parfait drôle: ouf! est-ce bien fini? (Baudelaire 1862: 1)

In this light, critics including Melvin Zimmerman (1968) and J. A. Hiddleston (1987) have interpreted the 'Pharisean prayer' of the fourth and final paragraph as 'inauthentic' and consciously duplicitous on the part of the writer, who chooses to present the hypocrisy rather than the humility involved in cultural practices of petition:

> Âmes de ceux que j'ai aimés, âmes de ceux que j'ai chantés, fortifiez-moi, soutenez-moi, éloignez de moi le mensonge et les vapeurs corruptrices du monde, et vous, Seigneur mon Dieu! accordez-moi la grâce de produire quelques beaux vers qui me prouvent à moi-même que je ne suis pas le dernier des hommes, que je ne suis pas inférieur à ceux que je méprise! (Baudelaire 1862: 1)

In such interpretations, the humour prompted by this ideological inconsistency — the prayer is fundamentally selfish rather than selfless — functions to satirise practices of self-improvement generally, and prayer more specifically. Critics tend to focus on the question of prayer, but it is not the only practice of self-improvement with which the poem is concerned. As we have discussed, Catholic methods of self-examination fed into the growth of the diary in nineteenth-century France, and it is a mistake, I argue, to ignore the growing significance and popularity of diary-writing in the period as a potential target for Baudelaire's irony. 'À une heure du matin' was first published in *La Presse* in 1862, the same year that Guérin's *Journal* appeared in print with Didier.[45] The suggestive links Stephens makes between 'À une heure du matin' and the *journal intime* become even more persuasive if we approach the poem as contemporaneous with one of the earliest, and most successful, commercial publications of a nineteenth-century diary.[46] Indeed, the poem itself first appears in a very public position, on the front page of the newspaper *La Presse*, in the *feuilleton* section (Figures 3.1 and 3.2). Marit Grøtta observes that, today, when we read Baudelaire's prose poems in book volumes, 'their relationship to the newspaper medium is easily lost' (2015: 33). If we reconsider this relationship, however, we see the situational irony created by the placement of the 'diary-poem' amplify the internal inconsistencies between solitude and multitude, privacy and publicity, and humility and pride which are constitutive of the text itself.

There are multiple textual and contextual indications that 'À une heure du matin' alludes to diary-writing. Diaries typically demonstrate a structural reliance on date and time: many of Barbey d'Aurevilly's entries in the *Memoranda*, for example, are marked by the date and more or less precise time of writing, usually late at night. The title 'À une heure du matin' is a clear nod to this convention, while at the level of reader reception, the placement of the poem on the front page of *La Presse* implicates it in the date displayed on the newspaper and *feuilleton* banner: 'Mercredi 27 août'. The combination of immediate present ('D'abord, un double tour à la serrure'), recapitulation ('Récapitulons la journée: avoir vu plusieurs hommes de lettres...'), and projection ('Je voudrais bien me racheter') reflect the content and tone of many of Barbey's entries, particularly those relating, appropriately, to his journalistic (and *feuilleton*) work. For example:

> Journée occupée, mais non comme j'aurais voulu. J'ai une foule de choses à faire et que je remets depuis huit jours tant mes damnés moments sont comptés! — Levé à huit heures. [...] Allé au Journal. [...] Rentré anéanti, et il faut pourtant que je griffonne ce satané feuilleton pour demain. — Je ne dormirai guères cette nuit. (*OCB* II: 928)

Barbey's entries frequently omit the first-person pronoun and employ abbreviations, bracketed interjections, and jargon, creating an impression of informality and familiarity. 'À une heure du matin' shares in these stylistic features: the poet's recapitulative list, building on the repetitive use of the infinitive, avoids the first-person pronoun and creates what Hiddleston has called a '"telegram" style' (1987: 84), as if the *faits divers* of *La Presse* and its prose had infiltrated the language of the poem. The poem also displays slang, interjections ('ouf!'), and bracketed asides which disrupt the regularity and rhythmic accumulation of the list: '(il prenait sans doute la Russie pour une île)'; '(pourquoi?)' (1862: 1).

Mid-century readers were used to seeing comic parodies of 'bourgeois' practices of self-analysis and self-improvement in the press. Graham Robb includes the 'examen de conscience où l'écrivain raconte sa journée à des fins satiriques et moralisants' as part of a 'répertoire connu' of journalistic tropes in the mid nineteenth century (1990: 17), and Scott has drawn attention to Daumier's 1839 series of caricatures, *La Journée du célibataire*, which follow the progress of a fictitious Monsieur Coquelot at

FIG. 3.1. Front cover of *La Presse*, 27 August 1862, Bibliothèque nationale de France

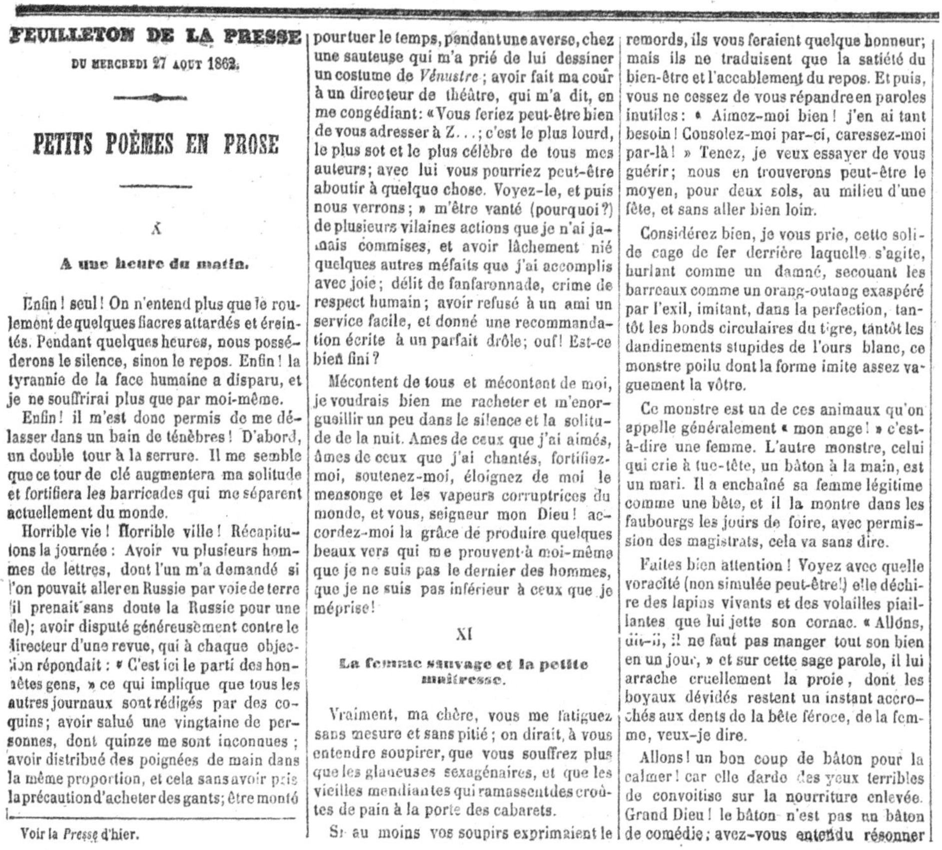

FEUILLETON DE LA PRESSE

DU MERCREDI 27 AOUT 1862.

PETITS POÈMES EN PROSE

X

À une heure du matin.

Enfin! seul! On n'entend plus que le roulement de quelques fiacres attardés et éreintés. Pendant quelques heures, nous posséderons le silence, sinon le repos. Enfin! la tyrannie de la face humaine a disparu, et je ne souffrirai plus que par moi-même.

Enfin! il m'est donc permis de me délasser dans un bain de ténèbres! D'abord, un double tour à la serrure. Il me semble que ce tour de clé augmentera ma solitude et fortifiera les barricades qui me séparent actuellement du monde.

Horrible vie! Horrible ville! Récapitulons la journée: Avoir vu plusieurs hommes de lettres, dont l'un m'a demandé si l'on pouvait aller en Russie par voie de terre (il prenait sans doute la Russie pour une île); avoir disputé généreusement contre le directeur d'une revue, qui à chaque objection répondait: « C'est ici le parti des honnêtes gens, » ce qui implique que tous les autres journaux sont rédigés par des coquins; avoir salué une vingtaine de personnes, dont quinze me sont inconnues; avoir distribué des poignées de main dans la même proportion, et cela sans avoir pris la précaution d'acheter des gants; être monté pour tuer le temps, pendant une averse, chez une sauteuse qui m'a prié de lui dessiner un costume de *Vénustre*; avoir fait ma cour à un directeur de théâtre, qui m'a dit, en me congédiant: « Vous feriez peut-être bien de vous adresser à Z...; c'est le plus lourd, le plus sot et le plus célèbre de tous mes auteurs; avec lui vous pourriez peut-être aboutir à quelque chose. Voyez-le, et puis nous verrons; » m'être vanté (pourquoi?) de plusieurs vilaines actions que je n'ai jamais commises, et avoir lâchement nié quelques autres méfaits que j'ai accomplis avec joie; délit de fanfaronnade, crime de respect humain; avoir refusé à un ami un service facile, et donné une recommandation écrite à un parfait drôle; ouf! Est-ce bien fini?

Mécontent de tous et mécontent de moi, je voudrais bien me racheter et m'enorgueillir un peu dans le silence et la solitude de la nuit. Ames de ceux que j'ai aimés, âmes de ceux que j'ai chantés, fortifiez-moi, soutenez-moi, éloignez de moi le mensonge et les vapeurs corruptrices du monde, et vous, seigneur mon Dieu! accordez-moi la grâce de produire quelques beaux vers qui me prouvent à moi-même que je ne suis pas le dernier des hommes, que je ne suis pas inférieur à ceux que je méprise!

XI

La femme sauvage et la petite maîtresse.

Vraiment, ma chère, vous me fatiguez sans mesure et sans pitié; on dirait, à vous entendre soupirer, que vous souffrez plus que les glaneuses sexagénaires, et que les vieilles mendiantes qui ramassent des croûtes de pain à la porte des cabarets.

Si au moins vos soupirs exprimaient le remords, ils vous feraient quelque honneur; mais ils ne traduisent que la satiété du bien-être et l'accablement du repos. Et puis, vous ne cessez de vous répandre en paroles inutiles: « Aimez-moi bien! j'en ai tant besoin! Consolez-moi par-ci, caressez-moi par-là! » Tenez, je veux essayer de vous guérir; nous en trouverons peut-être le moyen, pour deux sols, au milieu d'une fête, et sans aller bien loin.

Considérez bien, je vous prie, cette solide cage de fer derrière laquelle s'agite, hurlant comme un damné, secouant les barreaux comme un orang-outang exaspéré par l'exil, imitant, dans la perfection, tantôt les bonds circulaires du tigre, tantôt les dandinements stupides de l'ours blanc, ce monstre poilu dont la forme imite assez vaguement la vôtre.

Ce monstre est un de ces animaux qu'on appelle généralement « mon ange! » c'est-à-dire une femme. L'autre monstre, celui qui crie à tue-tête, un bâton à la main, est un mari. Il a enchaîné sa femme légitime comme une bête, et il la montre dans les faubourgs les jours de foire, avec permission des magistrats, cela va sans dire.

Faites bien attention! Voyez avec quelle voracité (non simulée peut-être!) elle déchire des lapins vivants et des volailles piaillantes que lui jette son cornac. « Allons, dit-il, il ne faut pas manger tout son bien en un jour, » et sur cette sage parole, il lui arrache cruellement la proie, dont les boyaux dévidés restent un instant accrochés aux dents de la bête féroce, de la femme, veux-je dire.

Allons! un bon coup de bâton pour la calmer! car elle darde des yeux terribles de convoitise sur la nourriture enlevée. Grand Dieu! le bâton n'est pas un bâton de comédie; avez-vous entendu résonner

Voir la *Presse* d'hier.

FIG. 3.2. 'À Une heure du matin', in *La Presse*, 27 August 1862, Bibliothèque nationale de France

regular intervals throughout the day (2005: 39). Given the textual markers discussed earlier, and the journalistic context of its initial publication, regular newspaper readers of the nineteenth century would, arguably, be primed to interpret 'À une heure du matin' as a form of diary entry. In *La Presse*, the text can be read as a ludic, but morally inflected, reflection on prosaic (both literally and figuratively) practices of self-improvement, exploited by Baudelaire for comic effect. Not only is the diarist-poet spectacularly unimproved by the end of his day, and the end of his poem, but his allusions to diary-writing as a solitary activity, safe from interruption or intrusion, are comically belied by its publishing context: 'Enfin! seul!'; 'Enfin! La tyrannie de la face humaine a disparu, et je ne souffrirai plus que par moi-même' (1862: 1). The poet's emphatic relief, conveyed, somewhat verbosely, through a combination of exclamation, metonym, and intertextual reference to Thomas De Quincey ('la tyrannie de la face humaine') is deflated by an awareness of the face of the reader bending over the pages of the newspaper, privy to the staged suffering, and self-torturing, of the diarist-poet.[47]

A Therapeutic Text

The above reading runs counter to interpretations of 'À une heure du matin' as an aestheticised, but largely authentic, fragment of life-writing to be placed alongside the aphorisms of Baudelaire's *Journaux intimes*. It argues that, in its journalistic context, 'À une heure du matin' amounts to a satire of the diary-writer and the nineteenth-century culture of self-improvement more broadly. However, the irony brought to bear on this diary-poem inevitably creates an indeterminacy which makes space for wide interpretive variation. If we adopt Murphy's position, outlined above, we might conclude that those who have assumed the authenticity of the voice of 'À une heure du matin', or explained the text by way of reference to Baudelaire's biography, lack the requisite scepticism to construct productive critical readings: they have fallen victim to an illusion of intimacy mischievously concocted by the poet.[48] Yet it is important to acknowledge that the poem can legitimately function, by virtue of its deployment of irony, both as a comment on confessional writing practices *and* as a powerful example of these same practices. Responses which conflate the first-person pronouns of the poem with Baudelaire as a biographical subject do not necessarily amount to communicational or critical failures, but testify rather to the discursive and affective complexity of a poem which can speak both to the ludic world of the nineteenth-century press — or that of postmodern play — and to the hermeneutic of intimacy which approaches literature as an essentially interpersonal encounter.

Indeed, 'À une heure du matin' exemplifies Stephens's view that the hybrid prose poems 'present Baudelaire's consciousness of boundaries and of the contours of different literary landscapes' (1999: 1) and — we might add — of different contexts and cultures of reception. While allowing for readings founded on suspicion, the poem has also, since its publication, appealed to readers as a sincere articulation of suffering, for which the *journal intime* offers an affectively potent, and culturally pertinent, form. In 1887, for example, referring to the prose poem in the new context of Baudelaire's *Œuvres complètes*, Paul Desjardins offers a 'confessional' interpretation: 'Voilà une instructive confession. Il m'a semblé qu'elle expliquait à merveille la misanthropie de Baudelaire'.[49] Rilke's inclusion of the poem in his own German-language *roman-diaristique*, *The Notebooks of Malte Laurids Brigge*, first published in 1910, suggests an intense identification between the fictitious Brigge and the diarist-poet of 'À une heure du matin' in which it is suffering, not satire, which functions as the point of contact. Before quoting the final paragraph of the prose poem in full, Brigge gives voice to a desperate sense of anguish which Baudelaire's poem is, it seems, able to assuage. He declares:

> I have fallen and cannot raise myself up again, because I am broken. I have always believed that there might yet be a rescue. What I prayed for, evening after evening, lies before me in my own handwriting. I have copied it out of the books in which I found it, so that I would have it close, issued from my hand as if they were my own words. And I want to write it down one more time, here, kneeling before my table, I want to write it; for that way I will have it for longer than if I read it and every word endures and has time to die away.

'Mécontent de tous et mécontent de moi, je voudrais bien me racheter et m'enorgueillir un peu dans le silence et la solitude de la nuit. Âmes de ceux que j'ai aimés [etc.]'. (Rilke 2016: 31)

Through transcribing, a mode of 'intimate reading' *par excellence*, Brigge is shown by Rilke to internalise the diary and appropriate its language, form, and sense. The potential ironic reception of the prose poem explored above does not, in Rilke's writing, preclude either an intensely emotional response to it, or the validity of the comfort afforded by it: the poem has become a therapeutic text. Such a response to the poem can be seen to be motivated by the highly emotive qualities of its content and formal structures. While the behaviour of the diarist-poet might be suspect, it is redeemed, at least partially, by his intense self-awareness: the self-loathing and desperation he expresses can incite pity, empathy, and even admiration in readers. At the discursive level, the incantatory repetitions and accumulations of the third paragraph have a noticeably childlike quality, suggestive of practices learned by heart, and testimony to the diary's use as an educational tool. These repetitions also prefigure the much-discussed 'prayer' which emerges in the prose poem's final paragraph. For readers familiar with practices of petition, the solemn, ritualised rhythms of this paragraph have the potential to activate recognition and a range of affective responses, from fear, despair, or boredom to hope and peace.

The association of diary-writing with childhood writing practices and the rhetoric of prayer thus helps to maintain the affective charge of 'À une heure du matin', despite the farcical misdeeds of the poet and the internal and situational ironies of the poem. The text thus confirms what has been an underlying hypothesis of this chapter: that irony is not necessarily opposed to emotion. In 1852, Flaubert asserted that 'l'ironie n'enlève rien au pathétique. Elle l'outre au contraire' (*CF* II: 172) and, read alongside this statement, it could be argued that the pathos of 'À une heure du matin' is in fact further heightened by the shadow of irony. Returning to the poem's initial site of publication, *La Presse*, the insertion of the personal language of introspection (the *journal intime*) into the discourse of the newspaper (the *journal*) creates an uncomfortable incongruity: the poet's intensely felt subjectivity is absorbed into the 'éternel bulletin' ('Le Voyage' (*OC* I: 133)) of human suffering, its significance offset and even undermined by news of Garibaldi's unification campaign, a rebellion in Shang-Hai or, closer to home, a factory fire in Paris. While this ironic imbalance is a potential trigger for humour, it also encourages an ethical reflection on the paradox surrounding the public placement of intimate literature, motivated, in part, by an increasingly market-driven economy in which the process of public self-disclosure has become profitable. The pathos-laden figure of the poet, forced to perform his *intimité*, albeit ironically, for all to see thus becomes a locus for readerly sympathy. In one reading, then, it is the poem's proximity to a 'genuine *journal intime*' (Stephens 2001: 140) which constitutes the appeal, and therapeutic function, of 'À une heure du matin', facilitating a sense of intersubjective identification with the voice of the diarist-poet, as depicted by Rilke. In another, it is the text's status as poetry which ultimately protects the writer from any definitive biographical interpretations. The diarist-poet's allusion to the 'double tour à la serrure' (1862: 1) is symbolic of the double-voiced (double-locked) nature of the text created by these divergent readings. Through its affinities with the diary, the poem invites the reader behind closed doors and into the everyday emotional world of the poet. Yet through a host of literary devices and contextual effects the poem simultaneously keeps its doors locked, eludes the autobiographical, and becomes a dramatisation — ironic, comic, and poignant — of the *journal intime*.

By deriding the diary as a 'literal' form (Sturrock 1993), twentieth-century critics cast doubt on the value of studying the *journal intime*. However, this chapter has argued that the diary's complex interactions with both known readers and the nineteenth-century literary sphere make it difficult to ignore the elements of 'audience-orientated' performativity evident in much diary-writing of the period, and thus question this assumption of 'literalness'. The diaries considered in this chapter may at times aspire to sincerity, but they nonetheless make use of a range of duplicitous writing techniques or editorial strategies in order to reconcile sincerity with the competing demands of modesty, narrative suspense, and critical distance. 'Tu as raison quand tu dis que je ruse un peu pour écrire mes cahiers' (*GJ*: 119), writes Guérin to Maurice, alluding to her decision to keep her diary-writing secret from her father. While motivated by different reasons, and taking different forms, ruses are at work too in diary-texts by Baudelaire and Barbey d'Aurevilly: writers occupying radically different positions from Guérin in literary history. This chapter has focused in particular on the uses and effects of irony, but argued that the presence of irony in the diaries in question does not negate their affective charge. Instead, such conflict and ambiguity amplifies their emotional tenor, reflecting tensions between the ideal of the diary as a tool of self-improvement or consolatory mode of communion and the frustrations and anxieties which the realities of the practice can entail.

The diary-texts written by Guérin, Barbey, and Baudelaire are each intertwined with domestic space and the comforts, or constraints, of home: the home is the place where they are crafted, and the backdrop, implicit or explicit, to the experiences they relate. Intimacy and domesticity are overlapping and often synonymous notions which gain much of their emotional resonance from each other. Yet, just as domestic space may easily be devoid of intimacy, intimacy can take shape at a distance from home, or be the means through which one distances oneself from it. When Guérin expresses her desire to Maurice to 'faire un tour dans les coins et les recoins de toi-même' (*GJ*: 83), for example, she imagines intimacy as a dynamic process or a journey which might allow her to escape the confines of her cloistered world. And in 'Confession', we have already seen Baudelaire depict a scene of intimacy between a couple as they walk the Parisian streets at night, illustrative of what Mikkel Bogh has called the 'small pockets of privacy [...] offered by the public space of city life' (2016: 240). The following two chapters pursue this conception of intimacy as a mobile, shapeshifting bond which, while frequently aligned with the domestic sphere, is not bound to it. By focusing on intimacy in the context of travel, these chapters will suggest mutually illuminating points of contact between two major impulses in nineteenth-century French culture: the desire for home, on the one hand, and for distance, or *dépaysement*, on the other. How can these two seemingly conflicting desires, visible across myriad cultural productions of the century, be brought to bear on the other?

Notes to Chapter 3

1. For a survey of historical criticisms and condemnations of irony, see Linda Hutcheon (1994), Chapter Two.
2. Irony is a notoriously 'slippery' concept (Hutcheon 1994: 140). It can refer to a classical rhetorical figure with a stable, recoverable meaning (the meaning being, in short, the opposite of what is said); the discrepancies of 'situational', 'historical', or 'dramatic' irony in which context undermines text, often to comic effect; or an overall evaluative attitude. It can also refer to what Philippe Hamon labels 'une ironie romantique-moderne' (1996: 130), a standpoint of uncertainty and non-commitment associated with German and subsequently French Romanticism. Although all these definitions pertain to my discussion, it is on Hutcheon's definition of what irony is *not*, 'something serious, solemn, and univocal' (1994: 27), that I base my principal understanding of irony as a linguistic and emotional effect brought about by textual 'duplicity', and the inconsistencies which can arise from multiple meanings or intentions operating at the same time. For more on irony, see D. C. Muecke (1980), Candace D. Lang (1988), Ross Chambers (1993), and Clare Colebrook (2004).
3. See Lejeune (2009: 147–67) for a survey of critical hostility towards the diary.
4. For discussion of the complex history of the categories of 'literature' and 'the literary', see Ann Jefferson (2007).
5. See Lejeune (2009), Part Two, for a discussion of the historical antecedents of the diary, ranging from account books and 'chronicles' in ancient Rome to sixteenth-century spiritual journals in France. See also Michel Foucault (1984a; 1984b: 340–72); Anne Martin-Fugier (1999: 177–80); and Françoise Simonet-Tenant (2004), Chapter Two.
6. Nonetheless, many studies continue to privilege male diarists, e.g. Girard (1963) and Pierre Pachet (1990).
7. See Rebecca Rogers (2010). Boys did not appear to keep diaries in the same way at school; see Philippe Lejeune: 'Ne concerne que les filles: aucun journal de garçon' (1993: 21).
8. Journals from the sixteenth, seventeenth, and eighteenth centuries were known and read in nineteenth-century France yet, often focusing on public events, these had little in common with nineteenth-century diaries; see Diaz and Diaz (2009: 133–34).
9. On the circulation of diaries amongst friends, so-called 'foyers d'intimisme', see Girard (1963: 70).
10. Lamartine went on to prepare his mother's diary for publication; it appeared two years after his death in 1871 as the *Manuscrit de ma mère*. For further discussion, see Aimée Boutin (2000).
11. On the link between letter-writing and diary-writing, see Paul Servais and Laurence Van Ypersele (2007) and Simont-Tenant (2009).
12. For differentiations between and discussions of these terms, see Simont-Tenant (2004: 24–29).
13. For a detailed table of the composition and publication dates of nineteenth-century diaries, see Girard (1963: 61–69). The mid-century emerges as a clear watershed: fragments and 'pensées' aside, nineteenth-century diaries did not begin to be published commercially until the 1860s. The 1860s saw the partial publication of diaries by Constant, Vigny, and Barbey d'Aurevilly in addition to those by Eugénie and Maurice de Guérin; by the late 1880s diaries by Amiel, Stendhal, Jules Michelet, and Marie Bashkirtseff had also been published.
14. To clarify: Guérin refers to Eugénie de Guérin; where mention is made of her brother, Maurice, his first name will be used.
15. This reference implies the existence of an earlier notebook, but this has not been found (*GJ*: 3, n.1).
16. As summarised in Simonet-Tenant (2004: 75–76).
17. Christianity has historically had an ambivalent relationship with friendship given its possible

associations with self-interest, exclusivity, and favouritism; in this way, friendship can in effect oppose the value of *caritas* or Christian love of the other; see Mark Vernon (2005).
18. On Guérin's diary as a method of survival, and the question of its textual afterlife, see Valerie Raoul (2001).
19. On the Romantic ideal of interchangeability between self, language, and paper, see Peter Simonsen (2007).
20. Paul Jouhanneaud (1856: 86). This sentiment is repeated in other Christian etiquette manuals, many inspired by the writings of Jean-Baptiste de La Salle; see e.g. *Petite civilité chrétienne* (Anon 1834: 54).
21. For a discussion of the correspondence between Trebutien and Barbey concerning the publication of the *Reliquiae*, see Christine Planté (1994); see also Raoul (2001: 144–45).
22. See Joanna Bourke (2009) on the question of Catholic 'scrupulosity'.
23. For further discussion of religious criticisms of the diary, see Girard (1963: 573–76). See also Agnès Cousson (2012) on the tension between analysis of, and disregard for, the self in the context of Port-Royal.
24. Alain Corbin (1999: 425).
25. Cf. Guérin's address to Maurice: 'Reprenons notre causerie, cette causerie secrète, intime, dérobée, qui s'arrête au moindre bruit, au moindre regard' (*GJ*: 119).
26. See Zachary Leader (1999) for a discussion of editorial practices, and the illusion of spontaneity, in Romantic-era writing.
27. While Barbey d'Aurevilly's later diaries were published during his lifetime, the first two *Memoranda* did not appear in public until the turn of the twentieth century. The *Premier Memorandum* was published in 1900 by A. Lemerre; the *Deuxième Memorandum* in 1906 by Stock. Prior to this, instalments of the first *Memorandum* appeared from 1898 to 1899 in the *Revue hebdomadaire*; the second in the *Renaissance latine* in 1903 (*OCB* II: 1457).
28. See Ronald Le Huenen (2010) and Marie-Françoise Melmoux-Montaubin (2002) on Barbey's melancholy.
29. Rainer Maria Rilke, *Fragments en prose*, trans. by Maurice Betz [1929], cited by Girard (1963: 84).
30. Mario Praz famously defines the 'fatal men' of Romantic literature, often associated in the nineteenth-century cultural imagination with Byron, as individuals who 'diffuse all round them the curse which weighs upon their destiny, they blast, like the simoon, those who have the misfortune to meet with them' (1970: 76–77). This type features strongly in Barbey's literary fiction, and is part of the vision of ideal masculinity which surfaces in the *Memoranda*, the title itself borrowed from Byron (Melmoux-Montaubin 2002: 367). Dandyism is another key model for Barbey, whose personal conduct and writings reveal a preoccupation with its characteristic qualities: 'Goût de la provocation, besoin de séduire, mépris du vulgaire, ironie, culte de soi, recherche vestimentaire, sens de la pose' (Le Huenen 2011: 43). Byronism and dandyism have points of similarity but also difference; in *Du dandysme et de G. Brummell* [1845], Barbey suggests that while Byron was a dandy, he had 'quelque chose de plus': poetic greatness (*OCB* II: 673).
31. Brigitte Diaz (2010a: 9).
32. Barbey explicitly links the diary to friendship when he writes in 1856 that 'l'amitié [...] est la vraie *confidente* du *Memorandum*' (*OCB* II: 1027–28).
33. For Barbey's analysis and partial defence of vanity, see *Du dandysme* (*OCB* II: 669–71). On Barbey's relationship with Catholicism from the 1840s onwards, see Patrick Avrane (2005), Chapter Four.
34. Cf. Philippe Berthier, who recommends that the biographer of Barbey should use the *Memoranda* 'avec quelque précaution, puisqu'écrits pour Maurice de Guérin et enjolivés ça ou là peut-être d'un certain narcissisme de la désolation' (1978: 22).
35. Christopher Prendergast (1986: 86).
36. On the fashion for irony in the wake of German Romanticism, see Hamon (1996). For further discussion of dandyism, see Sima Godfrey (1982), Anderson (2001: 159–62), Karin Becker (2010), and, most recently, Alain Montandon (2016).
37. In *S/Z*, Barthes describes the 'hermeneutic code' in relation to narrative as follows: 'Décidons d'appeler *code herméneutique* [...] l'ensemble des unités qui ont pour fonction d'articuler, de diverses

manières, une question, sa réponse et les accidents variés qui peuvent ou préparer la question ou retarder la réponse; ou encore: de formuler une énigme et d'amener son déchiffrement' (1970: 24).
38. On the shared preoccupations of Barbey's letters and literature, see Brigitte Diaz (2010b).
39. On Barbey's complex relationship with gender, and his misogyny, see Melmoux-Montaubin (2002) and Karen L. Humphreys (2012).
40. Mikhail Bakhtin (1981).
41. Thanks to Ann Jefferson for discussion of this point.
42. Sonya Stephens (2001: 140). Stephens's comment elucidates, in part, my choice to focus on Baudelaire's prose poetry here instead of the *Journaux intimes* (*Fusées, Hygiène, Mon cœur mis à nu*). Indeed, many critics refuse to consider the so-called *Journaux intimes* as diaries; Béatrice Didier asserts that 'ni les *Pensées* de Pascal, ni *Mon cœur mis à nu* de Baudelaire, ne sont des journaux et c'est fausser fondamentalement leur signification que de céder à ce genre d'interprétation. Il s'agit, dans l'un et l'autre cas, d'ouvrages destinés à être composés, organisés, en vue d'une démonstration' (1976: 14). While I do not believe that such an interpretation would necessarily falsify the meaning of *Mon cœur mis à nu*, the prose poem 'À une heure du matin' offers more productive points of comparison in the context of this chapter. However, I analyse *La Belgique déshabillée* in the following chapter: a text with obvious chronological and compositional affinities with the *Journaux intimes*.
43. Paraschas writes, for example, that 'critical readings of Baudelaire's prose poems have insisted on unearthing ever deeper levels of irony: irony directed against *Les Fleurs du Mal*, the narrator's irony towards his narrative, irony aimed at the narrator, or a constant self-ironization of the author and his aesthetic or political views' (2013: 104); this can be aligned with what Compagnon has called the emergence of a *Baudelaire postmoderne* in recent criticism (2003: 35–38).
44. Stephens probes the question of the intended reader in *Baudelaire's Prose Poems* (1999), Chapter One; she suggests that many of the poems present scenarios of miscommunication and mutual incomprehension between interlocutors which anticipate the collection's reception.
45. It is not known whether Baudelaire read Guérin's *Journal*, but his awareness of the earlier *Reliquiae* is confirmed by a letter sent from Barbey d'Aurevilly on 25 March 1856 asking Baudelaire to review the work; no evidence of a review, however, exists (Barbey d'Aurevilly 1985: 86).
46. See also Stephens (1998: 144).
47. The expression is from De Quincey's *Confessions of an English Opium-Eater*; see Zimmerman (1968: 104).
48. Claude Pichois, for example, observes that 'À une heure du matin' has 'un caractère autobiographique très prononcé' (*OC* I: 1314).
49. Paul Desjardins, 'Charles Baudelaire', in *Revue politique et littéraire*, 2 July 1887, reproduced in Guyaux (2007: 716). The first edition of Baudelaire's *Œuvres complètes* was published with Lévy between 1868 and 1870.

CHAPTER 4

Intercultural Encounters, or Intimacy at a Distance

Travelling generates what the anthropologist of tourism David Picard has called an 'emotionally heightened social realm' (2012: 3) in which feelings of anticipation, excitement, and fear begin long before the traveller sets out. Chapter Four considers the social bonds formed within this emotionally heightened landscape in the context of nineteenth-century France. It argues that the 'sorte d'intimité improvisée', in the words of Horace-Napoléon Raisson (1853: 103), experienced while travelling was a particular source of anxiety in this period, crystallising broader concerns about friendship. This anxiety is visible in a variety of nineteenth-century texts, from etiquette books and personal correspondence to travel journals and epistolary fictions. In much of this discourse, travelling is seen to engender friendships which are deficient, disingenuous, and sometimes even dangerous: it thus automatically throws light on an ideal standard of intimacy which writers employ, albeit implicitly, in their evaluations.

The chapter begins with an examination of nineteenth-century normative literature, namely the genre of the etiquette manual, and outlines one of its fundamental concerns: the establishment of the appropriate balance between intimacy and distance in human relations. It concentrates on the way in which these etiquette manuals treat the question of intimacy in the specific context of travel. The chapter then proceeds to analyse travel texts by Flaubert, Baudelaire, and Fromentin in light of this discussion: Flaubert's *Voyage en Égypte* (written in 1851, excerpts published from 1881 onwards); Baudelaire's *La Belgique déshabillée* (begun in 1864, excerpts published from 1887 onwards); and Fromentin's *Un été dans le Sahara* (published in 1854 in the *Revue de Paris* and in book form in 1857).[1] Flaubert recognises the circumstantial and enforced friendships formed on his outbound journey to Alexandria and chooses to exploit their comic potential, revelling in them as banal and vulgar imitations of intimacy. The comic potential of 'aped' intimacy is again mined in Baudelaire's notes for *La Belgique déshabillée*: in this text, the 'over-familiarity' of the Belgian people emerges as a form of debased intimacy which the writer seeks to satirise. Yet the aping of intimacy noted by both Flaubert and Baudelaire as a function of travel betrays an attachment to alternative models of intimacy which renders the relationships encountered abroad emotionally unsatisfying and at times distressing. The texts by Flaubert and Baudelaire remained at draft stage and neither one was published in the writers' lifetimes. The final part of the chapter, however, will examine how Fromentin deploys the motif of the *faux ami* in *Un été dans le Sahara*, his first published work. Fromentin's decision to structure parts of his travel account around the figure of the *faux ami* is indicative of the topicality of the phenomenon in nineteenth-century France, particularly heightened in the colonial context. The failure of the friendships depicted in his narrative, a result of intercultural misunderstanding and, at times, hostility, is alleviated not by humour but rather by the use of the epistolary form. In a way not tenable for Flaubert or Baudelaire, Fromentin invokes a form of intimacy firstly with the novel's dedicatee, his friend Armand du Mesnil, and, secondly, with his reading public, which provides him with the structural and affective impetus to complete the narrative.

The stakes of working with these three texts are, as Richard Terdiman highlights in relation to Flaubert, 'uncommonly high' (1985: 227): both Flaubert's and Fromentin's works are complicit with the ideological and cultural structures of Orientalism, while Baudelaire's notes for *La Belgique déshabillée* are explicitly xenophobic. However, this is not a reason to avoid the works. Their focus on the 'fellow traveller' throws into relief a cultural ideal of intimacy which the friendships formed *en voyage* fail to realise.[2] They also reveal how the language of friendship can work to repress or disguise power relations, and how cultures of intimacy define and encounter each other; in these texts, of course, such encounters are often the product of what Ann Laura Stoler calls 'colonial intimacies': 'first and foremost sites of intrusive interventions' (2006: 4). Working on travel texts has the added advantage of acknowledging and re-engaging with the spatial metaphors which lie behind the everyday language of personal relations; the phenomenon evoked by Georg Simmel in his essay 'The Stranger' that 'spatial relations are [...] the condition, on the one hand, and the symbol, on the other, of human relations' (1950: 402).

I. Travel Etiquette

Etiquette manuals flourished in post-Revolutionary France. In his research into nineteenth-century fashion, Philippe Perrot (1981) has identified the publication of at least sixty manuals between 1840 and 1875, many going through multiple editions but all coming together to establish a largely homogeneous corpus covering similar topics and giving similar advice.[3] This proliferation reflects what was, in Perrot's words, a 'demande sans précédent de la part des fractions non initiées de la bourgeoisie (puisqu'elles ont besoin d'apprendre), en ascension (réelle ou fictive), et en quête frénétique des signes d'appartenance qui doivent voir compléter leur réussite économique' (1981: 168). While Perrot concentrates on fashion, these signs were in reality as much behavioural as sartorial. Underlying many of the preoccupations palpable in these etiquette manuals is a concern with interpersonal relationships, and how to preserve the correct balance between intimacy and distance within these. This concern pertains to all forms of relationship but, in particular, extra-familial friendships and acquaintanceships.[4] Ideals of intimacy current in the nineteenth century could speak of 'true' or 'perfect' friendship as an unregulated and transparent union of souls which served to complete both individuals involved in the amicable encounter.[5] Yet these ideals sat uneasily alongside what Peter Gay has labelled the 'bourgeois cult of reserve and reticence' (1996: 343), in part necessitated by the social instability that marked post-Revolutionary France. For conservative social commentators such as Rostaing, the author of the *Manuel de la politesse*, the fall of the *ancien régime* had resulted in a 'mélange de toutes les classes [...] un assemblage confus, hétérogène, un pêle-mêle inextricable' ([18—]: 73) in which it was impossible to decipher an individual's social background or political persuasion. The sense of confusion that this caused (or was held to cause) was exacerbated by the violent sequence of changing governments and regimes following 1789. As a consequence, Rostaing advocates 'distance' in interpersonal interactions as a useful survival strategy:

> Notons qu'il y a danger, et danger sérieux à notre époque de trop se familiariser. Ce temps est si fertile en naufrages de toute sorte, que l'on s'y trouve exposé à de terribles avaries. Votre ami du jour peut être reconnu, le lendemain, pour un homme tout à fait indigne d'estime. (Rostaing [18—]: 22)

The etiquette manuals single out contexts in which the avoidance of familiarity and the cultivation of distance are even more important, and one of these is *en voyage*. As travel became an increasingly frequent activity amongst the middle classes, primarily within France but also abroad, many etiquette manuals featured guidelines for appropriate behaviour both during a journey — in diligence, train or boat — and at its destination.[6] These experiences occurred in public and could entail an alarming variety of encounters with strangers. Robbery was one obvious cause for concern, highlighted by the 1864 caricature by Daumier, 'Seul moyen de faire avec sécurité un voyage d'agrément', in which two men sitting side by side in a carriage eye each other suspiciously, pistols in hand. Yet less concrete, and thus subtly more threatening, fears were often what motivated the paranoid rhetoric of the etiquette manual. In transit or on holiday, the difficulty of deciphering an individual's background or political allegiance, already problematic in the modern city, was even further intensified. In recognition of this, the *Nouveau manuel complet de la bonne compagnie* (1839) by Elisabeth-Félicie Bayle-Mouillard is typical in including a section dedicated to travelling; here, passengers are urged to distinguish between the *connaissance intime* and the *voisin d'un moment*, and alter their behaviour accordingly: 'Un voyageur [...] mériterait le nom d'imprudent et de babillard, s'il causait avec ses voisins d'un moment comme avec des connaissances intimes' (1839: 244). Blanche Staffe, the author of the *Usages du monde* [1889], is later to repeat this advice, emphasising the need for prudence even when travelling with *intimes*:

> La prudence, toujours entièrement d'accord avec le bon goût, exige qu'on ne parle pas de ses affaires intimes aux parents, aux amis avec lesquels on voyage, en présence d'inconnus. On ne sait jamais devant qui l'on s'épanche et cet abandon peut avoir de graves conséquences. (Staffe 1897: 387)

There is some distinction between guides which admit to, and permit, a certain moral laxity while travelling and those which forbid it entirely. Raisson's *Code civil, manuel complet de la politesse*, for example, first published in 1828, approves of the sense of liberty, equality, and fraternity which public transport can inspire amongst passengers 'in the same boat' or train carriage.[7] Raisson asserts, somewhat idealistically, that:

> Sans doute, une voiture de chemin de fer est une sorte de petite république où l'étiquette sévère perd quelques-uns de ses droits, et après quelques heures de trajet faites en commun, il arrive d'ordinaire qu'une sorte de connaissance indirecte s'établit entre les voyageurs. (Raisson 1853: 104)

In 1861, Eugène Muller agrees, writing in *La Politesse française* that 'l'intimité est prompte à s'établir entre gens qui voyagent ensemble' (1861: 213). Yet even for writers who evaluate the relaxation of social hierarchy and convention in a positive light, there are limits. Raisson perceives these limits in temporal and moral terms: 'Dans ces rapports fortuits, dans cette sorte d'intimité improvisée, la bienséance doit toujours conserver ses droits' (1853: 103); moreover, 'la familiarité qui s'établit promptement entre commensaux d'une même diligence finit au terme du voyage. Quelques mots de compliment, un salut civil, voilà tout ce qu'on doit à ses compagnons de route' (1853: 106). This 'improvised' intimacy with the *compagnon de route* is one of chance and, as a consequence, has a certain charm. However, it should not trigger or eclipse the duties, loyalties, and affective investments which are both price and privilege of long-term ties, nor those owed to the 'eternal' principle of *bienséance*. It is the obsessive fear of the *faux ami* which appears to lie at the root of this rhetoric. As Rostaing anticipates, familiarity can be misinterpreted, and an offer of friendship made flippantly to social 'inferiors' could be taken seriously: 'De retour à Paris, ils ne manqueront pas de vous rendre visite' ([18—]: 188). Yet this, he continues, is not the greatest danger. While many of these individuals will be harmless, simply guilty of misreading a social situation, others may deliberately set out to manipulate and profit from their new-found friends:

> Admettons pour un instant que vous avez eu le malheur de tomber sur un ménage interlope, ou sur quelqu'un de ces aigrefins, homme ou femme, qui font métier de capter la confiance des familles pour s'en parer en public, et exploiter le reflet de leur honorabilité. Vous vous êtes laissé prendre à des dehors séduisants, vous avez été circonvenu sans aller toutefois jusqu'à l'intimité. (Rostaing [18—]: 188–89)

The alarmist advice palpable across this body of texts indicates the level of anxiety which surrounded novel forms of sociability in the nineteenth century and made intimacy and the sharing of confidences something to be resisted in these contexts, rather than privileged.[8] The once reassuring figure of the *confident* was being threatened by the spectre of the confidence man or swindler, embodied in American literature by Herman Melville's 1857 *The Confidence Man* (set, tellingly, on a Mississippi steamboat), with whom association could lead to financial or reputational ruin. According to the manuals' less-is-more logic, the increase in opportunities for forming context-specific and temporary friendships was leading to a degraded or deceptive intimacy. In addition to the 'fellow traveller', the nineteenth century also witnessed a proliferation of circumstantial, fleeting friendships in urban contexts (cafés, factories, and dormitories for migrant workers, for example) and amongst political activists or members of the military.⁹ For Corbin, increased mobility amongst these groups resulted in 'la fluidité et l'éparpillement de l'amicabilité' (1999: 474). Yet while in a twenty-first-century context the sociologist Morgan (2009) argues for the social and psychological benefits of the acquaintance, and Corbin's vocabulary might be seen to support this view, the figure was interpreted more suspiciously in nineteenth-century discourse, symptomatic of the acute levels of personal insecurity generated by post-Revolutionary political and social unrest. As Morgan writes, acquaintances often borrow 'some slight echoes or fragments of intimacy', whether these take the form of 'verbal exchanges, mutual recognition, knowledge of or by the other [...], [or] some slight physical intimacy' (2009: 4): Morgan uses the example of a doctor taking a patient's blood pressure, a professional procedure which evokes the kind of close and concentrated physical contact one might have, in a different context, with a loved one. It is the ambiguous slippage between stranger and intimate, or known and unknown stranger, this very 'fluidité [...] de l'amicabilité' (Corbin, 1999: 474) which can be seen to unsettle not only social convention, but the way in which emotional and embodied intimacy was experienced, understood, and desired in nineteenth-century society. The easy abandonment of reserve in the modern, mobile world was interpreted by some as a sort of intimacy 'à la légère' (Staffe 1897: 387), easily adopted but purely performative: a superficial mode of relation threatening to undermine the cultural privileges of intimacy even in its conventional or institutionalised forms.¹⁰ To guard against this threat, the manuals insist on a hierarchical difference between the two forms (while similar, they are of different orders) and thus seek to preserve the value of 'scripted' intimacy in the face of its 'improvised' counterpart.

The first part of this chapter has outlined anxieties surrounding the fellow traveller in nineteenth-century French culture. The second part considers how Flaubert treats the theme of 'intimité improvisée' (Raisson 1853: 103) in the context of his outbound journey to Egypt in 1849, documented both in his correspondence and his travel journal published posthumously as the *Voyage en Égypte*.¹¹ Feminist and postcolonial research into Flaubert's travels has tended to emphasise his holiday 'romances': unsurprising, given that Flaubert is, undeniably, what Naomi Schor labels a prototypical 'sex tourist' (1999: 57).¹² Yet Flaubert's writing also lends itself to an analysis of holiday friendships, revealing a marked interest in the way travelling affects non-sexual forms of intimacy. Motifs of travel and sociability recur throughout Flaubert's œuvre, and this interest is palpable both before and after his time in North Africa and the Middle East.¹³ Drawing on memories of family holidays in Trouville in his 1838 *Mémoires d'un fou*, for example, Flaubert presents familiarity as a commonplace feature of modern travel:

> Aux bains de mer, à la campagne ou en voyage, on se parle plus facilement — on désire se connaître. — Un rien suffit pour la conversation; la pluie et le beau temps bien plus qu'ailleurs y tiennent place. On se récrie sur l'incommodité des logements, sur le détestable de la cuisine d'auberge. (*OJF*: 489)

Thirty years later, the 1869 *L'Éducation sentimentale* opens with a description of the passengers on board *La Ville-de-Montereau*, for whom 'le plaisir tout nouveau d'une excursion maritime facilitait les épanchements' (*OF* II: 34); it is, moreover, Frédéric's 'chance' encounter with Jacques Arnoux on the boat that generates the narrative to follow. In this light, Flaubert's journey of 1849–51 emerges as a key instance in a thread of textual articulations which, formally but not thematically, move away from literary intimacy towards the 'exemplary impersonality' (Wall 2006: 1) of his later fiction.

II. Flaubert's *Voyage en Égypte*: 'Tout le monde est ami intime'

Analysing Intimacy

Flaubert set sail for Alexandria on 4 November 1849 on board the steam liner *Le Nil*. In place of the 'assemblage confus, hétérogène' or 'pêle-mêle inextricable' which Rostaing ([18—]: 73) sees manifest in modern society, or the 'petite république' which Raisson (1853: 102) associates with train travel, the spatial and temporal limiting factors of the crossing immediately serve to intensify social stratification for Flaubert. While Flaubert may be seeking to flee France, he has not done so yet, and rather than effect a process of gradual defamiliarisation, *Le Nil* instead produces a concentrated microcosm of familiar French hierarchies. In a letter to his mother, Anne Flaubert, of 17 November 1849, Flaubert describes life on board the liner: 'La vie y étant plus resserrée qu'à terre, y est plus dense. Le mépris des premières pour les secondes, des secondes pour les troisièmes, des troisièmes pour les quatrièmes, tout cela est fort plaisant' (*CF* I: 527–28). Consistent with his status as self-styled *bourgeoisophobus*, Flaubert's own behaviour does not seem marked by such open contempt; in direct contrast to the discretion demanded by social convention, he converses freely and openly with all those on board.[14] In an earlier letter to his mother of 7 November 1849, and somewhat contradicting his later observation, Flaubert explains:

> J'ai été un des plus gaillards, si ce n'est le plus gaillard des passagers. [...] Je ne sais pas ce que j'ai mais je suis adoré à bord. [...] Rien n'est plus drôle que notre bâtiment et la composition des passagers. Tout le monde est ami intime. On cause, on parlotte, on blague. (*CF* I: 524)

Writing to Louis Bouilhet on 1 December, he reinforces this impression in more explicit terms: 'Tout le temps de la traversée, 11 jours, j'ai mangé, fumé, blagué et été si aimable par mes histoires lubriques, bons mots, facéties, etc., que l'état-major m'adorait. Je crois que je repasserais sur le Nil gratis' (*CF* I: 539). Whether or not the letters are entirely accurate, they aim to present the impression of someone at ease with the quick establishment of intimacy, and able to form friendships effortlessly. References to 'causeries', familiar and unreserved chats, recur throughout the text of the *Voyage en Égypte* in relation to acquaintanceships struck up both on board *Le Nil* and amongst the French ex-patriot community of Cairo: 'Le lendemain autres causeries au clair de lune, sur du sable aussi' (*VE*: 325); later, 'Le soir à dîner conversation des plus libres' (*VE*: 240). These experiences occur primarily between men and thus exemplify what Vincent-Buffault has defined as a particular form of post-Romantic male sociability or 'virile friendship' in which sentimentality is replaced by a system of 'grivoiseries', obscenities, and often misogynistic jokes (1995: 236–37). Yet the unreserved nature of these interactions is nuanced by a cynical sense of detachment which pervades their description, and suggests that Flaubert is aware of them as a particular *style* of relation. Indeed, Flaubert's oxymoronic claim to his mother that 'tout le monde est ami intime' (*CF* I: 524) relies on a knowingly weakened definition of intimacy. At one point in the text of the *Voyage en Égypte*, Flaubert alludes to a 'best friend'. This assertion *could* be taken at face value: 'Mon meilleur ami était le second, Roux. Nous causions voyage par mer — récits du Cap Horn, homme jeté à la mer et enfoncé dans l'eau' (*VE*: 159). Yet another reference to Roux in the letter of 17 November suggests we are to read it ironically: 'Il y a le second du bord, une espèce de capitaine Barbey supérieur qui s'est pris de passion pour moi, et qui a été attendri hier en me quittant. C'est drôle comme je plais aux natures brutales' (*CF* I: 527).[15] Here, friendship takes on a knowingly modified meaning: what was in one location presented as a reciprocal intimacy (a 'best friendship') emerges elsewhere as one-sided; an affection and even *amitié-passion* which has been inspired in an object (Roux) without being felt or described in the same terms by the subject (Flaubert). In this passage, it is only Roux who seems to suffer the bitterness of the 'sympathies interrompues' that Flaubert will later appropriate for Frédéric in *L'Éducation sentimentale* (*OF* II: 448). What is an affective relationship for Roux is an instrumental one for Flaubert. The language of intimacy and friendship is used to disguise, yet simultaneously highlight, a power relation.

This analytic approach to intimacy recurs throughout the *Voyage en Égypte*, notably in Flaubert's evocations of the crossing to Alexandria, described as 'quelque chose de très fertile comme observations, quand on sait en faire' (*CF* I: 527). Intensified social stratification creates the effect of a laboratory in which Flaubert can observe and engage in the art of intimacy across social groups: far from being the dupe of a confidence-man or 'aigrefin' (Rostaing [18—]: 189), it is Flaubert who appears to be the trickster. A further example concerns Flaubert's interactions on board the boat with Codricka, the French consulate at Manilla. The *Voyage en Égypte* records the following interaction: 'Le mercredi soir, longue et intime causerie avec Codricka' (*VE*: 166). Flaubert observes:

> Elle commença comme toutes les causeries par le bordel, puis elle devint sentimentale — il me raconta de sa vie trois histoires d'amour — 1. à Paris, une maîtresse, dans le faubourg Saint Honoré [...]. – 2. en Grèce [...] — 3. adieux à Genève avec une femme qu'il aimait depuis longtemps. (*VE*: 166)

This staged dynamic from sex to sentiment nuances Vincent-Buffault's thesis regarding male sociability. While women still clearly function to facilitate bonds between men, Flaubert's reference to male sentiment questions her statement that, in the post-Romantic period, 'tout ce qui ressemble à de la sentimentalité [...] est banni des relations entre mâles' (1995: 236). Rather, the sentimental 'causerie intime' with Codricka is normalised by Flaubert to such an extent that it is imbued with a sense of routine inevitability. Given the scenario that Flaubert is faced with on board — passengers isolated for a defined period of time with little to do — intimate exchanges are bound, it seems, to occur. However, the relationship between Flaubert and Codricka has none of the uniqueness which Simmel sees as the property of intimate relationships, no 'inner or exclusive necessity' (1950: 407). Codricka is not a stranger to Flaubert, but no more significant a friend than Roux. Their acquaintanceship borrows 'echoes and fragments of intimacy' (Morgan 2009: 4) from more established or specific relationships but there is no mention of reciprocal confidences on Flaubert's part, or of a continued friendship once the boat docks in Alexandria.

Aping Intimacy

In the context of travel, therefore, Flaubert denies intimacy a privileged status. This absence of privilege also results from the relentlessly public nature of travelling. In the *Voyage en Égypte*, Flaubert records an incident which occurs during the first stage of his journey, in a diligence from Paris to Chalon-sur-Saône; an unknown, unnamed woman in the same carriage starts to cry, and shivers with cold: 'Je lui ai couvert les genoux avec ma pelisse de fourrure' (*VE*: 140), writes Flaubert. Next, 'elle s'est mise à vomir par [...] la portière' (*VE*: 140) and later, he notes, 'ma voisine endormie la bouche ouverte ronflait sur mon épaule — nous ne disions rien — on roulait' (*VE*: 142). In certain contexts, the action of resting one's head on another's shoulder could be interpreted as a sign of emotional closeness, but here this is not the case. While travelling, moments which might be the product of, or result in, enhanced intimacy — the witnessing and assuaging of another's vulnerability — occur in public and, via such exposure, become a source of humour. Flaubert's apparent delight at such debasement is demonstrated by his observations on board *Le Nil*: in a letter to his mother he describes how, in bad weather, 'on dégobille l'un devant l'autre, et le matin on se revoit avec des figures de déterrés qui rient les unes des autres' (*CF* I: 524). During a storm:

> J'essaie de me coucher à diverses places. [...] De temps à autre je ris malgré moi du grotesque qui se passe — gens qui gueulent et déguelent — craquements du navire — toutous errants — M. et Mme Codricka qui se disputent. (*VE*: 165)

The Codrickas' argument, raging against a backdrop of shouting and vomiting passengers, presents an incongruous image of domestic intimacy, on view for all to see. Here, Flaubert evokes, more literally, the social 'shipwreck' threatened by Rostaing in the *Manuel de la politesse*, and exploits it for dramatic, and comic, effect.[16]

Yet all this is not to say that Flaubert abandons a desire for more 'anchored' intimacy during his journey.[17] His allusions to fleeting familiarity implicitly posit another mode of intimacy and thus function in a similar way as do the references to 'improvised intimacy' in the etiquette manuals. Flaubert's new acquaintanceships with Codricka or Roux are represented within, and communicated via, private forms of writing constitutive of established, long-term ties: in letters sent home to family members and friends, for example, or travel notes written for private use. An attachment to long-term intimacy thus persists and is, moreover, thrown into relief by Flaubert's references to the formulaic, functional, and frequently curtailed experiences of familiarity which occur while travelling. Flaubert seemed untouched by his separation from Roux yet, in a letter of 15 January 1850, appears deeply moved by a letter from Bouilhet:

> Ce matin à midi, cher et pauvre vieux, j'ai reçu ta bonne et longue lettre tant désirée. — Elle m'a remué jusqu'aux entrailles. [...] Comme je pense à toi, va! inestimable bougre! combien de fois par jour je t'évoque, et que je te regrette! (*CF* 1: 567)

While interspersed with the obligatory obscenities, Flaubert's letters to Bouilhet imagine scenes of reciprocal and 'eternal' intimacy independent of the temporal and spatial constraints placed on friendships formed abroad. In the letter of 1 December 1849, Flaubert asks Bouilhet: 'Quand reprendrons-nous nos interminables causeries au coin du feu, plongés dans mes fauteuils verts?' (*CF* 1: 537). The same *effet d'intime* is employed in the letter of 15 January:

> Si tu trouves que je te manque, tu me manques aussi. Et marchant le nez en l'air dans les rues, en regardant le ciel bleu, les moucharabis des maisons et les minarets couverts d'oiseaux, je rêve à ta personne, comme toi dans ta petite chambre de la rue Beauvoisine, au coin de ton feu, pendant que la pluie coule sur tes vitres. (*CF* 1: 567)

Moreover, Flaubert is travelling with his friend Maxime du Camp, and, as he reassures his mother in a letter of 23 November 1849, 'Maxime me surveille et me soigne comme un enfant. Je crois qu'il me mettrait sous verre, s'il le pouvait, de peur qu'il m'arrive quelque chose' (*CF* 1: 536).[18] Yet, despite alluding to qualitative differences, his response to the new opportunities for intimacy produced by travel is not articulated in terms of disapproval. In his analysis of Flaubert as humourist, Terdiman has noted the 'constant presence within Flaubert's writing (but [...] largely confined within the "private sphere" of his correspondence) of an alternative discourse of *indecency*, of Bakhtin's "carnivalesque", which represents a simplified but gratifying return of the repressed' (1985: 223–24). Indeed, the 'grotesque' intimacies and fluid friendships of the *traversée*, unrestrained by social convention, emerge as a source of humour for Flaubert, which, by mediating his ambivalent response, allows him to withhold judgement: 'Rien n'est plus drôle que notre bâtiment' (*CF* 1: 524); 'Tout cela est fort plaisant' (*CF* 1: 528); 'C'est drôle comme je plais aux natures brutales' (*CF* 1: 527); 'Je ris malgré moi' (*VE*: 165).

Flaubert's travels in the Middle East took place in the mid-century, contemporaneous to the sudden rise and fall of the French Second Republic. Yet, at the level of personal chronology, the journey constituted a period of gradual development for the young writer in which he negotiated between the culturally motivated, but conflicting, ideals of intimacy and impersonality, and the implications of this conflict for his literary craft. Friendship was to remain a thematic preoccupation in Flaubert's fiction, but the writer-reader intimacy we see tested in the *Voyage en Égypte* was not to persist as a formal aspiration.[19] On his return to France, Flaubert largely abandoned the first-person form of his earlier fiction (*Mémoires d'un fou* and *Novembre*),[20] decided against publishing his travel diary, and began *Madame Bovary*.[21]

If travel writing can be considered part of Flaubert's 'apprenticeship', in the words of Adrianne Tooke (2004a: 64), it is typically seen to epitomise a sorrier period of decline for Baudelaire, who began drafting *La Belgique déshabillée* some three years before his death.[22] The two travel texts thus occupy different, even opposing, positions in relation to their writers' œuvres. Moreover, the plurality of places visited by Flaubert during his travels contrasts with Baudelaire's two-year stay, or stasis, in Belgium. And while Flaubert's journey appears motivated by the pursuit of pleasure, Baudelaire's visit to Belgium was undertaken for professional reasons: to present a series of lectures on Delacroix, and to make contact with Belgian publishers.[23] Despite these differences, however, both bodies of writing share a marked concern with the modes and meanings of familiarity in unfamiliar locations and both, I argue, articulate their observations in terms of humour. Yet this humour functions differently. For Flaubert, it emerges as a mediating force: a keen awareness of the limits of this commonplace intimacy does not necessarily render it unrewarding, or undesirable. Baudelaire states his intention to 'faire un travail amusant sur un sujet ingrat' (*BD*: 140); for him, then, Belgian forms of 'familiarity' are representative of the deeply negative and offensive qualities he associates with the nation. His use of parody, hyperbole, and the grotesque indicates a disgust with over-familiarity and a concomitant commitment to alternative modes of intimacy: restrained, discreet, and in large part the product of the imagination.

III. Baudelaire *belgophobe*

La Belgique déshabillée occupies a problematic position in Baudelaire's œuvre. Like much of Baudelaire's later work, including the *Journaux intimes*, the book on Belgium exists only in a fragmentary, unfinished state: a mixture of handwritten notes and annotated press cuttings from Belgian newspapers. Begun in 1864 on the writer's arrival in Brussels, *La Belgique déshabillée* had, in Guyaux's mind, 'réduit et englouti le vieux fantasme de faire pâlir *Les Confessions* de Rousseau, en tirant le projet vers d'autres formes littéraires, le récit de voyage, la satire' (1986a: 23). Unlike Baudelaire's previous projects, *Fusées*, *Hygiène,* and *Mon cœur mis à nu*, which attempt an exploration of the individual self, *La Belgique déshabillée* targets a country and viciously attacks its inhabitants as an emblem of human nature as a whole. Nudity has been transferred from Baudelaire's *cœur* to a country; as Guyaux writes, 'au lieu de retourner vers lui-même, Baudelaire s'est retourné contre le monde pour mieux se détourner de lui' (1986a: 17). The text was envisaged as something of a hybrid: part-satirical ethnography, part-mock tour guide, with occasional reference to first-hand experience, suggesting that the autobiographical impulse palpable in the earlier projects had not been entirely obscured. Popular cultural forms like the *journal de voyage, physiologie,* and even the etiquette manual were to be imitated: chapters on Brussels, the 'physionomie de la Rue' and its 'mœurs', interspersed with satirical sonnets (now collected as the *Amœnitates Belgicæ*), would be followed by discussions of politics, Belgian annexation and religion, finishing with chapters on the 'beaux-arts' and suggested walks in Anvers, Namur, and Bruges.[24] The text was to culminate with a section offering 'petits conseils aux Français condamnés à vivre en Belgique, pour n'être ni trop volés, ni trop insultés, ni trop empoisonnés' (*BD*: 277). However, it is less the hybrid form of the book and more its unrelenting tone of aggression which has caused so much anxiety amongst critics. The anger and hatred articulated in *Les Fleurs du Mal* and *Le Spleen de Paris* is, for many present-day readers, redeemed by the value of the poetry, and has become part of an acceptable Baudelairean aesthetic of disgust. Yet the bitterness and rage of *La Belgique déshabillée* is less easily understood by those uncomfortable with the anti-democratic and elitist strain of Baudelaire's thought, particularly prominent in his later years. Guyaux cites the critic Samuel de Sacy for whom the book is 'l'échec d'un échec' (1986a: 45). More recently, Rosemary Lloyd has described Baudelaire in Belgium, 'gathering a series of biting epigrams attacking what he presented as the materialism, stupidity, and gluttony of the entire nation' (2008: 170–71). These epigrams, however, lack the 'brilliance of language' which marks his prose poetry and other satires such as those by Juvenal (Lloyd 2008: 171). The biography of Baudelaire by Claude Pichois and Jean Ziegler attempts an excuse of *La Belgique déshabillée* by claiming that the text is the result of Baudelaire's physical and mental decline:

> La haine qu'il commence à exprimer contre la Belgique n'est qu'une forme de manie elle-même causé par les progrès de la syphilis [...]. Haïr quelques individus est une preuve de santé. Haïr un pays entier est un signe de maladie grave. (Pichois and Ziegler 1987: 511)

Many choose to ignore the book: Howells (1996) engages in a study of *Fusées*, *Hygiène*, and *Mon cœur mis à nu* but avoids *La Belgique déshabillée*, although it is part of the same network of texts. Guyaux, meanwhile, goes to the opposite extreme, positioning the book on Belgium as the founder of two literary lineages: the modern burlesque or *bouffonnerie* of Alfred Jarry, and the pamphlet of Paul Claudel, Léon Bloy, and Louis-Ferdinand Céline.

Despite the difficulties inherent in a study of *La Belgique déshabillée*, it is productive when considered in the light of Baudelaire's ambivalent approach to intimacy. The question of *pudeur* evident in his poetry, correspondence, and criticism, and the limits of decency at the moral and aesthetic level, retain their formal and thematic force in this hybrid travel text which, moreover, provides a complex catalogue of metaphors for these concepts. The text tells us very little, if anything at all, about Belgium, but a great deal about the Belgium which Baudelaire imagined, and its textual representation in terms of a culturally and personally constituted figurative framework. By highlighting a number of its obsessively repeated motifs, the following section seeks to elaborate on the paradoxes surrounding intimacy and familiarity as social and also literary modes. I suggest that Baudelaire identifies a culture of intimacy at work in Belgium which offends his personal vision of modesty and pudor. But while the practices described are grounded in Belgian culture, they also function, Baudelaire notes, as a comment on French society: 'À faire un croquis de la Belgique, il y a, par surcroît, cet avantage, qu'on fait une caricature des sottises de la France' (*BD*: 137). In reality then, the text is more, or less, than an investigation into intercultural relations. Rather than being disappointed by

Western cultural hegemony (the fate of Flaubert in Egypt), Baudelaire exploits the parallels he sees between Belgium and France to make a broader comment on an endemic degradation of an ideal of intimacy.[25]

Nudity and *pudeur*

The premise of *La Belgique déshabillée* is an undressing; the rendering naked of the other in an act of enforced exposure akin to violation: 'La vraie Belgique. La Belgique toute nue. La Belgique déshabillée' (*BD*: 138). For the purposes of his revelatory critique, Baudelaire needs to establish a level of proximity with the bodies and minds of the Belgian people, but a fundamental paradox underscores the text: his writing reveals a deep unwillingness and, at other times, a fundamental inability to do so. Both parties, Baudelaire and the Belgian people, are shown to share in a resolutely one-way curiosity which does not allow for a reciprocal return of interest, and thus makes communication between the two problematic. For Guyaux (1986a), Baudelaire embodies the figure of the *voyeur* or *espion*, stimulated and satisfied by covert and non-reciprocal observation. Yet, for Baudelaire, so do the Belgian people: Baudelaire's voyeurism is mirrored in what he identifies as a characteristically Belgian curiosity, a 'curiosité bestiale' (*BD*: 193), a 'curiosité de petite ville' (*BD*: 177), or 'une curiosité de village [qui] les pousse aux embarcadères pour voir qui arrive' (*BD*: 179). In a move typical of the writer, Baudelaire differentiates his own analytic inquisitiveness, purposely intended to contribute to a process of demystification or truth-telling, from the base and bestial nosiness of the Belgians; as with the question of *pudeur*, what is perceived as a trivial and vulgar trait in others is elevated, idealised, and exalted by Baudelaire in relation to his own conduct. Nevertheless the parallel between the two orders is clear, as is the aversion to being the object of another's curiosity. Baudelaire criticises the Belgians' hypocritical reticence and fear of inspection: while keen to study others, 'il [le Belge] craint d'être étudié. Il veut cacher ses plaies' (*BD*: 181); consequently, he demonstrates a 'haine de l'étranger', 'Atmosphère hostile. Le regard et le visage de l'ennemi, partout, partout. La calomnie, le vol, etc... Cependant, dans les premiers jours, curiosité bestiale, avec protestations d'amitié' (*BD*: 193).[26] In a passage which demonstrates the frequent slippage throughout the text between the generalising maxim and the personal anecdote, the apparent hostility of the Belgian people to the truth-seeking *étranger* is reflected in the hostility of Baudelaire towards the Belgian people. Baudelaire's fear of the gaze of the other is articulated, in paranoid terms, via the language of friendship. For Baudelaire, the friendship voiced and offered by the Belgian people is fundamentally false, obscuring the treacherous intentions of those who are, in reality, mere acquaintances or even enemies: mutual secrecy breeds mutual suspicion.

One cause of Baudelaire's hostility towards Belgium can be found in what the writer perceives there as an offensive, essentially unacceptable mode of corporeal and sentimental comportment. Paradoxically, the Belgian's desire to 'cacher ses plaies' from the critical foreign eye (which could, in one reading, be evidence of praise-worthy *pudeur*) co-exists, in Baudelaire's hyperbolic depiction, with a grotesque tendency towards exhibitionism. Baudelaire makes frequent allusions to Belgian 'barbarie et grossièreté *universelles*, sans exception, avec vive affectation [...] de manières civilisés. *Manières*!!!' (*BD*: 193). The attempt to *appear* modest, like the attempt to appear amicable, hides what is in fact a deep-rooted indecency. Here, the gendered nature of many of the criticisms levelled against Belgian behaviour emerges in full force, as Baudelaire aligns his disgust at so-called Belgian indiscretion with the negative cultural coding of 'femininity' in terms of bodily matter and fluids.[27] In Belgium, even women lack the *pudeur* which is labelled elsewhere as a quality, in its vulgar form, native to the female sex. A series of notes concentrates, with repetitive, obsessive force, on what he calls the 'histoire de Latrines, portes ouvertes' (*BD*: 194): '[L'] obscénité des Dames belges' (*BD*: 161), 'Des dames qui laissent, pendant qu'elles y *officient*, la porte des latrines ouverte' (*BD*: 172). This phenomenon is seen as symbolic of a national lack of *pudeur*: 'Pas de galanterie chez l'homme, pas de pudeur chez la femme. — La pudeur, objet prohibé, ou dont on ne sent pas le besoin' (*BD*: 161).[28] This vulgarity is rendered concrete in the figures of the *Cracheur* and *Manneken Pis*, two famous statues which adorn fountains near the Grand Place in Brussels: '*L'homme qui pisse. Le vomisseur*' (*BD*: 188), 'Pisseur et vomisseur. Statues nationales que je trouve symboliques' (*BD*: 186).[29] Baudelaire's desire to undress Belgium figuratively appears stumped by the 'obscenity' of the Belgian people who, by literalising his project before he does, render it futile.

The Baudelairean aversion to the display of bodily fluids in public recalls something of the etiquette manual's anxiety about the fluidity of modern-day relationships. While Baudelaire's projected *exposé* of Belgium demands first-hand knowledge of the country, it is fear of contagion or contamination by the liquids, and dilute insipidity, of the Belgians which prevents him from engaging with them. Liquidity is evaluated highly negatively in *La Belgique déshabillée*: the river Senne, which 'sert de vidange aux Latrines', is dirty and disgusting, and could not 'tant ses eaux sont opaques, réfléchir un seul rayon du soleil le plus ardent' (*BD*: 195). For Baudelaire, the inhabitants of Brussels, and Belgium more widely, share in this revolting liquid quality. The Belgian is a 'mollusque' (*BD*: 170), a spineless, slimy organism which is without intelligence but which can, through its very lack of form, appropriate that of others. Like the mollusc, the Belgian is inherently undefined, and thus relies, via a modification of the animal metaphor, on a process of aping or 'singerie' through which he or she copies and conforms to ideologies and behaviours without thinking: 'Il est singe *mais* il est mollusque' (*BD*: 170). As will be discussed in the following chapter, Baudelaire's art criticism expresses pleasure in figurative penetration by the particular foreign atmospheres which are able to produce a revitalising effect on the subject. However, penetration by the dull Belgian atmosphere, and the adoption of the unoriginality and conformism characteristic of it, is dreaded. Evoking in counterpoint 'des îles tropicales qui sentent la rose, le musc ou l'huile de coco' (*BD*: 294), Baudelaire proceeds to describe Brussels: '*Fadeur* générale de la vie. Cigares, légumes, fleurs, fruits, cuisine, yeux, cheveux, tout est *fade,* tout est triste, insipide, endormi. La physionomie humaine, vague, sombre, endormie. Horrible peur, de la part du Français, de cette *Contagion Soporeuse*' (*BD*: 294).³⁰ Fear of emotional and intellectual contagion and the loss of vitality is also articulated as a 'horrible peur de devenir bête' (*BD*: 146); 'On craint ici de devenir bête. [...] Atmosphère de sommeil. Lenteur universelle' (*BD*: 139).

Over-Familiarity and the *flâneur*

In *La Belgique déshabillée*, the conflict between impulses towards both intimacy and distance, palpable in Baudelaire's *œuvre* and nineteenth-century French culture more broadly, finds a locus in Baudelaire's response to the Belgian combination of over-familiarity and impenetrability. Baudelaire repeatedly criticises the 'présomption' (*BD*: 172, 297) and 'familiarité' (*BD*: 170, 297) of the Belgian people, a tendency noted in particular in relation to their behaviour towards social 'superiors'. For Baudelaire, the Belgian public's response to 'l'homme célèbre' is exemplary of this sort of comportment: he notes 'leur familiarité avec l'homme célèbre. Ils lui tapent tout de suite le ventre et le tutoient comme si, enfants, ils avaient roulé ensemble dans la poussière' (*BD*: 173). Here, the anti-egalitarian strain in Baudelaire's thought emerges defiantly:³¹ the over-familiarity singled out here as a sign of Belgian indecency chimes with the advice offered by the often socially reactionary etiquette manuals. The 'homme célèbre' in this passage is widely considered to refer to Félix Nadar, who visited Brussels in 1864 to display his new hot air balloon. In a letter to Nadar of 30 August 1864, Baudelaire warns him: 'Chacun dit ici: "Je monterai avec Nadar" (ces gens-là suppriment le "Monsieur", la familiarité étant le fait des brutes et des provinciaux)' (*BC* II: 401). These references reflect the immaturity, unsophistication, and idiocy associated in Baudelaire's mind with those who indulge in familiar behavioural practices in adulthood: we can see a connection here with the infantalisation of intimate writing practices in literary and cultural discourses of the time. Indeed, it is not only in Belgium that Baudelaire notes a worrying cultural shift towards the familiar or over-familiar. His 1861 critical essay on Léon Cladel's *Les Martyrs ridicules* establishes an analogy between literary and social immaturity, alluding to the same gestures of greeting noted in Belgium:

> On m'avait dit que l'auteur était un jeune homme, [...]. J'éprouve, au contact de la Jeunesse, la même sensation de malaise qu'à la rencontre d'un camarade de collège oublié, devenu boursier, et que les vingt ou trente années n'empêchent pas de me tutoyer ou de me frapper sur le ventre. Bref, je me sens en mauvaise compagnie. (*OC* II: 182)

For Baudelaire, therefore, the Belgian people as embodiments of over-familiarity are bad company. Moreover, their apparent excess of sociability masks what Baudelaire identifies as an utter incapacity for profound communion at the intellectual or emotional level. Belgium offers merely a simulacrum of intimacy: an aping or feigning which bespeaks its people's status as *singes*. Practically, this is the result of the perceived insularity and inhospitality of the Belgian people, and the lack of street-life in Brussels: 'Pas de vie dans la Rue. Beaucoup de balcons. Personne au balcon. [...] Chacun chez soi. Portes fermées' (*BD*: 150); '*Chacun chez soi!*' (*BD*:

151). While crude bodily acts may be performed in public, emotional life is lived firmly behind closed doors and windows, making 'flânerie, si chère aux peuples imaginatifs, impossible' (*BD*: 146). *Flânerie*, as the mode of imaginary intimacy evoked in Baudelaire's 1861 prose poem 'Les Foules', involves the act of figurative penetration into the minds of others (an act which, as the 1863 prose poem 'Les Fenêtres' also suggests, involves as much self-projection and self-gratification as it does empathy or identification with the other).[32] This penetration is, in the terms of 'Les Foules', the 'incomparable privilège' of the poet, imbued with the 'haine du domicile et la passion du voyage' (*OC* I: 291). Yet Baudelaire's literal journey to Brussels curtails the figurative voyage of *flânerie*, confronting the traveller with a culture which values the *chez soi* at the expense of the crowd. It is not only the lack of street life but Belgian 'emptiness' which, in Baudelaire's words, precludes penetration. Extending the misogynistic yoking of Belgium with the female, Baudelaire writes: 'Le Belge vous est incommunicable, comme la femme, parce qu'il n'a rien à vous communiquer, et vous lui êtes incommunicable, à cause de son impénétrabilité. — Rien de mystérieux, de profond et de bref comme le Néant' (*BD*: 193). Misunderstanding breeds misunderstanding, and Belgian forms of sociability remain fundamentally unproductive, and offensive, for the *flâneur*. The Baudelairean fusion with passers-by relies on the passivity, but also *profundity*, of the other: the perceived Belgian combination of over-familiarity and empty-headedness prevents this imagined intimacy.[33]

Indeed, the only *confidence* which appears possible in Belgium is one which occurs in an infectious, potentially fatal, form. In his section on 'Locutions Belges', Baudelaire discusses the Belgian deployment of the phrase 'maladies *confidentielles*' (*BD*: 207) to refer, euphemistically, to venereal disease. For Baudelaire, this euphemism is indicative of the absurd contradictions and hypocrisies of the Belgian character: simultaneously vulgar and prudish, receptive and reticent to the point of lexical and semantic inaccuracy. Baudelaire pursues the implications of this linguistic phenomenon, exploiting its comic potential:

> Ainsi je suppose que dans le grand monde de Bruxelles, une jeune fille ne dit pas:
> — *Ce jeune homme m'a foutu la vérole.*
> — Et qu'un jeune homme ne dit pas, en parlant d'une fille bien élevée: *Elle m'a poivré!*
> Ils préfèrent dire, l'une: [...] — *Ce jeune homme m'a fait une confidence si horrible que les cheveux m'en sont tombés!* et l'autre: *Elle m'a fait une confidence dont je me souviendrai longtemps!* ou bien: *Je lui ai fait ma confidence! Sa postérité s'en souviendra jusqu'à la troisième génération!*
> O Bons pharmaciens Belges! J'aime passionnément votre dictionnaire. (*BD*: 207–08)

The humour of this passage is triggered by the ambiguity of the *double entendre* which veils a pathological exchange of bodies behind a more edifying exchange of sentiments, or *confidences*. As we saw in relation to 'Confession', the verbal *confidence* may be 'étrange' or even 'horrible', but it can still fulfil a therapeutic function for those involved in the literary encounter. In Belgium, however, confiding is represented as a crudely corporeal process which leads to contamination, not cure; the medicalisation and sexualisation of the *confidence* undermines its connotations as a privileged mode of communion and a literary trope.

Baudelaire's experiences in Belgium exacerbated an acute sense of isolation already expressed by the writer in France: in a highly emotive letter to his mother of 6 May 1861, for example, he discusses suicide, claiming to be 'seul, sans amis, sans maîtresse, sans chien et sans chat' (*BC* II: 152). From a biographical perspective, Baudelaire's rejection of Belgian sociability can indeed be read as symptomatic of this heightened emotional state. Yet Baudelaire's marked disgust at, and fear of, the familiarity experienced abroad simultaneously exemplifies broader cultural anxieties expressed in the normative literature of the period. As with Flaubert, Baudelaire's ideal of intimacy differs from that posited in the etiquette manual, but it operates alongside over-familiarity in the same way: it functions as the original or authentic state for which the over-familiarity experienced while travelling is the foil. Like Flaubert's travel text, moreover, Baudelaire's *La Belgique déshabillée* exists only in manuscript form, and was not published during the writer's lifetime. While Baudelaire's illness may be the over-riding reason for this, it could be argued that the awareness palpable in both writers' work that over-familiarity is the debased, albeit at times entertaining, poor relation of intimacy curtails their engagement with what would effectively be the 'para-social' bond created between the writer and reader of these semi-autobiographical texts. It is in part the increasing antipathy felt by Flaubert and Baudelaire towards their reading public which prevents these first-person travel texts taking definitive and publishable shape. Writing to Bouilhet from Egypt, Flaubert explains: 'Autant travailler pour soi seul. On fait comme on veut et d'après ses propres idées, on s'admire, on se fait plaisir à soi-même, n'est-ce pas le principal? Et puis le public est si bête!' (*CF* I: 627). The final part of this chapter, however, proceeds to consider *Un été dans le Sahara*, the first literary work published by Fromentin, a writer who conceptualises his relationship with his readers in terms of affection rather than antagonism. It argues that familiarity fulfils a markedly different function in this semi-autobiographical work, deriving from Fromentin's commitment to the commercial publication of the narrative. Fromentin's decision to render 'false friendship' a theme of the travel account testifies to its topicality and anticipated interest for his envisaged readership. Familiarity abroad may be represented as dangerous at the level of plot, but Fromentin recuperates it formally through the employment of the epistolary mode, adopting a narrative device from the *roman intime*. The 'sens familier' (*OCF*: 13) which this technique results in, and which Fromentin acknowledges in the dedication to his friend, Armand du Mesnil, can be seen to compensate for the thwarted and frustrated attachments to people and place experienced in Algeria.

IV. Friendship in Fromentin's Travel Writing

Colonial Intimacies

Flaubert perceives existence on board *Le Nil,* en route for Egypt, in terms of French societal structures, while Baudelaire imagines Belgium as a caricature of France. By doing so, both writers subsume their host cultures under the auspices of France and deny them a unique or independent status. However, while Egypt and Belgium had previously been occupied by France, neither country was a French colony at the time of the writers' visits; Tooke claims that, in the mid-century, France was a 'relatively inoffensive' (2004b: 167, n. 2) presence in Egypt. The colonial context for Fromentin's travel writing is much more explicit. Following his visits of 1846 and 1847, Fromentin returned to Algeria for a third time in 1852 with his wife and stayed until the following year, seeking inspiration for the Orientalist paintings for which he was gaining an increasing reputation in France. *Un été dans le Sahara* — the narrative which this chapter will primarily focus on — is a semi-fictionalised, first-person account of this third visit to Algeria and, in particular, Fromentin's stay in the city of Laghouat in the summer of 1853. His second account, *Une année dans le Sahel,* published in serial form in 1858 and as a volume in 1859, focuses on the periods framing this summer.[34] Albeit in a markedly different context, the privileges and pains of friendship which later come to structure *Dominique* are, in these two texts, pre-empted by the terms in which Fromentin evokes North Africa: in terms, essentially, of intimacy.[35] *Une année dans le Sahel* highlights the narrator's desire to 'm'attacher à l'intimité des lieux' (*OCF:* 190), a statement which, via a shift in object, nuances Fromentin's intention in a letter of 4 October 1847 to his friend Paul Bataillard to 'pénétrer profondément dans l'intimité de ce peuple' (*CEF* I: 595). The narrator of *Une année dans le Sahel* desires to lead a static rather than peripatetic life in Algeria: 'Je veux essayer du *chez moi* sur cette terre étrangère, où jusqu'à présent je n'ai fait que passer' (*OCF:* 190). This desire is fundamentally ambiguous. On the one hand, as John Zarobell suggests, it produces a 'form of intimacy with Algeria and its inhabitants which was unprecedented' (2010: 77) at the time, offering a more nuanced model of colonial interaction than that of enforced domination and subordination. Yet, on the other hand, the lexicon of intimacy can be seen simply to veil what, in the colonial context, inevitably equates with an act of invasion and occupation and, as suggested by the metaphor of penetration, the violation of an objectifiable and generalisable other ('ce peuple'); we are reminded of Stoler's definition of 'colonial intimacies': 'first and foremost sites of intrusive interventions' (2006: 4). French control of Algeria had begun in 1830, and ongoing tensions between the French military and Algerian tribes had led to a siege of Laghouat and the violent repression of the city only six months before Fromentin's visit. In his memoirs, the French general François-Charles du Barail describes Laghouat after the siege, and his role in the ensuing French occupation:

> La ville que j'occupais était démantelée, éventrée par la brèche que nous lui avions faite pour la prendre [...]. Je n'avais rien à craindre matériellement de sa

population, réduite à l'état de troupeau tremblant [...]. Quant aux populations environnantes, elles étaient trop terrifiées par cette répression sanglante pour rien entreprendre d'immédiat, mais, dix fois domptées et dix fois insurgées, elles restaient profondément hostiles et prêtes à écouter le premier aventurier dont le souffle rallumerait en elle la haine du chrétien. (Du Barail 1897: 58)

Fromentin's language of intimacy must, therefore, be understood and interpreted within the context of the larger colonial power struggle, emerging as it does against a backdrop of French military dominance and brutality, and widespread hostility in the region.

Fromentin's *faux amis*

Un été dans le Sahara and *Une année dans le Sahel* both feature narratives of attempted integration which ultimately, and seemingly inevitably, end in failure. In the case of *Une année dans le Sahel*, the narrator admits that the majority of his friends in Mustapha d'Alger are, more precisely, acquaintances: 'Quant aux amis algériens dont j'ai parlé, [...] la plupart sont des connaissances du carrefour' (OCF: 215). It is the female figure of Haoûa who gradually becomes the locus for the narrator's hopes of intimacy, along with, to a lesser extent, the French ex-patriot Vandell who facilitates this relationship by acting as interpreter.[36] The narrator's bond with Haoûa is presented as one of egalitarian friendship ('J'ai revu Haoûa souvent depuis trois semaines, et décidément nous voilà bons amis' (OCF: 287)), although there are indications of the sexually charged and instrumental nature of this attachment which implicates it in the eroticised Orientalist visual repository linking Fromentin to Delacroix: 'Nous passons ainsi des après-midi chaudes ou des soirées, indolemment couchés sur des coussins. J'ai toute liberté de fouiller dans les meubles d'Haoûa, et j'en profite' (OCF: 288).[37] This friendship is curtailed by the tragic death of Haoûa at the hands of her violent husband, a loss for the narrator which is frequently foreshadowed in the text, and subsequently reinforced by the sudden departure of Vandell: 'Me voilà seul. Vandell m'a quitté' (OCF: 361). This double narrative of interrupted intimacy is, however, also foreshadowed extra-textually by the earlier publication of *Un été dans le Sahara*. Fromentin's first piece of published writing establishes the frustrated friendship as a prominent motif and structuring principle of the travel narrative, and thus confirms its place as a topical but anxiety-inducing feature of modern, colonial-era travel.

Un été dans le Sahara is constructed as a series of letters sent from a French traveller in Algeria to a male friend in France. While the letters are partly fictionalised, in the paratext to the work Fromentin explicitly equates the letter-writer, or narrator, with himself and the recipient with his friend Du Mesnil (OCF: 13); these are Fromentin's 'souvenirs de voyage' (OCF: 13), then, but altered to achieve particular narrative effects. Indeed, for the critic Anne-Marie Christin, the process of writing *Un été dans le Sahara* equates with 'une véritable prise de conscience littéraire pour Fromentin' (2009: 28). Comparisons between the draft manuscript and final published edition of the epistolary account reveal the progressive introduction of a number of narrative elements designed to give greater focus to the sequence of densely descriptive letters, and to create suspense.³⁸ The plotline surrounding the unnamed French Lieutenant N..., for example, beginning in Part Two as the narrator arrives in Laghouat, foregrounds both the latter's desire for intimacy with a construed social and implicitly racial 'equal' and his ambivalence concerning friendship with the Algerian people.³⁹ Unlike the comic degradation of friendship experienced by Flaubert on board *Le Nil*, intimacy retains its privileged position in Fromentin's work even as an unrealised aspiration. Friendship with Lieutenant N... is first described to the reader in hesitant and reverential terms: 'Grâce au lieutenant N..., devenu désormais mon compagnon de promenade, et, je crois pouvoir le dire, mon ami, je commence à me faire des connaissances' (*OCF*: 111). Friendship, positioned above companionship (*compagnon de promenade*) and acquaintanceship (*connaissance*), is conceptualised as a privilege which it would be immodest to assume, and which should not be rushed. As such, its slow realisation, delayed by multiple interruptions, provides a way for Fromentin to structure his narrative: the *confidence* which is figured as both proof and prize of intimacy becomes, through repeated deferrals, desired both diegetically by the narrator and extradiegetically by the reader: 'Ce soir-là, il [Lieutenant N...] avait repris une longue histoire interrompue dix fois, dix fois recommencée depuis un mois, et qui tôt ou tard finira, je l'espère, par une confidence' (*OCF*: 137). As with Haoûa, the friendship with the lieutenant appears to be valued as an end in itself. Yet it is also profitable, providing a means of establishing the friendships with the people of Laghouat which will be crucial if the narrator is to realise his ambition of accessing the Algerian *intime*.⁴⁰ He writes:

> Le lieutenant N... a beaucoup d'amis dans la ville; il connait ces gens-là par cœur; il sait leur histoire, leurs antécédents, leurs affaires de ménage, leur parenté; [...] il a ses entrées dans un grand nombre de maisons qui seraient fermées pour tout autre; privilège précieux pour moi, car il m'en fait obligeamment profiter.
> (*OCF*: 111)

With the help of the lieutenant, the narrator can go some way to penetrating 'l'intimité de ce peuple' (*CEF* I: 595). Friendship begets friendship, and the narrator thus seeks to establish an indirect or vicarious intimacy with the townspeople through the lieutenant's own knowledge 'par cœur' of them. Yet, after an initial conflation, Fromentin is quick to establish a cultural difference between 'amitié' as practised by the lieutenant and by the Laghouati population. Indeed, it is the lieutenant's capacity for friendship with the local population which allows him to know that, under the illusion of hospitality, these friendships are fundamentally false. The narrator refers to the lieutenant's description of his Algerian '"faux amis", comme il les appelle, avec la connaissance exacte des amitiés arabes' (*OCF*: 111): the lieutenant's instinctive knowledge *par cœur* of individuals morphing into a precise and apparently objective evaluation ('connaissance exacte') of cultural or racial traits. The overt stereotyping of the Arabic people as deceitful and untrustworthy builds on the earlier signposting of a revenge plotline against the lieutenant (Fromentin 2009: 224, n. 1), further creating a sense of narrative suspense which gradually crystallises around the figure of Ahmet, the narrator's servant. The sympathy the narrator directs towards his servant is rebuffed, and the vocabulary of suspicion infiltrates and eventually comes to outweigh that of intimacy: 'Au fond, je soupçonne Ahmet d'être contre moi et de trahir directement mes intérêts. [...] Ce qu'il y a de plus clair dans tout cela, c'est [...] qu'on épie tous les pas que je fais dans la ville' (*OCF*: 133). The patterns of mutual suspicion, even paranoia, evident in Baudelaire's *La Belgique déshabillée* are thus reproduced in *Un été dans le Sahara*. The narrator's desire for intimacy takes the form of semi-ethnographic observation, investigation, and verbal and visual documentation, albeit framed in the language of friendship, which troubles the Laghouati population and incites hostile reactions. The 'revenge plot' is resolved with the theft of the narrator's money by Ahmet, an incident which, the narrator claims, 'me sépare d'un domestique que j'aimais' (*OCF*: 142). While the narrator expresses regret at this outcome, the plot functions to confirm the (reliably) unreliable nature of attachments formed *en voyage*, exacerbated, it seems, in the colonial context.

'Le sens familier de ces récits'

Intercultural intimacy may be desired by Fromentin, yet in his travel writing it is seen to result in disingenuous, deceitful, and even dangerous relationships, affirming the worst fears of the etiquette manual. Fromentin's decision to render false friendship a prominent motif in his account gives tangible narrative shape to what he describes in a private letter to Du Mesnil of June 1853 as an experience of intense detachment in Laghouat:

> Ce n'est pas de la joie que j'éprouve ici, ni du bonheur. Il me serait difficile de t'expliquer cela. Je n'ai jamais éprouvé un tel détachement de lieu, malgré le vigoureux désir d'en tirer parti. Je visite ce pays comme on examine une proie, avidement, avec curiosité, satisfaction, mais sans amour. (*CEF* 1: 957)

Here, the vocabulary of predation and pillage reveals Fromentin's self-conscious complicity with the exploitative structures of colonisation, and the alienating and brutalising effects that this exploitation can have on coloniser and colonised alike. 'Amour' can be felt for neither people nor place in Laghouat, and is thus frustrated at the thematic level. Yet it is, I would argue, channelled instead into the epistolary form that the fictionalised account takes. As discussed in Chapter One, the epistolary form was explicitly associated with intimate literature in nineteenth-century French culture; the popularity of the epistolary novel from the eighteenth century onwards lay in its suggestion of verisimilitude and unmediated contact with the first-person letter-writer, chiming with the cultural apotheosis of nature and 'naivety'. In a retrospective account of the genesis of his travel writing in 1874, Fromentin describes his choice of narrative form: 'Il est clair que la forme de lettres, que j'adoptai pour les deux récits, était un simple artifice qui permettait plus d'abandon, m'autorisait à me découvrir un peu plus moi-même, et me dispensait de toute méthode' (*OCF*: 7). Fromentin's extensive work on the draft manuscripts questions this supposed lack of method. Nevertheless, his description shows the extent to which the positing of a friend or an intimate was essential to the realisation of the text. Christin writes:

> Cette écriture [...] apparaît seulement dans une situation de partage; c'est son destinataire qui la suscite [...]. Si la rêverie littéraire était nécessaire à Fromentin pour posséder le réel, l'intérêt d'un auditeur ami pouvait seul le déterminer à lui donner une forme. (Christin 2009: 27)

Intimacy with an 'other', whether present or imagined, lets the self articulate itself in an act of sharing which dilutes the focus on the *moi* by incorporating a *toi*.[41] And in a setting where both people and place prove resistant to intimacy, this other is found in a French friend — Du Mesnil — and worked into a favoured European literary form.

The friendship between Fromentin and Du Mesnil, evoked in the paratext of *Un été dans le Sahara*, is, it seems, of an entirely different order from the false friendships represented in the text itself. In his 1856 dedication to his 'cher ami' (*OCF*: 13), Fromentin claims to be returning these letters to their rightful owner, Du Mesnil. Moreover, 'c'est [...] indiquer l'origine particulière et le sens familier de ces récits, que de les publier sous le patronage d'une amitié qui rend nos deux noms inséparables' (*OCF*: 13). By displaying his friendship in an ideal and eternal form, Fromentin seeks to highlight the moral worth of both writer and work and also to justify the hybrid and frequently informal register of the narrative: seemingly unpremeditated anecdotes ('J'oubliais de te dire' (*OCF*: 177), 'J'ai su ce matin' (*OCF*: 33)) rub shoulders with frequent reference to shared memories ('Te souviens-tu' (*OCF*: 212), 'Si tu te rappelles' (*OCF*: 25)) and jokes. Yet this approach can also be seen to compensate for the disappointments experienced in Laghouat: by inscribing this travel account within the intimate paradigm, its emotionally ambivalent contents are rendered more palatable for both writer and reader. Fromentin's preface to the 1874 edition of the book extends this simultaneous idealisation and strategic deployment of friendship by applying it to the relationship between writer and reader. Fromentin evokes the process by which writers and readers befriend each other, through the medium of the text:

> Il n'est pas de livre un peu digne d'être lu qui n'ait son public et qui ne se l'attache, grâce à des affinités purement humaines. Il se forme ainsi quelquefois des amitiés qui se consolident, en raison de l'âge du livre, en souvenir de l'époque où l'on était jeunes ensemble. C'est à ce petit nombre d'amis connus ou inconnus d'ancienne date que je destine particulièrement cette édition. (*OCF*: 10–11)

Fromentin's travel narrative thus negotiates between the cultural idealisation of intimacy and a fear of its misuse or misplacement. His narrative exploits this fear through the insertion of plotlines which contrast cultures of intimacy (French and Algerian) and which focus on the false friendships seen to characterise these intercultural encounters. Yet by employing the epistolary form, and framing the narrative in terms of its French reception, Fromentin simultaneously promotes the virtues of those life-long friendships and affinities which are perhaps attained more satisfactorily through reading (a 'purely human' activity) than travelling.

This chapter has explored the tension between the idealisation of intimacy in nineteenth-century French culture and the anxiety surrounding over-familiarity, exacerbated by an acute sense of societal and political instability, and even further heightened in the context of travel. Etiquette manuals of the period forbade overfamiliarity with fellow travellers, advocating reserve and discretion, and these cultural concerns also surface in the travel texts of Flaubert, Baudelaire, and Fromentin. All three writers suggest that frustrated friendships are symptomatic of travel, yet articulate these frustrations differently. Flaubert and Baudelaire deploy humour while, for Fromentin, the epistolary form provides a means of combining the failure of friendship abroad with the consolatory effects of literary intimacy. While intimacy is unsuccessful at the diegetic level in Fromentin's text, it functions extradiegetically to construct an appealing — and thus marketable — form and tone for the narrative.

The following chapter will turn to another intercultural context in which the rhetorical usefulness of intimacy emerges: art criticism and, in particular, the act of comprehending and evaluating visual art from abroad. In 1874, Fromentin suggests that his life-long affinity with Algeria was in some ways beyond his control: 'J'avais visité l'Algérie à plusieurs reprises; je venais d'y pénétrer plus loin et de l'habiter posément. Une sorte d'acclimatation intime et définitive me la faisait accepter, sinon choisir, comme objet d'études' (*OCF*: 4). His ambivalent bond with the country is thus the product of those same 'fibres secrètes' which Flaubert sees at work in friendship (see n. 19 above), and which are also described in *Dominique* (*OCF*: 379–80). This process of gradual acquaintanceship and acclimatisation is also evoked, but actively *willed*, by Baudelaire in his mid-century art criticism, where it becomes a symbol and a method for critical engagement with foreign artwork. As the chapter will show, Baudelaire's mixed feelings towards intimate literature extend to its counterpart in the field of visual art. However, the transformative potential of intimacy as both an operation within the self ('acclimatation intime') and a figurative relation between the art critic and the art object is harnessed by Baudelaire in his art criticism, and takes on a new range of associations.

Notes to Chapter 4

1. Parts One and Two of this chapter reprise material originally published as an article, '"Une sympathie quittée": Holiday Friendships and Flaubert's *Voyage en Égypte*', in *Modern Language Review*; see Philippa Lewis (2015).
2. This chapter is indebted to the work of David Morgan (2009) on the sociology of acquaintanceship and the 'fellow traveller'.
3. See also Kent Puckett (2008), Chapter One. For Perrot, the interest of the manual as an object of study lies in the way it enables us to grasp the nebulous, generally unarticulated, 'grandes normes' of a social group (1981: 172).
4. For clarification, *amitié* is defined by the Littré dictionary as a 'sentiment qui affectionne, qui attache une personne à une autre'. *Connaissance* is defined as 'une personne que l'on connaît', or who participates in a 'liaison qui se fait entre des personnes qui se voient, qui se fréquentent'. Unlike friendship, acquaintanceship appears based on circumstance or habit, with no mention of affection.
5. On the nineteenth-century language of friendship, see Horowitz (2008: 136–51). See Vernon (2005) for a discussion of the philosophy of friendship from Antiquity to the present day.
6. On nineteenth-century holiday practices see Anne Martin-Fugier (1999: 205–12) and James

Buzard (1993). On the rise of the seaside and river holiday in particular see Alain Corbin (1988).
7. It is difficult to determine, in fact, whether Raisson personally penned this *Code*; Maurice Bardèche speaks of an 'atelier Raisson' responsible for many of the literary productions published under Raisson's name. For further discussion of Raisson's literary activities, and his friendship and possible collaboration with Balzac during the Restoration, see Bardèche (1940: 194–96, 204–05).
8. Similar concerns are evident in the advice books published specifically for railway travellers in the Second Empire, a genre discussed by Anne Green (2011), Chapter Three.
9. See Scott Haine (1996), Corbin (1999: 461–518), Anne Vincent-Buffault (1995), and Martin (2011).
10. In Victorien Sardou's Second Empire comedy *Nos intimes!*, for example, first performed on 16 November 1861, the character of the 'très-liant' Caussaude is shown to have an excessive number of friends, including 'aux Grandmenil, des amis que j'ai faits en chemin de fer' (1862: 33). Playing with the ambiguous nature of many of these bonds, the play ends with the warning, in the mouth of Tholosan, that 'nos intimes ne sont pas toujours nos amis' (1862: 157).
11. On the publishing history of the *Voyage en Égypte*, see Pierre-Marc de Biasi (1991: 14–18). The corrections Flaubert made to his manuscript, both additions and omissions, are marked in Biasi's edition; I have chosen to omit the markings when quoting from the *Voyage en Égypte* for ease of reading, but they can be consulted in Biasi's edition.
12. Flaubert's sexual encounters in the Middle East, primarily with Koutchouk-Hânem, have received extensive treatment in literary scholarship; see Edward Said (1985), Ali Behdad (1994), and Biasi (2009), Chapter Five.
13. For a discussion of the symbolism of transport in Flaubert's œuvre, see Kate Rees (2010).
14. Signing a letter of 26 December 1852 to his friend Louis Bouilhet, Flaubert writes 'Gustavus Flaubertus bourgeoisophobus'; see discussion in Gay (1998: 25) and Alan William Raitt (2005: 10).
15. Pierre Barbey was a retired sea captain whom the Flaubert family visited during their holidays in Trouville; see, for example, a letter to Flaubert from his sister Caroline of 1 July 1842 (*CF* I: 107).
16. 'Ce temps est si fertile en naufrages de toute sorte, que l'on s'y trouve exposé à de terribles avaries' (Rostaing [18—]: 22).
17. Erving Goffman (2009: 189).
18. On the friendship between Flaubert and du Camp, see Biasi (2009), Chapter Five.
19. Male friendship and the 'shifting patterns of intimacy and estrangement' (Williams 1987: 180) are key concerns of *L'Éducation sentimentale* and *Bouvard et Pécuchet*; see further discussion in J. Borie (1995) and Williams (1987), Chapter Seven. The friendship between Bouvard and Pécuchet is described by Flaubert in the following terms: 'Ainsi leur rencontre avait eu l'importance d'une aventure. Ils s'étaient, tout de suite, accrochés par des fibres secrètes. D'ailleurs, comment expliquer les sympathies? [...] Ce qu'on appelle le coup de foudre est vrai pour toutes les passions. Avant la fin de la semaine ils se tutoyèrent' (*OF* II: 719).
20. In the dedication to his friend Alfred Le Poittevin which opens *Mémoires d'un fou*, written in 1838, Flaubert expresses his original intention to 'faire un roman intime' (*OJF*: 465).
21. On Flaubert's decision not to publish his travel diary, partly due to the 'non-literary' and second-rate status of travel writing at the time, see Biasi (1991: 11–14).
22. Following André Guyaux's example, I use the title *La Belgique déshabillée* rather than *Pauvre Belgique!* to refer to these notes. Guyaux shows that *La Belgique déshabillée* was the last title envisaged by Baudelaire before his death (1986b: 58).
23. For information on Baudelaire's stay in Brussels, see Pichois and Ziegler (1987), Chapter 22.
24. Belgium officially became an independent state in 1830; on the history of Belgium in the nineteenth century, see Michel Dumoulin (2005).
25. See Behdad (1994).
26. The omissions and additions Baudelaire made to *La Belgique déshabillée* are signalled in Guyaux's edition; as with Flaubert's *Voyage en Égypte*, I have omitted these markings for ease of reading,

but it is important to appreciate the 'état velléitaire' (Guyaux 1986b: 48–49) of the manuscript, not prepared for publication. For a discussion of Guyaux's editorial approach, see Guyaux (1986b).
27. See, for example, Baudelaire's negative evaluation of George Sand's *'style coulant'* (Peter Dayan 1994: 416).
28. On the metaphor of the latrine in the Baudelairean critique of Sand, again see Dayan (1994).
29. For the history of *Manneken Pis* as a Belgian 'icon', see Catherine Emerson (2003, 2014).
30. On Baudelaire in the context of nineteenth-century theories of infection and hygiene, particularly in relation to odour, see Cheryl Leah Krueger (2012). For a discussion of Baudelaire's disgust with Belgian cuisine, linked to the notion of *fadeur* or blandness, see Andrea Schellino (2014).
31. *Tutoiement* was associated with the 1789 Revolution and Republicanism in nineteenth-century France; see the entry for *tutoiement* in E. Boursin and Augustin Challamel (1893: 849).
32. For example, 'Les Fenêtres' closes with the following rhetorical address: 'Qu'importe ce que peut être la réalité placée hors de moi, si elle m'a aidé à vivre, à sentir que je suis et ce que je suis?' (*OC* I: 339).
33. This has parallels with the distinction between 'conscious' and 'unconscious' contagion which Burgess (2011) relates to the discourse surrounding sympathy in late-eighteenth-century England. While conscious, imaginative contagion was seen as a desirable function of sympathy, cultural commentators feared the effect of involuntary contagion: that is, the migrancy or transmission of affect. Baudelaire privileges an intimacy which he is in control of, not one which is forced on him in the form of over-familiarity. Paradoxically, of course, he seeks to 'enforce' intimacy on the Belgian population.
34. Fromentin's painting *Une rue à El-Aghouat* was exhibited at the 1859 *Salon* in Paris, and received high praise from Baudelaire. On the ideological implications of Fromentin's visual and literary art, see Anne-Marie Christin (1982); Elwood Hartman (1994), Chapter Two; Vladimir Kapor (2005); and John Zarobell (2010), Chapter Four. Critics are divided over whether Fromentin's work perpetuates or subverts Orientalist conventions.
35. In 1874, Fromentin describes *Dominique* in relation to the earlier travel texts: 'Un volume de pur roman, publié quelques années plus tard, reproduisit sous une autre forme le côté tout personnel des ouvrages précédents' (*OCF*: 10).
36. On Assia Djebar's intertextual appropriation of the figure of Haoûa, see Sage Goellner (2004).
37. Cf. 'Il est 10 heures du matin, mon ami, et dans deux heures j'irai voir si l'appartement d'Haoûa ressemble à l'admirable tableau de Delacroix: *Les Femmes d'Alger*' (*OCF*: 275). Although he is referring in particular to Flaubert's writing, Edward Said draws attention to the 'almost uniform association between the Orient and sex' as 'a markedly persistent motif in Western attitudes to the Orient' (1985: 188).
38. See Anne-Marie Christin (2009: 28–39).
39. The paragraphs I discuss in this section are not present in the original manuscript of *Un été dans le Sahara* (Fromentin 2009: 247, n. 1); from this, we can extrapolate that the motif of friendship was considered of use to the narrative.
40. I use the word 'profit' figuratively yet it is also applicable in a literal, economic sense: Fromentin will gain financially from the sale of his texts and images inspired by Algerian private life.
41. Cf. Fromentin's private letter of 19 August 1853, which lists points for Du Mesnil to consider in his reading of the draft manuscript: 'Tu verras, s'il n'y a pas trop *je*. J'ai pourtant veillé à ce que le *moi* ne fût top embêtant. Si quelquefois il n'y a pas un peu de flon-flon. J'ai une peur affreuse de *la fanfare* à propos de trop peu, — comme des gens qui parlent trop haut' (*CEF* I: 968).

CHAPTER 5

❖

Experiencing Art: Baudelaire's Intimate Criticism

How was intimacy imagined in nineteenth-century France? In answering this question, this book has thus far focused on verbal articulations of the *intime*. Yet 'imagination' — the capacity to form and perceive images in the mind's eye — evidently encompasses a visual aspect. In the domain of visual art, intimacy is conventionally associated with the turn of the twentieth century, and the paintings of the French *intimistes* Pierre Bonnard and Édouard Vuillard. Writing in the *Gazette des Beaux-Arts* in December 1905, for example, André Gide describes his impression of four painted panels exhibited by Vuillard at the *Salon d'Automne*, one of which bears the title *L'Intimité* (Figure 5.1):

> Je reviens aux panneaux de M. Vuillard. — Je ne sais ce qu'il faut aimer le plus ici. C'est peut-être M. Vuillard lui-même. Il se raconte intimement. Je connais peu d'œuvres où la conversation avec l'auteur soit plus directe. [...] Cela vient surtout de ce qu'il parle à voix presque basse, comme il sied pour la confidence, et qu'on se penche pour l'écouter. Il est d'une mélancolie point romantique, point hautaine, discrète, et qui garde un vêtement de tous les jours, d'une tendresse caressante, et je dirais presque: timide, si ce mot se pouvait s'accorder avec déjà tant de maîtrise. (Gide 1905: 480)

Vuillard's panels depict dark, opulent interiors in shades of maroon and green; female figures calmly sew, read, or talk together, swallowed up by a backdrop of patterned wallpaper, thick carpets, and coloured textiles. Vuillard's panels are not presented as specific portraits or self-portraits, but Gide nevertheless experiences them as a confessional moment in which, to use Barthes's words from 'La Mort de l'auteur', 'la voix d'une seule et même personne, *l'auteur* [...] livrait sa "confidence"' (1984: 64). This, together with Gide's emphasis on the everyday, and on melancholy, tenderness, and timidity, clearly recalls the language of July Monarchy and Second Empire literary intimacy. Yet how did the language and hermeneutic of intimacy impact on the visual art of these periods themselves, and the critical discussion of it?

This chapter focuses principally on Baudelaire's art criticism and reveals two key strands to the mid-nineteenth-century art-critical articulation of the *intime*. The first part of the chapter considers the *genre intime* as an aesthetic category which, associated with still-life or genre painting, occupied a relatively lowly position in the academic hierarchy of genres. In his *Salons* of 1846 and 1859, Baudelaire withholds definitive judgement on this style of art and displays mixed feelings which echo his ambivalent approach to literary intimacy. The second part of the chapter turns to the less ambivalent role of intimacy in a network of terms pertaining to a profound, 'innermost' understanding between subject matter and spectator: intimacy as an instrument of aesthetic appreciation and interpretation. What Baudelaire refers to as the 'intelligence intime du sujet' (*OC* II: 432) visible in Eugène Delacroix's paintings becomes, I argue, a crucial method for the art critic, articulated most prominently in his *Exposition universelle – 1855*. As an aesthetic category, the *intime* is typically concerned with representations of the domestic sphere or private life, a concern still evident in Vuillard's turn-of-the-century canvases. Yet the art world of the Second Empire was one in which a wide variety of international subjects and artists were exhibited with ever-increasing frequency. In light of the challenges that this internationalism posed for critics, intimacy as a mode of analysis gained special resonance. In Baudelaire's international art criticism, intimacy comes to stand for an imaginative and empathetic encounter with artworks from different cultures and the radical transformation that this can entail in the viewing subject. Intimacy thus sidesteps the small-scale details of everyday domestic life and comes to refer to an exceptional critical gift akin to the 'grâce divine' (*OC* II: 576) of cosmopolitanism.

I. The *genre intime* in the Visual Arts

This book has been focusing on textual representations and evocations of intimacy in genres ranging from the *roman intime* and *poésie intime* to the diary and travel narrative. Nevertheless, figurative allusions to art have surfaced along the way, suggesting that the properties of written intimacy had a visual counterpart in nineteenth-century French culture. As discussed in Chapter Three, Guérin suggests an affinity between the *journal intime* and self-portraiture, emphasising the *petitesse* of the latter in comparison with history or religious painting. As she suggests, self-deprecatingly: 'Le petit peintre ne sait donner que son portrait à son ami, le grand peintre offre des tableaux' (*GJ*: 69). This distinction is corroborated by nineteenth-century dictionary definitions: the Littré dictionary defines the portrait not as a painting but rather as an image or likeness achieved 'à l'aide de quelqu'un des arts du dessin'. Baudelaire's *Salon de 1845* is set out according to the conventional academic hierarchy of genres in which history painting precedes portraiture, genre painting, landscape, sculpture, and drawing (*OC* II: 352–53). And while Fromentin exploits the *intime* in his literary fiction, he sees intimacy and excessive detail ('local colour') as symptomatic of a lack of technical skill and mental strength in relation to landscape painting. In a preparatory note for *Gustave Drouineau*, for example, he criticises:

> Les hommes trop intimes [qui] ne comprennent que le paysage intime, c.à.d [*sic*] un paysage rétréci le plus souvent mystérieux, dans lequel on peut aisément enfermer une idée ou un sentiment. [...] — Les campagnes découvertes, les grands horizons de plaine ou de mer, les montagnes leur causent une impression

FIG. 5.1. Édouard Vuillard, *L'Intimité*, 1896. Glue-bound distemper on canvas, 212.5 × 154.5 cm. Le Petit Palais, Musée des Beaux-Arts de la Ville de Paris (© RMN-Grand Palais/Agence Bulloz).

confuse, les troublent, les fatiguent. [...] — Au lieu d'en esquisser les contours, de les espacer, de les indiquer largement et à l'effet, — ils les fractionnent, cherchent à en étudier les détails, ôtent au paysage son unité, et tendent ainsi malgré eux à le réduire aux proportions du paysage intime. (Fromentin 1969: 102)

For Fromentin as a visual artist, a tendency towards the *intime* or small-scale in landscape painting is a limiting factor which destroys the visual harmonies and emotional impact of the 'campagnes découvertes' and indicates a fear of 'grands horizons', both literal and metaphorical. Fromentin's views speak, implicitly, of the deep schisms which marked the French art world of the nineteenth century in the form of ongoing conflicts between neo-classicism and Romanticism, idealism and realism, and universality and particularity. Each of these conflicts can be seen to pertain to the debated legitimacy of the detail. In her 'feminist archaeology' of the detail, Schor interprets the long-held Western hostility towards the small-scale as indicative of the 'sexual hierarchies of the phallocentric cultural order' (1987: 4) in which details are associated either with effeminate and decadent decoration or with the trivialities of the domestic sphere.[2] In contrast, the 'masculine' imagination has long favoured the universality of abstraction or generalisation and, it could be added, an aesthetic schema which equates *grand* dimensions with symbolic *grandeur* and greatness. The few references to Baudelaire in Schor's work place him firmly on the side of the detail-disparagers: Schor elides his dislike of the 'upstart detail' (1987: 21) with a fear of the feminine and a distrust of mimesis. However, while Baudelaire's praise of the detail is certainly far from fulsome, I suggest that references to the *intime* in his art criticism reveal a more nuanced appreciation of its potential than Schor allows. The references he makes to the concept, and the network of binaries within which he inserts it, throw light on the meaning and uses of intimacy for the nineteenth-century art world and, via analogy with the literary sphere, for French culture more broadly.

Baudelaire's references are underpinned by the same binary distinction between *grand* and *intime* as used by Fromentin. Nevertheless, unlike Fromentin's discussion, these references imply that grandeur and intimacy are two parallel, and potentially complementary, perspectives: much as beauty is composed of both eternal and contingent elements for Baudelaire, it can be attained through attention to either generality or detail, and through large-scale or small-scale artistic endeavours. Certain artists tend towards one mode or the other, although some, Baudelaire suggests, are adept at both. In Baudelaire's *Salon de 1846*, Jean-Auguste-Dominique Ingres is aligned with the *intime*. In this case, the compliment is clearly backhanded: Baudelaire's antipathy towards Ingres is well known, and his association of Ingres with intimacy emerges immediately as a correlate of imaginative deprivation. His discussion of Ingres's 1842 *Le Compositeur Cherubini et la Muse de la poésie lyrique* (Figure 5.2) perpetuates, while playing with, the hierarchical distinction between *portrait* and *tableau* alluded to by Guérin: 'Il est juste de dire que si M. Ingres, privé de l'imagination du dessin, ne sait pas faire des tableaux, au moins dans de grandes proportions, ses portraits sont presque des tableaux, c'est-à-dire des poèmes intimes' (*OC* II: 459). Ingres's portraits are almost tantamount to paintings,

FIG. 5.2. Jean-Auguste-Dominique Ingres, *Le Compositeur Cherubini et la Muse de la poésie lyrique*, 1842. Oil on canvas, 105 × 92 cm. Musée du Louvre, Paris.

although, crucially, not quite. In this passage filled with qualifications — and thus reminiscent of Baudelaire's review of Asselineau's *La Double Vie* — the analogy between literature and painting remains deliberately vague: are *poèmes intimes* equivalent to portraits or to paintings? The syntactical ambiguity suggests that, at best, *poèmes intimes* are equivalent to mediocre paintings and, at worst, competent portraits: hierarchical divisions are almost, but never entirely, blurred. The same tentative troubling of genre hierarchy occurs in Baudelaire's evaluation of sculpture. In the *Salon de 1846*, a distinction between large-scale sculpture and the form of the bust — the sculptural equivalent of the portrait — associates the *intime* with the same lack of imagination: 'Le buste est un genre qui demande moins d'imagination et des facultés moins hautes que la grande sculpture, mais non moins délicates. C'est un art plus intime et plus resserré dont les succès sont moins publics' (*OC* II: 489). Like Fromentin, Baudelaire equates intimate art with a process of reduction ('un art [...] plus resserré'), yet while Fromentin sees this as by definition reductive, Baudelaire partially redeems it. Not only can a process of reduction or concentration lead to increased intensity, but Baudelaire associates intimacy with delicacy and privacy: 'aristocratic' terms with a largely positive value in his lexicon.

The aesthetic potential of intimate art is, however, most evident in Baudelaire's discussions of work by the French artists Alexandre Gabriel Decamps and Delacroix in the *Salon de 1846*, and, turning first to the *Salon de 1859*, a cluster of English artists.[3] The idea that the aesthetic of intimacy was rooted in England, encouraged by Sainte-Beuve through his emphasis on the 'Lakistes' in his theorisations of *poésie intime*, is reinforced by Baudelaire in his art criticism. Baudelaire's experiences of English art centred on his visit to the 1855 *Exposition universelle* in Paris, where artists including William Henry Hunt, William Mulready, John James Chalon, and John Everett Millais, 'ce poète si minutieux' (*OC* II: 609), were exhibited. Many French critics displayed incomprehension or even hostility towards these English artworks.[4] In his 1855 *Voyage à travers l'exposition des beaux-arts*, for example, the French critic Edmond About claimed to be 'choqué par un certain nombre de tableaux excentriques' (1855: 4): certain English works are 'curieux' (1855: 20); English painting 'ressemble si peu à la nôtre qu'il faut toute une éducation pour l'apprécier' (1855: 26). About's emphasis on English singularity and eccentricity at the level of aesthetics was typical of many conservative French critics, and betrayed a more fundamental critique of English individualism. Reviewers also attacked the lack of '*grande peinture*' in the English school (Mainardi 1987: 106) and were quick to relate this phenomenon to the perceived lack of academic tradition in England and the weak position of state and Church, the bodies generally responsible for commissioning large-scale public art.

Despite this critical reaction, however, the English gallery was one of the best attended at the Universal Exhibition, and was popular with the French public. Baudelaire's interest in the exhibition is signalled by his plan to write an article on English visual art, evident in the intriguing draft of a title found amongst his notes: 'L'Intime et la féerique (Angleterre)' (*OC* II: xi). The ambiguity of the title precludes any conclusive interpretation: whether intimacy is an antonym or a synonym for the fairy-world is unclear, and the article never appeared. Nevertheless, reference *is* made to the English school of art in the *Salon de 1859*, in which intimacy features as a characteristic quality of English aesthetics. English artists had been scheduled to exhibit at the 1859 *Salon*, but withdrew at the last minute: it is likely that Baudelaire alludes to this disappointing absence when he evokes the concept of 'musées perdus et musées à créer' in his notes (*OC* II: xi). Indeed, the critic dedicates the opening pages of his *Salon de 1859* to regretting and thus, through a form of extended periphrasis, imaginatively recreating the exhibition that never was, drawing on memories of the 1855 display: 'Ainsi, ardeurs tragiques, gesticulations à la Kean et à la Macready, intimes gentillesses du *home*, splendeurs orientales réfléchies dans le poétique miroir de l'esprit anglais, [...] nous ne vous contemplerons pas, cette fois du moins' (*OC* II: 609).[5] Baudelaire describes the English as 'ces amis de l'imagination' (*OC* II: 609), for whom everyday domesticity and home life are as much of a source of inspiration as 'splendeurs orientales', indicating an abundance rather than a lack of imaginative capacity. By singling out the *intime* in his imaginary curatorship and criticism of the exhibition, Baudelaire turns the association between the *intime* and lack of talent on its head: intimacy is a quality to be valued, not veiled.

If we return to the *Salon de 1846*, we see both Decamps and Delacroix associated with differing modalities of the *intime*. In this analysis, the plasticity of the concept of the *intime* emerges fully: unlike the English artists referred to by Baudelaire in 1859, the *intime* of Decamps and Delacroix is not necessarily connected to the '*home*' (*OC* II: 609), but pertains rather to a way of seeing which, this chapter suggests, ultimately finds a parallel in Baudelaire's method of intercultural criticism. While Decamps and Delacroix are both admired by Baudelaire for their imaginative capacities, Decamps is, on occasion, contrasted with Delacroix. For Baudelaire, Decamps is an artist of the detail: 'Les tableaux de Decamps étaient [...] pleins de poésie, et souvent de rêverie, mais là où d'autres, comme Delacroix, arriveraient par un grand dessin, [...] M. Decamps arrivait par l'intimité du détail' (*OC* II: 450). Yet, on other occasions, this monolithic reading of Delacroix's skill is complicated and, as a 'homme complet' and 'universel', the *intime* is shown to be part of his repertoire as well: '[Delacroix] a fait des tableaux de genre pleins d'intimité, des tableaux d'histoire pleins de grandeur' (*OC* II: 435).

Intimacy, when equated with the detail and 'local colour' of genre painting, may be the antithesis of the grand works made for public places and public consumption. Yet the term nonetheless carries with it a body of positive connotations and possibilities stemming from Baudelaire's definition of Romanticism in the same *Salon*. Intimacy can connote genres and subjects on a small scale (portraits, busts, and interior and domestic scenes), yet, and sometimes at the same time, it can allude to a quality above and beyond subject matter. Baudelaire's definition in the *Salon de 1846* locates Romanticism not in a subject, but in the way the individual artist *feels* a subject: it is a 'manière de sentir' (*OC* II: 420) which encompasses the interiority of the artist at a deep level ('C'est en dedans qu'il était seulement possible de le trouver' (*OC* II: 420)) and thus, by etymological association, the notion of the *intime*: 'Qui dit romantisme dit art moderne, — c'est-à-dire intimité, spiritualité, couleur, aspiration vers l'infini' (*OC* II: 421). Baudelaire's definition speaks of the Romantic belief in the poet's ability to experience the infinite in the everyday, and the universal by way of a detail: William Blake's 'Infinity in the palm of your hand | And Eternity in an hour' (1972: 13), or Hugo's claim that 'la poésie c'est tout ce qu'il y a d'intime dans tout' (1867: 2). In this context, rather than connote triviality or materiality, intimacy provides the artist — verbal or visual — with symbolic access to the ideal. For Baudelaire, Delacroix's work epitomises this sense of the *intime*, which places him 'à la tête du romantisme' (*OC* II: 430): 'Delacroix part donc de ce principe qu'un tableau doit avant tout reproduire la pensée intime de l'artiste, qui domine le modèle' (*OC* II: 433).[6] Yet, at the same time, Baudelaire writes, 'il jouit pleinement d'une originalité insaisissable, qui est l'intimité du sujet' (*OC* II: 434). Together, these passages suggest that as a property of Romanticism, *intimité* lies in the way the artist and the subject of the artwork meet and connect with each other in the creative process. Understood in this way, and approached as a union of subjects rather than as a specificity of subject matter, intimacy in Baudelaire's language has the potential to transcend the domestic comforts and 'gentillesses du home' (*OC* II: 609).

The discussion thus far has illuminated the semantic suppleness of intimacy: arguably a factor in the mixed feelings and frustrations surrounding it in critical discourse. As we have seen, Baudelaire's art criticism proposes a two-fold vision of the *intime*. On the one hand, and more conventionally, the *intime* is a type and scale of subject matter which can be associated with triviality and a lack of imagination. Yet, when read in relation to Baudelaire's positive appraisal of certain French and English artists, the *intime* also comes to refer to a profound imaginative ability fundamental to creative inspiration. Maintaining the focus on intercultural encounters begun in Chapter Four, and already alluded to in the first part of this chapter, the second part will explore the applications and implications of intimacy's semantic plasticity in the context of the increasingly international nineteenth-century art world, and the art criticism which this generates. It will first elucidate Baudelaire's vision for art criticism as outlined in the *Salon de 1846*, suggesting that it is underpinned by an aspiration for intimacy between the art critic and art-object. It will then consider how the cosmopolitan character of the art world of the Second Empire, symptomatic of a cultural desire for imaginative distancing or *dépaysement*, challenges and reconfigures this critical aspiration, generating a tension in Baudelaire's writing between the desire to suppress nationalist sentiment but simultaneously develop a 'feel', or feelings, for the aesthetics of other cultures. In place of the comforts of home, intimacy thus comes to connote a radical and revitalising, although potentially destabilising, encounter between foreign subjects.

II. Intimacy and Distance

The *Salon de 1846*

As Baudelaire's first substantial piece of art criticism, the *Salon de 1846* as a whole, and the dedication and Chapter One, 'À quoi bon la critique?', in particular, function as statements of critical intent: alongside its comments on major artists of the period, the text is an extended discussion — playful, polemical, and unashamedly prescriptive — of the nature of art criticism itself. Nineteenth-century France witnessed a huge increase in published art criticism compared with the eighteenth century, particularly evident in newspaper and journal reviews of the state-sponsored *Salon*. Surveys of criticism published throughout the eighteenth and nineteenth centuries in France show just how extensively the number of *Salon* reviews increased in the mid-nineteenth century, and also reveal trends and shifts in the focus and presentation of these reviews. For the years 1699–1827, for example, archival work has located some 1,357 examples of *Salon* criticism, usually published in the form of pamphlets, averaging 10.6 reviews a year. However, for the period of the Second Empire alone, on average 90 reviews per year were published, evidence of a dramatic increase in journalistic output.[7] Despite his long-standing affiliations with the press, the *Salon de 1846* represents an attempt on Baudelaire's part to disassociate himself from journalism and forge his own brand of criticism, albeit one which bears the traces of both journalistic and literary critical conventions (Robb 1987: 416). The work is also clearly indebted to the Empire and Restoration *critique des beautés* or 'admiring criticism' advocated by, amongst others, Staël, Chateaubriand, and Hugo: this in itself a product of the aesthetic theories of German Romanticism.[8] The Baudelaire of 1846 appears committed to a mode or 'system' of sympathetic criticism in which positive qualities are more noteworthy than faults, and 'admiration', 'passion', and 'enthusiasm' are watchwords: 'N'est-il pas plus nouveau de voir les gens par leur beau côté?', he writes in relation to Delacroix:

> Les défauts de M. Delacroix sont parfois si visibles qu'ils sautent à l'œil le moins exercé. On peut ouvrir au hasard la première feuille venue, où pendant longtemps l'on s'est obstiné, à l'inverse de mon système, à ne pas voir les qualités radieuses qui constituent son originalité. (*OC* II: 441)

In keeping with their emphasis on sympathy, Empire and Restoration critics conceptualised criticism as an act of creative 'completion' which complemented rather than competed with the work of the artist (Glinoer 2009: 32–34). Much as the artist was to enter into a sympathetic relationship with his or her subject matter, the critic should engage personally and passionately with the artwork or artist in question, imbuing criticism with the same aesthetic, and affective, qualities as art. For Baudelaire, incorporating these ideas, 'la meilleure critique est celle qui est amusante et poétique; [...] — un beau tableau étant la nature réfléchie par un artiste, — celle qui sera ce tableau réfléchi par un esprit intelligent et sensible' (*OC* II: 418); this is criticism as a hall of mirrors in which the reflections of the artwork, and subsequent reflections *of* these reflections, are multiplied ad infinitum.

For Baudelaire, Delacroix's art lends itself particularly well to the critical process outlined above. In the *Salon de 1846*, Baudelaire contrasts the exhaustive detail of Hugo's poems with the suggestive qualities of Delacroix's art, which spark the creative critic's imagination: 'Dans ceux du premier [Hugo], il n'y a rien à deviner; [...] — Le second ouvre dans les siens de profondes avenues à l'imagination la plus voyageuse' (OC II: 431) (see Figure 5.3). Extending the comparison, Baudelaire continues: 'L'un commence par le détail, l'autre par l'intelligence intime du sujet; d'où il arrive que celui-ci n'en prend que la peau, et que l'autre en arrache les entrailles' (OC II: 432). Evoked in visceral terms which recall the metaphors of embodied intimacy in Guérin's *Journal*, the *intime* is used to counter the superficial and unnecessary detail with which it can, on other occasions, be paired: here, it establishes the intense intersubjective intelligibility evident in Delacroix's paintings. For Baudelaire, Delacroix's artwork combines a movement 'inwards' ('intelligence intime') with the potential for movement 'outwards' ('imagination [...] voyageuse'), a two-fold dynamic which encapsulates both the 'vertical' (self-orientated) and 'lateral' (other-orientated) axes of intimacy discussed in Chapter One. Moreover, through his recourse to travel imagery, Baudelaire gestures to the cultural context within which his critical theories were evolving. The imaginative journey he refers to is metaphorical, but the trope gains its pertinence from the reality of a period experiencing an increasingly mobile and globalised art world, in which questions of geographical proximity or distance were frequently provoked by the nationality of an artist, or the subject-matter of a painting. Baudelaire's engagement with intercultural aesthetics has already been suggested by his enthusiasm for English art: moreover, Delacroix's *œuvre* contains a large number of works inspired by his travels in Spain and North Africa, as does that of Decamps. If, following the Romantic paradigm, the work of the critic is closely modelled on, and reflects, that of the artist, how significant does this union between 'intelligence intime' and 'imagination [...] voyageuse' become to Baudelaire's critical project? An examination of travel metaphors in Baudelaire's art criticism reveals that his attempt to combine these two relational modes is a recurring preoccupation, and one in which the notion of intimacy — part of a network of terms pertaining to sympathy, shared sentiment, and sensibility — carries particular resonance. As suggested in Chapter Four, the concern with intimacy evident in nineteenth-century French culture is thrown into relief by, and thus gains new emphases from, the parallel cultural enthusiasm for the 'exotic'.

The *voyage au Salon*

The wayfaring or 'wanderlust' imagination ('l'imagination la plus voyageuse') which Delacroix's paintings display, and which in turn inspires Baudelaire, is a thread which runs throughout the *Salon de 1846*. The *Salon de 1846* introduces the metaphor of the critic as traveller, and while the theoretical implications of this figure are explored in more sustained fashion in Baudelaire's 1855 *Exposition universelle*, the earlier *Salon* establishes the significance of this metaphor both in relation to the changing nature

FIG. 5.3. Eugène Delacroix, *Le Sac du château de Front-de-Bœuf* [*Rébecca enlevée par le Templier*], 1846. Oil on canvas, 105 × 81 cm. Musée du Louvre, Paris.

of the art world and to Baudelaire's ideological position regarding nationalism, cosmopolitanism, and the role of the visual arts therein. Throughout the text, the figure of the voyager or *flâneur* is used repeatedly to represent the 'ideal' viewer of visual art: Baudelaire describes the hypothetical spectator as, variously, a 'flâneur désintéressé' (*OC* II: 442), a 'voyageur enthousiaste', an 'esprit cosmopolite' (*OC* II: 470), and a 'flâneur[s] enthousiaste[s]' with a 'cœur grand comme le monde' (*OC* II: 450). While the *voyageur* may, we presume, take journeys on a larger scale than the *flâneur*, and with greater focus, Baudelaire's decision to qualify both figures with similar adjectives suggests that, for him, they share an underlying synonymy of mindset which makes them both apt models for the artistic spectator.

The metaphorical application of physical movement to the art-critical process is certainly not unique to Baudelaire: from the 1840s onwards, French *Salon* criticism in journalistic, pamphlet or book form was beginning to employ the rubric of the *voyage au Salon*, updating the eighteenth-century motif of the philosophical 'promenade'.[9] The principal motivation for the growing use of the *voyage* analogy can be seen to lie in the increasingly international outlook of the *Salon*. Gautier's art journalism regularly cites the *peintre-voyageur* as a modern type who will establish a new genre of so-called 'ethnographic' landscape and figure painting, and regenerate the French school in the wake of neo-classicism. In a *Salon* review of 1859 dedicated to Fromentin's paintings of Algeria, Gautier describes 'la peinture ethnographique' as a possible replacement for history painting, noting that this trend, 'plus conforme à nos mœurs et au mouvement de la science se développe aujourd'hui dans l'art, recrutant des adeptes à chaque Salon' (1992: 38). As a genre that depicted the peoples and landscapes of foreign countries, typically the Middle East or Africa, but also European countries including Spain, 'ethnographic' painting was enabled by and thus tied to the French colonial project and developments in transport, particularly steam travel, as explored in Chapter Four. In a passage which frames art in the language of stasis and movement, Gautier describes how visual art had been 'réduit à l'immobilité. Alors la Vapeur est venue, qui lui a dit: "Prends ta palette, je t'emmène et je te ferai voir du pays"' (1992: 38). The regular *Salon* thus obtained an international atmosphere through the subject matter of many of its paintings, often, of course, heavily romanticised; neither Gros nor Ingres actually travelled in the Middle East or Africa yet both produced major ethnographic paintings, and many of Delacroix's works preceded his travels in Spain and North Africa, conditioned by and simultaneously conditioning French fantasies about life abroad. In addition to paintings by French artists, the *Salon* also began to exhibit an increasing number of works by artists from abroad. In a review of 1847 in *L'Illustration*, signed 'AJD', it is suggested that travel technologies will facilitate the movement and transfer of artworks and aesthetic ideas, and lead to an increasingly cosmopolitan art experience. Anticipating 'l'influence des chemins de fer sur les beaux-arts', the journalist suggests:

> Il est aisé de prévoir que la rapidité et la facilité de ces nouvelles voies de communication permettront aux produits artistiques aussi bien qu'aux produits industriels de se porter un jour d'un bout à l'autre de l'Europe. [...]

> Les expositions au lieu d'être exclusivement nationales prendront un aspect cosmopolite. [...] On se dépouillera des préjugés d'amour-propre exagéré. (AJD 1847: 155)

Baudelaire's metaphor of the critic as *voyageur* thus refers on one level to the experience of 'virtual travel' fostered by these infrastructural and cultural changes; to what Gautier describes in relation to the artist Léon Belly as the 'voyage de l'œil':

> On doit de la reconnaissance aux artistes qui nous rapportent, sur des toiles fidèles, les aspects des pays lointains [...]. On aime à faire avec eux ce voyage de l'œil qui ne coûte rien et ne fatigue pas. [...] M. Belly a bien mérité des cosmopolites sédentaires; il leur accroche l'Égypte au mur de l'exposition. (Gautier 1861: 50–51)

While the comic potential of this sedentary, vicarious cosmopolitanism, and the implied laziness of the *Salon* visitor, was mined relentlessly in the *petite presse*, Baudelaire seeks to preserve the potency of the trope by bringing it into dialogue with larger questions of cosmopolitanism and domestic nationalism.[10]

Cosmopolitanism and Criticism

Although seen by some as the salvation of French art, ethnographic painting was fiercely attacked by others on the grounds of its implicit 'escapism, lack of patriotism, abhorrence of social realities, [and] technical conservatism'.[11] Opposing these assumptions, Baudelaire's *Salon de 1846* firmly rejects the worth of patriotism in the domain of art, and the prestige of the travelling critic or 'voyageur enthousiaste' (*OC* II: 470) grows in proportion to this. While it is the artist Horace Vernet's propensity for superficial chic which partly motivates Baudelaire's antipathy for his work, it is principally his status as an 'artiste éminemment national' (*OC* II: 469) which incites the tirade against him in Chapter XI. Known for his military paintings, Baudelaire sees in the popularity of Vernet a dispiriting symptom of French nationalism and militarism, both of which tendencies are alien to the potential of art to transcend rather than strengthen national boundaries: 'Je hais cet art improvisé au roulement du tambour, [...] cette peinture fabriquée à coups de pistolet, comme je hais l'armée, la force armée, et tout ce qui traîne des armes bruyantes dans un lieu pacifique' (*OC* II: 469). The chapter aligns patriotism with egotism both at the level of the individual (in Baudelaire's eyes it is often symptomatic of a personal desire for gloire) and the collective: Vernet's paintings please because of their affirmation of French supremacy, and thus pander to aggressive *amour propre* on a national scale: they are 'une masturbation agile et fréquente' (*OC* II: 470). This kind of art is thus rejected on behalf of a '*nous* silencieux et invisible, — *nous*, toute une génération nouvelle, ennemie de la guerre et des sottises nationales' (*OC* II: 471). In the light of this virulent denial of national self-interest in art, Baudelaire's figuring of the art critic as a 'voyageur enthousiaste' or, elsewhere, an 'esprit cosmopolite qui préfère le beau à la gloire' (*OC* II: 470), takes on added moral and ethical significance; somewhat incongruously, admittedly, in light of the misanthropic tone to his later writing,

Baudelaire suggests that the appreciation of other cultures and aesthetic modes depends on a mindset which considers art from the point of view of the universal, from its potential to unite rather than divide humanity.[12]

Broadly speaking, 'cosmopolitanism' embodies three elements which have been central to understandings of the term since its origins in stoic and cynic thought, namely: reflective distance from one's 'primary cultural affiliation'; a broad understanding of other cultures and customs; and a belief in universal humanity (Anderson 2001: 64). Nineteenth-century French dictionaries define the *cosmopolite* as a 'citoyen du monde' and, by extension, an individual 'qui vit tantôt dans un pays tantôt dans un autre; qui adopte facilement les usages des divers pays' (Littré). As Anderson outlines, different periods and thinkers have accentuated different elements of the concept in response to changes in social, political, and intellectual spheres; in nineteenth-century Europe, for example, cosmopolitanism was increasingly defined in relation to nationalism, given the growth of the nation state in this period. In contemporary theory, 'cosmopolitanism' is often equated with an aspiration towards emotional distancing: at the turn of the twenty-first century, Anderson presents nineteenth-century cosmopolitanism as an exemplary mode of detachment.[13] By linking it with stoicism and dandyism, and related practices privileging emotional self-control, Anderson equates cosmopolitanism with the suppression of feeling, and with calculated and consistent disinterest. However, a glance at the words semantically tied to *cosmopolite* in Baudelaire's *Salon de 1846* suggests the question is, in this case, more complex: cosmopolitanism is associated with the qualities of *désintérêt* certainly, yet also *enthousiasme*, *passion*, and the figure of the *flâneur* with a 'cœur grand comme le monde' (*OC* II: 450). Given the significance of sentiment in Baudelaire's early criticism ('la critique doit être partiale, passionnée' (*OC* II: 418)), the concept of cosmopolitanism articulated therein is given an emotional emphasis.

The extent to which passion is productive and permissible is, however, carefully delimited by Baudelaire. Partiality is, on one level, natural and necessary for criticism, 'car pour être critique on n'en est pas moins homme' (*OC* II: 419). Yet the *nature* of these partialities is of varying value and, it seems, more or less controllable. An artistic partiality or preconceived preference which derives from an original or 'instinctive' attachment to nation, family, or indeed friendship runs counter to the ideals of Baudelaire's criticism. This view is defined as early as the *Salon de 1845*, in which the critic claims to lack the sentimental or instrumental ties which might result in bias: 'Nous serons [...] impartiaux. Nous n'avons pas d'amis, c'est un grand point, et pas d'ennemis' (*OC* II: 351). Baudelaire continues to pit himself against what he identifies as 'la critique des journaux, tantôt niaise, tantôt furieuse, jamais indépendante, [qui] a, par ses mensonges et ses camaraderies effrontées, dégoûté le bourgeois' (*OC* II: 351). The ideal of selective impartiality underlies the allusions to national disinterest in the chapter on Vernet in the *Salon de 1846* and, fifteen years later, Baudelaire's 1861 essay on Richard Wagner and *Tannhäuser*. In the latter, Baudelaire admits to a more complex relationship with the emotions of patriotism than expressed in the former, evoking the pain which accompanies the ongoing struggle to suppress nationalist sentiment, even when this sentiment is recognised, rationally, as flawed. In the following anecdote, the critic describes the humiliation felt on hearing French musical tastes mocked abroad:

> Je me souviens que, malgré que j'aie toujours soigneusement étouffé dans mon cœur ce patriotisme exagéré dont les fumées peuvent obscurcir le cerveau, il m'est arrivé, sur des plages lointaines, à des tables d'hôte composées des éléments humains les plus divers, de souffrir horriblement quand j'entendais des voix (équitables ou injustes, qu'importe?) ridiculiser la France. Tout le sentiment filial, philosophiquement comprimé, faisait alors explosion. [...] Or, pendant les scandales soulevés par l'ouvrage de Wagner, je me disais: 'Qu'est-ce que l'Europe va penser de nous, et en Allemagne que dira-t-on de Paris? Voilà une poignée de tapageurs qui nous déshonorent collectivement!' (OC II: 814)

The above passage articulates a concentrated attempt on the critic's part to stifle the sensations of patriotism which might obscure the critical faculties, even as it admits that this attempt can result in spectacular, explosive failure. Seen in this light, Baudelaire's critical ideal *could* correspond to Anderson's discussion of cosmopolitanism as an exemplary form of emotional detachment. Yet this detachment is only willed, we shall see, in order for new and voluntary attachments to be made. Indeed, Baudelaire's criticism reveals a parallel strand in which the cultivation and propagation of 'inter-national' emotion — intersubjective intimacy on a global scale — is both a means to and an end of proper criticism. While over-familiarity with the cultural world of an artist or subject can lead to lazy criticism, Baudelaire suggests that when faced with work from, or representative of, an unfamiliar culture, an elective affinity is both necessary for, and often a by-product of, a fair and sensitive evaluation of it. When a 'sentiment filial' (OC II: 814) exists 'naturally' it should be quashed, yet when it does *not*, it should be nurtured. It is this somewhat paradoxical approach which ultimately creates the particular configuration sought out by the 'critique raisonnable et passionnée' (OC II: 419), with internationalist rather than nationalist sympathies. The following sections of the chapter will focus on key passages from the *Salon de 1846* and *Exposition universelle – 1855* to explore how this aspiration for intimacy with alien cultures, materially and metonymically embodied in the artwork, is further theorised in Baudelaire's art criticism. While the focus is on the revitalising results of new aesthetic attachments, the pain which can be involved in distancing oneself from one's original cultural context or contexts — as conveyed in the passage above — needs, however, to be kept in mind.

The *Musée espagnol*

Baudelaire's dedication in the *Salon de 1846* evokes the personal, social, and political benefits which cross-cultural aesthetic appreciation can bring, amplified in the light of the anti-nationalistic rhetoric expressed in Baudelaire's discussion of Vernet. The status of the *dédicace* has long been controversial. Akin to the interpretative history of 'À une heure du matin', critics remain divided over whether to read the text as a sincere expression of sympathy towards the bourgeoisie, or as ironic or opportunistic.[14] What is not generally considered coloured by irony, however, is Baudelaire's tribute within it to the art institutions established during the reign of the 'bourgeois King' Louis-Philippe, in particular the *Musée espagnol*. In the *dédicace*, Baudelaire addresses his readers directly, praising the middle classes for their commitment to public art:

> Ce que vous avez fait pour la France, vous l'avez fait pour d'autres pays. Le musée espagnol est venu augmenter le volume des idées générales que vous devez posséder sur l'art; car vous savez parfaitement que, comme un musée national est une communion dont la douce influence attendrit les cœurs et assouplit les volontés, de même un musée étranger est une communion internationale, où deux peuples, s'observant et s'étudiant plus à l'aise, se pénètrent mutuellement, et fraternisent sans discussion. (*OC* II: 417)

The *Musée espagnol* opened in the Galeries de la Colonnade at the Palais du Louvre in 1838. The museum was a collection of Golden Age Spanish art purchased for Louis-Philippe at his request in the early years of the Carlist civil wars in Spain (1833–68), a period of social upheaval during which much Church property, including religious art, was sold for state profit. This upheaval facilitated French acquisitions for the collection, which featured major works by artists including Francisco de Zurbarán, Bartolomé Esteban Murillo, El Greco, and Francisco Goya.[15] Louis-Philippe's decision to gift the collection to the French public has been referred to as 'a monumental compensatory act':[16] a public apology for the return of much Spanish art after the fall of Napoleon and, more generally, for the questionable legitimacy of the Orléans monarchy. The critical reaction to the collection was mixed. Baudelaire's comments display a clear appreciation of it, however, as well as dismay at the decision to return the collection to the Orléans family in the wake of the 1848 revolution. In a letter of June 1864 to the fellow art critic Théophile Thoré, he reminisces, in a tone of bitter nostalgia: 'Nous jouissions de ce merveilleux musée espagnol que la stupide république française, dans son respect abusif de la propriété, a rendu aux princes d'Orléans' (*BC* II: 386).[17]

In 1846, however, prior to its dissolution, Baudelaire envisages the potential of the gallery in terms both individual and collective. The museum is able to enhance the individual's intellectual and imaginative funds by facilitating communication with other peoples and their ideas via the medium of the art: a process which leads to greater international understanding and co-operation. Although the rhetoric of fraternity will later be mocked by Baudelaire (for example, in the prose poem 'La Solitude'), here it provides a way for him to articulate an appreciation of the international goodwill that increased exposure to foreign art can, ideally, create. Verbal communication and multilingual mastery is unnecessary for this pre-eminently sensorial and spiritual communion 'sans discussion' (*OC* II: 417). Individual Spanish artists are not singled out as interlocutors in this silent communion; rather, through the cumulative effect of quiet engagement with the products of Spanish *esprits*, the spectator will come to feel at ease with a general sense of their 'school' and sensibility.[18] The critical encounter is thus imagined in terms of a virtual community in which individual ambitions ('volontés') are tempered, and friendships are gently fostered. While friendships which pre-date the critical encounter are identified in the *Salon de 1845* as a threat to the critic's integrity ('Nous n'avons pas d'amis, c'est un grand point' (*OC* II: 351)), the calm contemplation of a culture's artistic output can, it seems, result in the formation of new and more productive bonds of intimacy. These are not the shameless *camaraderies* alluded to in 1845 which reek of self-interest, but are rather friendships 'd'imagination' (*OC* II: 609), a term which Baudelaire uses in 1859 to refer to English artists, and which suggests at once a bond which blossoms from profound spiritual or creative kinship, and one which takes shape in the mind. When the French critic About talks of English art, he claims, with some bafflement, that 'il faut toute une éducation pour l'apprécier' (1855: 20). In contrast, when Baudelaire discusses Spain, he foregrounds a mode of understanding which is affective rather than academic, and engendered through sympathy and sentiment rather than scholarship. He does this by employing terms which, as seen in Chapter One, are constitutive of the spheres and semantic fields associated with *intimité* and the *intime*, both 'lateral' and 'vertical' (Montémont 2009: 28): affective relations (*fraterniser, douce influence, attendrir*); speech and verbal practices (*communion*); sociability and the structures of human relations ('deux peuples, s'observant et s'étudiant plus à l'aise'); and inwardness and interiority (*le cœur, pénétrer*). It is in terms of figurative intimacy, then, further heightened by the metaphorical allusions to bodily contact and interpenetration, or merging, that Baudelaire's talk of critical cosmopolitanism can be understood. This process emerges more fully in the 'Méthode de critique' of the *Exposition universelle – 1855*, to which the final section of the chapter will now turn.

The *Exposition universelle*

As we have seen, Littré defines the *cosmopolite* as a 'citoyen du monde' who 'adopte facilement les usages des divers pays'. The theory of comparative art criticism which opens the *Exposition universelle* has at its heart the issue of 'adopting' foreign customs or tastes, and the ease with which this can be done. These questions were of particular concern to art critics assigned to review the *Exposition universelle* which took place in Paris from May to November 1855.[19] While, as we have seen, foreign collections *had* previously been exhibited in the city, the *Exposition universelle* pursued this trend on an unprecedented scale. Inspired by the success of the 1851 Great Exhibition in London, Napoleon III sought to stage a fair which would enable France to present its industrial innovations and artistic talent to the world, but which, with an international emphasis, would also allow other countries to do so: the hope, of course, was that such cross-cultural comparison would function to affirm France's superiority. Over 5,000 artworks, almost half of them by French artists, were selected for display in a specially designed pavilion on the Avenue Montaigne.[20] For the first time, painters were to exhibit as representative of their nation and national school (Majluf 1997: 871), and some twenty-eight nations participated, from Peru to Prussia, and from Britain to Belgium. Many critics interpreted this ambitious international endeavour in a utopian light. Gautier's delight at the ability to 'franchir pour quelques instants la muraille de la Chine' (1855: 74) in the Chinese section of the exhibition was typical of the time. Charles

Perrier went further, asserting that: 'Désormais l'art ne sera plus circonscrit par ces étroites limites de nationalités qui le divisent depuis si longtemps' (1855: 15). Moreover:

> Quand l'art sera devenu cosmopolite, quand tous les artistes du monde en seront venus, sinon à se donner la main, du moins à se connaître et à produire en commun leur œuvre individuelle en présence de tous les critiques du monde, un grand pas aura été fait. (Perrier 1855: 16)

Perrier's rhetoric ignores the challenges that these 'critiques du monde' were faced with when asked to compare and rank works of art from diverse cultures or, as Margueritte Murphy states, to find a 'critical framework' (2012: 128) for the huge and unwieldy exhibition. Most critics made a nod to the ideal of impartiality and denied the existence of any blind patriotism which would affect their assessments: even About claims to consider the works 'sans préjugé' (1855: 37). Nevertheless, throughout his analysis of the English school, About firmly and explicitly retains his hold on his French identity, and perspective.[21] He is a French critic judging, somewhat uncomfortably, the work of other countries, remaining thoroughly embedded in French culture and aesthetics. His is not the *cosmopolite*'s journey, if we consider the *cosmopolite* as someone 'qui vit indifféremment dans tous les pays' or 'qui s'accommode de tous' (*Grand Robert* 1986).

Yet how, then, was the critic to become cosmopolitan? While many journalists employed travel imagery in their *Salon* criticism, few developed the implications of it at any length. Baudelaire's introduction to his survey of the *Exposition universelle*, however, published as the 'Méthode de critique' in *Le Pays* on 26 May 1855, does exploit the journey metaphor more fully. Building on the analogies established in the *Salon de 1846*, its opening address directs a series of rhetorical questions to the reader, 'pourvu qu'il ait un peu pensé et un peu voyagé', and proceeds to describe the ideal critic as one of those 'voyageurs solitaires, [...] sans autre compagnon que leur fusil, contemplant, disséquant, écrivant' (*OC* II: 576). Baudelaire suggests, at first, that the individuals most able to appreciate the diverse 'échantillon[s] de la beauté universelle' (*OC* II: 576) are those who have already travelled. However, the passage goes on to foreground a method of cosmopolitan criticism in which the metaphorical, or mental, voyage assumes precedence over the literal. Like Gautier, Baudelaire focuses on Chinese art:

> Que ferait, que dirait un Winckelmann moderne (nous en sommes pleins, la nation en regorge, les paresseux en raffolent), que dirait-il en face d'un produit chinois, produit étrange, bizarre, contourné dans sa forme, intense par sa couleur, et quelquefois délicat jusqu'à l'évanouissement? Cependant c'est un échantillon de la beauté universelle; mais il faut, pour qu'il soit compris, que le critique, le spectateur, opère en lui-même une transformation qui tient du mystère, et que, par un phénomène de la volonté agissant sur l'imagination, il apprenne de lui-même à participer au milieu qui a donné naissance à cette floraison insolite. Peu d'hommes ont, — au complet, — cette grâce divine du cosmopolitisme; mais tous peuvent l'acquérir à des degrés divers. (*OC* II: 576)

The imaginative travel alluded to here is not achieved with the ease assumed by the

Littré definition or that suggested in Gautier's allusion to country-hopping 'pour quelques instants' (1855: 74). Yet Baudelaire is careful to point out that, while not immediate, the experience of transformative cosmopolitanism — a 'grâce divine' — is within reach of everyone, and can be attained through a union of self and object which does not need the guidance of a tutor or pedagogue: this self-directed operation ('il appren[d] de lui-même') is far removed from the kind of formal education About believes necessary for an appreciation of English art. Instead of cloaking his criticism in a 'voile scolaire' (*OC* II: 576), Baudelaire privileges the imagination in order to make comparative art criticism appealing to an audience either lacking, or disillusioned with, classical education. As Murphy glosses (2012: 127–44), Baudelaire's methodology suggests that to engage with and understand the aesthetics of another culture, an inner and subjective transformation must be gone through on the part of the critic. Imaginatively removing him or herself from his or her native environment, the critic adapts to the 'milieu' from which the artwork has come, and in which it no longer seems strange but, rather, natural. The passage clearly abounds with allusions to racial and geographic determinism, but Baudelaire's attempts to go beyond the adjectives of 'étrange' and 'bizarre' nonetheless form a striking contrast to About's more dismissive responses to alternative aesthetics. And despite these allusions, Baudelaire claims that through a process of intimate engagement with foreign aesthetics, a subject's temperament and taste *can* change, with revolutionary results:

> Si, au lieu d'un pédagogue, je prends un homme du monde, un intelligent, et si je le transporte dans une contrée lointaine, je suis sûr que, si les étonnements du débarquement sont grands, si l'accoutumance est plus ou moins longue, plus ou moins laborieuse, la sympathie sera tôt ou tard si vive, si pénétrante, qu'elle créera en lui un monde nouveau d'idées, monde qui fera partie intégrante de lui-même, et qui l'accompagnera, sous la forme de souvenirs, jusqu'à la mort. Ces formes de bâtiments, qui contrariaient d'abord son œil académique [...], ces végétaux inquiétants pour sa mémoire chargée des souvenirs natals, [...] ces odeurs qui ne sont pas celles du boudoir maternel, [...] ces fruits dont le goût trompe et déplace les sens, et révèle au palais des idées qui appartiennent à l'odorat, tout ce monde d'harmonies nouvelles entrera lentement en lui, le pénétrera patiemment, comme la vapeur d'une étuve aromatisée; toute cette vitalité inconnue sera ajoutée à sa vitalité propre, quelques milliers d'idées et de sensations enrichiront son dictionnaire de mortel, et même il est possible que, dépassant la mesure et transformant la justice en révolte, il fasse comme le Sicambre converti, qu'il brûle ce qu'il avait adoré, et qu'il adore ce qu'il avait brûlé. (*OC* II: 576–77)

Baudelaire imagines an instance of real travel, but one which has implications for the critic's virtual journey at the *Exposition universelle*, and elsewhere. Despite an emphasis on labour and longevity, the adoption of foreign sensibilities is, in Baudelaire's hypothesis, a genuine possibility. It might be tempting to read this possibility of change as evidence of a progressive cultural relativism on Baudelaire's part: a rejection of objective or absolute values in the domain of art, and culture more broadly. However, while acknowledging and appreciating artistic diversity, Baudelaire ultimately interprets different aesthetics as fragments of the same 'beauté universelle' which operates above and beyond local difference. Indeed, it is his commitment to universalism which means Baudelaire can at times assert the possibility of intercultural 'accoutumance', but at others deny its very necessity; in 'Richard Wagner', for example, Baudelaire claims that 'rien de ce qui est éternel et universel n'a besoin d'être acclimaté' (*OC* II: 800). In 1855, this scientific lexicon or 'métaphore végétale' (*OC* II: 800) of acclimatisation, drawing on the biological and zoological concerns of the colonial era, is given a lyrical frame.[22] The subjective transformation of artistic taste occurs under the skin, deep within the body. The earliest bond of intimacy foregrounded in Object Relations theory, the bond with the mother, is here explicitly replaced by a new union with the external world which leads to internal changes within the self. The 'homme du monde' must distance himself from the 'souvenirs natals' of the 'boudoir maternel' and immerse himself in a new environment; in sensory language marked with a frisson of the sexual, harmonies of smell, taste, touch, and sight particular to this new climate penetrate the critic's body. This results in a figurative re-birth, independent of the mother, which revitalises the critic, much as sympathetic and silent communion with Spanish art in the *Salon de 1846* enriched the spectator's 'volume des idées générales' (*OC* II: 417). The shock of geographical distance and cultural difference is thus assuaged by the establishment of new intimate attachments.

In this context, impartiality and partiality, detachment and attachment, amount to two sides of the same coin for Baudelaire: impartiality does not necessarily signify a reasoned absence of preference, but rather the capacity to cultivate *new* preferences and worship new divinities. The truly impartial critic has, in Baudelaire's eyes, the capacity to convert: 'Il est possible [...], qu'il brûle ce qu'il avait adoré, et qu'il adore ce qu'il avait brûlé'. In Baudelaire's lexicon, this capacity depends on a quality of openness which is often associated with children. In the *Exposition universelle*, this association is created by the parallel drawn between the impressions and memories of childhood (the 'boudoir maternel') and the new and superior ones instigated by a change in environment. The infantalisation of the critic, and artist, is rendered more explicit in Baudelaire's study of Constantin Guys in *Le Peintre de la vie moderne* [1863]. Guys, an artist 'par nature, très voyageur et très cosmopolite' (*OC* II: 689), is a 'citoyen spirituel de l'univers' who 'veut savoir, comprendre, apprécier tout ce qui se passe à la surface de notre sphéroïde' (*OC* II: 698). For Baudelaire, Guys's exceptional abilities of observation and creation derive from his status as a 'homme-enfant' (*OC* II: 691). Here, childishness is evoked with less ambivalence than when Baudelaire sends Sabatier his *poème intime*, 'Confession', which 'sent horriblement l'enfantillage' (*BC* I: 225). In the context of criticism, to be childlike is not embarrassing but rather enviable, at once suggestive and symbolic of a constant curiosity about the world: the child 'voit tout en *nouveauté*; il est toujours *ivre*' (*OC* II: 690). The child, however, cannot help this state of fascination while, for Baudelaire, wonder and agency combine in the adult to produce genius: 'Le génie n'est que l'*enfance retrouvée à volonté*' (*OC* II: 690).[23] Guys's genius lies in his receptivity to the world around him. In keeping with the definition of cosmopolitanism suggested in the *Exposition universelle*, this receptivity is enabled not by detachment but rather passionate attachment to others at a local, national, and international level. For Baudelaire, Guys is not a dandy, aspiring to insensibility, but rather a subject who seeks to feel for and with all those he meets.[24] A capacity for new attachments is thus vital for the critical encounter, whether this takes place abroad or at home, in the street. Guys's love of crowds — the latter always feminised for Baudelaire — epitomises this capacity:

> La foule est son domaine [...]. Sa passion et sa profession, c'est d'*épouser la foule*. Pour le parfait flâneur, pour l'observateur passionné, c'est une immense jouissance que d'élire domicile dans le nombre, dans l'ondoyant, dans le mouvement, dans le fugitif et l'infini. Être hors de soi, et pourtant se sentir partout chez soi [...]. L'amateur de la vie fait du monde sa famille. (*OC* II: 691–92)

In the Introduction, we saw that Berlant's twentieth-century work on 'minor intimacies' (1998: 285) was concerned with sentimental and sexual ties which fall outside institutional or established frameworks but are, nonetheless, highly significant. For Berlant:

> Intimacy refers to more than that which takes place within the purview of institutions, the state, and an ideal of publicness. What if we saw it emerge from much more mobile processes of attachment? While the fantasies associated with intimacy usually end up occupying the space of convention, in practice the drive towards it is a kind of wild thing that is not necessarily organized that way, or any way. (Berlant 1998: 284)

Berlant's list of alternative intimacies includes 'workers at work, writers and readers, memorizers of songs, [...] listeners to voices who explain things manageably (on the radio, at conferences, on television screens, on line, in therapy), fans and celebrities' (1998: 284–85). In a nineteenth-century context, we could suggest that Baudelaire's art-critical intimacy is itself an alternative form of attachment. The sorts of intimacy which emerge from Baudelaire's art criticism are not literally sexual, romantic, filial, or fraternal: when these particular intersubjective bonds are referred to they operate figuratively, analogically, to communicate an ideal mode of relation between the art-object and the viewing subject. Pre-empting the dialogue of the 1862 prose poem 'L'Étranger', Baudelaire's art criticism imagines a mode of living independent of the inherited or institutional ties of family or *patrie*. The individual with a 'cœur grand comme le monde' (*OC* II: 450) is able to escape the constraints imposed on the physically, psychologically, socially, and geographically bounded body; this individual chooses to '*épouser la foule*' (*OC* II: 691), like Guys, instead of engaging in the institutionally sanctioned intimacy of a conventional marriage. Wishful thinking perhaps, yet voluntary *dépaysement* is imagined as a way of increasing opportunities for intimacy and, given its transformative potential, for a radical yet controlled and *chosen* revitalisation of the self.

This chapter has argued that as a mode of critical engagement rather than an aesthetic category or genre, intimacy becomes a potentially subversive way of making the foreign familiar. By elaborating a brand of cosmopolitanism which foregrounds attachment as a function of detachment, Baudelaire's art criticism suggests that intimacy can engineer encounters with novel ways of being. Baudelaire as an art critic can thus do what Delacroix does as an artist: start with 'l'intelligence intime du sujet' in order to 'en arrache[r] les entrailles' (*OC* II: 432); intimacy is intensified, becoming rebellious and 'wild' (Berlant 1998: 284) instead of comforting or reassuring. Of course, it is impossible to consider Baudelaire's theoretical discussions of cosmopolitanism without thinking of his later experiences in Belgium, discussed in Chapter Four, in which fusion with the host culture is a source of disappointment and disgust, rather than delight. The significance of Baudelaire's experiences in Mauritius and Réunion as a young man is also a moot point. The period left little direct trace on his work: the 'Critique de méthode' may indeed constitute one of the few allusions to it, but even this is uncertain.[25] It is thus in the realm of the imagination that intimacy appears to have the greatest use for Baudelaire as an art critic. It is an aspiration and an ideal which despite, or rather because of, the difficulties associated with realising it in practice, retains its power to compel in principle. This same mechanism emerges in the following chapter, which focuses on the one of the 'minor' intimacies (1998: 24) which Berlant *does* list, above: that between writer and reader. Rather than stress the marginal nature of this form of intimacy, however, Chapter Six presents it as a powerful model for the reading experience in nineteenth-century France, akin to the 'conversation [...] directe' between artist and spectator which Gide sees in operation in Vuillard's paintings (1905: 480). In particular, the chapter will examine the role of real and metaphorical friendship in literary criticism of the era, developing the discussion of partiality begun here. To do so, it takes a chronological step backwards to debates of the July Monarchy era before proceeding to an analysis of Sainte-Beuve's literary-critical 'portraits': a further analogy between visual and verbal worlds.

Notes to Chapter 5

1. For discussion of Bonnard, Vuillard, and post-Impressionist *intimisme*, see Elizabeth Wynne Easton (1989), Guy Cogeval (2002), and Katherine M. Kuenzli (2010). For broader explorations of the concept of intimacy in the context of art history, see Richard Rand (1997), Daniel Arasse (2008), and especially Bogh (2016).
2. See Arasse (2008) for a more recent study of the significance of the detail in Western visual art.
3. In this chapter I refer to 'English artists' and 'England' to maintain consistency with the French primary material, although it should be noted that some of the artists included by the French critics under this designation were in fact Scottish or American.
4. See Patricia Mainardi (1987: 103–07).
5. Edmund Kean and William Macready were English actors of the nineteenth century (*OC* II: 2386, n. 14).
6. In the *Salon de 1859*, Baudelaire reaffirms these ideas: Delacroix 'exprime surtout l'intime du cerveau, l'aspect étonnant des choses, tant son ouvrage garde fidèlement la marque et l'humeur de sa conception. C'est l'infini dans le fini. C'est le rêve!' (*OC* II: 636).
7. See Christopher Parsons and Martha Ward (1986), Neil McWilliam (1991a and 1991b).
8. See Anthony Glinoer (2009). For further discussion of these theories applied to literary criticism, see Raphaël Molho (1963) and Chapter Six.
9. For further analysis of the motif of the *voyage* in nineteenth-century art criticism, see Philippa Lewis (2013).
10. Cf. Bernard Comment (1999: 131). For twentieth-century theoretical work on the concept of

virtual travel, see Paul Virilio (1990) and Christopher Pinney (1992). On virtual travel and realist fiction in Victorian culture, see Alison Byerly (2012).
11. Roger Benjamin (2003: 25).
12. This is an echo of the liberal theories of cosmopolitanism associated in France with Staël and the Coppet circle; see Patrick H. Vincent (2004), Chapter Four.
13. Postcolonial criticism today is also quick to point out contemporary cosmopolitanism's complicity with capitalism. For a summary of recent critical theories of cosmopolitanism or transnationalism twinning it with 'neo-colonialism' see Anderson (2001: 63–65) and Timothy Brennan (1997). Richard Pope describes cosmopolitanism as 'some mystical sort of global citizenry' beholden to global capitalism (2010: 5).
14. See Chambers (1988: 5).
15. See Jeannine Baticle (2003) and Alisa Luxenberg (2008) for detailed histories of the *Musée espagnol*.
16. Gary Tinterow (2003: 37).
17. As with the English display, the *Musée espagnol* is the subject of a possible article for Baudelaire; see the notes already mentioned: 'Musées disparus/Musées à créer: musées espagnol, anglais etc.' (*BC* I: 449).
18. On the idea of coherent 'national schools' in the nineteenth century, see Natalia Majluf (1997: 871–72).
19. See Mainardi (1987) and Majluf (1997).
20. See Frank Anderson Trapp (1965: 300).
21. On French critical responses to the foreign 'schools', see Mainardi (1987), Chapter Ten.
22. On nineteenth-century French debates surrounding acclimatisation, see David N. Livingstone (1999) and Michael A. Osborne (2000).
23. On links between childhood and genius, with reference to Baudelaire and Freud, see Damian Catani (2013).
24. Pope (2010) further elucidates points of comparison and contrast between the dandy and the *flâneur*.
25. For biographical information concerning Baudelaire's journey to the Indian Ocean, see Pichois and Ziegler (1987), Chapter Nine, and Françoise Lionnet (1998).

CHAPTER 6

Literary Criticism and the Rhetoric of Friendship

Est-ce de la critique que nous faisons en esquissant ces portraits?
SAINTE-BEUVE, 'Madame de Charrière'[1]

In contemporary literary theory, we are more likely to hear the critic described as a lover than a friend. 'What does it mean to fall in love with a writer?' ask Eve Kosofsky Sedgwick and Adam Frank in their preface to the Tomkins reader (1995: 23). They continue: 'Some of what we're up to is the ordinary literary-critical lover's discourse: we want to propagate among readers nodes of reception for what we take to be an unfamiliar and highly exciting set of moves and tonalities' (1995: 23). This language is emblematic of a tendency within post-Freudian literary theory to describe readerly engagement with a text in erotic terms; for Sedgwick and Frank, the 'literary-critical lover' and his or her Barthesian *discours amoureux* have become 'ordinary'. Within the domain of structuralist and post-structuralist thought, Ross Chambers's notion of 'narrative seduction' (1984) draws on Barthes's concepts of *plaisir* and *jouissance*; for the queer theorist Joseph Boone, as Felski glosses, close reading is 'about intoxication rather than detachment, rapture rather than disinterestedness. [...] A yielding that is not abject or humiliating, but ecstatic and erotically charged' (2008: 51). This chapter shifts the historical parameters of this contemporary critical tendency, turning away from the twentieth- and twenty-first-century figure of the literary-critical lover towards the nineteenth-century figure of the literary-critical friend. Bringing together strands of thought which have been woven throughout the book, it focuses in a more sustained fashion on the pertinence and potency of intimacy as a model for literary criticism in nineteenth-century France. A conceptualisation of the critical process in terms of sympathetic interpersonal relationships was current in journalistic literary criticism of the July Monarchy and Second Empire, but articulated in terms of friendship and affection rather than erotic love or sexual delight. Such terms are rarely employed in professional criticism today. Faced with a journalist questioning the sympathetic qualities of her novel's protagonist in April 2013, for example, the writer Claire Messud replied, with some frustration, that 'if you're reading to find friends, you're in deep trouble. [...] The relevant question isn't "is this a potential friend for me?"'.[2] Within twentieth and twenty-first-century interpretative paradigms, such a question is, arguably, something of a category mistake. Yet within the culture of intimacy which operated, as this book has been arguing, in nineteenth-century France, the question of whether writers or protagonists were potential friends *was* a relevant question for readers and critics. And this, in turn, highlights larger social and cultural debates in the period concerning the value of friendship, criticism, and indeed reading.

To rephrase Sedgwick and Frank's question, then, what did it mean for a literary critic to *befriend* a writer in nineteenth-century France? The detrimental effect of certain sorts of friendship between authors and critics — Baudelaire's 'camaraderies effrontées' (*OC* II: 351) — was the subject of fierce polemic throughout the late Restoration and July Monarchy period; influential articles by Henri Latouche and Gustave Planche on the culture of the *cénacle* emphatically denied the possibility of reconciling literary-critical friendships with constructive, independent criticism. But a nuancing of these convictions can be found in the historical literary 'portraits' penned by Sainte-Beuve in the 1830s and 1840s in which *amitié* comes to operate as a textually articulated figure for the critical process.[3] Proust's reservations about Sainte-Beuve's criticism, in part responsible for the neglect of the latter in the twentieth century, rest on what he saw as its fundamental confusion of the 'moi profond' and the 'moi social'; discussing Sainte-Beuve's evaluation of Stendhal, for example, Proust asks: 'En quoi le fait d'avoir été l'ami de Stendhal permet-il de le mieux juger? Il est probable, au contraire, que cela gênerait beaucoup pour cela. Le moi qui produit les œuvres est offusqué pour ces camarades par l'autre' (1971: 222). However, to dismiss the rhetoric of friendship adopted by Sainte-Beuve in his literary portraits as necessarily misguided is to overlook his keen awareness of the privileged and indeed profitable place that the ideal of intimacy held for French readers of the nineteenth century. Whether or not it corresponds with our contemporary understandings of literature or selfhood, the rhetoric of friendship was undeniably productive for Sainte-Beuve, providing him with a means of gaining and claiming knowledge of his subject, and a means of attracting a readership. Viewed in this more generous way, Sainte-Beuve's literary portraits appear less rooted in critical confusion, and more alive to the social, or para-social, contexts in which literature can be created and consumed.

I. *Camaraderie* and Criticism

What is the role of friendship in the critical process? How critical can, or should, friends be with each other? Moreover, how critical should *criticism* be? Still asked today, these questions, straddling the domains of the social, professional, and ethical, fuelled intense debate in the pages of the nineteenth-century press.[4] Throughout the nineteenth century, literary criticism in France was undergoing an intense period of self-definition and self-justification. Less established than art or theatre criticism, it was dispersed across a range of media, written and oral (academic lectures both performed and published, books and pamphlets, newspaper articles), and adopted a variety of forms and styles: the brief mention in the *causerie* or the 'round-up'; the review of an individual work or *œuvre*; the literary portrait of the author.⁵ Critics were keen to elaborate on such differences and produced competing typologies of criticism which identified key trends in the period, often in reality more prescriptive than descriptive.⁶ Historians of literary criticism tend to follow suit, each producing his or her own typology of criticism to help the present-day reader map the critical terrain.⁷ For our purposes, Raphaël Molho's 1963 narrative of nineteenth-century literary criticism makes a useful distinction between the Romantic *critique des beautés* or *critique d'admiration* — already alluded to in relation to Baudelaire's art criticism — and the opposing vein of dogmatic or 'judgemental' criticism. As outlined in Chapter Five, 'admiring criticism', practised by Staël, Chateaubriand, and Hugo, amongst others, held that criticism with a default position of sympathy and enthusiasm was necessary for an appreciation of the increasing diversity of artistic approaches which blossomed with Romanticism. In contrast to the restrictive didacticism of the pre-Revolutionary period, *la critique d'admiration* aimed to understand works on their own terms rather than judge them according to pre-determined, often neo-classical, criteria: 'J'admire tout, comme une brute' writes Hugo in *William Shakespeare* (1864: 371). The opposing strand of criticism, whose practitioners included Planche, Nisard, and Barbey d'Aurevilly, was fundamentally hostile to this approach. As writers who conceived of criticism with a capital 'C' (what Barbey d'Aurevilly calls 'la Critique, cette grande chose de mesure et de poids, de principes et de certitude'), many were suspicious of reviewers who seemed only too happy to abandon their own system of values and principles in favour of those of the author.⁸

Concerns surrounding the culture of *la critique d'admiration* fed into an extended debate about literary sociability, launched by Latouche's polemical 'De la camaraderie littéraire' in the *Revue de Paris* on 11 October 1829.⁹ This debate concerned the close-knit relations between authors and critics in the *cénacle*. As discussed in Chapter One, the *cénacle* referred to an increasingly controversial social space in which a select group of individuals (generally men), affiliated with the same artistic movement, came together on a regular basis to talk and collaborate in a private setting 'propice à l'échange intime'.¹⁰ Throughout the 1820s, the *cénacle* was associated with Romanticism, and writers including Charles Nodier, Vigny, and Hugo, as well as Sainte-Beuve: opposition to cenacular culture thus often came from individuals hostile to the Romantic movement itself. Yet by the start of the July Monarchy, even those who had originally supported this continuation of aristocratic *salon* culture were beginning to turn against it. Glinoer (2008) reads this reaction as a result of the emerging 'personality cult' surrounding Hugo, the extension of the *cénacle* to 'undesirables', and the de-territorialisation brought about by public lectures and the infamous theatre battles of *Hernani*, all of which irrevocably altered the once-intimate atmosphere of the *cénacle*. Latouche's attack, however, is focused specifically on friendship as practised by the *cénacle* community, a bond which he describes as 'une des calamités de notre époque littéraire' (2008: 53). Honoré de Balzac's *Illusions perdues* may construct a binary opposition between the 'true' friendships of the *Cénacle de la rue des Quatre-Vents* and the hypocritical ones found in the world of journalism, but Latouche identifies a degradation of the bond across all spaces of literary sociability. His article paints a picture of faulty friendship in which true *amitié* — which should, above all, be honest — has descended into *camaraderie*, a weak and opportunistic, often self-serving, bond premised on superficial mutual appreciation, which is essentially unhelpful for the author: 'L'amitié qui loue: n'est-ce pas une dérision? ne serait-ce pas plutôt [...] une trahison véritable?' (2008: 58). Latouche attacks what he sees as the 'draguées de la critique' (2008: 54) and argues for a less flattering, but more constructive, mode of criticism which will ultimately improve the quality of French literary productions; a professional modification which demands an alteration in interpersonal practices.

Seven years later, Planche's 'Les Amitiés littéraires' [1836] draws similar conclusions regarding the possibility of friendship between critics and authors, yet with a different focus and emotional tenor, closer to nostalgia than polemic. The article, often read as a thinly veiled account of Planche's friendship with Hugo, begins by evoking an idyllic vision of a friendship between writer and critic. Planche suggests that, in the early stages of their mutual careers, writer and critic live together:

> Dans une intime familiarité, [ils] s'instruisent mutuellement et agrandissent chaque jour le champ de leur pensée. [...] Dans cette involontaire initiation, chacun donne et reçoit dans la même mesure; celui qui se montre et celui qui regarde, celui qui interroge et celui qui répond, s'enrichissent dans une proportion égale. (Planche 1853b: 279–80)

Reciprocity and equality are both preconditions and products of the 'intime familiarité' in which the interdependent writer and critic live and grow together. Yet this harmonious union is only described by Planche in such idealised terms for the fall, when it comes, to be all the greater. As the author in Planche's narrative begins to experience public success, the power balance shifts, as do his expectations and desires. The successful author, Planche suggests, becomes increasingly accustomed to the praise of the public and increasingly hostile to the honest criticism of his friend. And if honesty is no longer tenable, the friendship between the writer and critic must be — or rather, already has been — terminated:

> Dès que l'égalité fraternelle a cessé, dès que les deux intelligences, unies autrefois par une intimité de tous les instants, n'ont plus les mêmes droits et les mêmes devoirs, l'amitié n'est plus qu'une parole vide, qu'un nom sonore et menteur. (Planche 1853b: 296)

For both Latouche and Planche, the social reality and complicating factors of maintaining close bonds in the literary field make friendship incompatible with the practice of criticism. If the critic is to preserve his professional integrity, he must abandon any attempt to reconcile it with personal sympathies: the latter just as, if not more, problematic than the literary antipathies alluded to by Baudelaire in his 1846 'Conseils aux jeunes littérateurs' (*OC* II: 15–16). Sainte-Beuve was, of course, also aware of these problems: his initial involvement with, and subsequent disassociation from, the communitarian culture of the Romantic *cénacle* has been well documented; indeed, Glinoer writes that 'nul n'a vécu [...] la fin du Cénacle, plus douloureusement que Sainte-Beuve, parce que nul sans doute n'y avait plus investi, affectivement et institutionnellement' (2008: 130). Yet, claiming in 1832 that some of Latouche's concerns were exaggerated (*PL*: 295), Sainte-Beuve demonstrates a reluctance to abandon the role of friendship in the literary-critical process entirely. Rather than advocate a firmly impersonal criticism, we see Sainte-Beuve channel his 'affective investments' away from the contemporary *cénacle* and towards a figurative literary community, particularly visible in the historical literary portraits he published in the *Revue des deux mondes* between 1830 and 1845.[11]

II. Sainte-Beuve Befriends the Writer

The Consolations of Friendship

Sainte-Beuve was by no means the sole practitioner of the literary 'portrait' in the first half of the nineteenth century. For literary historians, the burgeoning 'portraitomanie', to use Hélène Dufour's term (1997: 3), of the period reflects a general personalisation of literary culture and, more specifically, an increasingly personal mode of biographical literary criticism.[12] In contrast to the dry *notice littéraire* of earlier criticism or the superficial *éloge académique*, the portrait encouraged an interest in the writer as much as his or her work, chiming with a growing move to conceive of the writer as an individual 'genius' rather than a copyist, craftsman, or rhetorical practitioner, as was typical in previous eras.[13] 'C'est le portrait de l'homme du quotidien, privé et familier, du génie ou du héros dans leur fragilité et leur humanité, qui intéresse le XIXe siècle', writes Dufour (1997: 190). This move was exciting and liberating, but simultaneously subversive and often controversial; in his list of nineteenth-century *antibiographistes*, Diaz includes philosophers, historians, and social humanitarians, all of whom deny that 'l'"homme" [...] puisse être l'explication de l'œuvre' (2011: 121–22). Despite these attacks, the popularity of the literary portrait persisted: testimony to what Patricia Meyer Spacks has referred to as the 'universal hunger to penetrate other lives' (1986: 93). Spacks's 'universal' might be contested here (the desire is surely greater or lesser at different historical moments, and felt differently by different individuals), but it is clear that personal reader-writer relationships *had* existed before: Michel de Montaigne's response to the writing of Seneca and Plutarch, for example, is such that he can talk of 'la familiarité que j'ay avec ces personnages icy' (1978: 721); 'familiarité' translated as 'intimacy' in Screech's English translation (1991: 817). Moreover, in his essay 'De l'amitié', it is Étienne de La Boétie as an author whom Montaigne befriends first: his writing 'me donna la première connoissance de son nom, acheminant ainsi cette amitié que nous avons nourrie' (1978: 184). However, Montaigne's response appears as a more isolated incident in contrast with the 'portraitomania' of the nineteenth century. The reader-writer relationship actively encouraged by the nineteenth-century literary machinery simultaneously incited and fed the reader's appetite for intimacy at a time when, as historians of friendship have shown, friendship was a highly prized and exemplary moral bond, in principle if not always in practice. As Diaz writes, nineteenth-century readers felt an increasing desire to 'connaître le grand écrivain dans son intérieur, [...] de l'approcher, de l'avoir pour ami' (2011: 85–86): the author, increasingly personalised and accessible, was becoming a new individual to 'befriend'. Here, however, Diaz is talking of the 'casual' reader. How did critics, as special, professional sorts of readers, address this impulse to befriend, both with regard to their audience's reading habits, and their own? How, for example, did Sainte-Beuve make sense of and legitimise it in the wake of the controversies surrounding contemporary literary sociability?

Glinoer's concept of 'affective investments' (2008: 130), alluded to earlier, offers us an initial way to articulate Sainte-Beuve's attempt to maintain friendship in the professional realm. Sainte-Beuve himself spoke of his critical approach as a combination of penchant and method, and Glinoer's phrase encapsulates this interplay between emotion and economics, sincerity and strategy, the personal and the professional.[14] The decision to redirect affection, albeit one-sided or imaginary, towards historical literary figures is one way in which Sainte-Beuve compensates for the lost consolatory qualities of community life in the *cénacle*. A subject of much of his work of the 1830s, Sainte-Beuve's creative and critical writing presents the *cénacle* as a safe and comforting haven for writers away from a hostile, tumultuous, and mercenary society, a trope perpetuated in Balzac's portrayal of the Restoration *cénacle* in *Illusions perdues*. For Sainte-Beuve, poetry is typically indicative of weakness or vulnerability on the part of its writer ('C'est un faible en ce monde que la poésie; c'est souvent une plaie secrète qui demande une main légère' (*PL*: 299)), and when this initial weakness is coupled with the increasing uncertainty of the poet's public place in society, the need for the consolations and compensations of the *cénacle* grows even greater. In 'Des soirées littéraires', Sainte-Beuve explains how the vulnerable:

> Ont senti le besoin de se rallier, de s'entendre à l'avance, et de préluder quelque temps à l'abri de cette société orageuse qui grondait alentour. *Ces sortes d'intimités* [...] *consolent*, elles soutiennent dans les commencements, et à une certaine saison de la vie des poètes, contre l'indifférence du dehors. (*PL*: 297, my emphasis)

In the verse poem 'Le Cénacle', from *Vie, poésies et pensées de Joseph Delorme,* this consolatory space is evoked through the material and sentimental signifiers of intimacy:

> Puis, les soirs quelquefois, loin des moqueurs barbares,
> Entre soi converser, compter les voix trop rares
> Et se donner la main;
>
> Et là, le fort qui croit, le faible qui chancelle,
> Le cœur qu'un feu nourrit, le cœur qu'une étincelle
> Traverse par instants;
> L'âme qu'un rayon trouble et qu'une goutte enivre,
> Et l'œil de chérubin qui lit comme un livre
> Aux soleils éclatants;
>
> Tous réunis, s'entendre, et s'aimer, et se dire:
> Ne désespérons point, poètes, de la lyre,
> Car le siècle est à nous. (Sainte-Beuve 1863b: 68)

However, as we have seen, these initially comforting 'sortes d'intimités' can become problematic. In the wake of his increasing disillusionment with the *cénacle*, we see Sainte-Beuve transfer his attention away from relationships with his cenacular contemporaries and towards the para-social, vicarious 'sortes d'intimités' possible with writers from the past. While the approach of the critic Nisard insists on, and relishes, the distance which separates him from the objects of his historical study ('Notre amour-propre [...] se tait devant cette distance infinie qui nous sépare des hommes supérieurs; le commerce de ces hommes accoutume à la modestie et apprend le respect' (1847: 385)), Sainte-Beuve's July Monarchy portraits aim to abolish temporal distance and enter into a more intimate 'commerce' with his chosen writers. For Baudelaire, intimacy was a state which enabled criticism across and between nations; here, it is used by Sainte-Beuve to transcend historical boundaries. Elucidating the critic's increasingly nationalistic conception of literature, Prendergast states that Sainte-Beuve 'carried French literature around in his head as a vast echo chamber, permitting all manner of varyingly probable filiations and associations. [...] No anxiety of influence here, but, precisely, a set of "conversational" exchanges within a perceived continuum of discourse' (2007: 8–9). Another way to conceive of this discursive 'echo chamber' would be to see it as a form of what John L. Caughey (1984), in a twentieth-century context, has called an 'imaginary social world'. As with all forms of para-social relation, these fantasy worlds (involving celebrities, for example, or characters from television series) often provide the subject with 'complementary attachments' which reaffirm and enhance actual attachments in his or her primary social group (by functioning, for instance, as shared cultural reference points). An imaginary social world, however, can also provide 'compensatory' attachments, a mechanism which sheds light on Sainte-Beuve's critical practice at this time; as Loïc Chotard proposes, succinctly: 'Plus il [Sainte-Beuve] se sent coupé de ses contemporains, plus il développe une conception communautaire [de la littérature]' (2000: 61).

The compensatory, and therapeutic, function of the historical portrait criticism is particularly evident in Sainte-Beuve's portrait of Diderot, first published in the *Revue des deux mondes* on 26 June 1831, a year before his article on the consolations of the *roman intime* in the same journal. Here, Sainte-Beuve introduces the reader to his critical methodology, conceived of as a process of gradual emotional attachment to the writer in question with, he suggests, parallels with the craft of the portrait painter or sculptor. After amassing a range of biographical and personal material concerning the writer (correspondence, biographies, and anecdotes), the critic:

> S'enferme pendant une quinzaine de jours avec les écrits d'un mort célèbre, poëte ou philosophe; on l'étudie, on le retourne, on l'interroge à loisir; on le fait poser devant soi; c'est presque si on passait quinze jours à la campagne à faire le portrait ou le buste de Byron, de Scott, de Goethe; seulement on est plus à l'aise avec son modèle, et le tête-à-tête, en même temps qu'il exige un peu plus d'attention, comporte beaucoup plus de familiarité. [...] Au type vague, abstrait, général, qu'une première vue avait embrassé, se mêle et s'incorpore par degrés une réalité individuelle, précise, de plus en plus accentuée et vivement scintillante; on sent naître, on voit venir la ressemblance; et le jour, le moment

où l'on a saisi le tic familier, le sourire révélateur, la gerçure indéfinissable, la ride intime et douloureuse qui se cache en vain sous les cheveux déjà clairsemés, — à ce moment l'analyse disparaît dans la création, le portrait parle et vit, on a trouvé l'homme. (*PL*: 166)

Alongside the notion of procreation at work in this passage ('on sent naître, on voit venir la ressemblance; [...] l'analyse disparaît dans la création') is the rhetoric of intimacy; as Dufour herself observes, ' "l'intime" — "l'intimité" — est l'un des mots clés de la technique du portrait chez Sainte-Beuve et ses successeurs' (1997: 190). Here, both the social practice of the *tête-à-tête*, and the process of sculpting a bust, which, as we saw in Chapter Five, Baudelaire labels an 'art plus intime' (*OC* II: 489), become metaphors for the critical process. Initially alluding to a close study or analysis of Diderot as mediated through his writing, the imaginative faculties of the critic come to clothe or 'flesh out' the text: criticism performs an imagined meeting between minds and bodies (a meeting which is, Sainte-Beuve qualifies, significantly more relaxed on paper than it would be in person). Indeed, the body is central to the way in which closeness is envisaged in this passage, and to how Sainte-Beuve evokes the gestures and reassuring sense of presence which accompany the physical proximity of a loved one. In his preface to the *Portraits contemporains*, Sainte-Beuve uses the language of touch to describe the sensitive nature of criticism. Citing lines from 'l'aimable Horace', Sainte-Beuve affirms that, as a critic, one should take care to 'se jouer autour du cœur de ceux même qu'on caresse, et montrer qu'on sait les endroits où l'on ne veut pas appuyer' (*PC*: 56). The immediacy and intensity of this imagined relation with the writer utterly absorbs the critic, allowing him to ignore, at least momentarily, the world outside. While there is, Sainte-Beuve claims, 'plaisir en tout temps à ces sortes d'études secrètes' (*PL*: 166), these pleasures are heightened, and perhaps best appreciated, in times of insecurity:

> En nous prenant cette fois à Diderot philosophe et artiste, en le suivant de près dans son intimité attrayante, en le voyant dire, en l'écoutant penser aux heures les plus familières, nous y avons gagné du moins, outre la connaissance d'un grand homme de plus, d'oublier pendant quelques jours l'affligeant spectacle de la société environnante, tant de misère et de turbulence dans les masses, un si vague effroi, un si dévorant égoïsme dans les classes élevées, les gouvernements sans idées ni grandeur, des nations héroïques qu'on immole, le sentiment de patrie qui se perd et que rien de plus large ne remplace, la religion retombée dans l'arène d'où elle a le monde à reconquérir, et l'avenir de plus en plus nébuleux, recélant un rivage qui n'apparaît pas encore. (*PL*: 167–68)

The Insights of Intimacy

The attractions and effects of intimacy as a social practice find, therefore, their textual analogue in the process of crafting, and subsequently reading, the literary portrait. Yet, befriending does more than provide affective consolation, or rather, the emotional benefits of befriending can be seen to engender cognitive rewards too, upsetting the modern, albeit increasingly contested, twinning of intellectual work with emotional detachment. Discussing the genre of biography in her study of gossip, Spacks argues that the 'biographical story-teller' must convince the reader of his or her 'right and power to control the story'; she adds that 'authority does not necessarily derive from the preservation of great height [...]; the narrator may claim, rather, the special awareness of intimacy' (1986: 93). Given the heavily biographical nature of Sainte-Beuve's literary criticism, this same need to assert and justify authority would seem to apply. Sainte-Beuve certainly attempts to use the 'special awareness of intimacy' to legitimise his studies of contemporary writers (to Proust's dismay); introducing the *Portraits contemporains*, he writes: 'Les noms les plus célèbres du jour s'y pressent: j'ai eu affaire à la plupart d'entre eux, d'assez près et plus d'une fois' (*PC*: 55). Yet such claims are problematic: Chotard (2000: 68) has discussed Alexandre Vinet's denial of friendship with Sainte-Beuve, despite the latter's assertion of it; and, as we have seen, many critics considered personal friendship something to be sacrificed, not advertised, for the sake of professional integrity. In his historical portraits, however, Sainte-Beuve's figurative approach enables him to benefit both professionally *and* personally from the powers of partiality, without the added complications surrounding contemporary literary sociability. The imaginary bond of friendship takes the place of the real bond, but fulfils the same function: to convince the reader that the critic has a special claim to closeness with the writer and has, by extension, the authority to speak. When dealing with historical subject matter — already temporally distant from the critic, and reader — it seems that affection and awareness can add to, rather than detract from, one another.

The reciprocal, symbiotic increase in emotion and knowledge is evoked in Sainte-Beuve's 1839 portrait of the eighteenth-century writer Isabelle de Charrière, already alluded to in Chapter One (and typically referred to as Madame de Charrière). Here, Sainte-Beuve describes the affection born of the effort to familiarise himself with an author from the past:

> Il résulte de ce soin même et de ce premier mystère de notre étude avec eux, que nous les aimons, et qu'il s'en répand un reflet de nous à eux, une teinte qui donne à l'ensemble de leur figure une certaine émotion. (*PF*: 490)

Introducing Mme de Charrière as the object of his study, he adds: 'Et voici un [nom] encore vers lequel le hasard nous a conduit, et auquel une connaissance suivie nous a attaché' (*PF*: 490). This gradual growth of feeling was one of the ways in which friendship could be distinguished from romantic love in the period. Sainte-Beuve's essay on Montaigne and La Boétie recalls La Bruyère's words that 'l'amour [...] naît brusquement, sans autre réflexion, par tempérament ou par faiblesse: un trait de beauté nous fixe, nous détermine. L'amitié, au contraire, se forme peu à peu, avec le temps, par la pratique, par un long commerce' (Sainte-Beuve 2003: 163). While Sainte-Beuve presents Montaigne and La Boétie as an exception to this rule (they fall subject to what he classifies as 'l'amitié-passion'), this understanding of friendship is exemplified by Sainte-Beuve's own critical practice which, through a long period of 'commerce' with the author in question and increasing 'connaissance', results in a bond of deep affection.[15] This process is reaffirmed in his preface to the *Portraits contemporains*:

> J'ai commencé par admirer pleinement, naïvement, ceux que j'aimais surtout à contempler et à pénétrer, et qui se déployaient d'eux-mêmes sous mon regard; ma curiosité se mêlait d'émotion à mesure que j'entrais plus avant dans chaque talent digne d'être étudié et connu. (*PC*: 55–56)

In Sainte-Beuve's 1831 portrait, the borders between the personal and the professional appear decidedly hazy, as do the borders between the critical subject (Sainte Beuve) and object (Mme de Charrière). Sainte-Beuve makes no gesture towards objectivity or impartiality, acknowledging that the image of Mme de Charrière which his criticism evokes is inevitably coloured by his fondness for her. In this, Sainte-Beuve can be seen to share in Michelet's belief in the scholarly advantages of affection, itself redolent of the Romantic *critique d'admiration*. In the 1869 preface to his *Histoire de France*, Michelet writes that, for the historian, 'en pénétrant l'objet de plus en plus, on l'aime, et dès lors on regarde avec un intérêt croissant. Le cœur ému à la seconde vue, voit mille choses invisibles au peuple indifférent. L'histoire, l'historien, se mêlent en ce regard' (1974: 14). In Sainte-Beuve's criticism, Michelet's *mélange* of history and historian, critical object and critical subject, is enacted at the textual level. Through his use of stylistic assimilation and pastiche — what he calls linguistic 'metamorphosis' — Sainte-Beuve clothes himself in the language of the writer; befriending ends in a stylistic becoming. Writing in his private notebooks, published posthumously in 1925 as *Mes Poisons*, he claims:

> La critique est pour moi une métamorphose: je tâche de disparaître dans le personnage que je reproduis. Je me fais à lui, même par le style, j'emprunte et je revêts sa diction: sentimental et à plaisir nuageux avec Mme de Krüdner, légèrement abstrait et serré avec M. Vinet, clair et courant à la façon dix-huitième siècle avec Mme de Charrière. C'est là que je vise. (Sainte-Beuve 1945: 126)

Moreover, in his 1851 'Nouveaux documents sur Montaigne', Sainte-Beuve describes Montaigne's style and finishes, with *faux* suprise: 'Mais voilà que, pour le définir, je suis presque amené à parler comme lui' (2003: 149).[16] The etiquette manual *La Politesse française* includes a nineteenth-century definition of friendship from Alphonse Karr: 'L'amitié ne doit pas être un pacte mais une assimilation; on ne doit pas prendre un ami, on doit devenir lui' (Muller 1861: 42). While the doomed critic-writer friendship sketched out by Planche was based on a (broken) pact between two complementary but fully individuated and autonomous beings, Sainte-Beuve's rhetoric foregrounds a critical persona with a more porous and protean conception of self, which allows for the kind of transformation advocated by Karr. This, in turn, allows Sainte-Beuve to envisage — and perform — a variety of interactions with writers, working according to a model of friendship in which it is critical interdependence, not independence, which is prized.

Intimacy and Enmity

Sainte-Beuve did not only produce literary portraits: he was often the object of them too. Planche's 1834 study of Sainte-Beuve appropriates the critic's rhetoric of metamorphosis: emphasising the figure of friendship, Planche describes the way in which, 'à force de contempler son nouvel ami, il [Sainte-Beuve] se transforme en lui; il se met à vivre de sa vie' (1853a: 274). Planche's words show that critics of the time actively recognised Sainte-Beuve's method of 'befriending'; they can also be read as Planche's own attempt at the stylistic assimilation of Sainte-Beuve's lexicon. Yet appropriation can be nuanced by more or less underhand critique.[17] Many were troubled by the implications of a protean or malleable conception of self: as we have seen, the possibility of uncontrollable influence by, or contamination from, others (the flip side of sympathy) was a major source of anxiety in the century. At times, Planche equates Sainte-Beuve's excessive adaptability or 'mobilité' (1853a: 273) with impiety, negatively coding the virtual voyage which, as we saw in Chapter Five, Baudelaire prized so highly:

> Chacune de ses biographies qu'il étudie lui devient, pour quelques semaines, un monde de prédilection, une atmosphère préférée où il respire à pleins poumons [...]. Chacune de ses études est un véritable voyage. Il nous revient de ses lectures aventureuses comme d'une course lointaine; il secoue de ses pieds le sable des rivages ignorés; il rapporte à la main la tige des plantes inconnues qu'il a cueillies sur sa route. Aussi ne faut-il pas s'étonner si, comme tous les voyageurs, il s'imprègne des mœurs et des passions des peuples qu'il a visités, s'il lui arrive de vanter tour à tour les temples de Bombay, de Memphis et d'Athènes, et de confesser tant de religions qu'on le prendrait pour un impie.
> (Planche 1853a: 273)

At other points, the analogy with impregnation ('il s'imprègne des mœurs') is extended, and Sainte-Beuve's critical approach is read explicitly as 'feminine'. For Planche, 'il étudie avec le cœur, comme les femmes; il se livre comme elles pour obtenir' (1853a: 274). While intimacy was frequently gendered as feminine, but nonetheless privileged, in a number of nineteenth-century contexts, the apparently female propensity to *abandon* or passive self-surrender ('se livrer') could become problematic in the field of criticism. Barbey d'Aurevilly's vitriolic attack, 'Sainte-Beuve', published shortly after Sainte-Beuve's death in 1869, further develops Planche's analogy between Sainte-Beuve's criticism and female corporeality. For Barbey, Sainte-Beuve is the 'chameleon critic': 'Sainte-Beuve, comme les femmes, et comme les actrices deux fois femmes, porte le reflet des personnalités qu'il avoisine; [...]. Il est le caméléon des œuvres qu'il étudie et qu'il scrute, mais c'est tout... Il n'outrepasse jamais cette nuance. Il *s'imprègne*' (1966b: 152, my emphasis). Barbey draws on the cultural tendency to perpetuate conceptions of female difference, often inferiority, through a focus on the body. As Matlock (1994) has shown, nineteenth-century medical discourse saw in hysteria, a condition associated predominantly with women, an exacerbation of what made women essentially different from men: differences which included impressionability and hypersensitivity.[18] When transferred to the reading context, this highly impressionable sense of self made female readers more suggestible than their male counterparts, and thus more subject to the dangers of readerly 'contagion'. Barbey's highly antagonistic attitude towards female writers in the literary sphere, overtly expressed in *Les Bas-Bleus* [1877], applies equally to Sainte-Beuve's critical endeavour.[19] The *Portraits de femmes* certainly testify to Sainte-Beuve's enthusiasm for the work of female writers, and he did at times actively, and positively, self-style himself as life-giver. Yet Barbey d'Aurevilly takes this analogy and subverts it according to his own misogynistic agenda, using it to degrade the critic in the eyes of posterity. In Barbey's rhetoric, Sainte-Beuve does not actively create his criticism, but is instead passively 'impregnated' with and by the author, like the body of the bestial — and not celestial — woman.[20]

One further way to explain such unsympathetic reactions to Sainte-Beuve's approach is to see them in the context of the emerging literary-critical profession, which was struggling to define itself, and was frequently accused of corruption and bias.[21] Subject to what Bourdieu has called the 'subordination structurale' (1992: 76) of the market (the power of sales, profits, positions), professional critics in the nineteenth century strove to assert what authority they could within the literary field and thus legitimise their place within it. Sainte-Beuve's apparent willingness to abdicate his own style, language, and viewpoint to that of the writer (his 'self-effacing submission to the voice of the other' (Prendergast 2007: 8)) might be seen to sit uneasily with, or even undermine, this project, throwing the originality and necessity of the critical voice into question. Yet, if we reconsider Sainte-Beuve's professed twinning of penchant and method ('Ç'a été à la fois, s'il m'est permis de le dire, un penchant et une méthode' (*PC*: 55)), we can see that his decision to foreground the affective and (para-)social dimensions of reading might be at once pleasurable for him, and useful: a strategy devised to enhance the popularity and indeed influence of the critic. For Chambers, 'to tell a story is to exercise power' (1984: 50). This power is not innate, however, but must be earned by the narrator: 'The maintenance of narrative authority implies an act of seduction, and a certain transfer of interest (on the narratee's part) from the information content to the narrating instance itself' (1984: 51). The critic, as a special kind of storyteller, must earn the right to narrate too and thus, using Chambers's language, also needs to 'seduce' his or her readership (another example of the twentieth-century critic preferring the lexicon of sexuality to that of friendship). Indeed, the need is perhaps even more urgent for the critic given the potential resistance by both writers and readers to critical encroachments into the literary sphere: if the reader wonders why he or she should read a writer's story, the question of why he or she should read a critic's story *about* this story — why the intimacy of the writer-reader dyad needs to be triangulated by the critic — poses itself even more insistently.

Instrumental Intimacies

Aside from the added insights and authority which friendship can bring, Sainte-Beuve's use of the trope is employed to engineer the 'seduction' which operates in literature and, by extension, literary criticism. While Sainte-Beuve's portraits were later gathered together into volumes, they were initially published in the press: a space where the language of intimacy wielded not simply affective charge, but also symbolic and economic power. Melmoux-Montaubin writes that much nineteenth-century journalism at once created and responded to an 'exigence de familiarité' (2004: 482): journalists worked at cultivating a friendly, light-hearted, and flattering tone to appeal to the reader. The hope was that this would create an affective bond or attachment, ensuring the reader's loyalty towards the newspaper in an increasingly crowded marketplace. Corinne Saminadayar-Perrin links this familiar tone ('la connivence et l'intimité avec le lecteur') to journalism's decision to fashion itself as the rightful inheritor of the eighteenth-century *salon* and 'l'art ancien de la conversation' (2007: 169), considered by many nineteenth-century social commentators to have been lost in modern times. Certainly, Sainte-Beuve's portraits and *causeries* of the period show an awareness of criticism as an act: an awareness that his para-social interactions with writers of the past occur within the larger context of his interactions with present-day readers in the form of an ongoing conversation mediated through the pages of the press.[22] In his portrait of Sainte-Beuve, Barbey d'Aurevilly admits that the latter had successfully 'séduit le dix-neuvième siècle' thanks to his 'vivacité d'impression, l'imagination *coloriante*, la sensibilité nerveuse, [...] l'anecdote, l'amusette' (1966b: 151), qualities and techniques which are, for Barbey, highly superficial and, consequently, an indictment of the century at large. Barbey's critique suggests, implicitly, that much as Sainte-Beuve as a critic responds sentimentally to his authors, his own writing produces sentimental responses in his readers (undeservedly, in Barbey's eyes). It is the former phenomenon which, I suggest, partly results in the latter. According to Sainte-Beuve's 1832 discussion of Délécluze's *Mademoiselle Justine de Liron*, it is the eponymous heroine's ability to love which in turn makes her lovable to readers of the novel. By a similar logic, Sainte-Beuve can present a critical persona endowed with sentimental prowess — exemplified by his ability to form long-lasting (albeit fictitious) bonds of friendship with his subjects — and thus make himself more attractive to the reading public. Planche writes of Sainte-Beuve that 'chacun des modèles qu'il fait poser devant nous gagne notre affection en révélant à nos yeux des mérites inattendus' (1853a: 274). Yet it is not just affection for these authors which is gained. By establishing himself as the crucial, mutual, friend of both reader and writer, Sainte-Beuve compels the readers of his criticism to befriend his chosen — often neglected — authors and, at the same time, himself. This technique, combined with articles which speak more explicitly about Sainte-Beuve as a subject in his own right ('Un mot sur moi-même' (*PL*: 707–08)), can explain a comment like that of Henry James who, contradicting Barbey's characterisation of Sainte-Beuve as a critical 'caméléon' (1966b: 152), argues that 'his work offers a singularly complete image of his character, his tastes, his temper, his idiosyncrasies. It was from himself always that he spoke — from his own personal and, as they say in France, intimate point of view' (1880: 52).[23] Valued for his sentimental ability as much as his analytical skill, Sainte-Beuve can thus create affective ties with his reading public: the rhetoric of intimacy works simultaneously, but surreptitiously, to create commercial loyalty.

The trope of friendship continued to be used throughout the century, embedded and exploited differently in different critical contexts. A later example comes from Olympe Audouard's literary portrait of Jules Janin, which appeared in her newspaper *Le Papillon* on 25 October 1861.[24] Here, Audouard frames her encounter with the writer and his work in terms of a slowly blossoming friendship.

Told in the first-person, the article crafts a retrospective narrative which traces Audouard's friendship with Janin from its imaginary beginnings in childhood, inspired by weekly readings of his articles, through thwarted attempts to enter into correspondence with him, to its ultimate resolution as a reciprocated relationship in Paris in adulthood.[25] Audouard elucidates the feelings of friendship which were inspired by her childhood reading material:

> Les enfants ont un instinct qui les guide tout de suite vers le beau; au milieu de bien d'autres articles ceux de Jules Janin me frappèrent; mon journal arrivé, bien vite je regardais s'il contenait un article de celui que j'appelais mon ami Janin, et avec raison... On appelle souvent du nom d'amis des gens qui n'ont rien fait pour vous autres, dont la présence même est pour vous plutôt une importunité qu'un plaisir, tandis que Janin me faisait passer des soirées charmantes avec ses nouvelles aussi amusantes qu'instructives et écrites avec ce style brillant, élégant, qui distingue cet auteur... N'avais-je pas raison de l'appeler mon ami Janin? (Audouard 1861: 458)

While it may evoke genuine memories, and say much about the emotional and social possibilities of reading, Audouard's portrait is also strategic on a number of counts. Exemplary of the increasing personalisation of journalistic literary criticism evident in the period, already discussed, Audouard's emphasis on her childhood can be seen as a device designed to move and amuse her readers and, by extension, create her own bonds of figurative friendship with them. Moreover, Janin himself was associated with *Le Papillon*: in this light, the piece aims to flatter and encourage further contributions from an established writer whose involvement added prestige to the fledgling newspaper. Although Audouard's imaginary friendship with Janin is clearly associated with childhood, and is thus partly complicit with a developmental narrative in which real, reciprocal relations supersede fantasy ones, her discussion goes some way to defending the legitimacy of imaginary friendships: rather than see them as problematic, she instead seeks to justify them. Audouard's imagined friendship with Janin ('un homme que je ne connaissais pas' (1861: 459)) is described as more meaningful than many of her reciprocated friendships ('des gens [...] dont la présence même est pour vous plutôt une importunité qu'un plaisir'). Moreover, it incites real emotions and suffering within her; when Janin's articles stop appearing in the newspaper, her younger self is distraught: 'J'étais triste, contrariée, je parcourais les autres articles d'un œil distrait!...Il est peut-être malade, me disais-je. Cette idée me peinait' (1861: 458). Ultimately, the eventual reciprocation of Audouard's friendship for Janin in adulthood does not alter the bond in quality, but merely strengthens it: 'Son aimable bienveillance, son caractère gai, enjoué, son esprit toujours jeune et brillant, ont augmenté encore l'amitié que, petite fille, j'avais ressentie pour lui en lisant ses articles' (1861: 459). Audouard's imaginary friendship is useful for her as a critic, performed in *Le Papillon* as a sign of her 'natural' intuition and divination, qualities culturally associated with children and women.[26] Yet by presenting friendship as a function of childhood, and specifically girlhood, reading practices, Audouard's article simultaneously points to the very reasons for which Sainte-Beuve's use of the trope could be critiqued: on grounds of effeminacy, immaturity, and apparent artlessness.

Over time, Sainte-Beuve turned increasingly to the paradigms offered by naturalism in order to evaluate his subjects, partly as a response to such attacks.[27] Yet even these later *causeries*, such as his 1862 'Chateaubriand jugé par un ami intime', perpetuate the rhetoric of friendship; indeed, a given writer's circle of friends or 'groupe naturel littéraire' (*NL* III: 23) becomes central to Sainte-Beuve's explanatory theories of genius as outlined in the essays on Chateaubriand. In a culture which continued to prize the virtues of intimacy as an ideal, and the moral support which it could provide, literary critics continued to employ the language of *amitié*. While undoubtedly used to render criticism more palatable, or even to disguise criticism, this language also functioned to encourage emotional bonds between writers, readers, and critics, and to construct relations more comforting and less fraught than those carried out in the literary field itself. Profiting from the emotional and ethical charge which talk of friendship carried with it, critics could thus fight against literary indifference, generating appreciation of — and affection for — their chosen writers and also, at times, for themselves.

Notes to Chapter 6

1. *PF*: 489.
2. Annasue Wilson (2013).
3. Sainte-Beuve's critical output is extensive and varied, and his method of literary criticism — and way of conceptualising it — inevitably changed over time. Rather than attempt an exhaustive study of his critical approaches, this chapter focuses on one significant trope in his writing; consult, for example, Molho (1963), Roxana Verona (1999), or Prendergast (2007) for more wide-ranging discussions of his critical contribution as a whole.
4. These questions are discussed in a twentieth-century context by Tobin Siebers (1988) and Julie Ellison (1990).
5. See Marie-Françoise Melmoux-Montaubin (2003).
6. See, for example, Gustave Planche's 'De la critique française' (1853c). Planche lists the following types of criticism: 'la critique marchande', 'la critique indifférente', 'la critique spirituelle', 'la critique érudite', 'la critique écolière', and finally, the only one approved of, 'la critique indépendante'.
7. See Glinoer (2009) and his model of 'critique donné(e), critique prostitué(e)'; also Melmoux-Montaubin (2003, 2004). For a larger overview of the history of literary criticism in the West, see René Wellek (1955–92).
8. Barbey d'Aurevilly cited by Molho (1963: 167).
9. See Anthony Glinoer (2008) for a thorough analysis of the 'querelle de la camaraderie littéraire' and reproductions of key texts difficult to locate outside France. I refer to the article by Latouche as reproduced in Glinoer.
10. The *cénacle* was defined by Glinoer in this way at the Nineteenth-Century French Studies Conference in Raleigh, North Carolina, 8 October 2012.
11. These individual portraits were gathered together into the collection *Critiques et portraits littéraires* between the years 1832 and 1839. In 1844, this collection was divided into separate volumes: the *Portraits littéraires*, dedicated to deceased authors; the *Portraits de femmes*, which focused on women writers; and the 1846 *Portraits contemporains* which discussed living authors, and went through multiple re-editions in the years to come. For further details, see the chronology in Gérald Antoine (1993).
12. Cf. Melmoux-Montaubin (2004). For analysis of the links between the written 'portrait' and nineteenth-century French visual culture, see Dufour (1997); also Kathrin Yacavone (2017) for discussion of the development of the photographic portrait at this time and its implications for literature.

13. Cf. José-Luis Diaz (2007: 233–89). On the concept of genius in modern France, see Kete (2012) and Jefferson (2015).
14. Cf. Sainte-Beuve's preface to the *Portraits contemporains*: 'Je débute le plus souvent par la louange', 'ç'a été à la fois, s'il m'est permis de le dire, un penchant et une méthode' (*PC*: 55).
15. This is also how we saw Flaubert describe the friendship between Bouvard and Pécuchet (see Chapter 4, n. 19).
16. Another note in *Mes Poisons* confirms that Sainte-Beuve's stylistic imitation is more deliberate than he suggests elsewhere: 'J'ai toujours pensé qu'il faut prendre dans l'écritoire de chaque auteur l'encre dont on veut le peindre' (1945: 126).
17. Indeed, Henry James observes that Sainte-Beuve's sympathetic, and subtle, manner could itself hide covert criticisms: '[his] subtility [...] led him to analyze motives with a minuteness which was often fatal to their apparent purity, it led him to slip in — to *glisser*, as he always says — the grain of corrosive censure with the little parcel of amenities' (1880: 54–55).
18. On this history of male hysteria, however, see Mark S. Micale (2008).
19. See Humphreys (2012).
20. James would also write of Sainte-Beuve that 'there is something feminine in his tact, his penetration, his subtility and pliability, his rapidity of transition, his magical divinations, his sympathies and antipathies, his marvelous art of insinuation' (1880: 53); certain contemporary critics continue to describe Sainte-Beuve unproblematically in these gendered terms, for example, Gérald Antoine (1998: 8).
21. On the ties between publishing, publicity, and criticism from the 1820s onwards and the suspicion this cast on the professional, remunerated critic, see Glinoer (2009); such ties are dramatised in Balzac's *Illusions perdues*.
22. For a detailed analysis of the metaphors of conversation which underpin Sainte-Beuve's criticism, particularly the *causerie*, see Verona (1999).
23. Cf. Melmoux-Montaubin on the personalisation of journalism: 'Parler de soi apparaît comme une ruse critique propre à susciter la sympathie du lecteur' (2004: 492).
24. Much work on the female journalist and, in particular, the female critic in nineteenth-century France remains to be done. For discussion of the nineteenth-century *presse féminine*, see Eve Sullerot (1963) and Hélène Eck and Claire Bandin (2011); for some discussion of the female literary critic in the French context, see Jeanne Brunereau (2000) and Alison Finch (2000).
25. Friendship is a recurrent theme in Audouard's work; she will later write a novel on female friendship: *L'Amie intime* (1873).
26. See Ellison (1990) and Michèle Le Dœuff (1998) on the cultural construction of female intuition. For a survey of research into child cognition and 'magical thinking', see Karl S. Rosengren, Carl N. Johnson, and Paul L. Harris (2000).
27. See Molho (1963: 15–21).

CONCLUDING REMARKS

Baudelaire *intime*

The legacy of Sainte-Beuve's biographical criticism and its rhetoric of friendship lives on, hesitantly, in Baudelaire's own critical studies. Indeed, the relationship between Baudelaire and biography more broadly — whether articulated in his own 'portraits' of contemporaneous artists or in certain biographically orientated studies of *him* — offers us one further perspective on the themes of this book: unsurprising, when we consider that the growing popularity of biography as a genre in nineteenth-century France is itself inextricably bound up with 'le goût croissant pour l'"intime"' (Diaz 2011: 7). In these concluding remarks, I begin by considering the articulation of friendship and biography in Baudelaire's criticism, suggesting that the differences between Sainte-Beuve and Baudelaire in this regard crystallise a central tenet of my argument: that writers continued to aspire to intimacy as a relational model and literary mode throughout the nineteenth century, but that conflicting behavioural, ideological, and aesthetic demands forced them to reimagine intimacy in new and sometimes surprising ways. Moreover, the process of reimagining coincided with, and contributed to, a hierarchisation of intimacy in the nineteenth-century imagination. While *Intimacy and Distance* has focused primarily on the periods of the July Monarchy and Second Empire, intimacy continued to be reimagined in the late nineteenth century, and throughout the twentieth century. The twentieth-century sexualisation of intimacy, and, to an extent, literary criticism, is reflected in Nadar's biography of Baudelaire, *Charles Baudelaire intime: le poète vierge* [1911]. Indebted to the increased interest in sexuality in *fin-de-siècle* France as well as early developments in psychoanalysis, Nadar seeks to explain Baudelaire's creative impulse in terms of sexual function and, by simultaneously maintaining the idiom of intimacy, recasts the concept in ways suited to the emerging preoccupations of the age. Nadar's *Charles Baudelaire intime* can thus be read as a prefiguration of the shape intimacy will take in twentieth- and twenty-first-century cultural and critical discourses: a shape which risks obscuring the wider range of associations the concept encapsulated in the pre-Freudian era.

Baudelaire and Biography

Much as *Les Fleurs du Mal* bears traces of Sainte-Beuve's *poésie intime*, Baudelaire's critical studies share Sainte-Beuve's vision of criticism as an intersubjective encounter in which intimacy is both a means and an end. Intimacy is, as we have seen, of conceptual use to Baudelaire's intercultural art criticism, evoked to explain the way in which a spectator can relate to an art-object and, by extension, the culture or country from which the object originates. In these cases, the critical rapport takes place between the viewing subject and the national school or 'spirit' in question, channelled through individual artworks. In Baudelaire's separate studies of writers, artists, and composers, however, the rhetorical and analytical uses to which the *intime* is put are inevitably altered.[1] In Chapter Five, we saw Baudelaire deny the existence of friendships or, more specifically, *camaraderies*, in the *Salon de 1845* (OC II: 351). Yet in his portraits, friendship is not only tolerated, but emerges as a crucial methodological and analytical tool. In his analyses of Gautier, Delacroix, and Wagner, for example, Baudelaire is quick to emphasise his own associations with the celebrated individuals. For a critic who seeks to reveal the defining quality, the *sui generis*, of a particular artist's genius, intimacy between the artist and the critic increases, and authorises, critical insight (and evidently enhances the critic's reputation by association). While Sainte-Beuve's historical portraits necessitated purely imaginary friendships, Baudelaire's focus on his contemporaries allows him to highlight meetings and conversations with the subjects of his criticism: visits to Delacroix's workshop, for example (OC II: 761), or formative conversations with Gautier (OC II: 107). Where personal affiliation cannot be claimed, as in the case of Wagner, Baudelaire acknowledges the use of biographical material (OC II: 787). The kind of biographical information which Baudelaire considers relevant, however, can be seen to position him somewhat, although not entirely, apart from the 'portraitomanie' (Dufour 1997: 3) of the nineteenth century, and indeed from Sainte-Beuve's critical practice. Baudelaire's early essays equate the nineteenth-century vogue for biography with an egalitarian impulse. In his 1851 study of the song-writer Pierre Dupont, he theorises:

> Le public aime à se rendre compte de l'éducation des esprits auxquels il accorde sa confiance; on dirait qu'il est poussé en ceci par un sentiment indomptable d'égalité. 'Tu as touché notre cœur! Il faut nous démontrer que tu n'es qu'un homme et que les mêmes éléments de perfectionnement existent pour nous tous.' (OC II: 28)

Baudelaire's own interventions into the biographical, however, are concerned with the exception rather than the norm. By this token, anecdotes suggesting the commonality of the artist can quickly become petty and belittling. Eight years later, his 1859 portrait of Gautier asserts:

> Il importerait bien peu, à la rigueur, que j'apprisse ou que je n'apprisse pas à mes lecteurs que Théophile Gautier est né à Tarbes, en 1811. Depuis de longues années j'ai le bonheur d'être son ami, et j'ignore complètement s'il a dès l'enfance révélé ses futurs talents par des succès de collège [...]. De ces petitesses je ne sais absolument rien. (OC II: 104)

As this use of paralipsis suggests — Gautier *was* born in Tarbes in 1811 — Baudelaire's opinions regarding the value of biographical anecdote in criticism are inconsistent and at times contradictory. Like Sainte-Beuve, Baudelaire seeks to illuminate the individuality of the artist in question; like Sainte-Beuve, he often turns to pastiche to evoke the style of the artist he is discussing, and as 'proof of his own gymnastic skill' (Lloyd 1981: 178).[2] Yet whereas Sainte-Beuve can talk easily of the *amour* which the critical encounter generates, Baudelaire's criticism seeks to perpetuate an emotion which, in the case of Gautier, he is careful to distinguish as 'admiration' (*OC* II: 103). Aligning himself elsewhere with 'ces hautains solitaires qui ne peuvent se faire une famille que par les relations intellectuelles' (*OC* II: 769), Baudelaire concentrates on the intellectual, spiritual, and moral qualities of the artists he studies. His portrait of Gautier is, in reality, he claims, the 'histoire d'une *idée fixe*' (*OC* II: 104) and, consequently, biographical information regarding the material details of his childhood or home life, which Sainte-Beuve is happy to provide, is unproductive and, often, unpalatable. What Baudelaire rejects, fundamentally, is the sensational or salacious. He warns his readers against the 'vampirish' posthumous biographies of Poe ('Il n'existe donc pas en Amérique d'ordonnance qui interdise aux chiens l'entrée des cimetières?' (*OC* II: 298)), and, in his 1861 essay on Wagner, is shown to filter carefully the plethora of biographical articles produced to accompany the Parisian première of *Tannhäuser*: 'Parmi ces documents fort connus aujourd'hui, je ne veux extraire que ceux qui me paraissent plus propres à éclairer et à définir la nature et le caractère du maître' (*OC* II: 787). In the conclusion to his portrait of Gautier, Baudelaire asserts that biographies of artists amount to far more than the mere compilation of dates and facts:

> Il y a des biographies faciles à écrire; celles, par exemple, des hommes dont la vie fourmille d'événements et d'aventures; là, nous n'aurions qu'à enregistrer et à classer des faits avec leurs dates; — mais ici, rien de cette variété matérielle qui réduit la tâche de l'écrivain à celle du compilateur. Rien qu'une immensité spirituelle! La biographie d'un homme dont les aventures les plus dramatiques se jouent silencieusement sous la coupole de son cerveau, est d'un travail littéraire d'un ordre tout différent. [...] Qui pourrait concevoir une biographie du soleil? (*OC* II: 103–04)

Orders of Intimacy

What can Baudelaire's two-fold conception of biography tell us about intimacy in the nineteenth-century cultural imagination? Lloyd suggests that Baudelaire was 'not someone for whom friendship came particularly easily' (2002: 114). Yet friendship is a figure throughout Baudelaire's critical work, a 'faculté divine' (*OC* II: 768) which, when used in moderation, facilitates the divining work of the critic and grants him access 'sous la coupole [du] cerveau' (*OC* II: 104); 'sous le ciel du crâne, dans le laboratoire étroit et mystérieux du cerveau' (*OC* II: 429). However, his vision of friendship is one in which head is emphasised as much as heart, intelligence stressed alongside emotion, and whose appeal is ultimately generated by the apparently rare and elite nature of the bond rather than its egalitarian or communitarian potential: it is only possible, moreover, between men. This view of friendship is thus in no way comparable to the *camaraderies* he was quick to denounce in his early *Salon*. As this study has argued, such careful delineation on the part of Baudelaire bespeaks the historical position of a cluster of writers who worked with literary modes and representations of intimacy during the July Monarchy and Second Empire, but for whom the implications of these writing and reading practices generated significant ideological conflicts. On the one hand, the expression of shared emotion could offer affective, aesthetic, and economic rewards for writers, evoking a superior and sublime form of communion. Yet, on the other hand, intimate writing practices could be culturally stigmatised as feminine, infantile, frivolous, even sinful. To cope with these contradictions, particularly heightened for men, writers reimagined intimacy in ways which accommodated their competing concerns. As explored in Chapters Two and Three, the embarrassments associated with the defining genres of intimacy — *poésie intime*, the *roman intime*, and the *journal intime* — called for certain compensatory strategies: the self-conscious textual thematisation of embarrassment, authorial or editorial omissions and rewritings, and an emphasis on irony as an antidote to the *intime*. Chapters Four, Five, and Six demonstrated that, in the genres of travel writing, art criticism, and literary criticism, intimacy was both privileged and problematised: writers alluded to 'superior' modes of intimacy (real or imagined) to counteract the flawed versions also documented in these texts.

By focusing on a variety of cultural and literary forms, this book has demonstrated that this hierarchisation of intimacy was characteristic not of one particular generic practice, but rather of French culture more broadly. The societal, cultural, and technological changes which shaped nineteenth-century France, and the new opportunities for intimacy these offered citizens both in person and on paper, called for classification and categorisation: impulses which served both a regulatory and a reassuring function. A two-fold vision of the *intime* thus emerged which allowed individuals to distinguish their version of intimacy from forms considered trivial, or even dangerous. Indeed, the more disappointing or threatening intimacy appeared in practice, the more precious it became as an ideal. The effort at qualitative distinction or gradation epitomised in Baudelaire's critical writing — there are different orders of intimacy, like different orders of biography or 'travail littéraire' (*OC* II: 104) — thus reflects, I argue, the anxieties generated by the upheavals of the post-Revolutionary period. Yet it also demonstrates that the aspiration towards intimacy in the literary field did remain, countering narratives which present the cultivation of detachment as the exemplary impulse of the age. The tendency towards impersonality and impassivity in nineteenth-century literature has received much critical attention in recent years. But this tendency needs to be understood as a reaction to the self-conscious culture of intimacy which existed in tension with it. In order to illuminate this culture and the conflicts it generated, *Intimacy and Distance* has focused on a core of writers in the July Monarchy and Second Empire. However, the French cultural preoccupation with intimacy would only intensify under the Third Republic. As Diaz and Diaz have shown, the publication of diaries, correspondence, biographies, and critical works following the titular model 'proper name + *intime*', accelerated in the post-1880 period (2009: 131).[3] It is, therefore, unsurprising that Baudelaire's textual afterlife was absorbed into the public appetite for intimacy which showed no sign of abating but instead adopted new interpretative paradigms and vocabularies as the century wore on. Nadar's *Charles Baudelaire intime* was published in 1911, a year after Nadar's death. The work, part of an ambitious and unrealised project on Nadar's part to write the 'memoirs' of his generation, is a blend of anecdotes, correspondence, and draft poetry; the 1990 Obsidiane edition also includes Nadar's photographs and drawings of the poet.[4] To a certain extent, this 'weird tribute', in the words of Nigel Gosling (1976: 25), to the writer mirrors Baudelaire's own critical quest to 'pénétrer sous le vernis' (*OC* II: 757) of the artist in question. Yet by focusing on what Nadar admits to be 'détails scabreux' (1990: 12) rather than Baudelaire's aesthetic creations or theories, the text comes close to offering the sensationalist version of biography which Baudelaire derides. At the same time, it anticipates the twentieth-century sexualisation of intimacy which still endures today.

Le poète vierge?

Nadar's early-twentieth-century biography denotes the continued appeal and marketability of intimacy in the literary sphere. It also provides evidence, if further was needed, that the veiling strategies put in place by Baudelaire in his published writing served only to increase, rather than inhibit, public interest in the author's private life. Through a series of internal inconsistencies concerning the level of intimacy between Nadar and Baudelaire, *Charles Baudelaire intime* highlights, and perpetuates, this paradox. To begin with, certainly, it is Nadar's status as a close friend of Baudelaire which generates and authorises this posthumous account of the writer's life. Nadar's friendship with Baudelaire is a recurring motif throughout the study, as are allusions to Baudelaire's 'tressaillante réserve de sensitif' (1990: 11); Baudelaire's reserve thus enhances the value of Nadar's friendship with him in a way which mirrors Baudelaire's own evocations of familiarity with Delacroix, whose 'austère sentiment de l'amitié' (*OC* II: 767) was reserved 'pour les grandes occasions' (*OC* II: 768). Yet while Baudelaire might have maintained a 'masque d'imperméabilité' (Nadar 1990: 61) in public, Nadar suggests that, once attained, his friendship was far from austere. Nadar begins by painting a charmingly carefree picture of his interactions with Baudelaire which carries echoes of Flaubert's depictions of male sociability: 'On s'était immédiatement tout raconté puisque rien à cacher, tout en commun par ce coin de bohème' (1990: 31). In private, Nadar puns, Baudelaire was someone happy to share the details of a sexual encounter ('Incontinent, il me narra avec abondance tous les détails de la rencontre' (1990: 17)), but who was equally capable of restraint:

> Ceux qui n'ont pas connu Baudelaire intime ont pu, ont dû devant sa réserve d'attitude prendre pour sécheresse de cœur ce qui n'était que circonspection et certaine pudeur jalouse. Mais mieux encore que la sensibilité, chez notre ami se révélaient des délicatesses rares. (Nadar 1990: 61)

As the text proceeds, however, the intimacy between the two writers is curiously undermined. While possibly representative of a genuine distancing, the shift also underlines the need for Nadar to create narrative in *Baudelaire intime*, and the uses to which intimacy — gained, lost, recalled — can be put as a plot device. References to Baudelaire's solitary nature gradually pervade the text, and in place of a Baudelaire *intime*, Nadar substitutes a secretive, 'sombre figure' (1990: 87). Idealised descriptions of the 'clans bohèmes' (1990: 90) of the July Monarchy, their transparency expressed by the simile of the glass dome, now function to throw into relief Baudelaire's essential difference:

> Tout en commun, sans réserve, sans secret, nos existences individuelles n'en faisant qu'une, nous vivions en pleine clarté, comme sous une coupole de verre, dans une intimité de toutes les heures et de toutes les minutes à laquelle rien n'eût échappé. D'où l'inattendue révélation...
> Dès les premiers temps de notre rencontre, nous n'avions pu manquer d'observer la réserve de Baudelaire sur certain chapitre. (Nadar 1990: 90)

The particular mystery which crystallises around the poet is sexual in nature. Despite Baudelaire's cryptic allusions to erotic encounters, Nadar notes Baudelaire's 'froideur glaciale au moindre leste propos' (1990: 90), his indifference to women during trips to the Folies-Bergère and other areas of 'galanterie courante' (1990: 90), and his apartment at the hôtel Pimodan, resolutely 'vierge de tout pas féminin' (1990: 91). Based on this accumulation of evidence, Nadar asks, might it be surmised that Baudelaire was sexually inactive; perhaps even, like his apartment, a perpetual virgin?

The enigma functions in a similar way to Barbey d'Aurevilly's nameless suffering in the *Memoranda*, and exerts a powerful pull on Nadar and, by extension, the reader. 'Mais je m'aperçois que je reviens encore à ce caractère tant de fois fouillé,' writes Nadar, 'et c'est malgré moi que je me retourne vers la chère et sombre figure' (1990: 87). In his *Memoranda*, as we saw in Chapter Three, Barbey maintains control of his unnamed 'secret', yet Nadar concludes *Baudelaire intime* with a triumphant explanation of Baudelaire's failings. In terms which pre-empt Sartre's critique of 1946, these include the poet's inability to maintain relationships with women and his deep-seated misogyny. Influenced by turn-of-the-century psychopathology, Nadar presents a solution which is part-physiological, part-psychological in nature. On the one hand, he suggests, an answer for Baudelaire's 'abstinence' may lie in sexual impotence or dysfunction: 'Devions-nous chercher et trouverions-nous à l'article "Cas rares" du Dictionnaire des Sciences Médicales l'explication de ce nihilisme spécial?' (1990: 91). On the other, he links Baudelaire's 'recul devant la femme' (1990: 88) to a lack of maternal love. The reasons for the 'attractions et répulsions du névrosé' (1990: 87) can thus be located in Baudelaire's childhood:

> La première de nos émotions humaines et qui ne restera pas la moindre, douce, tendre, échange d'épanchements et de caresses entre sa mère et l'enfant: 'Maman! — Mon chéri!' cette exquise communion, à tous dévolue, avait été refusée à notre déshérité. (Nadar 1990: 87)

And in light of his analysis, Nadar concludes, admittedly with sympathy, that Baudelaire was a 'cas pathologique avéré' (1990: 89), the erotic encounters of his poetry functioning as fantasy substitutes for sexual 'abnormality' or failure: 'C'est le verbe qui supplée le geste, le rêve qui se venge de la réalité' (1990: 92).

Nadar's theory is somewhat far-fetched and, according to Stéphanie de Saint Marc, 'farfelu[e]' (2010: 324). Nonetheless, *Charles Baudelaire intime* is of interest for what it reveals of the changing models of intimacy at the turn of the twentieth century. From a focus on Baudelaire's friendships to an analysis of his psychic and sexual life couched in the normative discourse of medical science, the text enacts the transition of intimacy from a pre-Freudian world into one in which affection, attachment, and artistic creation would be explained more frequently, and explicitly, in terms of sexual function. Nadar's text bears witness to the growing liberalisation of *fin-de-siècle* and early-twentieth-century French society, while Nadar's vocabulary of fantasy and pathology bespeaks developments in psychology in the period and, potentially, the growing influence of Freudian theories of creativity.[5] As Kristeva (1997) notes, classical psychoanalysis does not discuss intimacy as a specific concept. However, its theoretical emphasis on infantile sexuality and sexual development determined which bonds were considered significant and healthy for individuals, and typically reduced the importance of non-sexual relationships by considering them as by-products or displacements of primary sexual drives, a move later challenged by Object Relations and Attachment Theory. In the case of imaginary relationships conceived by writers, these were forms of infantile wish-fulfilment which shared a common root with neurosis and psychosis. I do not mean to suggest that psychoanalytic readings of the nineteenth century are untenable, but I do propose that intimacy in nineteenth-century France was shaped by a number of different models and invested with a variety of cultural meanings which it is important to acknowledge. The nineteenth-century interest in the intimacies of friendship and acquaintanceship, writing and reading, and creativity and criticism is not, I argue, best interpreted as a symptom of displaced sexuality, but as an illustration of the continued and complex legacy of the sentimental paradigm in nineteenth-century France. Rather than bring the twentieth-century conflation of sexuality and intimacy to bear on this pre-Freudian era, historical investigations into intimacy in the nineteenth century are enriched and rendered more accurate by a focus on the full spectrum of real and imaginative bonds documented in the period. In particular, as my study has argued, literature was actively envisaged and valued as a space which represented, facilitated, and created interpersonal relationships, into which sexuality surely entered, but not as the dominant note or defining feature. The bonds mediated through literature could provide emotional consolation and even compensation, as was suggested in Chapter Six, yet they need not be interpreted as delusional or testament to psycho-sexual disorder, the conclusion which Nadar draws from his study of Baudelaire. Instead, these bonds can be understood as a product of the culture of intimacy manifest in nineteenth-century France.

Intimate Reading: Past and Present

Although the focus of *Intimacy and Distance* has been historical, the conflicted relationship between intimacy and literature is not restricted to the nineteenth century: readers today certainly continue to experience their reading in terms of consolation, and companionship. The twentieth-century separation of 'everyday' and academic literary practices, however, has made discussion of reading as an interpersonal encounter a contentious issue at least in the field of literary criticism. For Diaz, this separation is illustrated by the opposing attitudes to authorship which hardened in the twentieth century. He identifies:

> Un clivage très marqué, conséquence du processus d'autonomisation de la littérature commencé au milieu du siècle précédant [le dix-neuvième siècle], entre 'grand public' et élite: le premier, friand de révélations sur l'"homme", en trouve pâture grâce aux médias, nouveau moteur de la machine biographique; la seconde propose par réaction une mystique de l'œuvre sans auteur. (Diaz 2011: 219)

The same rift can be noted in relation to intimate reading practices more broadly. At the beginning of the twentieth century, as we saw in Chapter Two, Proust argued that both Sainte-Beuve and Baudelaire were wrong to conflate literature with life, or the artistic self with the social self.[6] With the ascendancy of 'new criticism' and structuralist thought in the mid-century, the 'hermeneutic of intimacy' (Mole 2007) was to become a cardinal sin in the academic sphere, reductive and complicit with capitalism (Barthes 1984). If intimacy could exist in literary criticism, it could only do so in academically sanctioned, largely theoretical ways: as intertextuality, for example, or in terms of the erotics of reading alluded to in Chapter Six. Subsequent critical tendencies, such as *écriture féminine* and indeed Barthes's own experiments with autobiography in the 1970s, spoke of the limitations of such approaches and a desire to renegotiate the relationship between literature and subjectivity. Yet in the twenty-first century, Felski still identifies a need to 'build better bridges' (2008: 13) between literary theory and everyday reading experiences, suggesting that a dichotomy persists. *Intimacy and Distance* has deployed the methods of cultural history and close reading in its analysis of the role of intimacy in nineteenth-century French literature and culture. In doing so, it has brought to light overlooked configurations of, and connections between, writers, revealing the shared aspiration for intimacy — wrought by conflict, fear, and failure — which unites writers as diverse as Guérin, Baudelaire, and Flaubert, or Barbey d'Aurevilly, Sainte-Beuve, and Audouard. But its findings also support attempts to expand the way academic disciplines are willing to think about literature in the present day: its uses and effects, and its modes of intersection with people's emotional and social lives.[7] Felski has argued for a serious engagement with those:

> Ordinary motives for reading — such as the desire for knowledge or the longing for escape — which are either overlooked or undervalued in literary scholarship. [...] My argument is not a populist defense of folk reading over scholarly interpretation, but an elucidation of how, in spite of their patent differences, they share certain affective and cognitive parameters. (Felski 2008: 14)

More precisely, she calls for a shift away from what Sedgwick, citing Paul Ricœur, has labelled the 'hermeneutics of suspicion' omnipresent in literary criticism, and demands an enriched vocabulary for discussing the affirmative effects of reading. She holds that:

> There is no reason why our readings cannot blend analysis and attachment, criticism and love. In recent years, however, the pendulum has lurched entirely too far in one direction; our language of critique is far more sophisticated and substantial than our language of justification [for literature]. [...] Is it possible to discuss the value of literature without falling into truisms and platitudes, sentimentality and *Schwärmerei*? We shall see. (Felski 2008: 22)

Intimacy and Distance has uncovered a language for speaking about, and often valuing, literary culture in nineteenth-century France which resonated in both private and public spheres, both personal and professional. Specifically, it is a language which reveals the points of convergence and divergence which existed (and which still exist) between intimacy with known family members, friends, or lovers, and intimacy with 'unknown' others, be these celebrated writers from history, hypothetical but hoped-for readers, or even the 'amis imaginaires' alluded to by Baudelaire in his cryptic dedication to *Les Paradis artificiels*: 'J'ai, quant à moi, si peu de goût pour le monde vivant que, pareil à ces femmes sensibles et désœuvrées qui envoient, dit-on, par la poste leurs confidences à des amis imaginaires, volontiers je n'écrirais que pour les morts' (*OC* I: 399–400). The nineteenth-century paradigms which underpin this language of intimacy may sit uncomfortably with our twenty-first-century perspectives; nonetheless, if approached judiciously, they may also offer us new but historically grounded ways to conceptualise the uses and effects of literature in the present; new or revitalised lines of continuity with the past.

Notes to the Conclusion

1. Baudelaire's literary criticism and biographical writings remain relatively under-researched areas of his *œuvre*, perhaps because they might be seen to resist the kind of 'proto-modernist' recuperation possible with his poetry. Important studies, however, include Margaret Gilman (1943), Lloyd (1981), and, more recently, Alain Vaillant (2011).
2. For further discussion of Baudelaire's use of pastiche, see Lloyd (1981: 276–78)
3. See also Elizabeth Emery (2012, 2015) on the growth of interest in 'at home' interviews with authors and other public figures in this period.
4. On Nadar's writing projects, see Stéphanie de Saint Marc (2010). While not necessarily the overriding motivation for the memoirs, Nadar had suffered financial hardship in the years after the Paris Commune and he thus hoped to 'gagner un peu d'argent de sa plume' (2010: 319).
5. Freud published *The Interpretation of Dreams* in 1899 and *Three Essays on Sexuality* in 1905. Specific theories of creativity are articulated in, for example, 'Creative Writers and Daydreaming' [1907] and 'Leonardo de Vinci and a Memory of his Childhood' [1910]; see Sigmund Freud (1995). The ebbs and flows of Freud's influence in France are charted by Alain de Mijolla (2010).
6. In 'Sainte-Beuve and Baudelaire' (Proust 1971: 248).
7. Cognitive literary studies, for example, is an emerging interdisciplinary research area which examines and analyses the cognitive responses generated by reading; key texts include Lisa Zunshine, *Why We Read Fiction: Theory of Mind and the Novel* (2006); Blakey Vermeule, *Why Do We Care About Literary Characters?* (2011), and Isabel Jaén and Julien Jacques Simon (eds), *Cognitive Literary Studies: Current Themes and New Directions* (2012).

BIBLIOGRAPHY

Primary Texts

Barbey d'Aurevilly, Jules-Amédée

1966A. *Œuvres romanesques complètes*, ed. by Jacques Petit, 2 vols (Paris: Gallimard)
1966B. *Le Dix-neuvième siècle: des œuvres et des hommes*, ed. by Jacques Petit, 2 vols (Paris: Mercure de France), II
1985. *Correspondance générale*, ed. by Philippe Berthier and Andrée Hirsch, 9 vols (Paris: Les Belles Lettres), V
2013. *Lettres à Trebutien 1832–1858*, ed. by Philippe Berthier (Paris: Éditions Bartillat)

Baudelaire, Charles

1862. 'À une heure du matin', *La Presse*, 27 August 1862
1973. *Correspondance de Baudelaire*, ed. by Claude Pichois, 2 vols (Paris: Gallimard)
1975–76. *Œuvres complètes*, ed. by Claude Pichois, 2 vols (Paris: Gallimard)
1980. Letter to Armand Fraisse, 12 August 1860, reproduced in *Les Cahiers obliques* 1.5: 5–6
1986. *Fusées, Mon cœur mis à nu, La Belgique déshabillée*, ed. by André Guyaux (Paris: Gallimard)

Flaubert, Gustave

1951. *Œuvres de Flaubert*, ed. by A. Thibaudet and R. Dumesnil, 2 vols (Paris: Gallimard)
1973–2007. *Correspondance de Flaubert*, ed. by Jean Bruneau and Yvan LeClerc, 6 vols (Paris: Gallimard)
1991. *Voyage en Égypte*, ed. by Pierre-Marc de Biasi (Paris: Bernard Grasset)
2001. *Œuvres complètes*, I: *Œuvres de jeunesse*, ed. by Claudine Gothot-Mersch and Guy Sagnes (Paris: Gallimard)

Fromentin, Eugène

1969. *Gustave Drouineau: sur un 'romantique libre'*, ed. by Barbara Wright (Paris: Minard)
1984. *Œuvres complètes*, ed. by Guy Sagnes (Paris: Gallimard)
1995. *Correspondance d'Eugène Fromentin*, ed. by Barbara Wright, 2 vols (Paris: CNRS-Éditions)
2009. *Un été dans le Sahara*, ed. by Anne-Marie Christin (Paris: Flammarion)

Guérin, Eugénie de

1855. *Reliquiae*, publié par Jules Barbey d'Aurevilly et G. S. Trebutien (Caen: Imprimerie de A. Cardel)
1862. *Eugénie de Guérin, Journal et lettres*, publiés avec l'assentiment de la famille par G.-S. Trebutien (Paris: Didier)

Sainte-Beuve, Charles Augustin

1863A. *Les Consolations, Pensées d'août, Notes et pensées, Un dernier rêve* (Paris: Michel Lévy Frères)
1863B. *Vie, poésies et pensées de Joseph Delorme* (Paris: Michel Lévy Frères)
1879. *Œuvres de C.-A. Sainte-Beuve: poésies complètes*, ed. by Anatole France, 2 vols (Paris: Alphonse Lemerre), II
1883–86. *Nouveaux lundis*, 13 vols (Paris: Calmann Lévy)
1945. *Mes Poisons* (Paris: Plon)
1993. *Portraits littéraires*, ed. by Gérald Antoine (Paris: R. Laffont)
1998. *Portraits de femmes*, ed. by Gérald Antoine (Paris: Gallimard)
2003. *Causeries sur Montaigne*, ed. by François Rigolot (Paris: Honoré Champion)
2008. *Portraits contemporains*, ed. by Michel Brix (Paris: Presses de l'université de Paris-Sorbonne)

Secondary Sources

ABOUT, EDMOND. 1855. *Voyage à travers l'exposition des beaux-arts* (Paris: Hachette)
ADAMS, JAMES ELI. 1995. *Dandies and Desert Saints: Styles of Victorian Masculinity* (Ithaca, NY, & London: Cornell University Press)
AJD. 1847. 'Beaux-Arts — Salon de 1847', *L'Illustration*, 8 May 1847
ALLEN, JAMES SMITH. 1987. 'Towards a History of Reading in Modern France', *French Historical Studies*, 15.2: 236–86
——1991. *In the Public Eye: A History of Reading in Modern France* (Princeton, NJ: Princeton University Press)
ANDERSON, AMANDA. 2001. *The Powers of Distance: Cosmopolitanism and the Cultivation of Detachment* (Princeton, NJ: Princeton University Press)
ANON. 1834. *Petite civilité chrétienne, ou règles de la bienséance* (Paris: L. Hachette, Firmin Didot Frères)
——1837. 'Note de l'éditeur', in Julie de Krüdener, *Valérie: roman*, 2 vols (Paris: Ollivier), I, VII–XIV
——1903. Untitled notice in 'Second Mémorandum de J. Barbey d'Aurevilly', *La Renaissance latine*, 2.5: 340
ANSEL, YVES, PHILIPPE BERTHIER, and MICHAEL NERLICH (eds). 2003. *Dictionnaire de Stendhal* (Paris: Champion)
ANTOINE, GÉRALD. 1993. 'Chronologie', in Charles Augustin Sainte-Beuve, *Portraits littéraires*, ed. by Gérald Antoine (Paris: R. Laffont), pp. LXXXV–CXLIV
——1998. 'Préface', in Charles Augustin Sainte-Beuve, *Portraits de femmes*, ed. by Gérald Antoine (Paris: Gallimard), pp. 7–33
ARASSE, DANIEL. 2008. *Le Détail: pour une histoire rapprochée de la peinture* (Paris: Flammarion)
AUDOUARD, OLYMPE. 1861. 'Jules Janin', *Le Papillon*, 1st ser., 20: 458–59
AVRANE, PATRICK. 2005. *Barbey d'Aurevilly: solitaire et singulier* (Paris: Campagne première)
BAKHTIN, MIKHAIL. 1981. *The Dialogic Imagination: Four Essays*, trans. by Caryl Emerson and Michael Holquist (Austin: University of Texas Press)
BARBÉRIS, PIERRE. 1987. 'Introduction', in Eugène Fromentin, *Dominique*, ed. by Pierre Barbéris (Paris: Flammarion), pp. 13–54
BARDÈCHE, MAURICE. 1940. *Balzac romancier: la formation de l'art du roman chez Balzac depuis la publication du Père Goriot, 1820–1835* (Paris: Plon)
BARLOW, NORMAN H. 1964. *Sainte-Beuve to Baudelaire: A Poetic Legacy* (Durham, NC: Duke University Press)

BARTHES, ROLAND. 1970. *S/Z* (Paris: Seuil)
—— 1972. *Le Degré zéro de l'écriture, suivi de Nouveaux essais critiques* (Paris: Seuil)
—— 1977. *Fragments d'un discours amoureux* (Paris: Seuil)
—— 1984. 'La Mort de l'auteur', in *Le Bruissement de la langue* (Paris: Seuil), pp. 63–69
BATICLE, JEANNINE. 2003. 'The Discovery of the Spanish School in France', in *Manet/ Velázquez: The French Taste for Spanish Painting*, ed. by Gary Tinterow and Geneviève Lacambre (New York: Metropolitan Museum of Art), pp. 175–90
BAUDRILLARD, JEAN. 1986. 'La Sphère enchantée de l'intime', *Autrement*, 81: 12–15
BAUMAN, ZYGMUNT. 2000. *Liquid Modernity* (Cambridge: Polity Press)
—— 2003. *Liquid Love: On the Frailty of Human Bonds* (Cambridge: Polity Press)
BAYLE-MOUILLARD, ÉLISABETH-FÉLICIE. 1839. *Nouvel manuel complet de la bonne compagnie, ou Guide de la politesse et de la bienséance [...] par Mme Celnart* (Paris: Roret)
BECKER, KARIN. 2010. *Le Dandysme littéraire en France au XIXe siècle* (Orléans: Paradigme)
BEHDAD, ALI. 1994. *Belated Travelers: Orientalism in the Age of Colonial Dissolution* (Cork: Cork University Press)
BELENKY, MASHA. 2008. *The Anxiety of Dispossession: Jealousy in Nineteenth-Century French Culture* (Lewisburg, NJ: Bucknell University Press; Associated University Presses)
BENJAMIN, ROGER. 2003. *Orientalist Aesthetics: Art Colonialism and North Africa, 1880–1930* (Berkeley & Los Angeles: University of California Press)
BERLANT, LAUREN. 1998. 'Intimacy: A Special Issue', *Critical Inquiry*, 24.2: 281–88
—— 2008. *The Female Complaint: The Unfinished Business of Sentimentality in American Culture* (Durham, NC, & New York: Duke University Press)
BERSANI, LEO. 1977. *Baudelaire and Freud* (Berkeley & London: University of California Press)
BERSANI, LEO, and ADAM PHILLIPS. 2004. *Intimacies* (Chicago, IL: University of Chicago Press)
BERTHIER, PHILIPPE. 1978. *Barbey d'Aurevilly et l'imagination* (Geneva: Droz)
BERTRAND, ANDRÉ. 1999. *Droit à la vie privée et droit à l'image* (Paris: Litec)
BIASI, PIERRE-MARC DE. 1991. 'Introduction', in Gustave Flaubert, *Voyage en Égypte*, ed. by Pierre-Marc de Biasi (Paris: Bernard Grasset), pp. 8–112
—— 2009. *Gustave Flaubert: une manière spéciale de vivre* (Paris: Grasset)
BLAKE, WILLIAM. 1972. *The Pickering Manuscript* (New York: The Pierpont Morgan Library)
BLATTERER, HARRY. 2015. *Everyday Friendships: Intimacy as Freedom in a Complex World* (New York: Palgrave Macmillan)
BLIN, GEORGES. 1939. *Baudelaire* (Paris: Gallimard)
—— 1958. *Stendhal et les problèmes de la personnalité* (Paris: Librairie José Corti)
BOGH, MIKKEL. 2016. *Closer: Intimacies in Art, 1730–1930* (Copenhagen: Statens Museum for Kunst)
BOITARD, PIERRE. 1861. *Guide-manuel de la bonne compagnie, du bon ton, et de la politesse* (Paris: Passard)
BOLOGNE, JEAN-CLAUDE. 1986. *Histoire de la pudeur* (Paris: Hachette littératures)
BORIE, J. 1995. *Frédéric et les amis des hommes* (Paris: Grasset)
BOURDIEU, PIERRE. 1992. *Les Règles de l'art: genèse et structure du champ littéraire* (Paris: Seuil)
BOURKE, JOANNA. 1999. *An Intimate History of Killing: Face-to-Face Killing in Twentieth-Century Warfare* (London: Granta Books)
—— 2009. 'Divine Madness: The Dilemma of Religious Scruples in Twentieth-Century America and Britain', *Journal of Social History*, 42.3: 581–603
BOURSIN, E., and AUGUSTIN CHALLAMEL (eds). 1893. *Dictionnaire de la révolution française* (Paris: Jouvet et Compagnie)
BOUTIN, AIMÉE. 2000. 'Confessions of a Mamma's Boy: Lamartine's *Manuscrit de ma mère*', in *The Mother in/and French Literature*, ed. by Buford Norman (Amsterdam: Rodopi), pp. 125–38

BOWLBY, JOHN. 1969–80. *Attachment and Loss*, 3 vols (London: Hogarth Press & Institute of Psycho-analysis)
BRENNAN, TIMOTHY. 1997. *At Home in the World: Cosmopolitanism Now* (Cambridge, MA, & London: Harvard University Press)
BROWN, MARSHALL. 1991. *Preromanticism* (Stanford, CA: Stanford University Press)
BRUNEREAU, JEANNE. 2000. *Presse féminine et critique littéraire, 1800–1830* (Paris: Ève et son espace créatif)
BURGESS, MIRANDA. 2011. 'On Being Moved: Sympathy, Mobility, and Narrative Form', *Poetics Today*, 32.2: 289–321
BURKE, PETER. 1990. *The French Historical Revolution: The Annales School, 1929–89* (Cambridge: Polity Press)
BURT, E. S. 2009. *Regard for the Other: Autothanatography in Rousseau, De Quincey, Baudelaire, and Wilde* (New York: Fordham University Press)
BUZARD, JAMES. 1993. *The Beaten Track: European Tourism, Literature and the Ways to Culture* (Oxford: Clarendon Press)
BYERLY, ALISON. 2012. *Are We There Yet? Virtual Travel and Victorian Realism* (Ann Arbor: University of Michigan Press)
CATANI, DAMIAN. 2013. 'The "Spleen" and "Idéal" of Opium: Baudelaire and Thomas de Quincey', *Dix-Neuf*, 17.3, <http://www.maneyonline.com/doi/abs/10.1179/1478731813Z.00000000037> [accessed 31 October 2016]
CAUGHEY, JOHN L. 1984. *Imaginary Social Worlds: A Cultural Approach* (Lincoln & London: University of Nebraska Press)
CHAMBERS, ROSS. 1984. *Story and Situation: Narrative Seduction and the Power of Fiction* (Manchester: Manchester University Press)
—— 1988. 'Baudelaire's Dedicatory Practice', *Substance*, 17.2: 5–17
—— 1993. *The Writing of Melancholy: Modes of Opposition in Early French Modernism* (Chicago & London: University of Chicago Press)
CHARTIER, ROGER. 1988. *Cultural History: Between Practices and Representations*, trans. by Lydia Cochrane (Ithaca, NY: Cornell University Press)
CHASE, KAREN, and MICHAEL LEVENSON (eds). 2000. *Spectacles of Intimacy: A Public Life for the Victorian Family* (Princeton, NJ: Princeton University Press)
CHOTARD, LOÏC. 2000. *Approches du XIXe siècle* (Paris: Presses de l'Université de Paris-Sorbonne)
CHRISTIN, ANNE-MARIE. 1982. *Fromentin conteur d'espace: essai sur l'œuvre algérienne* (Paris: Sycomore)
—— 2009. 'Présentation', in Eugène Fromentin, *Un été dans le Sahara*, ed. by Anne-Marie Christin (Paris: Flammarion), pp. 7–54
CLERVAL, ALAIN. 1984. 'Eugène Fromentin, l'antiromantique,' *La Nouvelle Revue Française*, 378: 118–24
COGEVAL, GUY. 2002. *Vuillard: Master of the Intimate Interior* (London: Thames and Hudson)
COHEN, MARGARET. 1999. *The Sentimental Education of the Novel* (Princeton, NJ: Princeton University Press)
—— 2002A. 'Introduction', in Sophie Cottin, *Claire d'Albe*, trans. by Margaret Cohen (New York: Modern Languages Association of America), pp. vii–xxi
—— 2002B. 'Sentimental Communities', in *The Literary Channel: The Inter-National Invention of the Novel*, ed. by Margaret Cohen and Carolyn Dever (Princeton, NJ: Princeton University Press), pp. 106–32
COLEBROOK, CLARE. 2004. *Irony* (London: Routledge)
COMMENT, BERNARD. 1999. *The Panorama* (London: Reaktion Books)
COMPAGNON, ANTOINE. 2003. *Baudelaire devant l'innombrable* (Paris: Presses de l'université de Paris-Sorbonne)

CONNELL, R. W. 1995. *Masculinities* (Cambridge: Polity)
CORBIN, ALAIN. 1988. *Le Territoire du vide: l'Occident et le désir du rivage, 1750–1840* (Paris: Aubier)
—— 1999. 'La Relation intime et les plaisirs de l'échange', in *Histoire de la vie privée*, ed. by Philippe Ariès and Georges Duby, 5 vols (Paris: Seuil), IV, 461–518
CORBIN, ALAIN, JEAN-JACQUES COURTINE, and GEORGES VIGARELLO (eds). 2016. *Histoire des émotions*, 2 vols (Paris: Seuil)
COUDREUSE, ANNE. 1997. 'Flaubert lecteur du XVIIIe siècle: pathos, ironie et apathie dans la *Correspondance*', *La Licorne*, 43: 129–42
—— 1999. *Le Goût des larmes au XIX siècle* (Paris: Presses universitaires de France)
COUSSON, AGNÈS. 2012. *L'Écriture de soi: lettres et récits autobiographiques des religieuses de Port-Royal* (Paris: Honoré-Champion)
CURTIS, SARAH ANN. 2000. *Educating the Faithful: Religion, Schooling, and Society in Nineteenth-Century France* (Dekalb: Northern Illinois University Press)
DAYAN, PETER. 1994. 'Baudelaire at his Latrine: Motions in the *Petits poèmes en prose* and in George Sand's Novels', *French Studies*, 48. 4: 416–24
DECKER, MICHELINE. 2001. *Aspects internes et internationaux de la protection de la vie privée en droits français, allemand et anglais* (Aix-en-Provence: Presses universitaires d'Aix-Marseille)
DE QUINCEY, THOMAS. 2013. *Confessions of an English Opium-Eater and Other Writings*, ed. by Robert Morrison (Oxford: Oxford University Press)
DESJARDINS, PAUL. 1887. 'Charles Baudelaire', *Revue politique et littéraire*, 2 July 1887
DIAZ, BRIGITTE. 2010A. 'Avant-propos', in *Barbey d'Aurevilly en tous genres*, ed. by Brigitte Diaz (Caen: Presses universitaires de Caen), pp. 7–18
—— 2010B. 'Barbey d'Aurevilly épistolier: la lettre contre le livre', in *Barbey d'Aurevilly en tous genres*, ed. by Brigitte Diaz (Caen: Presses universitaires de Caen), pp. 45–60
DIAZ, BRIGITTE, and JOSÉ-LUIS DIAZ. 2009. 'Le Siècle de l'intime', in *Pour une histoire de l'intime et de ses variations*, ed. by Anne Coudreuse and Françoise Simonet-Tenant (Paris: L'Harmattan), pp. 117–46
DIAZ, JOSÉ-LUIS. 1994. 'Cher auteur...', *Textuel*, 27: IX–XXI
—— 2007. *L'Ecrivain imaginaire: scénographies auctoriales à l'époque romantique* (Paris: H. Champion)
—— 2011. *L'Homme et l'œuvre: contribution à une histoire de la critique* (Paris: Presses universitaires de France)
DIDIER, BÉATRICE. 1976. *Le Journal intime* (Paris: Presses universitaires de France)
DIXON, THOMAS. 2015. *Weeping Britannia: Portrait of a Nation in Tears* (Oxford: Oxford University Press)
DU BARAIL, FRANÇOIS-CHARLES. 1897. *Mes Souvenirs*, 3 vols (Paris: E. Plon, Nourrit), II
DUFIEF-SANCHEZ, VÉRONIQUE. 2010. *Philosophie du roman personnel: de Chateaubriand à Fromentin 1802–1863* (Geneva: Droz)
DUFOUR, HÉLÈNE. 1997. *Portraits, en phrases: les recueils de portraits littéraires au XIXe siècle* (Paris: Presses universitaires de France)
DUMOULIN, MICHEL (ed.). 2005. *Nouvelle histoire de Belgique*, 4 vols (Brussels: Complexe), I
DUPONT, JACQUES. 1991. 'Introduction', in Baudelaire, *Les Fleurs du Mal*, ed. by Jacques Dupont (Paris: Flammarion), pp. 9–39
DUVERGIER DE HAURANNE, PROSPER. 1879. Untitled review, in *Œuvres de C.-A. Sainte-Beuve: poésies complètes*, ed. by Anatole France, 2 vols (Paris: Alphonse Lemerre), II, 131–43
EASLEY, ALEXIS. 2004. *First-Person Anonymous: Women Writers and Victorian Print Media, 1830–70* (Aldershot: Ashgate)
EASTON, ELIZABETH WYNNE. 1989. *The Intimate Interiors of Édouard Vuillard* (London: Thames and Hudson)

ECK, HÉLÈNE, and CLAIRE BANDIN (eds). 2010. *La Vie des femmes: la presse féminine au XIXe et XXe siècle* (Paris: Panthéon-Assas)

EDWARDS, TIM. 2006. *Cultures of Masculinity* (London: Routledge)

ELIAS, NORBERT. 1994. *The Civilizing Process*, trans. by Edmund Jephcott (Oxford: Blackwell)

ELLISON, JULIE. 1990. *Delicate Subjects: Romanticism, Gender and the Ethics of Understanding* (Ithaca, NY, New York & London: Cornell University Press)

—— 1999. *Cato's Tears and the Making of Anglo-American Emotion* (Chicago & London: University of Chicago Press)

EMERSON, CATHERINE. 2003. 'The Infant of Brussels: The *Manneken Pis* as Christ Child', *The Irish Journal of French Studies*, 3: 95–108

—— 2014. *Regarding Manneken Pis: Culture, Celebration, and Conflict in Brussels* (Oxford: Legenda)

EMERY, ELIZABETH. 2012. *Photojournalism and the Origins of the French Writer House Museum (1881–1914): Privacy, Publicity, and Personality* (Farnham, & Burlington, VT: Ashgate)

—— 2015. *En toute intimité... Quand la presse people de la Belle Époque s'invitait chez les célébrités* (Paris: Parigramme)

FELSKI, RITA. 2008. *Uses of Literature* (Malden, MA, & Oxford: Blackwell)

FEYDEAU, ERNEST. 1858. *Fanny* (Paris: Amyot)

FINCH, ALISON. 2000. *Women's Writing in Nineteenth-Century France* (Cambridge: Cambridge University Press)

FORD, CAROLINE C. 2005. *Divided Houses: Religion and Gender in Modern France* (Ithaca, NY, & London: Cornell University Press)

FOUCAULT, MICHEL. 1984A. *Le Souci de soi* (Paris: Gallimard)

—— 1984B. *The Foucault Reader*, ed. by Paul Rabinow (London: Penguin)

FRAISSE, ARMAND. 1973. *Armand Fraisse sur Baudelaire, 1857–1869*, ed. by Claude Pichois and Vincenette Pichois (Gembloux: Éditions J. Ducolot)

FRANCE, ANATOLE. 1879. 'Sainte-Beuve', in *Œuvres de C.-A. Sainte-Beuve: poésies complètes*, ed. by Anatole France, 2 vols (Paris: Alphonse Lemerre), I, I–XXXIX

FREUD, SIGMUND. 1995. *The Freud Reader*, ed. by Peter Gay (London: Vintage)

GAUTIER, THÉOPHILE. 1855. 'L'Art chinois', *L'Artiste*, 5th ser., 16: 71–74

—— 1861. *Abécédaire du Salon de 1861* (Paris: E. Dentu)

—— 1992. *Exposition de 1859*, ed. by Wolfgang Drost and Ulrike Henninges (Heidelberg: Carl Winter Universitätsverlag)

GAY, PETER. 1996. *The Bourgeois Experience, Victoria to Freud*, 5 vols (New York: W. W. Norton), IV

—— 1998. *The Bourgeois Experience, Victoria to Freud*, 5 vols (New York: W. W. Norton), V

GERSON, STÉPHANE. 2006. 'In Praise of Modest Men: Self-Display and Self-Effacement in Nineteenth-Century France', *French History*, 20.2: 182–203

GIDDENS, ANTHONY. 1992. *The Transformation of Intimacy: Love, Sexuality, and Eroticism in Modern Societies* (Oxford: Polity Press)

GIDE, ANDRÉ. 1905. 'Promenade au Salon d'Automne', *Gazette des Beaux-Arts*, 3.34: 475–85

GILL, MIRANDA. 2009. *Eccentricity and the Cultural Imagination in Nineteenth-Century Paris* (Oxford: Oxford University Press)

—— 2015. 'Self-Control and Uncontrollable Passion in Stendhal's Theory of Love', *French Studies*, 69.4: 462–78

GILMAN, MARGARET. 1943. *Baudelaire the Critic* (New York: Columbia University Press)

GIRARD, ALAIN. 1963. *Le Journal intime* (Paris: Presses universitaires de France)

GLINOER, ANTHONY. 2008. *La Querelle de la camaraderie littéraire* (Geneva: Droz)

—— 2009. 'Critique donné(e), critique prostitué(e) au XIXe siècle', *Études littéraires*, 40.3: 29–41

GODFREY, SIMA. 1982. 'The Dandy as Ironic Figure', *SubStance*, 11.3: 21–33

GOELLNER, SAGE. 2004. 'Assia Djebar and Eugène Fromentin's Haoûa: Cultural Betrayal and Intertextual Transformation', *Equinoxes*, 2, <https://www.brown.edu/Research/Equinoxes/journal/issue2/eqx2_goellner.html> [accessed 31 October 2016]
GOFFMAN, ERVING. 2009. *Relations in Public* (New Brunswick, NJ: Transaction Publishers)
GOSLING, NIGEL. 1976. *Nadar* (London: Secker and Warburg)
GREEN, ANNE. 2011. *Changing France: Literature and Material Culture in the Second Empire* (London & New York: Anthem Press)
GREENBERG, JAY R., and STEPHEN A. MITCHELL. 1983. *Object Relations in Psychoanalytic Theory* (Cambridge, MA, & London: Harvard University Press)
GRØTTA, MARIT. 2015. *Baudelaire's Media Aesthetics: The Gaze of the Flâneur and 19th-Century Media* (New York & London: Bloomsbury Academic)
GUYAUX, ANDRÉ. 1986A. 'Préface' in Charles Baudelaire, *Fusées, Mon cœur mis à nu, La Belgique déshabillée*, ed. by André Guyaux (Paris: Gallimard), pp. 7–46
—— 1986B. 'Notice sur le texte et l'édition', in Charles Baudelaire, *Fusées, Mon cœur mis à nu, La Belgique déshabillée*, ed. by André Guyaux (Paris: Gallimard), pp. 47–62
—— (ed.). 2007. *Un demi-siècle de lectures des Fleurs du mal, 1855–1905* (Paris: Presses universitaires de la Sorbonne)
HABERMAS, JÜRGEN. 1989. *The Structural Transformation of the Public Sphere: An Inquiry into a Category of Bourgeois Society*, trans. by Thomas Burger (Cambridge: Polity)
HAINE, SCOTT. 1996. *The World of the Paris Café: Sociability among the French Working Class, 1789–1914* (Baltimore, MD: John Hopkins University Press)
HALL, CATHERINE. 1999. 'Sweet Home', in *Histoire de la vie privée*, ed. by Philippe Ariès and Georges Duby, 5 vols (Paris: Seuil), IV, 47–76
HAMON, PHILIPPE. 1996. *L'Ironie littéraire: essai sur les formes d'écriture oblique* (Paris: Hachette)
HARKNESS, NIGEL. 2011. 'The *roman personnel*', in *The Cambridge History of French Literature*, ed. by William Burgwinkle, Nicholas Hammond, and Emma Wilson (Cambridge: Cambridge University Press), pp. 441–49
HARPMAN, JACQUELINE. 2008. *Ce que Dominique n'a pas su* (Paris: Grasset)
HARRIS, RUTH. 1999. *Lourdes: Body and Spirit in a Secular Age* (London: Allen Lane)
HARRIS, TREVOR A. LE V. 1993. 'Fromentin's *Dominique*: Who's Complaining?', *French Studies Bulletin*, 13.47: 8–10
HARTMAN, ANNE. 2005. 'Confession as Cultural Form: The Plymouth Inquiry', *Victorian Studies*, 47.4: 535–56
HARTMAN, ELWOOD. 1994. *Three Nineteenth-Century Writers/Artists and the Maghreb* (Tübingen: Narr)
HIDDLESTON, J. A. 1987. *Baudelaire and Le Spleen de Paris* (Oxford: Clarendon)
HILGER, STEPHANIE M. 2006. 'Epistolarity, Publicity and Painful Sensibility: Julie de Krüdener's *Valérie*', *The French Review*, 79.4: 737–48
HOLMES, JEREMY. 1993. *John Bowlby and Attachment Theory* (London: Routledge)
HOROWITZ, SARAH. 2008. 'States of Intimacy: Friendship and the Remaking of French Political Elites, 1815–1848' (unpublished doctoral thesis, University of California at Berkeley)
HORTON, DONALD, and RICHARD WOHL. 1956. 'Mass Communication and Para-Social Interaction: Observations on Intimacy at a Distance', *Psychiatry*, 19: 215–29
HOWELLS, BERNARD. 1996. *Baudelaire: Individualism, Dandyism and the Philosophy of History* (Oxford: Legenda)
HUGO, VICTOR. 1864. *William Shakespeare* (Paris: Librairie internationale)
—— 1867. *Odes et ballades* (Paris: J. Hetzel)
HUMPHREYS, KAREN L. 2012. 'Bas-bleus, filles publiques, and the Literary Marketplace in the Work of Barbey d'Aurevilly', *French Studies*, 66.1: 26–40

HUNT, LYNN. (ed.). 1989. *The New Cultural History* (Berkeley & London: University of California Press)
—— 2007. *Inventing Human Rights: A History* (New York: W. W. Norton & Co)
HUTCHEON, LINDA. 1994. *Irony's Edge: The Theory and Politics of Irony* (London: Routledge)
IACUB, MARCELA. 2008. *Par le trou de la serrure: une histoire de la pudeur publique (XIXe–XXI siècle)* (Paris: Fayard)
JAÉN, ISABEL, and JULIEN JACQUES SIMON (eds). 2012. *Cognitive Literary Studies: Current Themes and New Directions* (Austin: University of Texas Press)
JAMES, HENRY. 1880. 'Sainte-Beuve', *The North American Review*, 130.278: 51–68
—— 1986. *The Art of Criticism: Henry James on the Theory and Practice of Fiction*, ed. by Susan M. Griffin and William R. Veeder (Chicago, IL, & London: University of Chicago Press)
JAMIESON, LYNN. 1998. *Intimacy: Personal Relationships in Modern Societies* (Cambridge: Polity Press)
JAUSS, HANS ROBERT. 1970. 'Literary History as a Challenge to Literary Theory', trans. by Elizabeth Beninger, *New Literary History*, 2.1: 7–37
JEFFERSON, ANN. 1988. *Reading Realism in Stendhal* (Cambridge: Cambridge University Press)
—— 2007. *Biography and the Question of Literature in France* (Oxford: Oxford University Press)
—— 2015. *Genius in France: An Idea and Its Uses* (Princeton, NJ: Princeton University Press)
JOUHANNEAUD, PAUL. 1856. *Nouvelle civilité chrétienne, ou Traité élémentaire de politesse à l'usage des enfants pieux. Extrait et revu du traité des bienséances du B. de La Salle* (Limoges: M. Ardant Frères)
KANG, MATHILDE. 2009. *Le Parcours transatlantique du journal d'Eugénie de Guérin: un cas de transfert culturel (1850–1950)* (Oxford: Peter Lang)
KAPOR, VLADIMIR. 2005. 'La Couleur anti-locale d'Eugène Fromentin', *Nineteenth-Century French Studies*, 34.1: 63–74
KEEN, SUZANNE. 2007. *Empathy and the Novel* (New York & Oxford: Oxford University Press)
KETE, KATHLEEN. 2012. *Making Way for Genius: The Aspiring Self in France from the Old Regime to the New* (New Haven, CT, & London: Yale University Press)
KLEIN, MELANIE. 1997. 'On the Sense of Loneliness', in *Envy and Gratitude and Other Works, 1946–1963* (London: Vintage), pp. 300–13
KRUEGER, CHERYL LEAH. 2012. '*Flâneur* Smellscapes in the *Spleen de Paris*', *Dix-Neuf*, 16.2: 181–92, <http://www.maneyonline.com/doi/full/10.1179/12Z.00000000016> [accessed 31 October 2016]
KRISTEVA, JULIA. 1997. *La Révolte intime: (discours direct)* (Paris: Fayard)
KSELMAN, THOMAS A. 1993. *Death and the Afterlife in Modern France* (Princeton, NJ: Princeton University Press)
KUENZLI, KATHERINE M. 2010. *The Nabis and Intimate Modernism* (Farnham: Ashgate)
LAMARTINE, ALPHONSE DE. 1845. *Souvenirs, impressions, pensées et paysages, pendant un voyage en Orient (1832–1833), ou Notes d'un voyageur*, in *Œuvres complètes*, 8 vols (Paris: C. Gosselin), VII
—— 1849. *Les Confidences* (Paris: Perrotin)
—— 1879. Letter to Sainte-Beuve, in *Œuvres de C.-A. Sainte-Beuve: poésies complètes*, ed. by Anatole France, 2 vols (Paris: Alphonse Lemerre), II, 147–49
—— 1954. *Jocelyn: épisode, journal trouvé chez un curé de village* (Paris: Garnier)
LANE, CHRISTOPHER. 1999. *The Burdens of Intimacy: Psychoanalysis and Victorian Masculinity* (Chicago, IL: University of Chicago Press)
LANG, CANDACE D. 1988. *Irony/Humour: Critical Paradigms* (Baltimore, MD: John Hopkins University Press)

LANGFORD, PAUL. 2000. *Englishness Identified: Manners and Characters, 1650–1850* (Oxford: Oxford University Press)
LATOUCHE, HENRI DE. 2008. 'De la camaraderie littéraire', reproduced in Anthony Glinoer, *La Querelle de la camaraderie littéraire* (Geneva: Droz), pp. 53–61
LEADER, ZACHARY. 1991. *Revision and Romantic Authorship* (Oxford: Clarendon Press)
LEAKEY, FELIX. 1992. *Baudelaire: Les Fleurs du Mal* (Cambridge: Cambridge University Press)
—— 1998. 'A Conversation Piece: Baudelaire's 'Causerie'', in *The Art of Reading: Essays in Memory of Dorothy Gabe Coleman*, ed. by Philip Ford and Gillian Jondorf (Cambridge: Cambridge French Colloquia), pp. 135–41
LEBON, HUBERT. 1857. *Cœur à cœur avec Jésus, ou Pieuses affections d'une âme aimante se plaçant en toute intimité avec son Dieu* (Lyon: Périsse Frères)
—— 1872. *Heart to Heart with Jesus: or, Pious Affections of a Loving Soul Placing Herself in Tender Intimacy with Her God*, trans. by Samuel Cooke (London: Thomas Richardson and Son)
LE DŒUFF, MICHÈLE. 1990. *Le Sexe du savoir* (Paris: Aubier)
LEGAULT, MARIANNE. 2008. *Narrations déviantes: l'intimité entre femmes dans l'imaginaire français du dix-septième siècle* (Quebec: Presses de l'Université Laval)
LEHMANN, A. G. 1962. *Sainte-Beuve: A Portrait of the Critic, 1804–1842* (Oxford: Clarendon Press)
LE HUENEN, RONALD. 2010. 'Mélancolie de Barbey d'Aurevilly: les deux premiers *Memoranda*', in *Barbey d'Aurevilly en tous genres*, ed. by Brigitte Diaz (Caen: Presses universitaires de Caen), pp. 33–44
LEJEUNE, PHILIPPE. 1993. *Le Moi des demoiselles: enquête sur le journal de jeune fille* (Paris: Seuil)
—— 2009. *On Diary*, ed. by Jeremy D. Popkin and Julie Rak, trans. by Katherine Durnin (Honolulu: University of Hawaii Press)
LETHBRIDGE, ROBERT. 1979. 'Fromentin's *Dominique* and the Art of Reflection', *Essays in French Literature*, 16: 43–61
LEWIS, ANN. 2009. *Sensibility, Reading and Illustration: Spectacles and Signs in Graffigny, Marivaux and Rousseau* (Oxford: Legenda)
LEWIS, PHILIPPA. 2013. 'The 'Voyage au Salon': The Virtual Journey in Nineteenth-Century French Art Criticism', *HARTS and Minds*, 1.2, <http://media.wix.com/ugd/30 89fd_934769007d15e855bc9b195c686e4371.pdf> [accessed 30 November 2016]
—— 2015. '"Une sympathie quittée": Holiday Friendships and Flaubert's *Voyage en Égypte*', *Modern Language Review*, 110.1: 104–20
LINKE, GABRIELE. 2011. 'The Public, the Private, and the Intimate: Richard Sennett's and Lauren Berlant's Cultural Criticism in Dialogue', *Biography*, 34.1: 11–24
LIONNET, FRANÇOISE. 1998. 'Reframing Baudelaire: Literary History, Biography, Postcolonial Theory, and Vernacular Languages', *Diacritics*, 28.3: 63–85
LIVINGSTONE, DAVID. 1999. 'Tropical Climate and Moral Hygiene: Anatomy of a Victorian Debate', *The British Journal for the History of Science*, 32: 93–110
LLOYD, ROSEMARY. 1981. *Baudelaire's Literary Criticism* (Cambridge: Cambridge University Press)
—— 2002. *Baudelaire's World* (Ithaca, NY, & London: Cornell University Press)
—— 2008. *Charles Baudelaire* (London: Reaktion Books)
LOCKE, JOHN L. 2010. *Eavesdropping: An Intimate History* (Oxford: Oxford University Press)
LUHMANN, NIKLAS. 1986. *Love as Passion: The Codification of Intimacy* (Stanford, CA: Stanford University Press)
LUKES, STEVEN. 1971. 'The Meanings of Individualism', *Journal of the History of Ideas*, 32.1: 45–66

LUXENBERG, ALISA. 2008. *The Galerie Espagnole and the Museo Nacional, 1835–1853: Saving Spanish Art or the Politics of Patrimony* (Aldershot: Ashgate)

LYONS, MARTYN. 1999. 'New Readers in the Nineteenth Century: Women, Children, Workers', in *A History of Reading in the West*, ed. by Gugleilmo Cavallo and Roger Chartier, trans. by Lydia G. Cochrane (Oxford: Polity Press), pp. 313–43

——2008. *Reading Culture and Writing Practices in Nineteenth-Century France* (Toronto: University of Toronto Press)

MCMILLAN, JAMES F. 2000. *France and Women 1789–1914* (London & New York: Routledge)

——2005. 'Catholic Christianity in France from the Restoration to the Separation of Church and State, 1815–1905', in *The Cambridge History of Christianity*, ed. by Sheridan Gilley and Brian Stanley (Cambridge: Cambridge University Press), VIII, 215–32

MCWILLIAM, NEIL. 1991A. *A Bibliography of Salon Criticism in Paris from the July Monarchy to the Second Republic, 1831–1851* (Cambridge: Cambridge University Press)

——1991B. *A Bibliography of Salon Criticism in Paris from the Ancien Régime to the Restoration, 1699–1827* (Cambridge: Cambridge University Press)

MADELÉNAT, DANIEL. 1989. *L'Intimisme* (Paris: Presses universitaires de France)

MAINARDI, PATRICIA. 1987. *Art and Politics of the Second Empire: The Universal Expositions of 1855 and 1867* (New Haven, CT, & London: Yale University Press)

MAJLUF, NATALIA. 1997. '"Ce n'est pas le Pérou" or, the Failure of Authenticity: Marginal Cosmopolitans at the Paris Universal Exhibition of 1855', *Critical Inquiry*, 23.4: 868–93

MARTIN, BRIAN JOSEPH. 2011. *Napoleonic Friendship: Military Fraternity, Intimacy and Sexuality in Nineteenth-Century France* (Durham: University of New Hampshire Press)

MARTIN-FUGIER, ANNE. 1999. 'Les Rites de la vie bourgeoise', in *Histoire de la vie privée*, ed. by Philippe Ariès and Georges Duby, 5 vols (Paris: Seuil), IV, 175–241

MATLOCK, JANN. 1994. *Scenes of Seduction: Prostitution, Hysteria, and Reading Difference in Nineteenth-Century France* (New York: Columbia University Press)

——1995. 'Censoring the Realist Gaze', in *Spectacles of Realism: Body, Gender, Genre*, ed. by Margaret Cohen and Christopher Prendergast (Minneapolis: University of Minnesota Press), pp. 28–65

MATT, SUSAN J. 2011. 'Current Emotion Research in History: Or, Doing History from the Inside Out', *Emotion Review*, 3.1: 117–24

MAZA, SARAH. 2003. *The Myth of the French Bourgeoisie: An Essay on the Social Imaginary* (Cambridge, MA, & London: Harvard University Press)

MELMOUX-MONTAUBIN, MARIE-FRANÇOISE. 2002. 'Les *Memoranda* de Jules Barbey d'Aurevilly: de la féminité comme apprentissage d'écriture', in *Masculin/Féminin dans la poésie et les poétiques du XIXe siècle*, ed. by Christine Planté (Lyon: Presses universitaires de Lyon), pp. 365–75

——2003. 'Autopsie d'un décès: la critique dans la presse quotidienne de 1836 à 1891', *Romantisme*, 121: 9–22

——2004. '"Contes de lettres" et écriture de soi: la critique littéraire dans le journal au XIXe siècle', in *Presse et plumes: journalisme et littérature au XIXe siècle*, ed. by Marie-Ève Thérenty and Alain Vaillant (Paris: Nouveau monde)

MELTZER, FRANÇOISE. 2011. *Double Vision: Baudelaire's Modernity* (Chicago: University of Chicago Press)

MELVILLE, HERMAN. 1857. *The Confidence-Man: His Masquerade* (New York: Dix, Edwards & Co.)

MICALE, MARK S. 2008. *Hysterical Men: The Hidden History of Male Nervous Illness* (Cambridge, MA, & London: Harvard University Press)

MICHELET, JULES. 1845. *Du prêtre, de la femme, de la famille* (Paris: Hachette)

——1974. *Œuvres complètes*, ed. by Paul Viallaneix, 21 vols (Paris: Flammarion), IV

MIJOLLA, ALAIN DE. 2010. *Freud et la France: 1885–1945* (Paris: Presses universitaires de France)
MOËLO, HERVÉ. 2004. 'L'Ordinaire et le littéraire', *Les Actes de lecture*, 85: 34–41
MOLE, TOM. 2007. *Byron's Romantic Celebrity: Industrial Culture and the Hermeneutic of Intimacy* (Basingstoke: Palgrave Macmillan)
MOLHO, RAPHAËL. 1963. *La Critique littéraire en France au XIXe siècle* (Paris: Buchet/Chastel)
MOLHO, RAPHAËL, and PIERRE REBOUL (eds). 1976. *Intime, Intimité, Intimisme* (Lille: Éditions universitaires, Université de Lille III)
MONNIOT, VICTORINE. 1867. *Le Journal de Marguerite ou Les Deux années préparatoires à la première communion* (Paris & Brussels: Régis Ruffet)
MONTAIGNE, MICHEL DE. 1978. *Les Essais de Michel de Montaigne*, ed. by V.-L. Saulnier, 2 vols (Paris: Presses universitaires de France), I
—— 1991. *The Essays of Michel de Montaigne*, trans. by M. A. Screech (London: Allen Lane)
MONTANDON, ALAIN (ed.). 2016. *Dictionnaire du dandysme* (Paris: Honoré Champion)
MONTÉGUT, ÉMILE. 1855. 'Types modernes en littérature: Werther', *Revue des deux mondes*, 2nd ser., 11: 333–44
—— 1858. 'Le Roman intime de la littérature réaliste (*Fanny* de M. Feydeau)', *Revue des deux mondes*, 2nd ser., 18: 196–213
MONTÉMONT, VÉRONIQUE. 2009. 'Dans la jungle de l'intime', in *Pour une histoire de l'intime et de ses variations*, ed. by Anne Coudreuse and Françoise Simonet-Tenant (Paris: L'Harmattan), pp. 15–38
MONTÉMONT, VÉRONIQUE, and FRANÇOISE SIMONET-TENANT (eds). 2013. *Intime et politique* (Paris: L'Harmattan)
MORETTI, FRANCO. 2013. *The Bourgeois: Between History and Literature* (Brooklyn, NY: Verso)
MORGAN, DAVID. 2009. *Acquaintances: The Space Between Intimates and Strangers* (Maidenhead: Open University Press)
MORTELETTE, YANN. 2005. *Histoire du Parnasse* (Paris: Fayard)
MUECKE, D. C. 1980. *Irony* (London: Methuen)
MULLER, EUGÈNE. 1861. *La Politesse française: traité des bienséances et du savoir-vivre* (Paris: Garnier-Frères)
MURPHY, MARGUERITTE. 2012. *Material Figures: Political Economy, Commercial Culture, and the Aesthetic Sensibility of Charles Baudelaire* (Amsterdam & New York: Rodopi)
MURPHY, STEVE. 2003. *Logiques du dernier Baudelaire: lectures du Spleen de Paris* (Paris: Honoré Champion)
MUSSET, ALFRED DE. 1973. *La Confession d'un enfant du siècle*, ed. by Gérard Barrier (Paris: Gallimard)
NADAR, FÉLIX. 1990. *Charles Baudelaire intime: le poète vierge* (Paris: Obsidiane)
NEUSCHEL, KRISTIN B. 1989. *Word of Honor: Interpreting Noble Culture in Sixteenth-Century France* (Ithaca, NY: Cornell University Press)
NIETZSCHE, FRIEDRICH. 1990. *Beyond Good and Evil*, trans. by R. J. Hollingdale (London: Penguin)
NISARD, DÉSIRÉ. 1847. 'Les Historiens romains', in *Revue des deux mondes*, new ser., 17: 383–96
—— 1891. *Essais sur l'école romantique* (Paris: Calmann Lévy)
NYE, ROBERT. 1998. *Masculinity and Male Codes of Honor in Modern France* (Berkley & London: University of California Press)
O'RAWE, CATHERINE. 2014. *Stars and Masculinities in Contemporary Italian Cinema* (New York: Palgrave Macmillan)

ORR, MARY. 2000. *Flaubert: Writing the Masculine* (Oxford: Oxford University Press)
—— 2003. *Intertextuality: Debates and Contexts* (Cambridge: Polity Press)
OSBORNE, MICHAEL A. 2000. 'Acclimatizing the World: A History of the Paradigmatic Colonial Science', *Osiris*, 2nd ser., 15: 135–51
PACHET, PIERRE. 1990. *Les Baromètres de l'âme: naissance du journal intime* (Paris: Hatier)
PARASCHAS, SOTIRIOS. 2013. *The Realist Author and the Sympathetic Imagination* (Oxford: Legenda)
PARDAILHÉ-GALABRUN, ANNIK. 1988. *La Naissance de l'intime: 3000 foyers parisiens, XVII–XVIIIe siècles* (Paris: Presses universitaires de France)
PARSONS, CHRISTOPHER, and MARTHA WARD. 1986. *A Bibliography of Salon Criticism in Second Empire Paris* (Cambridge: Cambridge University Press)
PEARSON, ROGER. 1988. *Stendhal's Violin: A Novelist and his Reader* (Oxford: Clarendon Press)
—— 2016. *Unacknowledged Legislators: The Poet as Lawgiver in Post-Revolutionary France* (Oxford: Oxford University Press)
PERRIER, CHARLES. 1855. 'L'Art à l'exposition universelle', *L'Artiste*, 5th ser., 15: 15–17
PERRIER, LOUIS. 1980. 'Intime, Intimité', in *Le Vocabulaire du sentiment dans l'œuvre de Jean-Jacques Rousseau*, ed. by Michel Gilot and Jean Sgard (Geneva: Slatkine), pp. 428–31
PERROT, MICHELLE. 1999. 'La Famille triomphante', in *Histoire de la vie privée*, ed. by Philippe Ariès and Georges Duby, 5 vols (Paris: Seuil), IV, 81–107
PERROT, PHILIPPE. 1981. *Le Dessus et les dessous de la bourgeoisie: une histoire du vêtement au XIXe siècle* (Paris: Fayard)
PICARD, DAVID. 2012. 'Tourism, Awe and Inner Journeys', in *Emotion in Motion: Tourism, Affect and Transformation*, ed. by David Picard and Mike Robinson (Farnham: Ashgate), pp. 1–19
PICHOIS, CLAUDE, and JEAN ZIEGLER. 1987. *Baudelaire* (Paris: Julliard)
PINNEY, CHRISTOPHER. 1992. 'Future Travel: Anthropology and Cultural Distance in an Age of Virtual Reality; or a Past Seen from a Possible Future', *Visual Anthropology Review*, 8.1: 38–55
PLAMPER, JAN. 2010. 'The History of Emotions: An Interview with William Reddy, Barbara Rosenwein, and Peter Stearns', *History and Theory*, 49.2: 237–65
—— 2015. *The History of Emotions: An Introduction*, trans. by Keith Tribe (Oxford: Oxford University Press)
PLANCHE, GUSTAVE. 1853A. 'Sainte-Beuve', in *Portraits littéraires*, 2 vols (Paris: Charpentier), I, 267–89
—— 1853B. 'Les Amitiés littéraires', in *Portraits littéraires*, 2 vols (Paris: Charpentier), II, 271–300
—— 1853C. 'De la critique française', in *Portraits littéraires*, 2 vols (Paris: Charpentier), II, 301–24
PLANTÉ, CHRISTINE. 1994. 'L'Intime comme valeur publique', in *La Lettre à la croisée de l'individuel et du social*, ed. by Mireille Bossis (Paris: Kimé), pp. 82–90
POPE, RICHARD. 2010. 'The *Jouissance* of the *Flâneur*: Rewriting Baudelaire and Modernity', *Space and Culture*, 13.1: 4–16
PRAZ, MARIO. 1970. *The Romantic Agony*, trans. by Angus Davidson (London & New York: Oxford University Press)
PRENDERGAST, CHRISTOPHER. 1986. *The Order of Mimesis: Balzac, Stendhal, Nerval, Flaubert* (Cambridge: University of Cambridge Press)
—— 2007. *The Classic: Sainte-Beuve and the Nineteenth-Century Culture Wars* (Oxford: Oxford University Press)
PRIEST, ROBERT D. 2014. 'Reading, Writing, and Religion in Nineteenth-Century France: The Popular Reception of Renan's *Life of Jesus*', *The Journal of Modern History*, 86:2: 258–94
PROBYN, ELSPETH. 2005. *Blush: Faces of Shame* (Sydney: UNSW Press)

PROUST, MARCEL. 1971. *Contre Sainte-Beuve* (Paris: Gallimard)
PUCKETT, KENT. 2008. *Bad Form: Social Mistakes and the Nineteenth-Century Novel* (Oxford: Oxford University Press)
RAISSON, HORACE-NAPOLÉON. 1853. *Code civil, manuel complet de la politesse, du ton, des manières de la bonne compagnie* (Paris: Renault)
RAITT, ALAN WILLIAM. 2005. *Gustavus Flaubertus bourgeoisophobus: Flaubert and the Bourgeois Mentality* (Oxford: Peter Lang)
RAND, RICHARD. 1997. *Intimate Encounters: Love and Domesticity in Eighteenth-Century France* (Hanover, NH: Hood Museum of Art, Dartmouth College; Princeton, NJ: Princeton University Press)
RAOUL, VALÉRIE. 2001. 'Women's Diaries as Life-Savings: Who Decides Whose Life is Saved? The Journals of Eugénie de Guérin and Elisabeth Leseur', *Biography*, 24.1: 140–51
REBREYAND, ANNE-CLAIRE. 2008. *Intimités amoureuses: France 1920–1975* (Toulouse: Presses universitaires du Mirail)
—— 2009. 'Représentations des intimités amoureuses dans la France du XX siècle', in *Pour une histoire de l'intime et de ses variations*, ed. by Anne Coudreuse and Françoise Simonet-Tenant (Paris: L'Harmattan), pp. 149–61
REDDY, WILLIAM. 1997. *The Invisible Code: Honor and Sentiment in Postrevolutionary France, 1814–1848* (Berkeley & London: University of California Press)
—— 2001. *The Navigation of Feeling: A Framework for the History of Emotions* (Cambridge: Cambridge University Press)
REES, KATE. 2010. *Flaubert: Transport, Progression, Progress* (Oxford & New York: Peter Lang)
RENAN, ERNEST. 1873. *Vie de Jésus* (Paris: Michel Lévy)
RIGAUX, FRANÇOIS. 1990. *La Protection de la vie privée et des autres biens de la personnalité* (Brussels: E. Bruylant)
RILEY, DENISE. 1988. *'Am I That Name?' Feminism and the Category of 'Women' in History* (Minneapolis: University of Minnesota)
RILKE, RAINER MARIA. 2016. *The Notebooks of Malte Laurids Brigge*, trans. by Robert Vilain (Oxford: Oxford University Press)
RISKIN, JENNIFER. 2002. *Science in the Age of Sensibility: The Sentimental Empiricists of the French Enlightenment* (Chicago, IL, & London: University of Chicago Press)
ROBB, GRAHAM. 1987. 'Le *Salon de 1846*: Baudelaire s'explique', *Nineteenth-Century French Studies*, 15.4: 415–24
—— 1990. 'Les Origines journalistiques de la prose poétique de Baudelaire', *Les Lettres romanes*, 44.1–2: 15–25
ROGERS, REBECCA. 2010. *From the Salon to the Schoolroom: Educating Bourgeois Girls in Nineteenth-Century France* (University Park: Pennsylvania State University Press)
ROSENGREN, KARL S., CARL N. JOHNSON, and PAUL L. HARRIS. 2000. *Imagining the Impossible: Magical, Scientific, and Religious Thinking in Children* (Cambridge: Cambridge University Press)
ROSENWEIN, BARBARA H. 2002. 'Worrying about Emotions in History', *The American Historical Review*, 107.3: 821–45
ROSTAING, JULES. [18—]. *Manuel de la politesse des usages du monde et du savoir-vivre* (Paris: Delarue)
ROUNDING, VIRGINIA. 2003. *Les Grandes Horizontales: The Lives and Legends of Marie Duplessis, Cora Pearl, La Païva and La Présidente* (London: Bloomsbury)
ROUSSEAU, JEAN-JACQUES. 1959. *Œuvres complètes*, ed. by Bernard Gagnebin and Marcel Raymond (Paris: Gallimard), I
SABIN, MARGERY. 1976. *English Romanticism and the French Tradition* (Cambridge, MA: Harvard University Press)

SAID, EDWARD. 1985. *Orientalism* (Harmondsworth: Penguin)
SAINT MARC, STÉPHANIE DE. 2010. *Nadar* (Paris: Gallimard)
SAINT-ALBIN, ALEXANDRE DE. 1851. *Une confession publique* (Paris: C. Douniol)
SAMINADAYAR-PERRIN, CORINNE. 2007. *Les Discours du journal: rhétorique et médias au XIXe siècle (1836–1885)* (Saint-Étienne: Publications de l'Université de Saint-Étienne)
SAMUELS, MAURICE. 2004. *The Spectacular Past: Popular History and the Novel in Nineteenth-Century France* (Ithaca, NY: Cornell University Press)
SAND, GEORGE. 1865. *La Confession d'une jeune fille* (Paris: Calmann-Lévy)
SARDOU, VICTORIEN. 1862. *Nos intimes! comédie en quatre actes* (Paris: Michel Lévy Frères)
SARTRE, JEAN-PAUL. 1975. *Baudelaire* (Paris: Gallimard)
SCHEER, MONIQUE. 2012. 'Are Emotions a Kind of Practice? (And is That What Makes Them Have a History?)', *History and Theory*, 51.2: 193–220
SCHELLINO, ANDREA. 2014. 'Baudelaire, la cuisine belge, et les "omelettes de M. Nadar"', *French Studies Bulletin*, 35: 68–71
SCHOLAR, RICHARD. 2005. *The Je-Ne-Sais-Quoi in Early Modern Europe: Encounters with a Certain Something* (Oxford: Oxford University Press)
SCHOR, NAOMI. 1987. *Reading in Detail: Aesthetics and the Feminine* (London: Methuen)
——1993. *George Sand and Idealism* (New York: Columbia University Press)
——1999. 'Domestic Orientalism', in *Corps/décors: femmes, orgie, parodie*, ed. by Catherine Nesci (Amsterdam, Rodopi), pp. 57–65
SCHULTZ, GRETCHEN. 1999. *The Gendered Lyric: Subjectivity and Difference in Nineteenth-Century French Poetry* (West Lafayette, IN: Purdue University Press)
SCOTT, MARIA. 2005. *Le Spleen de Paris: Shifting Perspectives* (Aldershot: Ashgate)
SEDGWICK, EVE KOSOFKSY. 1990. *Epistemology of the Closet* (Berkeley: University of California Press)
SEDGWICK, EVE KOSOFSKY, and ADAM FRANK. 1995. *Shame and its Sisters: A Silvan Tomkins Reader* (Durham, NC, & London: Duke University Press)
SEGAL, NAOMI. 1988. *Narcissus and Echo: Women in the French Récit* (Manchester: Manchester University Press)
SENNETT, RICHARD. 1993. *The Fall of Public Man* (London: Faber and Faber)
——1995. *Les Tyrannies de l'intimité*, trans. by Antoine Berman and Rebecca Folkman (Paris: Seuil)
SERVAIS, PAUL, and LAURENCE VAN YPERSELE (eds). 2007. *La Lettre et l'intime: l'émergence d'une expression du for intérieur dans les correspondances privées, 17e–19e siècles* (Louvain-la-Neuve: Academia Brulant)
SIEBERS, TOBY. 1988. *The Ethics of Criticism* (Ithaca, NY: Cornell University Press)
SIMMEL, GEORG. 1950. 'The Stranger', in *The Sociology of Georg Simmel*, trans. and ed. by Kurt Wolff (Glencoe: Free Press), pp. 402–08
SIMONET-TENANT, FRANÇOISE. 2004. *Le Journal intime: genre littéraire et écriture ordinaire* (Paris: Téraèdre)
——2009. *Journal personnel et correspondance (1785–1939) ou Les Affinités électives* (Louvain-la-Neuve: Academia Brulant)
SIMONSEN, PETER. 2007. *Wordsworth and the Word-Preserving Arts: Typographic Inscription, Ekphrasis and Posterity in the Later Work* (Basingstoke: Palgrave Macmillan)
SMITH, MAXWELL A. 1920. *L'Influence des Lakistes sur les romantiques français* (Paris: Jouve & compagnie)
SMITH, VANESSA. 2010. *Intimate Strangers: Friendship, Exchange, and Pacific Encounters* (Cambridge: Cambridge University Press)
SPACKS, PATRICIA MEYER. 1986. *Gossip* (Chicago & London: University of Chicago Press)
STAFFE, BLANCHE. 1897. *Usages du monde: règles du savoir-vivre dans la société moderne* (Paris: Harvard)

STAROBINSKI, JEAN. 1957. *Jean-Jacques Rousseau: la transparence et l'obstacle* (Paris: Plon)
STENDHAL. 1980. *De l'amour*, ed. by V. Del Litto (Paris: Gallimard)
STEPHENS, SONYA. 1998. 'Voices in the Night: "À une heure du matin"', in *The Art of Reading: Essays in Memory of Dorothy Gabe Coleman*, ed. by Philip Ford and Gillian Jondorf (Cambridge: Cambridge French Colloquia), pp. 143–53
—— 1999. *Baudelaire's Prose Poems: The Practice and Politics of Irony* (Oxford: Oxford University Press)
—— 2001. 'Contingencies and Discontinuities of the Lyric I: Baudelaire as Poet-Narrator and Diarist', in *Baudelaire and the Poetics of Modernity*, ed. by Patricia A. Ward (Nashville, TN: Vanderbilt University Press), pp. 134–43
STERNBERG, ROBERT J., and WEIS, KARIN (eds). 2011. *The New Psychology of Love* (New Haven, CT, & London: Yale University Press)
STOLER, ANN LAURA. 2006. 'Intimidations of Empire: Predicaments of the Tactile and Unseen', in *Haunted by Empire: Geographies of Intimacy in North American History*, ed. by Ann Laura Stoler (Durham, NC, & London: Duke University Press), pp. 1–22
STURROCK, JOHN. 1993. *The Language of Autobiography: Studies in the First-Person Singular* (Cambridge: Cambridge University Press)
SULLEROT, ÉVELYNE. 1963. *La Presse féminine* (Paris: A. Colin)
SUSSMAN, HERBERT. 1995. *Victorian Masculinities: Manhood and Masculine Poetics in Early Victorian Literature and Art* (Cambridge: Cambridge University Press)
SWART, KOENRAAD W. 1962. 'Individualism in the Mid-Nineteenth Century (1826–1860)', *Journal of the History of Ideas*, 23.1: 77–90
TAYLOR, CHARLES. 1989. *Sources of the Self: The Making of the Modern Identity* (Cambridge: Cambridge University Press)
TERASHIMA, MIYUKA. 2011. 'Le Discours de "l'intime" dans *Les Rougon-Macquart*. Étude d'une trilogie romanesque: *La Joie de vivre, L'Œuvre, Le Docteur Pascal*' (unpublished doctoral thesis, Université Sorbonne Nouvelle — Paris 3)
TERDIMAN, RICHARD. 1985. *Discourse/Counter-Discourse: The Theory and Practice of Symbolic Resistance in Nineteenth-Century France* (Ithaca, NY: Cornell University Press)
TEXIER, EDMOND. 1842. *Physiologie du poëte par Sylvius* (Paris: J. Laisné)
TINTEROW, GARY. 2003. 'Raphael Replaced: The Triumph of Spanish Painting in France', in *Manet/Velázquez: The French Taste for Spanish Painting*, ed. by Gary Tinterow and Geneviève Lacambre (New York: Metropolitan Museum of Art), pp. 3–66
TODD, JANET. 1986. *Sensibility: An Introduction* (London: Methuen)
TOMBS, ISABELLE, and ROBERT TOMBS. 2008. *That Sweet Enemy: Britain and France, The History of a Love-Hate Relationship* (New York: Vintage Books)
TOOKE, ADRIANNE. 2004A. 'Flaubert's Travel Writings', in *The Cambridge Companion to Flaubert*, ed. by Timothy Unwin (Cambridge: Cambridge University Press), pp. 51–66
—— 2004B. 'Flaubert: Views of the Orient', in *Eastern Voyages, Western Visions*, ed. by Margaret Topping (New York: Peter Lang, 2004), pp. 167–86
TRAPP, FRANK ANDERSON. 1965. 'The Universal Exhibition of 1855', *The Burlington Magazine*, 107.747: 300–05
TREBUTIEN, G. S. 1862. 'Avertissement de l'éditeur', in *Eugénie de Guérin, Journal et lettres, publiés avec l'assentiment de la famille par G. S Trebutien* (Paris: Didier), pp. I–XII
VAILLANT, ALAIN. 2009. 'Baudelaire, artiste moderne de la "poésie-journal"', *Études littéraires*, 40.3: 43–60
—— 2011. *Baudelaire journaliste: articles et chroniques* (Paris: Flammarion)
VALÉRY, PAUL. 1957. *Œuvres*, ed. by Jean Hytier, 2 vols (Paris: Gallimard), I
VERMEULE, BLAKEY. 2011. *Why Do We Care About Literary Characters?* (Baltimore, MD: John Hopkins University Press)
VERNON, MARK. 2005. *The Philosophy of Friendship* (Basingstoke: Palgrave Macmillan)

VERONA, ROXANA. 1999. *Les Salons de Sainte-Beuve: le critique et ses muses* (Paris & Geneva: Champion)
VINCENT, PATRICK H. 2004. *The Romantic Poetess: European Culture, Politics, and Gender, 1820–1840* (Durham: New Hampshire University Press)
VINCENT-BUFFAULT, ANNE. 1986. *Histoire des larmes: XVIII–XIX siècles* (Marseille: Rivages)
―― 1995. *L'Exercice de l'amitié: pour une histoire des pratiques amicales au XIXe siècle* (Paris: Seuil)
VIRILIO, PAUL. 1990. *L'Inertie polaire* (Paris: C. Bourgois)
WALL, GEOFFREY. 2006. 'The Invisible Man: An Essay on Flaubert and Celebrity', *Cambridge Quarterly*, 35.2: 133–50
WALLER, MARGARET. 1993. *The Male Malady: Fictions of Impotence in the French Romantic Novel* (New Brunswick, NJ: Rutgers University Press)
WATT-SMITH, TIFFANY. 2014. *The Book of Human Emotion* (London: Profile Books)
WELLEK, RENÉ. 1955–92. *A History of Modern Criticism 1750–1950*, 8 vols (New Haven, CT: Yale University Press)
WHIDDEN, SETH. 2007. *Leaving Parnassus: The Lyric Subject in Verlaine and Rimbaud* (Amsterdam: Rodopi)
WHITE, NICHOLAS. 2013. *French Divorce Fiction from the Revolution to the First World War* (Oxford: Legenda)
WILLIAMS, D. A. 1987. *The Hidden Life at its Source: A Study of Flaubert's 'L'Éducation sentimentale'* (Hull: Hull University Press)
WILLIAMS, RAYMOND. 1976. *Keywords* (London: Fontana)
WILSON, ANNASUE. 2013. 'An Unseemly Emotion: PW Talks with Claire Messud', *Publishers Weekly*, <http://www.publishersweekly.com/pw/by-topic/authors/interviews/article/56848-an-unseemly-emotion-pw-talks-with-claire-messud.html> [accessed 11 October 2016]
WRIGHT, BARBARA. 2000. *Eugène Fromentin: A Life in Art and Letters* (Bern & Oxford: Peter Lang)
YACAVONE, KATHRIN. 2017. '"Une corde de plus à l'arc de tout le monde": l'usage de la photographie chez Balzac et Hugo', in *L'Écrivain vu par la photographie. Formes, usages, enjeux (XIXe–XXIe siècles): actes du Colloque de Cerisy-la-Salle*, ed. by David Martens, Jean-Pierre Montier, and Anne Reverseau, pp. 51–57
YOUSEF, NANCY. 2013. *Romantic Intimacy* (Stanford, CA: Stanford University Press)
ZAROBELL, JOHN. 2010. *Empires of Landscape: Space and Ideology in French Colonial Algeria* (University Park: Pennsylvania State University Press)
ZELDIN, THEODORE. 1994. *An Intimate History of Humanity* (London: Sinclair-Stevenson)
ZIMMERMAN, MELVIN. 1968. 'Critical Notes', in Charles Baudelaire, *Petits poèmes en prose*, ed. by Melvin Zimmerman (Manchester: Manchester University Press), pp. 93–157
ZUNSHINE, LISA. 2006. *Why We Read Fiction: Theory of Mind and the Novel* (Columbus: Ohio State University Press)

Modern Dictionaries

Le Grand Robert de la langue française: dictionnaire alphabétique et analogique de la langue française, ed. by Alain Rey, 9 vols (Paris: Le Robert, 1985)
Le Petit Robert de la langue française: dictionnaire alphabétique et analogique de la langue française, Nouvelle édition millésime 2017, ed. by Josette Rey-Debove and Alain Rey (Paris: Le Robert, 2016)

Historical Dictionaries

The asterisked dictionaries have been accessed via the *Dictionnaires d'autrefois* website provided by the Project for American and French Research on the Treasury of the French Language (ARTFL), Centre national de la recherche scientifique (CNRS), University of Chicago, <http://artfl-project.uchicago.edu/content/dictionnaires-dautrefois> [accessed 26 May 2017]

*NICOT, JEAN. *Le Thresor de la langue françoyse*, 1606
*FÉRAUD, JEAN-FRANÇOIS. *Dictionaire critique de la langue française*, 1787–88
**Dictionnaire de l'Académie française*: 1st ed. (1694); 4th (1762); 5th (1798); 6th (1835)
LITTRÉ, ÉMILE. *Dictionnaire de la langue française* (Paris: Hachette, 1873–74). Electronic version created by François Gannaz, <http://www.littre.org> [accessed 26 May 2017]

Online Resources

Dictionnaire électronique des synonymes, Centre de recherche inter-langues sur la signification en contexte (CRISCO), Université de Caen, <http://www.crisco.unicaen.fr/des/> [accessed 26 May 2017]
Frantext database, ATILF — CNRS and Université de Lorraine, <http://www.frantext.fr> [accessed 26 May 2017]

INDEX

abandon 17, 48, 56, 72, 80, 95, 150
About, Edmond 122, 133, 134, 135
acquaintance 94–97, 100, 110–11, 114 n. 2 & 4
Aïssé, Charlotte-Élisabeth 31
Algeria 109–14, 128
Amiel, Henri-Frédéric 68, 90 n. 13
ancien régime 26, 95
Anderson, Amanda 7, 12 n. 2, 64 n. 9, 91 n. 36, 130
Antoine, Gérald 154 n. 11, 155 n. 20
anxiety 6, 74, 93, 96, 105, 110, 150
Asselineau, Charles 40, 48–49
Attachment Theory 6, 162
Audouard, Olympe 152–53, 155 n. 25
autobiography 8, 32–36, 48, 55, 57–58, 65 n. 25 & 28, 77, 89, 92 n. 48, 102, 108, 163
Avrane, Patrick 80, 91 n. 33

Bakhtin, Mikhail 80, 101
Balzac, Honoré de 10, 11, 30, 43 n. 51, 115 n. 7
   Illusions perdues 142–43, 145, 155 n. 21
Banville, Théodore de 7
Barbéris, Pierre 57
Barbey d'Aurevilly, Jules Amédée:
   Du dandysme et de G. Brummell 79, 91 n. 30 & 33
   Les Bas-Bleus 150
   Memoranda 67, 76–81, 84, 91 n. 27, 30, 32 & 34, 161
   'Sainte-Beuve' 150
Barthes, Roland 13 n. 26, 57, 65 n. 28, 67, 79, 91 n. 37, 117, 140, 163
Bashkirtseff, Marie 71, 90 n. 13
Baudelaire, Charles:
   'Conseils aux jeunes littérateurs' 143
   Études sur Poe 158
   Exposition universelle – 1855: 118, 134–38
   Fusées 92 n. 42, 102, 103
   Hygiène 92 n. 42, 102, 103
   La Belgique déshabillée 42 n. 32, 93, 94, 102–08, 112, 115 n. 22 & 26
   '*La Double Vie*, par Charles Asselineau' 40, 48, 49, 122
   Le Peintre de la vie moderne 136–37
   Le Spleen de Paris 81–82, 103
      'À une heure du matin' 67, 81–89, 92 n. 42 & 48, 131
      'Assommons les pauvres !' 81
      'L'Étranger' 137
      'La Solitude' 132
      'Le Mauvais Vitrier' 81
      'Les Foules' 107
   Les Fleurs du Mal 44, 49–52, 55, 56, 65 n. 21, 81, 82, 83, 92 n. 43, 103, 156
      'Au Lecteur' 83
      'Causerie' 51
      'Confession' 44, 49, 52–56, 58, 59, 64, 89, 107, 136
      'Je n'ai pas oublié, voisine de la ville' 51
      'L'Examen de minuit' 82
      'L'Invitation au voyage' 51
      'La Cloche fêlée' 51
      'Le Balcon' 50–51
      'Le Voyage' 88
      'Semper eadem' 51
      'Sonnet d'automne' 51
   Les Paradis artificiels 56, 164
   Mon cœur mis à nu 65 n. 13, 92 n. 42, 102, 103
   'Pierre Dupont [I]' 157
   'Richard Wagner et *Tannhäuser* à Paris' 130–31, 136, 157, 158
   Salon de 1845: 118, 130, 133, 157
   Salon de 1846: 34, 117, 120, 122, 123–29, 130, 131–33, 134, 136
   Salon de 1859: 116 n. 34, 117–18, 122–23, 133, 138 n. 6
   'Théophile Gautier [I]' 47, 48, 157–58
Baudrillard, Jean 12 n. 9
Bauman, Zygmunt 4–5, 6
Behdad, Ali 115 n. 12 & 25
Belgium 102–08, 115 n. 24, 133, 138
Berlant, Lauren 4–5, 6, 13 n. 13, 21, 137–38
Bersani, Leo 11, 13 n. 17
Berthier, Philippe 91 n. 34
Biasi, Pierre-Marc de 115 n. 11, 12, 18 & 21
biography 8, 28, 30, 65 n. 25, 156–61, 163–64
   biographical criticism 144–54
Blake, William 124
Blanchot, Maurice 67
Blin, Georges 14 n. 32, 50–52, 56, 64 n. 8
Bloy, Léon 103
body 6, 45, 46, 72, 77, 104, 107–08, 126, 133, 136, 146–47, 150
Bogh, Mikkel 43 n. 53, 89, 138 n. 1
Bologne, Jean-Claude 46
Bonnard, Pierre 117
Bouilhet, Louis 98, 101, 108
Bourdieu, Pierre 41 n. 21, 151
Bourke, Joanna 12 n. 8, 91 n. 22
Bowlby, John 6

Britain 7, 12 n. 10, 23, 27, 42 n. 24, 133
  see also England
Brummell, George 79, 91 n. 30
Brussels 102, 105–07, 115 n. 23
  see also Belgium
Burt, E. S. 55
Byron, George Gordon 9, 76, 78, 91 n. 30, 146

camaraderie 17, 130, 133, 141–44, 154 n. 9, 157
caricature 51, 84–86, 95, 103, 109
Catholicism 22, 28–29, 42 n. 27, 46, 68, 71–74, 83, 91 n. 22 & 33
Caughey, John L. 146
causerie 19, 29, 51, 59, 80, 91 n. 25, 98–101, 141, 152, 154, 155 n. 22
celebrity 4, 5, 9, 38, 47, 106, 137, 146–48, 157, 164
Céline, Louis-Ferdinand 103
cénacle 26–27, 40, 141–47, 154 n. 10
Chambers, Ross 56, 90 n. 2, 139 n. 14, 140, 151
Charrière, Isabelle de 31, 148–49
Chateaubriand, François-René de 31, 125, 142, 154
childhood 6, 23, 38, 45, 47, 55, 68, 88, 136, 139 n. 23, 153, 155 n. 26, 158, 161
  see also immaturity
children's literature 69–70, 82
China 133–34
Chotard, Loïc 146, 148
Christianity 42 n. 28, 73, 90 n. 17, 91 n. 20
  see also Catholicism, Protestantism
Christin, Anne-Marie 110, 112–13, 116 n. 34 & 38
Cladel, Léon 106
Claudel, Paul 103
Clerval, Alain 57
Cohen, Margaret 12 n. 3, 14 n. 30, 21, 31, 32, 37, 42 n. 38
Compagnon, Antoine 14 n. 33, 57
confession:
  as literary mode 32, 39, 44, 48–64, 64 n. 12, 65 n. 27, 77, 87, 107–08
  as religious practice 29, 42 n. 32, 65 n. 14
  see also Baudelaire, 'Confession'
confidence 17, 19, 29, 32, 48, 51, 55, 56, 58, 60, 62–63, 64 n. 12, 68, 70, 77, 80, 96, 107–08, 111, 117, 164
confident 17, 62, 70, 91 n. 32, 96
Connell, R. W. 45, 64 n. 3
Constant, Benjamin 31, 68, 90 n. 13
contagion 105–06, 116 n. 33, 150, 116 n. 30
conversation 19, 35, 51, 78–80, 97–98, 117, 146, 152, 155 n. 22, 157
Corbin, Alain 13 n. 22, 97, 115 n. 6
cosmopolitanism 12 n. 2, 128–31, 133–38, 139 n. 12 & 13
Cottin, Sophie 37
Coudreuse, Anne 8, 14 n. 28, 42 n. 40
crowds 52, 107, 137

dandyism 7, 12 n. 1, 65 n. 22, 76, 78–79, 80, 91 n. 30 & 36, 130, 137, 139 n. 24
Daumier, Honoré 35, 84, 95
David, Jules A. 31, 36
Dayan, Peter 116 n. 27 & 28
De Quincey, Thomas de 64 n. 12, 86, 92 n. 47
Decamps, Alexandre Gabriel 122, 123, 126
Delacroix, Eugène 102, 110, 116 n. 37, 123–28, 138, 138 n. 6, 157, 160
Delécluze, Étienne-Jean, Mademoiselle Justine de Liron 31, 33, 37–38, 152
dépaysement 90, 124, 137
Desbordes-Valmore, Marceline 49
Desjardins, Paul 87
detachment 2, 7–8, 64 n. 9, 66, 112, 130–31, 136, 138, 147, 159
detail 35, 118, 120, 123–24, 126, 138 n. 2, 160
diary 1, 2, 8, 30, 66–90, 90 n. 3 & 11, 91 n. 23 & 32, 118, 159
  gendering of 68–69, 75, 90 n. 6 & 7
  history of 68–70, 90 n. 5
  and literary theory 66, 67, 89
  and publication 70, 73, 75, 82, 84, 88–89, 90 n. 13, 91 n. 18 & 27
  see also examen de conscience, roman-diaristique
Diaz, Brigitte 2, 8, 9, 13 n. 24, 19, 39, 40, 53, 69, 80, 90 n. 8, 92 n. 38, 159
Diaz, José-Luis 2, 8, 9, 10, 13 n. 24, 19, 34, 39, 40, 43 n. 51, 53, 69, 80, 90 n. 8, 144–45, 156, 159, 163
Diderot, Denis 31, 37, 146–47
Didier, Béatrice 73, 92 n. 42
disgust 103, 105, 108, 116 n. 30
domesticity 24–25, 29, 35, 40, 50–51, 69, 89–90, 100, 120, 123–24
Drouineau, Gustave 58, 65 n. 26, 118
Du Barail, François-Charles 109–10
Du Camp, Maxime 101, 115 n. 18
Du Mesnil, Armand 94, 108, 110, 112–13, 116 n. 41
Dufour, Hélène 144, 147, 154 n. 12, 157
Dupont, Jacques 12, 14 n. 32, 51
Dupont, Pierre 157
Duras, Claire de 31
Duvergier de Hauranne, Prosper 35, 38, 39–40

Egypt 97, 98, 104, 109. 129
Ellison, Julie 14 n. 28, 21, 154 n. 4, 155 n. 26
embarrassment 44, 46, 53, 55–56, 58, 63–64, 159
Emery, Elizabeth 164 n. 3
emotions 7–8, 22–23, 24
  see also history of emotions
empathy 9, 88, 107
England 21, 27–28, 35, 42 n. 23, 38 & 46, 116 n. 33, 122–23, 126, 133, 138 n. 3 & 5, 139 n. 17
  see also Britain
enigma 79, 81, 161
Enlightenment 4, 7, 9, 22

epistolary fiction 31, 37, 69, 110–11, 112–14
  see also letter-writing
etiquette manuals 2, 24–25, 41 n. 15, 47, 91 n. 20, 93,
  94–98, 100, 102, 105, 106, 108, 112, 114, 149
examen de conscience 68, 82, 84

family 2, 3–5, 12 n. 7, 24–25, 28, 30, 35, 70, 75, 78,
  100, 130, 137, 164
fan mail 11, 38–39, 43 n. 51
Felski, Rita 12 n. 5, 140, 163–64
femininity 23, 28–29, 36, 40, 46, 48, 55, 64 n. 9, 73,
  76, 80, 105, 120, 150, 155 n. 20, 159
Feydeau, Ernest, *Fanny* 14 n. 31, 25, 41 n. 17, 42 n. 37
flâneur 107, 128, 130, 137, 139 n. 24
Flaubert, Gustave:
  Bouvard et Pécuchet 115 n. 19, 155 n. 15
  L'Éducation sentimentale 97–98, 99, 115 n. 19
  Madame Bovary 101
  Mémoires d'un fou 97, 101, 115 n. 20
  Novembre 101
  Voyage en Égypte 93, 97, 98–102, 114 n. 1, 115 n. 11 & 26
Fraisse, Armand 51, 55–56
France, Anatole 35
Freud, Sigmund 11, 139 n. 23, 162, 164 n. 5
friendship 23, 59–60, 114 n. 4 & 5, 140–45, 158
  amitié-passion 99, 148
  and Christianity 90 n. 17
  dangers of 25, 93–97, 130, 132–33
  false friendship 94, 96, 104, 108, 110–12
  history of 8, 13 n. 22 & 25, 144–45
  ideals of 36, 94–95, 101, 112–14, 132–33, 149, 158
  between men 17, 26, 58, 63, 81, 98–102, 115 n. 19, 160
  as narrative device 58, 62–63, 110–14, 116 n. 39
  and reading 37–39, 140–41, 144–45
  and role in criticism 130, 140–54, 157–58
  between women 71, 155 n. 25
  and writing 76–78, 91 n. 32, 112–14
  see also *camaraderie*, *cénacle*, sociability
Fromentin, Eugène:
  Dominique 44, 57–64, 65 n. 23, 24 & 27, 109, 114, 115 n. 35
  Gustave Drouineau 58, 65 n. 26, 118
  Un été dans le Sahara 93, 94, 108, 109–13, 116 n. 39
  Une année dans le Sahel 109, 110

Gautier, Théophile 47, 48, 128–29, 133–34, 135, 157–58
Gay, Peter 95, 115 n. 14
Gazette des Beaux-Arts 117
genre painting 118–24
Gerson, Stéphane 47
Gide, André 117, 138
Gill, Miranda 41 n. 5 & 22, 64 n. 9
Girard, Alain 68, 76, 90 n. 6, 9 & 13, 91 n. 23 & 29
Girardin, Delphine de 34

Glinoer, Anthony 125, 142, 143–44, 145, 154 n. 7, 9 & 10, 155 n. 21
Goethe, Johann Wolfgang von 31, 146
Gosling, Nigel 160
Green, Anne 115 n. 8
Grøtta, Marit 84
Guérin, Eugénie de:
  Journal et lettres 66–67, 70–76, 77, 84, 89, 90 n. 13, 91 n. 18, 118, 126
  Reliquiae 73, 91 n. 21, 92 n. 45
Guérin, Maurice de 34, 70–71, 72–73, 74, 76, 77, 78, 79, 80, 90 n. 13
Guizot, François 27–28, 42 n. 25
Guyaux, André 14 n. 33, 102, 103, 104, 115 n. 22 & 26
Guys, Constantin 136–37

Habermas, Jürgen 3–5, 6, 33, 41 n. 10
Hamon, Philippe 90 n. 2, 91 n. 36
'happy few' 11, 34, 42 n. 43, 82
  see also Stendhal
Harkness, Nigel 32
Harris, Trevor A. Le V. 58
Heredia, José-Maria de 7
heteronormativity 5, 29
Hiddleston, J. A. 83, 84
history of emotions 8, 13 n. 22, 41 n. 7
Holmes, Jeremy 6
home 3–4, 24–25, 27–28, 35, 50–51, 89, 123, 124, 164 n. 3
honnêteté 47
honour 2, 44, 46, 47
Horowitz, Sarah 13 n. 22 & 25, 27, 42 n. 25, 114 n. 5
Howells, Bernard 49, 65 n. 13 & 14, 103
Hugo, Victor 26, 30, 31, 34, 42 n. 33, 53, 124, 125, 126, 142, 143, 13 n. 25
humiliation 9, 46, 47, 48, 52, 54, 61, 131
Hunt, Lynn 13 n. 21, 22–23
Hutcheon, Linda 79, 90 n. 1 & 2
hysteria 150, 155 n. 18

Iacub, Marcela 46
illness 54, 55, 71, 107, 108
immaturity 52, 54, 60, 65 n. 19, 76, 136, 106, 153, 159
impartiality 130, 134, 136, 149
impersonality 2, 4, 7–8, 13 n. 18, 98, 101, 144, 159
individualism 5, 7, 27, 41 n. 20, 122
Ingres, Jean-Auguste-Dominique 120, 121, 128
interiority 5–6, 16, 17, 18, 72, 123, 133
intersubjectivity 3, 5, 16, 17, 70, 88, 126, 131, 137, 156
intertextuality 13 n. 15, 50, 57, 82, 86, 116 n. 36, 163
intimacy:
  dangers of 20, 94–97, 110–12, 150
  definitions of 1–3, 16–18
  effet d'intime 8, 13 n. 24, 40, 53, 80, 101
  'hermeneutic of intimacy' 9, 36, 37, 43 n. 53, 55, 57–58, 82, 87, 117, 163

ideological appeal in nineteenth-century France 21–30
Intimism 117, 138 n. 1
'lateral intimacy' and 'vertical intimacy' 17, 28, 36, 71, 126, 133
'minor intimacies' 5, 137, 138
and reading 37–41, 88, 163–64
in scholarship 2, 3–10, 12 n. 6 & 7, 13 n. 12, 14 & 25
semantic plasticity of 2–3, 28, 30, 123, 124
word histories of 16–21
inwardness 17–18, 33, 126, 133
irony 66, 67, 70, 72–73, 74, 75, 76, 77–90, 90 n. 1 & 2, 91 n. 36, 92 n. 43, 131, 159
Italy 27, 44 n. 22

James, Henry 1, 12 n. 1, 152, 155 n. 17 & 20
Jamieson, Lynn 3
Janin, Jules 152–53
Jarry, Alfred 103
Jefferson, Ann 41 n. 5, 42 n. 39, 43 n. 49, 90 n. 4, 92 n. 41, 155 n. 13
journal de voyage 69, 101, 102, 115 n. 21
journal intime, see diary
journalism 30, 78, 84, 86, 87, 88, 102, 125, 128, 134, 140, 143, 145, 151–53, 155 n. 23 & 24
July Monarchy 2, 10, 15, 26, 27, 30, 34, 42 n. 24, 46, 69, 78, 117, 140, 141, 142, 146, 156, 159, 161

Kang, Mathilde 69, 73
Karr, Alphonse 149
Kete, Kathleen 64 n. 10, 155 n. 13
Klein, Melanie 6
Kristeva, Julia 5–6, 13 n. 15, 18, 162
Krüdener, Julie de, *Valérie* 31, 32, 33, 38, 42 n. 36

La Boétie, Étienne de 144, 148
La Morvonnais, Hippolyte de 34
La Presse 67, 82, 84, 85, 86, 88
La Renaissance latine 77, 91 n. 27
Lake Poets 35, 122
Lamartine, Alix de 68–69, 71, 75, 90 n. 10
Lamartine, Alphonse de 26, 28, 34, 38–40, 68–69, 75, 90 n. 10
Latouche, Henri 141, 142–44, 154 n. 9
Le Globe 35
Le Papillon 152–53
Le Pays 134
Leakey, Felix 51
Leconte de Lisle, Charles 7
Lejeune, Philippe 67, 90 n. 3, 5 & 7
letter-writing 1, 8, 31, 49, 50, 52–54, 70, 74–75, 77, 78, 90 n. 11, 101, 112–13, 146, 153, 159, 164
Lewis, Ann 22, 36, 41 n. 6
literary criticism, history of 141–44
see also biographical criticism

Lloyd, Rosemary 64 n. 11, 103, 158, 164 n. 1 & 2
loneliness 6, 56, 59
Luhmann, Niklas 5, 13 n. 12
Lyons, Martyn 13 n. 23, 39

Madélenat, Daniel 3, 8, 30, 42 n. 46, 43 n. 47, 50, 51
Magnin, Charles 34
Mainardi, Patricia 122, 139 n. 21
Majluf, Natalia 133, 139 n. 18
marriage 24–25, 45, 137
Martin, Nicolas 34
masculinity 7, 21, 29, 44, 45–48, 54, 58, 61, 63, 64, 64 n. 3, 76, 78, 91 n. 30, 120
maternal love 6, 136, 161
Matlock, Jann 14 n. 29, 43 n. 51, 150
Mauritius 138
melancholy 20, 36, 53, 61, 68, 73, 79, 91 n. 28, 117
Melmoux-Montaubin, Marie-Françoise 91 n. 28 & 30, 92 n. 39, 151, 155 n. 23
Melville, Herman 96
Michelet, Jules 29, 90 n. 13, 149
modernity 14 n. 33, 33, 34, 45, 57, 59, 97, 98, 105, 110, 123, 128, 136
modesty 35, 46–48, 49, 55, 59, 60, 64, 89, 103
Mole, Tom 9, 36, 37, 163
Molho, Raphaël 138 n. 8, 142, 154 n. 3
Monniot, Victorine 69, 70, 82
Montaigne, Michel de 144, 148, 149
Montégut, Émile 14 n. 31, 42 n. 37, 43 n. 50
Montémont, Véronique 8, 16–19, 41 n. 2, 69, 70, 133
Montpensier, Mademoiselle de 31
Morgan, David 97, 100, 114 n. 2
Murphy, Margueritte 134, 135
Murphy, Steve 81–82, 87
Musée espagnol 131–33, 139 n. 15 & 17

Nadar, Félix 106, 156, 160–62, 164 n. 4
Napoleonic Code 45
nationalism 27–28, 124, 128, 129–31, 146
Nietzsche, Freidrich 44, 58
Nisard, Désiré 31, 142, 146
nostalgia 15, 26, 27, 35, 132, 143
Nye, Robert 45, 46

O'Rawe, Catherine 64 n. 3
Orientalism 94, 109, 110, 116 n. 34 & 37

paranoia 24, 95, 104, 112
Paraschas, Sotirios 43 n. 49, 81, 92 n. 43
para-social bonds 9, 13 n. 27, 37, 108, 141, 146, 152
Parnassianism 2, 7, 13 n. 18
patriotism 27–28, 129–31, 134
Pearson, Roger 13 n. 25, 42 n. 43, 43 n. 49 & 52
Perrier, Charles 133–34
Perrier, Louis 23
Perrot, Michelle 24

Perrot, Philippe 94, 114 n. 3
Picard, David 93
Pichois, Claude 92 n. 48
Pichois, Claude, and Jean Ziegler, *Baudelaire* 103
Planche, Gustave 141, 142, 143, 149–50, 152, 154 n. 6
Poe, Edgar Allan 158
poésie intime 1, 8, 11, 34–36, 51, 53, 55, 57, 59, 61, 77, 79, 118, 122, 156
prayer 83, 87–88
Praz, Mario 91 n. 30
Prendergast, Christopher 65 n. 15, 146, 151, 154 n. 3
prose poetry 67, 81–82, 84, 87, 92 n. 42, 43 & 44, 103, 107, 132, 137
Protestantism 22, 28–29
Proust, Marcel, *Contre Sainte-Beuve* 42 n. 41, 49–50, 141, 148, 163
psychoanalysis 5–6, 18, 156, 162
public and private spheres 3–4, 7, 8, 24–25, 40, 52–56, 64, 69, 73–76, 77, 84, 88–89, 90 n. 8, 95, 100, 101, 107, 123, 159, 164
Puckett, Kent 114 n. 3
pudeur 46–47, 48–49, 52, 54, 58, 60, 61, 63, 103, 104–06, 160

Raisson, Horace-Napoléon 93, 95–96, 98, 115 n. 7
Raoul, Valérie 73, 91 n. 18
realism 7, 10, 11, 12 n. 2, 14 n. 29 & 31, 120
Reddy, William 2, 7, 23, 45, 46, 47, 64 n. 6
  'emotional refuge' 13 n. 20, 24, 25, 26
  'emotional regime' 13 n. 19
Restoration France 26, 30, 34, 125, 141, 145
Réunion 138
Revue de Paris 93, 142
Revue des deux mondes 14 n. 31, 31, 43 n. 50, 44, 55, 65 n. 20, 144, 146
Revolution of 1789: 7, 21, 23, 24, 45–47, 95, 97, 116 n. 31, 159
Revolution of 1830: 10, 39
Revolution of 1848: 101, 132
Richardson, Samuel 22, 31
Rilke, Rainer Maria 76, 87–88
Robb, Graham 84, 125
roman intime 1, 8, 11, 14 n. 31, 25, 30–34, 35, 36, 37, 39, 42 n. 37, 44, 57–59, 64 n. 12, 65 n. 16, 66, 77, 79, 108, 115 n. 20, 118, 146, 159
roman-diaristique 68, 69, 87
Romanticism 7, 9, 11, 21, 26, 34, 35, 42 n. 46, 54, 57, 61, 71, 81, 90 n. 2, 91 n. 19, 91 n. 26, 91 n. 30 & 36, 99, 120, 123–24, 125, 126, 142, 143, 149
Rousseau, Jean-Jacques 9, 22, 23–24, 31, 39, 43 n. 51, 48–49, 64 n. 12, 77, 102

Sabatier, Apollonie 44, 52, 53, 54, 55, 65 n. 17 & 18, 136
Sacy, Samuel de 103
Sagnes, Guy 59

Said, Edward 115 n. 12, 116 n. 37
Saint Augustine of Hippo 28, 64 n. 12, 71
Saint Marc, Stéphanie de 162, 164 n. 4
Saint-Albin, Alexandre de 46
Saint-Chéron, Alexandre de 34, 61
Sainte-Beuve, Charles Augustin:
  '*Dominique*, par M. Eugène Fromentin' 57–58, 59, 60, 61, 62
  Les Consolations 35, 36, 39, 50, 51, 53, 65 n. 29
    'A Madame V. H.' 53
    'Sonnet VII' 51
  Les Pensées d'août 50
  Mes Poisons 149, 155 n. 16
  'Nouveaux documents sur Montaigne' 149
  Portraits contemporains 26, 33, 147, 148–49, 154 n. 11, 155 n. 14
  Portraits de femmes 150–51, 154 n. 11
    'Du roman intime ou Mademoiselle de Liron' 31–34, 37–38, 39, 146, 152
    'Madame de Charrière' 140, 148–49
  Portraits littéraires 154 n. 11
    'Des soirées littéraires ou Les poètes entre eux' 40, 145
    'Diderot' 146–47
  Vie, poésies et pensées de Joseph Delorme 50, 51, 145
    'Causerie au bal' 51
    'Le Cénacle' 145
  Volupté 31, 32, 65 n. 16
Sales, Francis de 71
salon 25–27, 41 n. 21, 47, 52, 65 n. 17, 78, 142, 152
  see also *cénacle*
Salon criticism 57, 116 n. 34, 117–18, 120–29, 130, 131, 133, 134, 136, 138 n. 6, 157, 158
Saminadayar-Perrin, Corinne 152
Sand, George 31, 33, 42 n. 23, 64 n. 12, 116 n. 27 & 28
Sardou, Victorien 115 n. 10
Sartre, Jean-Paul 65 n. 19, 161
Schellino, Andrea 116 n. 30
Schlegel, August 81
Scholar, Richard 19, 21
Schor, Naomi 32, 97, 120
Scott, Maria 65 n. 21, 81–82, 84
Scott, Walter 146
sculpture 118, 122, 123, 146–47
Second Empire 2, 26–27, 28, 41 n. 21, 44, 56, 63, 69, 117, 118, 124, 125, 140, 156, 159
Second Republic 101
secrecy 4, 9, 16, 17, 19, 20, 32, 53, 74, 76, 91 n. 25, 104, 107, 114, 115 n. 19, 145, 147, 161
Sedgwick, Eve Kosofsky 41 n. 11, 140, 141, 164
Segal, Naomi 57, 58
Ségalas, Anaïs 34
self-portrait 74, 117, 118
Sennett, Richard 4–5, 6, 7, 8, 13 n. 11, 24, 25, 25
sensibility 2, 15, 21–24, 28, 30, 31, 33, 36, 41 n. 6, 45–47, 68, 80, 126

sentimental fiction 10, 21, 31, 32, 37
Sévigné, Madame de 31
sexuality 1, 2, 5, 6, 16, 17, 18, 29, 42 n. 32, 46, 62, 97, 107–08, 110, 115 n. 12, 136, 137, 140, 151, 156, 160–62
shame 3, 10, 44, 46–48, 53, 55, 59, 61, 64, 74, 75
  see also *pudeur*
shyness 46, 60
siblings 70–76
sincerity 4, 23, 39, 48, 72, 78, 82, 87, 89, 131, 145
silence 63, 80
Simmel, Georg 94, 100
Simonet-Tenant, Françoise 8, 90 n. 5 & 16
Smith, Adam 37
sociability 25–28, 59–60, 78, 96, 97, 99, 106–07, 133, 142–43, 145–46, 148, 160
Spain 126, 128, 132, 133, 136
Spacks, Patricia Meyer 144, 148
Staël, Germaine de 21, 26, 125, 139 n. 12, 142
Stendhal 10, 11, 20, 27, 33, 34, 37, 41 n. 22, 42 n. 39, 41 & 43, 43 n. 49, 46, 64 n. 8, 68, 80, 90 n. 13, 141
Stephens, Sonya 84, 87, 88, 92 n. 42 & 44
Stoler, Ann Laura, 'colonial intimacies' 94, 109
Sturrock, John 66, 89
Sussman, Herbert 64 n. 3
sympathy 9, 22, 27–28, 37, 71, 99, 116 n. 33, 125, 126, 131, 142, 150, 155 n. 23
syphilis 103, 107

Taylor, Charles 17, 21, 22, 25, 28
tears 33–34, 42 n. 40, 72
Terashima, Miyuka 11
Terdiman, Richard 94, 101
tête-à-tête 60, 146–47
Texier, Edmond 35–36

Third Republic 30, 159, 162, 164 n. 3
Tinterow, Gary 139 n. 16
Todd, Janet 21, 23
Tomkins, Silvan 61, 140
Tooke, Adrianne 102, 109
Tourte-Cherbuliez, Marie 69
travel, culture of 94–98, 126–29
Trebutien, G.-S. 67, 69, 73, 75, 76, 77, 91 n. 21
tutoiement 24, 25, 51, 116 n. 31

Universal Exhibition of 1855: 118, 122–23, 133–37

Vaillant, Alain 52, 65 n. 20, 164 n. 1
Valéry, Paul 14 n. 32
vanity 10, 28, 64 n. 8, 74, 76, 77, 91 n. 33
Vernet, Horace 129, 130, 131
Vigny, Alfred de 26, 90 n. 13, 142
Vincent-Buffault, Anne 14 n. 28, 42 n. 40, 99
Vinet, Alexandre 148, 149
violation 104, 109
voyeurism 41 n. 17, 104
Vuillard, Édouard 117, 118, 119, 138, 138 n. 1
vulnerability 29, 40, 54, 67, 100, 145

Wagner, Richard 130, 131, 136, 157, 158
Waller, Margaret 54
Whidden, Seth 12 n. 4, 13 n. 18
White, Nicholas 64 n. 5
Wilson, John 9

Yousef, Nancy 9

Zarobell, John 109, 116 n. 34
Zeldin, Theodore 12 n. 8
Zimmerman, Melvin 83, 92 n. 47
Zola, Émile 7, 11

www.ingramcontent.com/pod-product-compliance
Lightning Source LLC
LaVergne TN
LVHW061251060426
835507LV00017B/2019